It's More Than Shootouts and Car Chases

Memoirs of a Montgomery Police Officer

by

Cpl. (Ret.) Stephen Z. Smith

authorHOUSE®

AuthorHouse™
1663 Liberty Drive
Bloomington, IN 47403
www.authorhouse.com
Phone: 1-800-839-8640

Cover photography by Stephen Z. Smith
Graphics by Emile Mattison
Back cover photography by Jenny Gola-Smith

First published by AuthorHouse 2/11/2010

ISBN: 978-1-4490-5738-1 (e)
ISBN: 978-1-4490-5736-7 (sc)
ISBN: 978-1-4490-5737-4 (hc)

Library of Congress Control Number: 2009913052

The badge pictured on the front cover is similar to the badge given to me
when I retired from the Montgomery Police Department. Depiction of
said badge does not constitute or imply an endorsement by the Montgomery
Police Department, City of Montgomery or its elected officials.

Printed in the United States of America
Bloomington, Indiana

This book is printed on acid-free paper.

DEDICATION

This book is dedicated to the men and women who have worked for the Montgomery Police Department and have served the citizens with pride and dignity and those who have paid the ultimate sacrifice and to the dedicated chaplains who serve the officers.

A percentage of the proceeds from this book will go toward supporting the River Region Chaplain Service. This is a non-profit organization that ministers to our public safety officers. www.riverregionchaplains.org

CONTENTS

ACKNOWLEDGEMENTS

AND

SPECIAL THANKS

To my wife Nancy, who supported me through the academy, all the late nights working and all the early morning call-outs,

To my daughters, Stacy and Kelly for being patient with me as I worked long hours and was not always home when they wanted Daddy to be there,

To my Mom, who didn't like the idea of me becoming a police officer, but understood it was a calling from God and supported and encouraged me, not only in my career but to write this book and for the many, many hours she spent proof reading...with that dang red pen,

To my Dad, who spent many hours listening to the scanner to make sure I made it off a dangerous call unscathed,

To Lieutenant Paul Walker, "King of the Motormen" and one of my academy classmates who spent countless hours reading, editing and helping make a good story better,

To all my partners, who I patrolled endless hours with; they watched my back and I watch theirs,

To my friends and church family who lifted me up in prayers throughout my career,

To my Lord and Savior who protected me from harm as I served the citizens of Montgomery, Alabama.

AUTHOR'S NOTE

All the events in this book are actual events. Through my research of field notes, statements, affidavits and talking with many of my former partners, I have tried to ensure that the events are as truthful and accurate as humanly possible. I have changed the names of all but two suspects and citizens so not to cause undo problems of those who may have had only one brush with the law. The names of suspects used are variations of my family's names.

Forward

From September **1981** until September 2001, I worked for the Montgomery Police Department in Montgomery, Alabama serving the people. Over the years, I have seen and experienced some amazing things. Many of my friends have suggested that I write a book about my experiences. I have always talked about writing a book and have kept somewhat detailed field notes and saved statements thinking I might actually write a book, *one day*. At the suggestion of my mom I wrote one story about a call I answered and sent it to her to read and critique. She liked the story and suggested that I write a few more. She also pointed out my grammatical errors with a bright red pen. One story led to two and two to a dozen and before I knew it I was doing something I had never done before, I was writing. Once I made the decision to write this book I began to look through all my field notes, statements and compiled two legal pads worth of possible stories to share.

For over five years, I have been researching and compiling information to make this book as truthful and accurate as humanly possible. As I did my research I discovered a lot about myself. I had been involved in many more life and death situations than I had realized. I experienced things that most people would never dream of, seen things that I will never forget and things that I wish I could erase from my memory forever.

Throughout my career, I have wished that people could see some of the things I have seen and get a real look at what a police officer *really* experiences. People think they know but they don't.

I have written about my experiences as a police officer giving as much detail as possible of what it has been like to wear the uniform, ride in a black and white patrol car and deal with the public day in and day out. I came into this job as a naïve nineteen year old cadet and retired as a 39 year old street wise cop. I have had to do things that I really did not want to do but did them anyway because it was my job. I have made good decisions and not so good decisions. But like every police officer who wears the badge, I am only human.

I came into this job as a Christian, and on more than one occasion asked God, *"Why did you place me in this occupation?"* As I look back, I see the path I have taken and no longer question God *why*, but say *thank you* for the blessings and adventures. My faith has grown in more ways that I can count and I pray that He will continue to use me as a witness.

As you read this book, think back to the dates and times I have written about and ask yourself, "What was I doing then?" Police officers don't get enough credit for the little things they do that make a difference in people's lives and are only brought into the spotlight by the media for the most news worthy events, whether it is good or bad.

I hope you enjoy reading about my career and will see police officers as just regular people doing a sometimes impossible job and sometimes risking their lives for someone they don't even know.

Over my twenty years of being a police officer, I have learned a lot about people and human nature. But for those who think they know what police officers do everyday or are thinking about being a police officer, one thing I can tell you for sure, <u>It's More than Shootouts and Car Chases.</u>

"Greater love hath no man than this: "That he gives his life to save a friend." Law enforcement offices do even more, sometimes they give their lives to save a stranger.

Author unknown

Engraved on the Police Memorial "Duty Called" on the Capital grounds in Montgomery, Alabama.

We are the Class of 83-A

AFTER GRADUATING FROM SIDNEY LANIER High School in May of 1980, I, as many seniors will do upon graduation, made a pilgrimage to the beach with two good friends, Jamie Reynolds and Jeff Manley. We spent a week in Destin, Florida, staying with Jamie's uncle, which for three gainfully unemployed and recently graduated seniors was a great deal because it was much cheaper than a motel.

After returning from the beach, I planned to relax the whole summer and wait for college to start in the fall. After all, I was a high school graduate and after twelve years of school and three summers of summer school, I felt I deserved a break. I'd been accepted to Auburn University of Montgomery and was not really looking forward to starting school again, but it was something that was expected of me when I graduated.

After being back a couple of days, I was sitting on the couch watching television. Actually, I was more slumped down on the couch relaxing when my mom walked in and asked me a profound question.

She looked at me and said, "You don't think you're just going to sit around all summer and do nothing, do you?"

I replied back somewhat jokingly, "Yes, that was the plan. I'm a graduate and I deserve a break."

"You need to go out and find a job. You're not going to just sit around the house all summer."

"Okay." I said, after some thought. "First thing in the morning I'll go out and look for a job."

The next morning, I got up, went out and began filling out applications. One of the many places I went was First Alabama

Bank downtown on Commerce Street. My girlfriend, Julie, knew someone who worked there and thought they might hire me. After a couple of weeks I received a call from the bank to come in for a job interview. I was really surprised to receive a call so quickly. After the interview process, I was hired in July to work in Checking and Information. This section consisted of about eight to ten women who verified signatures on cancelled checks over five hundred dollars, pulling checks that had "stop pays" on them, and verifying business checks requiring more than one signature. They would then file them in massive cabinets in large bundles. My partner, Theodore and I would then pull the bundles and sort them on a large sorter in account number order. We would then feed them into a machine that would stuff into envelopes to be mailed out.

Working with the ladies wasn't so bad, it was just the job was so boring. The only good part was that I got to sit at the tables and talk. Sometimes I would have to encode check amounts on checks with a machine, the most boring of all jobs.

After six months, I knew this was not the job I wanted to do for the rest of my life. Working full-time eventually took the place of entering college, but working at the bank was not what I wanted for myself. I began to pray for the Lord to lead me in the direction of what He wanted me to do. At the time, I truly had no idea of what I wanted, or what the Lord had in mind for me.

One afternoon, while returning from lunch, I saw several police cars in the area of the Atlanta Highway converging on the Popeye's Chicken near Federal Drive and figured it must have gotten robbed. Later, on the news, I saw that it had been robbed. That was something of a revelation for me—an epiphany if you will—but it was then I realized what I wanted to do. I wanted to be a police officer.

I learned that you had to be twenty-one to become a police officer because that was the legal age in Alabama to carry a firearm. I was only eighteen at the time and couldn't see myself working at the bank for another three years.

Then I learned that the police department had a cadet program. The department hired prospective police officers between eighteen and twenty and put them to work in administrative positions at headquarters learning different non-hazardous aspects of the job.

Upon turning twenty-one, however, the cadet would be reassigned to the Montgomery Police Academy to begin formal training. Anyone who could not make that transition would then be terminated.

I went down to the police department during my lunch hour and got an application. The lady in the recruiting office was at lunch in the break room, but one of the cadets I knew from high school told me to ask her if she would get me an application. She got up and got me one, reluctantly. I took the application home, filled it out and turned it in a day or two later.

I was excited to think that I could be working at the police department in a few weeks. After all, I applied with the bank and was called back about three weeks later and was working there shortly thereafter.

I found out some time later that the police department was under a federal hiring freeze. That wasn't what I wanted to hear. I hated working at the bank to the point that when I awoke on Saturday morning and realized I didn't have to go to work, I'd be so excited I couldn't fall back to sleep. Whenever anyone asks how long I worked at First Alabama Bank, I would always say that I worked there "a *lifetime* one year."

I found out the police department regularly conducted a firearms familiarization course for civilians where anyone could learn in a couple of Saturday mornings how to shoot a pistol and at the same time receive instruction about Alabama's gun laws. I thought I could get a head start on my police career by learning to shoot a pistol. I found out later that cadets never handle firearms and that marksmanship was taught in a weeklong class at the police academy.

I called the police department and asked about enrolling into the program. I was told that I had to call Anita Folmar, the mayor's wife and sponsor of the program, at her residence to sign up. Emory Folmar had been mayor of Montgomery since I was in the tenth grade and was a tough, no-nonsense leader. He was pro-active on crime and took great pride in the police department, often boasting that Montgomery had the best-trained police department in the nation.

After speaking with Mrs. Folmar, I decided to take a chance and ask to speak with the mayor himself. She put him on the phone. I told him who I was and that I wanted a job with the police department.

He said that he liked the fact that I was a "go-getter" by asking him personally for the job and told me to reapply as soon as the hiring freeze was lifted. I was delighted that he took the time to speak with me and thanked him for it. Julie was not at all happy with my plan to become a police officer. She said, "I can't live with the idea of you being shot at everyday and me getting a call in the middle of the night that you've been killed!"

I replied, "What makes you think I'm gonna be shot at every day? Police officers are not shot at *every* day!"

I don't know where she got her information, but it was obviously wrong. I think she just wanted me to work some eight-to-five job at the bank, or some other boring office job. She was a year older than I and wanted to get married. Her friends were older and had boyfriends and some of them were engaged, but marriage wasn't even a consideration for me at that time. I just wanted to find a career.

Someone from the recruiting office at the police department finally called. I went down, filled out the required paperwork, and interviewed for the job. Corporal Sandi Pierce interviewed me and completed my background check. During my initial interview, she asked a lot of questions about my personal life, including my religious affiliation. I told her, among other things, that I was preaching at my church the following Sunday during our Youth Sunday service, where younger members take over the duties of the pastor and the church leaders.

She asked me if I could shoot someone even with my strong Christian convictions. I referred her to Romans 13:1-4, where the Bible talks about the police officer as being "God's minister to you for good."

I told her, "I believe the Lord has led me to this job and if I have to shoot someone, then I believe I can."

I had to go in one evening to take a polygraph test and after two sets of questioning, the officer administering the polygraph test stated, "You're not lying. There is no need to run a third time."

The final interview is called "Staff." This is where the applicant comes into a closed conference room and sits at the end of a long table. The department's highest ranking officers, usually captains and majors, are seated along either side of the table and proceed to interrogate, sometimes harshly, the prospective police officer. They questioned me about leaving the bank and coming to work with the police department. They wanted to know why I would take a pay cut to become a police cadet.

For some reason people think that banks pay well. This isn't always true. There is a significant gap between the wages paid to the rank-and-file employees and the upper level administrators. If someone can cross that gap, that employee will make good money, but the majority of the employees don't make that much. I know this because as part of my job at the bank, I saw everyone's paycheck.

I told the staff that I would not be taking a pay cut, but, in fact, I would be making about five thousand dollars more a year as a police cadet than I made at the bank. I then heard one of the major's whisper to another, "This guy is too clean. There has to be some dirt on him." One of them then asked me if I had ever gotten any tickets.

I stated, "No traffic tickets, but I have gotten some parking tickets, but I've paid all of them."

"How many parking tickets have you gotten over the last year?" he asked.

"About two hundred or so," I replied, with some hesitation.

"Two hundred!" the major said, with disbelief. "Why did you get two hundred parking tickets?"

I explained. "There's limited parking near the bank and we have to park at the civic center parking lot and walk. I would sometimes run a little late or it would be raining and I did not want to walk that far. So I would park at a meter and get a ticket. I paid all the tickets every payday."

After looking at some paperwork they said that was all. I was notified a day or two later that I had been hired. They gave me a hire date of September 9th. I would begin my new job within three and a half weeks.

All the ladies at the bank were happy for me and they had a little party on my last day. The ladies I worked with were nice, and I missed them, of course, but I never missed the job at all. I had worked there a lifetime one year and now it was over.

I began my new job on Tuesday, September 9th, 1981, assigned to the Supply and Evidence Room working for Leroy Ducker and

James Story. Mr. Ducker was a reserve officer in charge of the Supply and Evidence room. He had a son who was also a police officer for the department.

Mr. Ducker has a great sense of humor. He hated bicycles though, because he had so many in the evidence room and could never find their owners. He told me on many occasions that when he died and went heaven he was going to find the guy who invented the bicycle and kick his butt.

Mr. Story was retired from the Air Force and was a civilian employee. I learned that Mr. Story, while in the Air Force, had been in charge of loading the bomb that was dropped on Hiroshima, Japan, during World War II. He said he had no idea what he was loading but he knew it was top secret. He later found out exactly what it was. He added he was glad he didn't know at the time. He shared this and many other stories, about the war with me.

1981 or 1982 — Working as a police cadet in the Supply and Evidence Room. Mr. Story is pictured on the left.

The Supply and Evidence Room was in the basement of police headquarters and was where all the evidence collected in criminal investigations was brought and stored for court. I was assigned to log in all the evidence from the night before as well as what came in during the day, and release evidence to officers for presentation in court. I would also release impounded property back to the rightful owners if it wasn't needed as evidence.

The "supply" part of supply and evidence referred to the volumes of blank paperwork and forms printed and distributed throughout the department as well as the equipment and uniform gear issued to the trainees during the academy.

My first dose of reality working at the police department came on January 5, 1982. Narcotics Investigators Tony Burks and Mary McCord were shot on Traction Avenue in north Montgomery. Mary succumbed to her wounds on the scene. I had never been exposed to death in this way. Someone who worked at the same place I did had been killed and another seriously wounded. I didn't know either one at the time and I did not know how to deal with it. I witnessed sadness, anger and bitterness in the other officers, but I really didn't know how to act. I was there when Mary's friends and fellow officers brought in her uniforms to the supply room. I also signed in some of the evidence from the case. I was sad for both of them but this was something I had never experienced.

The only person I had ever known who had been shot and killed was my grandfather, Homer Smith. He was shot and killed on January 17, 1974 in Pell City, Alabama. I was eleven years old when he died. Many people have asked, including my mother, if this was why I joined the police department. No other relatives had ever been police officers. I told them I felt led by the Lord to join.

Robbery May Have Been Motive In Smith Slaying

Robbery was the apparent motive in the daytime slaying of Homer Carl Smith, 58, who was found dead at his home in West Pell City last Thursday evening, a fatal bullet wound in his head.

Swift work by law enforcement officers resulted in the apprehension and arrest of Michael Carl Gwin, 22, of Rt. 1 Ragland less than nine hours after the body was discovered. Gwin has been charged with first degree murder.

Smith's body was discovered at about 3 p.m. by his wife, Mrs. Elizabeth L. Smith, who had come home from work a short time earlier. She found him lying partially inside a chicken house on a hill at the rear of the home, where he raised game chickens.

According to Sheriff Clemons Roe, the victim had apparently been shot with a .22 caliber pistol, and a search for the weapon in the area of the Smith

HOMER SMITH

home has thus far proved fruitless.

Mr. Smith had for a number of years conducted a lucrative business in the raising of game roosters, and reportedly, sold them throughout the U.S. and in some South American countries as well.

He was known to have carried large sums of money on his person and according to members of his family, had such a sum of money on the day he was killed, which was missing when the body was found.

Sheriff Clemons Roe, Coroner Jimmy Davis and District Attorney Charles Robinson were summoned to the scene. They began an extensive investigation, along with members of the Pell City Police Department, ABC Agents, and State Investigator Lt. Raines.

Sometime Thursday night, Gwin, an Avondale Mills employee, who had in the past worked with Mr. Smith in the raising and grooming of his chickens, was brought in for questioning, Sheriff Roe said. At around midnight, Gwin was

placed under arrest at the Pell City Courthouse.

Funeral services for Mr. Smith were held Saturday, January 19, from the Eden Methodist Church with interment in Valley Hill Cemetery. Rev. Bill Hitt and Rev. Harris officiated, Kilgroe directing.

He is survived by his wife, Mrs. Elizabeth L. Smith; one son, L. Zane Smith of Montgomery, two daughters, Mrs. Sybil Bynum of Birmingham and Mrs. Kay Hendricks of

Gadsden; one brother, Joe Smith of Pendleton, Oregon; two sisters, Mrs. Dorothy Meehan and Mrs. Kathryn Johnson, both of Cropwell; six grandchildren.

January 17, 1974 – Newspaper article on the murder of my grandfather, Homer Smith, Pell City, Alabama (Courtesy of St. Clair – News Aeiges)

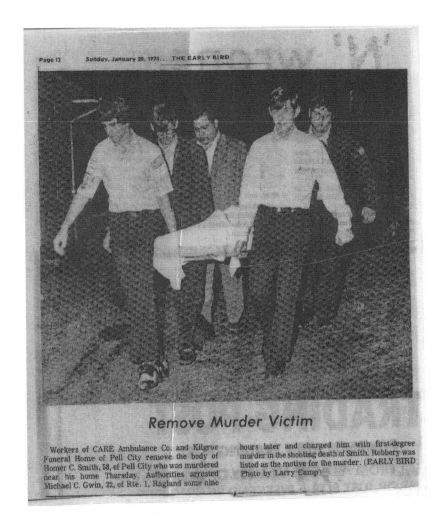

Remove Murder Victim

Workers of CARE Ambulance Co. and Kilgroe Funeral Home of Pell City remove the body of Homer C. Smith, 58, of Pell City who was murdered near his home Thursday. Authorities arrested Michael C. Gwin, 22, of Rte. 1, Ragland some nine hours later and charged him with first-degree murder in the shooting death of Smith. Robbery was listed as the motive for the murder. (EARLY BIRD Photo by Larry Camp)

January 17, 1974 — My grandfather being carried away from the scene. (Photo courtesy of St Clair — News Aeiges)

9

Verdict due today in Smith murder

BULLETIN

St. Clair County Jury in Pell City on Wednesday, March 30, at 5:40 p.m. returned a verdict of second degree murder in the trial of Michael Guinn. The jury sentenced Guinn to a term of twenty years imprisonment at the State Penitentiary.

As of NEWS press time Wednesday, a 13-member, all-male St. Clair County jury was expected to receive the first-degree murder case of Michael Carl Gwin late Wednesday or early today after Gwin took the stand himself.

Courthouse sources said the jury should receive the case by 3 p.m. Wednesday.

Gwin, a 22-year-old Ragland native, is accused of murdering Homer Carl Smith, a Pell City businessman, on Jan. 17, 1974, at Smith's residence.

St. Clair District Attorney Charles Robinson, in testimony taken Tuesday, submitted a confession obtained from Gwin by State Investigator O.M. Raines, a move which drew an immediate request for mistrial from Gwin's defense attorney Billy L. Church.

After the jury was excused,

Church told Circuit Judge L.P. Waid the statement was taken while Gwin was intoxicated and that his client was not informed of his constitutional rights at the proper time.

Waid ruled however, that the prosecution could enter the confession and the jury was recalled.

According to testimony given Tuesday, the alleged murder weapon was stolen by Gwin from the residence of Charles Smith before the day of the murder of Homer Smith.

St. Clair Sheriff Clemmons Roe testified that the weapon allegedly stolen from Charles

(See Murder Page 5)

Smith, after repeated searches, could not be found.

When Raines took the stand Tuesday, several objections were raised by Church on the grounds that the statement had been taken unconstitutionally.

In the alleged confession, the charge was made that (Homer Smith) "had tried to mess with my wife." The statement described being taken Smith's death with the words "I let him have it."

Defense attorney Church moved for a mistrial again when testimony was being taken from James T. Stewart on grounds that the deputy prosecutor, Gerald Swann, was "feeding the testimony " to Stewart. Waid denied the motion.

Wednesday, the defendant, Gwin took the stand in his own defense and, upon questioning, recounted the events prior to and after Smith's death.

Gwin said he and his wife had gone to Ragland with Smith some two months before the slaying and that, during the ride, Smith had said he "wanted

to ...my wife," Gwin testified.

Gwin said he had not talked to Smith since that time until the morning of the shooting. He said he had stolen a pistol from the residence of Charles Smith and was going to sell it when Smith (Homer) picked him up. He added that after they had gone to the bank where Smith cashed a money order, they went to another residence but the occupants were not at home.

Then, according to Gwin, they returned to Homer Smiths home where he began helping Smith catch chickens to have their combs cut.

"While I was helping him he said he wanted to proposition my wife," Gwin said. He said "Smith and I got into an argument about it and Smith began shaking the scissors in my face and reaching into his pocket... and I stepped to his side and pulled the gun from my belt, and shot him," Gwin said.

Under cross examination from Robinson Gwin said he ran because he was scared. "If it was like that, it would be self defense," Robinson said. "Why didn't you tell the sheriff instead of running?" Robinson quired. "I was scared," Gwin said.

As of NEWS press time Wednesday, the court was dismissed for lunch with Gwin expected to resume the stand following the break.

March 1974 – Newspaper article on trial verdict
(Courtesy of St. Clair – News Aeiges)

10

My mother wasn't exactly thrilled with the idea of her son being a police officer. Especially since none of the men on my grandmother Smith's side of the family (Lill) have died natural deaths. My grandmother's brother was killed in the war, a great-uncle was killed trying to hobo a ride on a moving train and other relatives have been killed in vehicle accidents. The Lill men did not have a good track record and now, I was pursuing a career as a police officer. Mom was not crazy about the idea, but she said it was my life and I had to live it.

Julie and I broke up shortly after I was hired. I don't know if it was because of my job or the fact that we seemed headed in different directions. She wanted marriage and a family, but I was looking for something else entirely. I didn't take marriage so lightly. As young as I was, I had to be sure it was the right thing to do, and at the time it wasn't.

After about a year I was transferred to the Investigative Division on the second floor. I learned to write reports and saw the variety of suspects brought in for interrogation on felony investigations.

Working as a police cadet really opened my eyes to what was going on in the world. I was raised in a Christian home and had been active in the youth group at Highland Avenue Baptist Church. I guess I lived a fairly sheltered life and was oblivious too much of what transpired every day in the real world. I got to know the investigators with whom I worked and I saw how really dangerous the job is. Something occurred three days before I went to the police academy that drove home the point for me. This would be my second dose of law enforcement reality.

Two of the investigators I knew well, Les Brown and Eddie Spivey, were assaulted and nearly killed while investigating a missing persons case on Todd Road on February 28, 1983. This event would later become known in the media as the "The Todd Road Incident."

Les and Eddie, who are both white, were taken hostage, shot, cut, and severely beaten by at least twenty-five to thirty members of a black family from Michigan, who were in town for a funeral. Les was shot twice with his own .357 magnum revolver, and Eddie's throat was slashed open. Les nearly died and both men took several

11

months to recover from their injuries. However, both survived and continued working for the police department.

I read the statement Eddie wrote about the incident in total disbelief of the brutality they had endured. I would read part of the statement and have to put it down to clear my head before continuing. These two guys deserve to go to Heaven, because they've both already been through Hell.

The assault on Todd Road widened the racial divide in the city following allegations that several police officers physically assaulted several of the suspects who were arrested for the crime that night. The controversy was fueled by some of the black leaders in Montgomery and northern newspaper reporters writing about Montgomery as if it were still the 1950's. The history of Montgomery began way before 1955, but you can't convince some people of that. A northern reporter who covered the case later wrote a book about it called *The Todd Road Incident*. I read it, and it was full of errors.

I started the Montgomery Police Academy on March 3, 1983, with twenty other trainees. This was one of the smallest classes at the time to start the academy. Class began that morning at 7:30 sharp with inspection, then a memory test.

March 3, 1983 – The first day at the Montgomery Police Academy. I'm third from the left standing. (Photo by Montgomery Police Dept.)

While attending the academy, I visited Les in the hospital. He encouraged me to finish the academy. I remember to this day, as he lay in the hospital bed, he was upbeat and told me, "Stick with it. It's worth it."

I thought to myself, *if he can tell me it was worth it after all he had been through, then this must be a great job.* Les Brown's bloody hazardous duty check was framed and still hangs on the wall in the detective division as a memorial to their suffering to this day.

The police academy lasted sixteen weeks. It was a combination of college classes and boot camp. The academy, on Mildred Street, was located in one of the highest crime areas of the city. On our daily runs we had to be escorted by one of our instructors in a marked patrol vehicle after Kelly Summers, the trainee from Hoover Police Department, was nearly kidnapped by a couple of thugs who attempted to pull her into a vehicle near the academy.

The first three weeks of training were the toughest. This was the period when the instructors weeded out all those who weren't fit or serious about becoming police officers. As a cadet, I was fortunate that I had the memory work given to me ahead of time, so I had already memorized it and was ahead of the game. I was running and doing push-ups in preparation for the physical training, but it was still extremely tough. I cannot imagine anybody starting the academy *then* deciding to get into shape. I was running a mile to a mile and a half each day after work before I started the academy, and still I struggled to keep up with the class.

On our first day of physical training, known to us as "P.T.," one of the instructors announced, "We are only going to run a mile. If you all finish together, you can all go home."

I thought to myself, *Alright! Just one mile, I can do that.*

Of course the instructors knew this wasn't going to happen. This was just one of those mind games they played on us that seemed to amuse them.

Well, we ran the first mile and I stayed with the group pretty well. They ran a faster pace than I was used to, but it was only one mile. The mile course was around the block and crossed over the interstate. The hardest part was the uneven pavement and concrete we had to negotiate during the run. As we returned to the academy one by one, I was in the second group of about ten trainees. After you ran into the parking lot and caught up to your classmates, you had to march in a circular formation around the lot until everyone else returned.

The instructors then informed us that since we didn't all finish together, we were going to run the mile again. Lieutenant Frank Mitchell said, "We will finish together even if we have to run in the dark. We have flashlights we can issue out if we need to."

I saw the overweight trainees gasping and the heavy smokers wheezing, and I knew that there was no way we would all finish together. We were going to have to run in the dark, I just knew it. We ran the second mile, and again, we didn't finish together. The overweight and heavy smokers finished even later on the second run than on the first. They never even got a chance to rest before we ran again. Lieutenant Mitchell told us that the last five to finish the run would have to stay and do remedial P.T. When we started the third mile, I started counting classmates to make sure I was not in the last five. This was the rule for the next several weeks. I never was one of the fastest runners but I gave it everything I had, every day. I couldn't quit because I had nowhere else to go.

Near the end of the academy when there were only six of us left, we took off on our daily run one afternoon, and I was feeling pretty good. John Mann, our class president, had told us, "Today we are not going to let the instructors out run us. We are going to run *them* into the ground."

We took off from the academy at a pace faster than normal. I wasn't going to let the class down, so I did everything I could to keep up. About four miles into the six-mile run, Lieutenant Mitchell finally reached his limit and stopped running. He turned to us breathing heavily with his hands on his knees and said, "Let's stop for a minute and check our packages."

John told us later that we had done it. We ran the instructors to the point that they had to stop. What a great day! And what made it better was the fact that it was my birthday. I turned twenty-one.

One of the directives that trainees at the academy were expected to follow was the "stand clear" rule. Anytime a police officer, visitor, or other civilian came down the hallway, the trainees were to snap to attention with their backs to the wall and yell, "Stand clear!" No matter what we were doing, our orders were to clear a path that way.

We could only resume what we were doing after they passed or if the person said, "Carry on," or "As you were."

We were also required to know the names of the mayor, the chief and deputy chief, all of the majors and captains of the police department and where they lived. This is where I had the advantage. Since I had been a cadet for a year and a half, I knew each one. So when one of us saw a person walking up from the parking lot, I could tell my fellow classmates who they were, their rank and the division they worked, in case we were asked, as often was the case.

There were many nights where I only got four hours sleep from doing homework. The Dickie type uniforms we had to wear had a big yellow patch on the front that said "Police Trainee." They were used and worn out. Of the four sets issued to me, only two were in good enough condition to pass morning inspection. I would come home each night after doing P.T., take a shower and eat dinner. I would put my uniform and my P.T. clothes in the washer then do my homework. After three or four hours of homework, I would shine my shoes and leather gear to a mirror finish, iron my uniform with a crease sharp enough to cut flesh, go over my memory work once or twice, then go to bed. If I was able to get five hours of sleep I was doing great.

The academy encouraged us to study together as a team. At first we would do this over the weekends, especially during criminal law week. After ten weeks in the academy there were only six of us left, so it was easier to do the work at home instead of getting together each night. We would still get into study groups on the weekends before our major exams to study together and test each other. I think having a small class brought us closer together.

One of the more interesting days in the academy happened on April 18th. Narcotics officers came and taught us about the drug enforcement. I was raised in a Christian home and had never been exposed to illegal narcotics. My father was a pharmacist who worked for a major pharmaceutical company, so I was somewhat familiar with prescription drugs. I was never around anyone who used alcohol or drugs so I was never tempted to use them myself. I saw people who came to school high and I would hear the stories of when people got drunk and the stupid things they did and it was just not what I wanted in my life. My dad also told me if I ever used drugs, when he found out it would be the worst day of my life. So I saw no reason to use drugs.

After a day of being taught about more drugs than I ever knew existed, Corporal Ronnie Davis came and taught us about marijuana. I was familiar with the smell of marijuana from the locker room in high school. I did not know at the time but I was told by one of my classmates that was the smell of weed (marijuana).

After an hour or two of learning about marijuana, Corporal Davis said that because we were in a classroom setting and it was a learning environment that we needed to know what marijuana smelled like. He also said that since it was a learning environment that we could take a couple of drags of the burning marijuana cigarettes.

I'd never been around anyone smoking marijuana, but here I was at the police academy around my fellow police trainees smoking marijuana. Corporal Davis lit two joints and passed them around the classroom. I was sitting on the end of the row of seats and when he handed me the lit joint I just passed it on to Mike McCree who was sitting next to me. I had never smoked in my life and I wasn't going to start now, even if it was in a 'classroom' setting. Several of my classmates had apparently smoked a little weed in the past. I could hear them taking long drags from the joints. After the joints were gone we went on a break.

I could not tell who took the long drags until later in the day when they started raiding the snack machine. I had always heard about people who smoke marijuana getting the munchies and on every break, they were buying candy bars, chips, whatever it took to satisfy their hunger. They don't allow the trainees to try marijuana in the classroom setting anymore. As far as I know, we were the last class.

It seemed like that the further into the academy I got, the easier it got. Later I figured out that it wasn't getting easier, I was just becoming accustomed to the stress and the physical training. As I heard someone once say about the academy, "The only easy day... was yesterday."

Out of the twenty students attending, only five officers from Montgomery graduated. John Mann, Mike Morand, Paul Walker, Mike McCree and I graduated from the academy on June 15, 1983. I served as chaplain for my class, and I can honestly tell people that I graduated in the top five. Kelly Summers, training for service with the Hoover Police Department, graduated with us.

June 1983 – The Class of 83-A, (l to r) John Mann, Mike Morand, Kelly Summers (Hoover Police Dept.), me, Mike McCree, Paul Walker. (Photo by Montgomery Police Dept.)

June 1983 – Academy graduation photo (Courtesy of Wimberly Photography)

After graduation we were assigned to third shift patrol. Starting salary for a police officer was $11,574.00 and would top out at $14,917.00. After graduation we would receive a monthly hazardous duty check of $150.00. Later on, we went back to the academy to see our class photos framed and hanging on the wall of the police academy with all the other classes. Someone, we assumed one of the instructors, had put a nameplate inside the frame with the saying that was to become our class motto, "Quality Tells."

We are the class of 83-A.

MY FIRST NIGHT AS A
MONTGOMERY POLICE OFFICER

ON **FRIDAY, JUNE 17, 1983,** I worked my very first tour as a sworn Montgomery Police officer. I was twenty-one years old and assigned to the night shift. I arrived at headquarters early, wearing my brand new class-B uniform. My trousers were bloused and my newly issued combat boots were shined to a high-mirror gloss. We wore black baseball caps with the letters MPD stitched in silver on the front. A stainless steel Smith & Wesson .357 revolver in a Tex Shoemaker breakfront holster hung heavily on my side.

My leather gear was brand new and stiff and had that distinctive squeak of fresh leather. I had purchased a second set of handcuffs for my duty belt on the advice of a more experienced officer who told me while I was in the academy, "You'll need more than one pair of cuffs. Juveniles travel in packs."

The police department didn't issue body armor to its officers at that time, so I purchased a slightly used ballistic vest from Officer Larry Pugh to give me some added protection. After strapping on all my equipment, I came to the conclusion that only two other professions seemed to require more equipment—astronauts and scuba divers.

Since this was the first night on the street for my newly graduated academy class, our training officers met with all of us and went over the nightly procedure for checking out equipment. Roll call was at 10 p.m. sharp, but we were told to arrive at 9:30. I think I arrived at 9:15 so as not to be late. I also met my first training officer, Corporal Johnny McBride.

During roll call, the group of about thirty-five officers stood in formation in the assembly room facing the podium where the small group of supervisors and our shift commander stood. We stood at attention behind our training officers and, after opening the ranks in military fashion, were welcomed to the shift. We all listened attentively at parade rest as the senior sergeant briefed us on current lookouts, changes in departmental policies, and other various announcements of interest to the third shift.

Johnny was assigned to District Two, a downtown district bordered by Madison Avenue on the north, interstate I-85 by the south, Ann Street on the east and South Jackson Street on the west. It was the smallest district but, at times, the busiest. Among the businesses and located within it were Victor Tulane housing project, Jackson Hospital, and Cramton Bowl, the city's largest football stadium. During football season, Thursday, Friday and Saturday nights were busy in the area with traffic from the competing local high school fans leaving the games. The emergency room at Jackson Hospital stayed busy with gunshot and stabbing victims, and it was our job to respond to the hospital whenever one of them showed up for treatment.

During our time together, Johnny instructed me on proper use of the radio, patrol techniques, traffic stops, and just minding my surroundings. Back then we didn't have mobile computers in the car or the ultra-bright LED strobes flashing on the roof and every corner of the cruiser. Our only source for information was a dispatcher's voice on the radio, and our overhead lights were just spinning mirrors around bright bulbs beneath a blue plastic dome. I still remember the whirring sound of the tiny motors as they spun whenever I flipped the toggle on the light bar control box on a traffic stop.

Our cars were black and white, but that was just a recent change. Just a couple of years earlier, marked vehicles with the MPD had all been painted a soft baby blue. When Mayor Folmar took office in the late seventies, he wanted our department to look more modern and more professional—similar to the LAPD, so we copied their color scheme and adapted our uniforms to more closely match theirs.

As we started the night on patrol, it was a warm summer night, we stopped occasionally and talked to several people walking the streets. I watched Johnny and noted his ability to put people at ease while talking to them, but, at the same time, find out why they were out in the middle of the night and what they were up to.

Around 2:30 in the morning, we received a dispatch to Rigsby Missionary Baptist Church on Fairground Road on a report of someone drunk in public. Fairground Road is in a neighboring district, but that unit was busy on another call. When we arrived, we observed a man in his fifties lying on the front porch of the church. He was propped up against the front door, dirty, disheveled and reeking of cheap wine. Over the years, I would come to know these smells very well as I dealt with a never-ending procession of less-than-clean people in my career.

Johnny began to question the guy, but he only replied with a drunken slur. Johnny told me to ask the guy for his name, address and date of birth. This was my first time talking to a drunken person, so it was a unique experience for me. Neither of my parents drank alcohol, nor did I. I never hung out with people in high school who drank, so I had no experience with this. Yet somehow I was able to get the necessary information from the man, and I ran a warrant check on him on the radio.

While we waited on the dispatcher, Johnny tried to make idle conversation with him. As they talked, Johnnie tried to learn how the man got to this point in his life. The warrant check came back negative. The guy needed to go to jail anyway, so Johnny told me to place him under arrest for Public Intoxication.

My first arrest!

I told the guy to stand so I could place the handcuffs on him. But due to his state of intoxication, he couldn't stand on his own. I had to help him up, lean him against the building and place the cuffs on him. This wouldn't be a problem for me today, but my first time arresting a drunken person offered something of a challenge.

Johnny held him up against the wall as I clicked the cuffs around his wrists. Practicing in the academy on my classmates was entirely different than arresting a real criminal in the field. I assisted him to the car and placed him in the back seat. Back then our patrol cars weren't equipped with safety cages, so our prisoner sat on the passenger side, and I sat behind Johnny. I had to ride to headquarters in the backseat with him, holding him upright. He stank! Not the worse I would ever smell in my career but, nevertheless, he *stank*.

We placed the man in jail and I filled out all the necessary paperwork that accompanies each arrest, the arrest report, the affidavit, and the misdemeanor warrant. I found out quickly that rookies are responsible for *all* the paperwork during their training period.

The rest of the night was pretty uneventful. Johnny and I got to know each other a little better as we patrolled and watched and listened to the city growing quieter and less active with each passing hour. At about 6:30 that morning, we made our way back to headquarters, turned in our paperwork, and checked in our gear. I was tired, but satisfied that I had successfully finished the night. It was an exciting first tour.

My first night on the streets, and I had made my first arrest. It may not seem like a big deal to most people, and I don't know how many officers remember their first arrest, but I remember mine. This was my first night as a Montgomery Police Officer.

1984 – Montgomery Police Dept yearbook photo, third shift patrol

It Doesn't Take a Genius
to Figure that One Out

SUNDAY, SEPTEMBER 11, 1983, I was on third shift patrol and assigned to my third training officer, Corporal Kinney Bishop. Officially I guess he was my second training officer because I'd only ridden with my first one for two weeks. Kinney patrolled District Eleven in the very heart of the city. District Eleven could be characterized as a low-income, high-crime area; always very active and itself surrounded by other busy districts. At one time the area was a bustling center of commerce for the city, but the late sixties and seventies had seen it decline into a shadow of its former self as industry and new business moved eastward.

It is a good training district, however, and provided quite an education for me on many levels. Both Cloverdale Junior High and Sidney Lanier High School were located there. Between these two schools, I'd spent six years working toward graduation. I thought it ironic that just a few years earlier I'd been a student at these schools; now I was a police officer patrolling the neighborhoods that surrounded them.

From the ninth grade until I graduated high school I was basically raised in church, so talking to prostitutes, homeless people, drug addicts and other "street people" provided quite a culture shock for me. No matter how much you learn in the academy, nothing quite prepares you for face-to-face contact with those who exist on the fringe of civilized society.

Around 3 a.m., on that warm, balmy night, Kinney and I weren't especially busy and were on our way to meet Unit 112, Corporal Steve Thompson and his partner, Officer Paul Walker, one of my

24

classmates from the academy. We were supposed to meet them behind Lanier High School on Court Street to shoot the breeze and kill some time.

On our way there, the dispatcher detoured us to a code 34 (theft) from a vehicle in progress at the Courtyard Apartments on the corner of Howard Street and South Court Street directly across the street from the school. The dispatcher said that the subject was attempting to break into a car in the parking lot of the complex. This call should have gone out as a code four (vehicle burglary) in progress, and we approached it as such. Prowlers are often burglars on the hunt for targets of opportunity like an unlocked door or an opened window.

We turned off South Perry Street and crept up to the edge of the parking lot with our headlights out. Kinney parked the patrol car on Howard Street, next to a brick wall bordering the complex. We walked slowly around the wall into the back parking lot of the apartments and saw a black male subject wearing a blue shirt standing behind a car across the empty parking lot.

As he slowly opened the trunk of the car, I crouched over and began to sneak up on him. There was nothing to hide behind across the open expanse of parking lot, so I was completely exposed in the pale glow of the streetlight. Being crouched and sneaking up on the guy didn't aid my concealment at all, but I guess it's just human nature to do so.

The subject removed a large television from the trunk. Then I guess he noticed Kinney and me creeping up on him. He calmly placed the television on the ground, turned and suddenly bolted away in a panicked sprint. I took off after him. I heard Kinney tell the dispatcher that I was in foot pursuit of the suspect.

I had only chased him about fifteen feet when the suspect suddenly drew a pistol, aimed it over his right shoulder, and fired a shot at me. The bright flash from the muzzle and the loud pop of the discharge took me by surprise, and I dove onto the asphalt.

"*Shots fired. My partner's down!*" Kinney shouted on the radio.

I lay on the ground for about a second or two, then got back up and took off after the guy again.

I heard Kinney's voice on my radio, "My partner's back up and in foot pursuit!"

I chased the subject around the corner of the building in time to see him cross Court Street and turn left, where I momentarily lost sight of him. As I trotted into the middle of the street and stopped, I spotted him rounding the corner of the school by the gym still sprinting like an Olympic athlete. He was at least a hundred yards away from me by this time, so I knew I'd never catch him.

I heard the dispatcher advise our unit to switch to channel three, so I switched over. Channel three was the unit-to-unit channel separate from the main dispatch channel that supervisors used to collect detailed information from units in the field. My adrenaline was still pumping, and in my confused state I couldn't find the right channel. While desperately turning the channel knob on my hand-held radio, the dispatcher attempted to call me on channel one, but since I was on another channel, I never heard her. Kinney, along with the other units, probably assumed that something had happened to me. I walked back to the parking lot where the television sat on the ground and found Kinney.

"Do you have your radio on?" he yelled as I approached.

"Yes, I've got it on," I shouted back.

"Why did you not answer the dispatcher when she called?" he asked, the frustration evident in his tone.

I didn't understand why he seemed so angry. I had just chased a burglar and been shot at and he's yelling at me. "I was on channel *three*," I said.

"Why were you on channel three? You're supposed to stay on channel one," he said, still scolding.

"The dispatcher *said* to switch to channel three." I couldn't understand why he seemed so upset.

"You're supposed to stay on channel one when you're in foot pursuit, and *I'm* supposed to switch to channel three," he said a little more calmly.

"I heard the dispatcher say switch to channel three and I switched," I explained.

Steve and Paul roared up in their car and screeched to a halt next to us. Paul jumped out of the vehicle and ran up to me, "Are you okay?" he blurted in his excitement.

"I'm okay."

"Man, you got shot!"

"No. I got shot *at*," I said smiling. "Being shot and being shot at are two totally different things."

"Yeah, that's what I meant."

"Where exactly did he run when he crossed the street?" Steve asked. "We were behind the school and when we heard the radio traffic we came around and saw him cross Court Street. We couldn't find him after that."

I pointed across the street and showed him exactly where he ran and described what he was wearing. Steve said they'd found a blue shirt on the ground in the parking lot.

Lieutenant Scarborough, our supervisor, showed up a minute later. Kinney and I told him exactly what had happened. He wanted to know if we were sure the burglar had fired a shot or if it could have been fireworks.

Kinney and I looked at each other then looked at him in disbelief.

Fireworks? What the heck is he talking about? I thought to myself.

Once we explained again in more detail how it all went down, he seemed to understand.

Kinney explained to me later about staying on channel one during a foot pursuit and how the dispatcher and the other units need to be kept abreast of the suspect's location and more importantly *my* location. It was more important to know my location in case I needed help. It's all a part of the learning process for a rookie police officer. Kinney was concerned about me, like any good training officer would have been.

This was the first serious incident that someone from my academy class had encountered. You spend sixteen weeks together in the academy and you develop a very close bond. Whenever something serious happens to a classmate you always pay special attention because it's like a close family member is in trouble.

The same subject attempted to break into several other cars in the same area over the next couple of weeks. The officers who responded began to notice that the suspect would always take the same escape route whenever he got spooked. One night, Corporal Jack Clark was driving down Court Street when another call went out on the same guy. Jack hid at the corner of the building on Court Street along his usual escape route and waited for him. As he ran by, Jack stepped out from the shadows and slammed him hard in the chest with a riot stick, knocking him to the ground. The suspect had no idea what hit him.

Detectives interviewed him later when he could speak again but couldn't tie him to any specific break-in. He, of course, denied breaking into any vehicles and said he only ran because he was scared.

It's funny how things like that work out. He said he never broke into any cars, but once he was arrested, the burglaries stopped. It doesn't take a genius to figure that one out.

The Po-lice is Santa Claus!

Saturday, December 24, 1983 was the first Christmas I ever worked. During my time as a police cadet, I was considered an administrative employee and entitled to have holidays off. No one likes to work on Christmas, especially officers with wives and children waiting impatiently at home, but I didn't mind. I was single and still living at home with my parents.

That night I was assigned to ride with Officer Kevin Putnam in District Twelve. Kevin was a somewhat quiet and reserved man who never said much. I didn't know him well at the time, but Officer Les Moore, with whom I'd worked with as a cadet told me, "I think y'all will be good partners because both of you are very religious people."

I had only been out of the academy for about six months and hadn't met any other officers who were very open about their religious beliefs.

The weather was frigid that night. The previous night had seen the temperature plunge to around ten degrees. The forecast for Christmas Eve was more bitter cold down into the single digits. I don't remember exactly when weathermen began adding the wind chill factor to their forecasts, but I know the wind chill had to be well below zero that night. I don't like being out in cold weather. I was hoping for a quiet night in the cozy confines of the heated patrol car, but I wore thermals just in case.

We left headquarters at 10:30 p.m. for our eight-hour shift. The temperature was already in the low twenties and dropping steadily in the wake of a fierce north wind that seemed to suck the heat out of everything. On the way to our district, we stopped a driver for a traffic violation. We were only out of the car for about three minutes, but during that time my ears had gone completely numb from the cold. I decided I needed a toboggan to wear to keep my ears warm.

Toboggans weren't approved uniform clothing, but this was an unusual circumstance. I ran into the Bellas Hess department store and found a black toboggan for three dollars. An off-duty deputy sheriff working security in the store let me through the line ahead of the crowd of last-minute Christmas shoppers. When I emerged from the store after only ten minutes or so, the temperature felt like it had tumbled another ten degrees with the wind howling even more intensely than before.

Having never worked on Christmas, I really didn't know what to expect or how busy we might be. About midnight we received a family disturbance call to West Edgemont Avenue. The dispatcher advised us that a black male subject was in the front yard and wouldn't let the caller take the children's Christmas presents inside the house.

We were about ten minutes away. During the drive I asked Kevin, "What kind of person would not let someone take presents to their children?"

"I don't know," he replied softly.

Since he didn't seem to want a conversation, I didn't say anything else.

We arrived at a small two-story brick duplex and saw a man in his early thirties standing in the yard. We got out of the car, and I told the man we'd speak to him in a moment after we spoke with the female complainant. She told us that the man in the yard was the father of her kids and was refusing to let her bring in the children's Christmas gifts from the trunk of her car.

She said that she didn't have much money and that she'd been paying for the presents on layaway for several months. She had picked them up and just wanted to get them inside.

She wasn't wearing a coat so I assumed she must have waited until she thought the kids were asleep before running outside to retrieve the presents. The whole time we were speaking with the mother, the father stood unsteadily in the yard repeating, "Them kids don't need no presents!"

The man's speech was somewhat slurred, so I had a feeling he had been indulging in too much holiday cheer.

Now I am a patient man, but there are certain things that make me angry enough to lose my cool. The mistreatment of children is one of those things. So many times children are the innocent victims of adults who just can't get along, and it seems the adults rarely take a child's feelings into account.

We walked over to the father and asked him the nature of his problem. The odor of alcohol was strong on his breath. His clothes smelled musty, and his appearance was generally disheveled as he swayed back and forth. When we asked him why he wouldn't let the kids have their presents, he replied angrily, "Them kids don't need no presents. Them kids is bad!"

"Why don't you just go home and let her take the presents inside," Kevin asked in voice just barely loud enough to be heard over the unrelenting wind.

"Them kids don't need no presents and I ain't gonna let them get none! Them's bad kids!"

"It's Christmas. Just let the kids have their presents and you go home," Kevin said.

"I ain't leaving, and they ain't gettin' *nothin'*!" the man ranted.

While Kevin spoke to the man, I stood to the man's right about two feet away. In spite of the blowing wind, the smell of the alcohol was strong and unmistakable.

The more my partner tried to reason with this drunk, the more irritated I became. Then I began to get angry. It was Christmas Eve, and this mother of two young children was trying to bring whatever Christmas joy she could afford to her children, likely without his help and he had the nerve, or should I say the *stupidity*, to stand in the yard and prevent it.

I don't know if it was the cold, or the fact that the kids were once again innocent victims of an unfit parent, or a combination of the two, but I'd had enough of this idiot. I stepped in between Kevin and the man, and got right up in the drunk's face.

The anger ground my teeth together, and in Clint Eastwood style, I looked him straight in the eye and said in a low growl, "Let me tell you something! You are *not* going to ruin these kids'

Christmas with your stupidness, and you have two choices. You can either walk away right now, or I'm going to take this police baton and beat you to death right here in the yard and they'll find your dead frozen body here in the morning!"

We stood there looking at each other for a few seconds as my words worked their way through his liquor-induced haze. I couldn't really tell if he was weighing his options or simply in shock in response to my threat, but I could tell that he knew I was dead serious.

Threatening to beat people to death, especially on Christmas Eve, is not standard police procedure, but police officers are only human. Dealing with calls day in and day out we learn to keep our cool and remain calm, but there are times when our buttons get pushed and we react. Officers are like anyone else, and we all have different things that set us off.

The man decided to leave. He turned slowly and unsteadily ambled down the street into the night. Kevin and I helped the mother unload the presents from the trunk of her car. She had two small matching pink metal ironing boards with little pink irons and two baby dolls. There were also a couple of children's books. Not much by some people's standards but it was all she could afford.

As we carried the gifts inside and helped set them up, I thought about all the Christmases I'd had as a kid. I had never gotten to play Santa Claus, so this was a new experience. As we were setting up the gifts in the small living room I heard soft whispers coming from the stairs. I looked up and saw two little faces about four and five years old peeping around the wall half way down the stairs. Both girls wore faded pink flannel pajamas. I pretended not to see them.

"I hope there aren't any kids out of bed right now," I said loud enough for them to hear.

Then I heard one whisper to the other, "The *po*-lice is Santa Claus! The *po*-lice is Santa Claus!"

Both girls then scurried back up the stairs.

The lady thanked us and we left.

Kevin told me as we got in the car that it wasn't a good idea to threaten to beat people to death. It wasn't professional. He warned me that if I continued to talk to people like that, I'd get myself into trouble. Of course, as the senior officer in the car, it was his job to correct me.

I told him that the guy was being a jerk and had made me angry. "I don't like people doing children wrong, and he was doing those kids wrong," I said.

"Well, if he complains, then you will have to tell the supervisors what you said."

"If he complains then I will tell them what happened," I said. "And if I get into trouble, then I will get into trouble."

We drove down West Edgemont Avenue and came upon the man stumbling against the frigid wind trying to make his way down the street. We stopped him to see where he was headed. Because of his intoxication level and the bitter cold of the night, we decided to put him in jail for his own safety. Another hour or so in the chilly wind, and hypothermia probably would have killed him.

After placing him in jail, we left headquarters headed back to our district. I couldn't help but smile at the thought of the man's kids telling their friends they knew who Santa Claus really was.

When their friends ask, "Who is really Santa Claus?"

I can picture them saying together in a matter-of-fact tone, "The PO-lice is Santa Claus!"

Christmas 1983 – Mom and me

Don't Have an Affair!

O N FRIDAY, DECEMBER 30, 1983, my partner, Officer Kevin Putnam, and I were riding District Seven on third shift patrol. When we weren't answering calls our primary job was to check buildings. Looking for burglars was our number-one priority. While patrolling on Carter Hill Road we pulled into the parking lot of Palomar Insurance and noticed a van parked in the middle of the lot. Since it wasn't in a parking space, that made it suspicious. It also had a tag from outside the county, so that added to our suspicions, that the van didn't belong there.

The van was unlocked, and I noticed a purse on the front passenger seat. We began to walk around the building, checking the doors and windows. I had only been out of the police academy six months, so I was the one who did most of the work. As I pulled on the doors one by one checking them, they were locked. The majority of businesses we check we find the doors and windows secure, so checking the doors can become routine. As I pulled on the last door, it came open. I looked at my partner and he saw that I had found an unlocked door. Kevin radioed in that we had a code 16 (open door) but there was no sign of forced entry. The door was probably left open but we had to check the building to make sure. As we entered the door we saw pieces of clothing strewn down the long hallway. We saw a woman's shoe on the carpet. Kevin and I both looked at each other and grinned. Then another woman's shoe lying next to a pair of men's shoes. A woman's blouse, a man's shirt and a skirt were on the floor as we slowly walked down the hallway. As we got half-way down the hall we could hear giggling coming from one of the offices. We stopped at the office door where the clothes ended. There were four tickets to the 1984 Sugar Bowl, Auburn vs. Michigan.

My partner called out, "Police department!"

The giggling stopped immediately. "Who is it?" came a voice from a dark office. With pistols and flashlights in hand, we slowly opened the door and saw a guy sitting in the chair behind the office desk. To our left was a woman's head sticking up from behind the desk. "I'm Ray Blake * I work here," he said.

"You two need to get dressed and come out here and talk to us," my partner told them.

"We need our clothes," Mr. Blake said.

I gathered up all the clothes in one big bundle and placed them on the desk. We closed the door and waited a few minutes for them to get dressed and come up with a story. They both came out and the young woman was embarrassed. We got both of their names and checked them for warrants.

"I work here," he said as he pointed to his name plate on the wall next to the door. The female identified herself as Marlene Bynum**.

While we were waiting on the warrant check to come back, they were telling us about how they came to be there in the wee hours of the morning. In these situations, the stories get kind of lame and then it always ends with the statement "you know how it is."

He wanted to know if his wife would have to know. Up until that question, I was giving him the benefit of the doubt that they were both single and they just stopped by his office to mess around. I recognized the last name of the woman and asked, "Are you related to Elizabeth Bynum***?" She covered her face with her hands and cried out, "Oh my God, you know Elizabeth!" Elizabeth was in my Algebra class at Lanier my senior year. I was a senior and she was a junior.

She asked me if I was going to mention this to her sister.

"No," I replied. "I hadn't seen her since high school."

The warrant check came back and Miss Bynum was negative,

---

*   Name changed to protect the unfaithful

**   Name changed

*** Name changed

but Mr. Blake had a capias warrant for an unpaid traffic ticket. He said he had forgotten about the ticket and thought it had been paid. We arrested him and took him to jail. She followed us down to police headquarters driving his van and was going to bail him out. While en route to headquarters, he began to get mad and told us, "I'm best friends with the Mayor, and if you want to keep your jobs you better let me go."

Since I'd only been out of the academy a short time, I wasn't sure who really knew the mayor and who didn't. As time went on, however, I found out that *everybody* was the Mayor's best friend, and they were *all* after my job.

I explained to him that we were only doing our job.

"You won't have your jobs in the morning!" he replied.

I turned to him. "Well, if you've got that much pull," I said calmly, "Then just have me fired."

After we arrived at headquarters, Mr. Blake began to apologize for threatening us and said, "I understand that you are only doing your job, and that's what you get paid for."

We took Mr. Blake upstairs to jail and then met Miss Bynum in the back parking lot and told her how much his bail would be. She did not have any idea how to bail someone out of jail.

"Forget it!" she said. "I'm tired of the whole thing and he can get himself out of jail! I'm through with him!"

She then got into his van and left. I guess she took his van to wherever her car was parked and left his van for him to find. I can only imagine what he told his wife. Every time I ride by Palomar Insurance, I remember that night and wonder how long he waited for her to bail him out.

My advice to anyone who wants to have an affair; if you stop by your office for a midnight rendezvous, make sure you lock the door behind you. Also, you might want to make sure you have all your unpaid tickets paid. Or better yet, if you are married, then be faithful to your spouse and don't have an affair!

THE WINDOWS OF GIRLS

SUNDAY, JANUARY 8, 1984, I was assigned to ride with Officer Bill Morris in District Three. My regular partner, Kevin Putnam, had taken the night off. Around 11:30 that night we received a call to Withers Street on the report of someone shot. When we arrived at the run down duplex, we found James Scott,* a twenty-four-year-old man lying face down in one of the doorways.

We rolled him over and he looked up at us and gasped, "I been *stobbed*."

"No," I corrected. "You've been shot!"

The paramedics arrived and began to treat the small wound in his chest that trickled a steady stream of blood onto the worn wood floor. Investigators Richard Teague and James Hamner, of the robbery-homicide bureau, arrived on the scene and began questioning the other people in the house. Teague told us to be careful because there was probably a gun somewhere in the house. I did a quick search of each room but didn't see a gun anywhere. Then I blocked the other doorway next to the victim and began a crime scene log by taking down the names of everyone present at the crime scene.

After taking down all their names, I decided to ask the only question that no one was asking. "Does anybody know who shot the guy in the next room?"

A young woman sitting on a dirty musty couch replied, "Larry Russell**shot him."

"How do you know he shot him," I asked.

"James said he did."

"Where does Larry Russell live?"

---

*   Not his real name

**   Not his real name

"He lives on French Street."

I called Teague into the room. "You need to talk to *her*," I said, indicating the woman. Then I turned to her. "Tell him what you told me about who shot him."

"Larry Russell shot him," she said. "James dates Larry's daughter."

Teague and I went over to French Street to try and locate Mr. Russell. We found him at home. He calmly answered the door and told us what happened.

It seems that James had been sneaking into his sixteen-year-old daughter's window and having sex with her. James would throw small rocks at his daughter's window and signal her to open the window and let him crawl inside. When Russell's daughter finally confessed this to her father, he had her sleep in the bed with her mother. He armed himself and lay in wait in his daughter's room. When the small rocks once again clattered against the window in the dead of night, Mr. Russell unlocked the window and waited for James to creep into the room. He then shot the young man with a .22 caliber pistol. James fled the house, ran home to Withers Street a couple of blocks away and collapsed in the doorway.

I placed Mr. Russell under arrest, and we returned with him to the house where James was being treated for the gunshot wound. At the house I spoke with two women as investigators photographed the scene and interviewed the other witnesses.

One of the ladies said, "I was shot in the head three years ago." She pointed at the scar between her eyes.

The other woman pointed out a scar on her shoulder, "I was shot too."

I don't know if Mr. Russell was ever charged or what ultimately happened to James, but I bet from then on he thought twice about sneaking into the windows of girls.

WE WORKED WELL AS A TEAM

WHEN WORKING THE NIGHT SHIFT, a police officer must be able to do a little bit of everything. During my time on the night shift, there were two detectives working after midnight and no traffic units. If anything other than a major felony occurred, we were supposed to be able to handle it. The day and evening shift had traffic units working to handle speeders and fender-benders, but at night it was just us. That gave us skills other patrolmen didn't share, but the state accident report was always quite a chore to complete and get correct. Filling out an accident report was time-consuming and tedious, and a new version of the report that came out a few months earlier was still a little unfamiliar to most of us.

On Tuesday, October 23, 1984, Officer Pat Sides and I were riding in District Four in the northeast corner of the city. Pat was an experienced veteran officer and one of the few women employed by the department at that time.

Shortly after we went on duty, we were dispatched to Twain Curve at the Eastern Boulevard on a traffic accident. The dispatcher advised us that a truck had overturned. Pat and I had worked out a deal between us that I would work all the traffic accidents and she would write all incident-offense reports when we responded to any other call. I thought this was a great idea because we worked very few accidents in comparison to the number of offense reports written.

When we arrived we found a large panel truck turned over on its side in the ditch between the service road and the main highway of the Eastern Boulevard. A twenty-year-old man was standing on top, or actually on the side of the truck when we arrived.

"Are you hurt?" I yelled up at him as we got out of the car.

"No!" he shouted back.

"Is anyone else in the truck?"

"No!"

"Come down off that truck!"

"Sure, man," he replied gleefully. "Comin' right down." He then leaned over and did an awkward half-dive half-jump off the truck and fell clumsily to the ground. He landed with a hard thud but then sprang up to his feet. "Oh, Wow!" he muttered. He seemed somewhat surprised that gravity had caught him so unaware.

"Do you have a driver's license or any type of ID?" I asked.

"No," he replied with a broad grin. "But I got some joints. Ya want some?" He seemed very enthusiastic at the prospect of providing us with these.

I slipped into character rather quickly and surprised myself. "Yeah, I'll take some joints!" I answered, mimicking the enthusiasm he seemed to exude.

He then handed me a bag of marijuana he pulled from his left front pocket. I took the bag and placed it in my back pocket.

"Hey, put your hands behind your back," I said with renewed eagerness.

"Why do I have to put my hands behind me?" he asked. He now seemed a little puzzled.

"Oh, we handcuff everyone who has marijuana," I told him calmly. I was suddenly a cop again.

"Wow! That's great!" He seemed just as happy as if I'd just fired up a joint and shared my wildest dreams with him.

The more I talked to the guy, the more apparent it was that he wasn't just drunk but extremely stoned on some type of drug, probably some of the marijuana he was trying to share with us.

I placed him in the back seat of our patrol vehicle and started to question him about the cause of the accident, but he didn't want to talk about the accident. He really wanted Pat and me to go party with him.

"I got three dollars and we can go and buy a six pack and get drunk," he exclaimed.

As I filled out the accident report and waited for the wrecker, the young man continued to bask in the euphoria of the drug. He rambled on about partying, drinking beer and getting high. He also mentioned that he worked with the traveling fair and was on his way to Birmingham. Needless to say, he spent the remainder of the night enjoying his high in the comfort of our city jail.

I responded to many accidents while I worked the night shift with Pat, but this one stood out as one in particular that made me wonder what some people are thinking, and smoking, when they get behind the wheel.

As I worked more traffic accidents, I got pretty proficient and didn't mind all the paperwork. Typically, Pat would get all the necessary information, such as the vehicle identification numbers (VIN's) and other vehicle information and call for wreckers if we needed them while I interviewed the drivers and filled out the lengthy report.

We had a great system and we worked well as a team.

I Need to See Your Driver's License

NOT MUCH HAPPENS IN MONTGOMERY after midnight during the week. On the weekends, it usually dies off after 2 a.m. when most people are at home asleep. This clears the highways of nearly all traffic. The only problem is that drag racers sometime take advantage of these open roadways to engage in a little competition with their fast cars. Sometimes we're able to catch drag racers, but it's usually the slower guy who lost the race.

Tuesday, October 30, 1984, Officer Pat Sides and I were riding District Seven in southeast Montgomery, which consisted mostly of quiet neighborhoods with businesses lining the South Boulevard. Most of our patrol time is spent checking businesses along the bypass.

As we drive in between and around closed businesses checking for burglaries, we can see and hear the traffic on the Bypass. You can hear the roaring of engines as vehicles speed by or the racing of engines as drivers wait for the traffic lights to change to green. The squealing rubber and smoke billowing off the tires, signaled us to traffic violations in progress.

As we drove through the parking lot of the Governors Square Shopping Center and stopped at the traffic light at Wallace Drive and the Boulevard, we saw two vehicles drag racing. They flew through the intersection traveling west in front of us and we immediately pulled out and began to pursue them. We turned on our blue lights and siren and the driver of the Chevrolet Camaro pulled over. The maroon Gran Prix won and got away.

The passenger, a young man of about nineteen to twenty years old, stepped out from the driver's seat and walked back to my vehicle. The driver, a young female whom I recognized from high school, followed. She was one year behind me and was one of the popular girls, a who's who in high school. "You obviously don't know who my father is," he stated firmly like I was suppose to be impressed. What's the deal with people thinking that police will tremble in their boots if they mention who their father is or who they know? But, I will play along and always ask, "So who is your father?"

"He is a Colonel at Maxwell Air Force base," he said, with a cocky attitude and smirk on his face.

"Your father has jurisdiction on the base, but off the base he *has* no jurisdiction. As a matter of fact, it doesn't matter who your father, mother, grandmother, or great uncle is. I have the final say so on what happens on these streets in Montgomery," I told him with authority. He just bowed his head, walked back to the car, got in and closed the door.

His date then stepped up and stated, "You *obviously* don't know who *my* father is." *Okay, here we go again,* I thought. Tired of the 'Do you know who my father is' game I replied, "It doesn't matter to me who he is."

"He's a major with the state troopers!" she said defiantly. I took her driver's license and went back to the car and wrote her a ticket for Reckless Driving while Pat talked to her. She calmed down during their conversation and by the time I walked back up to her she was acting nice. She told my partner who her father was and he was in fact a major with the Alabama State Troopers. She also explained that the maroon Gran Prix was trying to run them off the road. I don't know if this was the truth or if she was just grasping at straws, trying to get out of the ticket by blaming her driving on someone else. It didn't appear to me that anyone was trying to run anybody off the road when I saw them race by. "My fathers goin' to be mad when he sees you gave me a ticket," she told me as she signed the ticket.

"I get off at 6:30 this morning. Have your father call me before I get off, and if he feels that I gave you this ticket unfairly then I will tear it up," I explained.

"Oh, no. He will kill me and take away my car if I tell him I got a ticket. I'll just pay it and not tell em," she stated.

"Okay, it's your choice."

I gave her, her copy of the ticket and explained that she would have to appear in court since it was a mandatory court appearance ticket and the court date was on the ticket. "If you feel you got the ticket unjustly then you can plead not guilty and the judge will set up a court date and both of us will appear before the judge. You can tell your side and I will tell mine," I explained.

"No. I will just pay it and hope my dad doesn't find out," she said quietly.

As I gained experience as a police officer, I made many traffic stops and from time to time I would hear, especially from teenagers and young adults, "Do you know who my father is?" I came up with a snappy comeback for that question by asking, "No, do you know who my father is?" They would get this puzzled look on their face and say, "Ah, no, I don't." I would then say, "Okay, then we're even. Now, I need to see your driver's license, please."

He Lived in the Building Next Door

Tuesday, November 13, 1984, was a slow night, typical back then for a weeknight on third shift. I was assigned to District Eight which at that time was the area located west of Troy Highway and South of the boulevard. I was paired up with Officer David Salum that night. My regular partner and Dave's had both taken the night off, so the sergeant paired us up for the evening. Dave had been out of the academy for less than a year, so I was the senior officer.

Dave was a sports fan and a really huge basketball fan, especially college basketball. Now, when I say huge, I mean HUGE! He knew everything there was to know about college basketball, or at least he seemed to. I wasn't a big sports fan, especially when it came to basketball. When I was in high school, I played in two different church basketball leagues for three years. In my entire career I scored *one* basket. I was the worst basketball player in history.

I can usually hold my own in a conversation about football or baseball, but I was always a little lost on basketball or hockey. But Dave's knowledge of teams, players and stats left my head spinning. He really knew his stuff and even though I knew very little about the sport, the conversation helped pass the time on that slow night.

Around 2:30 that morning the basketball talk was interrupted by the dispatcher's voice. She sent us on a burglary in progress call to the Stonebridge Apartments on Strathmore Drive. The victim had called and said that a subject was trying to break down the front door. It took less than three minutes for us to arrive at the scene. We ran from our vehicle and found the apartment on the second floor.

We found a very intoxicated young man on the balcony

46

attempting to force his way into the sliding glass door. Dave went around to the front door to speak with the complainant, and got the man's attention from the stairway immediately adjacent to the balcony. From his loud slurred speech and having to hold onto the railing, I could tell that he was extremely drunk.

He told me that he was trying to get inside his apartment but that his girlfriend wouldn't let him in. I notified the dispatcher that the call wasn't a burglary but a simple disturbance and to cancel any back-up units.

I ordered the subject down. He stepped from the balcony onto the staircase with his right foot. It had been sprinkling rain off and on all night and the wood was wet and slippery. When the suspect tried to climb down, he lost his footing and fell, landing hard with a splash in the puddle of water from the rainspout. He was so drunk, however, it didn't seem to faze him. He pulled himself up and began staggering and yelling. I had to physically push him against the railing of the ground level stoop to control him. Sergeant Willie Echols, our supervisor, arrived on the scene and went upstairs where Dave was to meet the complainant. Dave called down a moment later and asked me to find out the man's name. He said his name was Alex Kendall.*

While Dave and Sergeant Echols continued to speak with the complainant, Alex became belligerent and kept trying to leave. I grabbed him and he stumbled to the ground with me in tow. We both fell in the wet grass and mud.

Struggling with a belligerent drunk is never an easy task. They tend to be limp and don't feel much pain. I finally got him handcuffed, thinking all the while that Dave or the Sergeant would hear the commotion and come down to assist me. I sat him down at the bottom of the stairs and eventually Dave and Sergeant Echols came down.

"What happened to you?" Dave asked. "You look like crap!"

"The guy got unruly and I had to wrestle him to the ground. What were y'all doin' while I was dealin' with this guy?"

"Run a twenty-nine on him and if he's clean, then make sure

---

*   Name changed just to be nice

he gets home," Sergeant Echols interrupted, as he walked by the subject.

"Man, you should have come upstairs and seen these girls. They are foxes!" Dave said, with great excitement.

"I was dealin' with this knuckle head." I replied in disgust.

"I ain't no knuckle head," Alex muttered in his drunken stupor.

"Both ladies were about twenty-two and came to the door with nothin' on!" Dave said in a loud whisper. "I kept trying to get your attention but you would never look up at me. Man, you missed it."

Fortunately for Alex, he didn't have any warrants.

Dave said, "Let's just take him home."

I don't know why the sergeant wanted us to take him home instead of arresting him for public intoxication. We must have been short handed that night and it was easier to take him home than put him in jail and be tied up with paperwork for several hours. After all, he was close to home anyway.

While Dave was talking to the complainant he found out that Alex was at the wrong apartment. All the buildings look alike, and due to the level of inebriation, he had gone to the wrong apartment. He lived in the building next door.

No One Was Hurt

WEEKNIGHTS ON THIRD SHIFT PATROL are usually not busy, with the possible exception on the eve of a holiday. Wednesday, November 21, 1984, was one of those nights. We came on duty at 10:30 p.m. and when the clock passed midnight into Thursday, it was Thanksgiving. I was riding in District Eleven with Officer Ronnie Felder, who had been with the department less than a year. We were just finishing the paperwork on a traffic accident when we were dispatched to an address on South Decatur Street to investigate a hang-up call.

The dispatcher advised us that a woman had called and stated only that she needed the police before hanging up. This kind of call can be anything from siblings arguing to a homicide. As police officers, however, we're obligated to respond to all calls for help, and we have to be prepared for anything when we arrive. It was also difficult to prepare my rookie partner on what to expect when I didn't know what to expect myself.

We arrived at the address given and found that the house we were looking for was actually located behind the house where the call originated. Some of the older houses downtown have smaller houses behind them that can't be seen from the street. I contacted the dispatcher and updated the address and the exact location of the house. If things turned bad, I wanted any back-up unit to know without a doubt where we were.

We cautiously walked to the door and knocked. A woman answered the door and as she did so she handed me the phone receiver. "Listen to this," she whispered.

I could hear two people talking, but I couldn't quite understand what they were saying.

We stepped inside and she explained her situation. A young girl about nine-years old stood silently in the living room.

"My husband and I went to the Alabama State University alumni dance at the Civic Center earlier this evening, and I danced one dance with an old schoolmate," the woman explained. "My husband got real jealous and has been angry with me ever since we left the dance. Now he's in the back bedroom with a pistol."

We were standing in the living room right in front of the hallway that led to the bedrooms in the back of the house.

"Are there any more kids in the back of the house?" I asked.

"Yes, there are two more back there, but he won't hurt the kids," she said. "He's just mad at me."

I sent the child in the room with us to get the other two and bring them back to the living room.

Suddenly, one of the kids in the back came running down the hall from the back room with terror on his face. "Daddy's coming down the hall and he's gonna shoot the police and anybody else in the house!"

I immediately called for back-up and had Ronnie quickly take the kids outside. The woman refused to go outside, so I pushed her to the floor away from the hallway, drew my Smith & Wesson .357 revolver and took up a defensive position to the left of the hallway. I was prepared to shoot the man if he came down the hallway with a gun. I figured since they had been to a party that he might have had too much to drink and he probably wasn't using the best judgment.

My sergeant called me on the radio, and I quickly briefed him on what I had. Corporal Denson of the K-9 unit arrived moments later as our back-up. The man never did come down the hall, and it was probably a bluff to get us to leave. I ordered the wife out of the house, and I slowly backed out making sure he didn't try to shoot at us.

We took the woman and her frightened children to the grandmother's house on Southmont Drive. While en route to the house the wife told me that her husband had attempted suicide by shooting himself in the chest a couple of years earlier. This information could have been useful had there been an armed standoff with the man.

This is one of those calls that could have gone downhill quickly but actually ended on a good note. We left the man in the house alone so he could calm down and sober up. It was the best possible outcome for the situation.

Jealousy is an ugly thing, and this was something that needed to be worked out between the husband and the wife without the kids around. When you mix healthy doses of alcohol and jealousy, then add a gun, nothing good can happen. Fortunately, everything worked out and no one was hurt.

"Guns! Guns!"

SOME NIGHTS, AFTER MY SHIFT ended, I would often wonder how I survived. Wednesday December 5, 1984, turned out to be one of those nights.

My partner that night, Officer Jerome White, a massive and powerful man. A former star football player in college, he stood only five eleven, but was two hundred and fifty pounds of lean, pure muscle. His arms are the size of most men's legs, and he looks as if he could bench press a Buick. He was definitely a guy I wanted on my side when things got ugly.

On this particular night, ugly seemed to be just one call away. As the night began, every call which we responded to involved a gun. The MPD radio terminology for someone with a gun was code 8, and after nine or ten of those, we were somewhat relieved to be dispatched to a code 29 instead. That was the code for a stranded motorist—usually someone broken down with a flat tire or someone out of gas, nothing we normally consider dangerous. We headed toward the call on the North Boulevard at Sixth Street with a welcome sigh of relief.

The dispatcher gave us a description of a red and white pick-up pulling a U-Haul trailer stuck in the ditch. As we arrived, we noticed that the vehicle was resting at a forty-five degree angle down in a ditch adjacent to the roadway where the driver had pulled off in the darkness looking for a shoulder and found a four-foot deep trench instead. A man in his fifties sat behind the wheel of the sloping vehicle. I saw that the window was about halfway down as I approached.

"Hey, how are you doing?" I asked.

"Okay," he replied, without looking up.

52

I had to step down into the ditch and lean against the truck with the right side of my hip and shoulder to open the door to help him out of the truck. I opened the door with my left hand and a security guard who had walked up held the door open.

"Can you get out on your own, or do you need some help?" I asked.

"I can get out by myself," the man replied.

I stepped away from the truck and the man quickly grabbed the door, closed and locked it. He began to dig around into the middle console between the seats as if looking for something.

I looked at the security guard and he gave me a look that said, 'I'll hold the door and you get him.'

I reached in the half-open window, unlocked the door, and opened it. That's when I saw the man pull a revolver from the console in his right hand and swing it around toward me.

It is amazing how fast my training ran through my mind before I reacted. I was leaning on my holster and right shoulder preventing me from drawing my own weapon, but I noticed the man's weapon was a revolver. I recalled in an instant from my training that by grabbing the cylinder and preventing it from rotating as the trigger was pulled, it wouldn't fire. I grabbed the pistol around the cylinder and squeezed with everything I had.

"GUN!" I yelled, hoping Jerome could hear me.

The man and I struggled for possession of the pistol and after a moment or two I was able to pull it from his grasp. I stepped back from the truck, held up the gun. "I got it! I got it!" I yelled.

Jerome, with only his left hand, reached into the cab of the truck, grabbed the man's shirt and jacket and yanked him out of the truck. My partner held him off the ground for a moment, and he dangled there like a puppet, completely helpless and at Jerome's mercy. Jerome held him suspended in the air for what seemed like a couple of seconds, then he gently set him on the ground and placed him in custody. My powerful partner could have broken every bone in the man's body with very little effort, but I learned that all that strength was under the command of a gentle giant.

We arrested the man and took him to jail. Jerome and I had survived another call involving a gun. That night, even the calls that weren't suppose to involve guns, involved guns. Maybe that was the Lord's way of preparing us to be alert for guns when we encountered this gentleman. In the police academy your instructors repeat the mantra, "Watch their hands!" This was a perfect example of why that rule is so important.

From that night on, every time I see Jerome or he sees me, we always say to each other, "Guns! Guns!"

But Then the Lord
Sets Me Straight

I MET SOME INTERESTING PEOPLE WHILE working the midnight shift. In the wee hours of the morning people were scarce, except maybe on the weekends when the bars stayed open most of the night. On occasion, however, I ran across someone just trying to make it through life—one day at a time.

Our primary function on the late shift after the calls died down was to check businesses to make sure they were secure—and to hunt for burglars. Most home burglaries take place during the day when residents are at work and the homes are vacant. Business burglaries, however, occurred mostly at night when the owners and employees are home asleep. Burglars who hit businesses prefer to do so on Friday and Saturday nights because usually the crime wouldn't be discovered until Monday morning.

Saturday, February 9, 1985, I met someone who taught me something I would never forget. On this particular night the temperature had dropped to the low twenties with an icy wind that sent the wind chill plummeting into the single digits. On nights like this, I always avoided getting out in the weather whenever possible. If I had to get out for any length of time I found myself complaining about the bitter cold and freezing wind.

"Who in their right mind would be out in this cold?" I often heard myself say before quickly retreating to the warm confines of the patrol car.

The new master worksheet had just come out the night before and Officer Jon G. Shultz and I had just been assigned District Seven. District Seven was mostly neighborhoods with small to mid-sized homes with manicured lawns and businesses along the main roads. We were anxious to learn the new district and make sure no businesses were burglarized on our watch.

We patrolled on the Eastern Boulevard around 2:30 that morning, driving behind building after building checking the back doors to make sure they were all secure. While driving behind Forbes Piano Company, we pulled up behind a green station wagon with wood grain sides parked in the back. I radioed in our location then got out to check the car. The station wagon didn't seem to be the type of vehicle a thief might use to burglarize a piano store, but I've learned that anything is possible.

I walked down one side of the car while my partner walked down the other, lighting up the car's interior with our flashlights. I noticed that the windows seemed unusually fogged when I heard a noise come from the dumpster behind us. Jon and I redirected our beams toward the dumpster just in time to see a large flattened cardboard piano box fly out of it.

Then a man wearing a black toboggan, who looked to be in his thirties, dressed in a green camouflage coat zipped up to the neck, climbed out of the dumpster without noticing our presence. When he bent to pick up the box he saw us and froze.

I asked him what he was doing. He replied that he was getting cardboard to take home with him. He motioned toward the roof of his car. Stacked on top were about eight to ten flattened boxes.

"Why are you out in the middle of the night collecting boxes from the dumpster?" I asked, already numb from the cold.

"My house has cracks in the walls and the cardboard keeps the wind out," he replied respectfully.

"What do you mean keeps the wind out?"

"When it's really cold and windy, sir, the wind blows in the cracks of the walls and my family gets cold," he said, motioning toward the car.

I lit up the interior of the car again and noticed a woman sitting in the front passenger seat and two children sitting in the back, bundled in clothing that appeared tattered and worn. The children, a boy about eight and a girl maybe six or so, were curled up tightly, arms folded under them trying desperately to keep warm.

"How exactly do you use the cardboard to keep warm?" I asked him. "Are you burning it or what?"

"Oh no, sir," he replied. "I use it as insulation. I nail it up on the inside walls of my house. It covers up the cracks and keeps the wind out."

"Where do you live?"

"Traction Avenue, sir," he replied. "I didn't think I was stealing it because it was in the trash. I'll put it back if it's not okay for me to get it. I was just trying to take care of my family the best I could."

I was familiar with the houses on Traction Avenue and most are in bad shape. They are old, wooden structures, probably built during the post-war years of the late forties and early fifties. A lot of them are rotting and falling in.

By this time my partner had gone back to the patrol car to run a warrant check on the man. I walked to the passenger side where my partner was sitting and told him, "I think he's okay. C'mon, let's give him a hand."

My partner looked up at me with a puzzled expression. "What do you mean give him a hand?"

"Help him load his car with the cardboard."

We walked back to where the man was standing. "If you throw the cardboard out of the dumpster," I said, "We'll put it on top of the car for you."

"Thank you, sir! I really 'preciate it! It'll really help keep the wind out."

He climbed into the dumpster and threw out more boxes. I handed them to my partner who stacked them neatly on top of the man's car. After loading about a dozen or more boxes, we helped him tie them down.

He shook our hands and walked away toward his car.

In that moment, something compelled me to call out to him again. "Hey, wait a minute," I yelled. I walked over to him and handed him a ten-dollar bill out of my wallet. "Make sure the kids get something hot to eat tonight."

"You don't have to do this, sir," he said. "We'll be okay,"

It was obvious that his pride was interfering with the well being of his family.

"No, just take it for the kids." I said.

He took the money with a sad smile, thanked us again, then left.

My heart goes out to those who must endure such hardship. It seems whenever I complain about the troubles I face, I always meet someone whose truly tragic situation puts my own in perspective. I may have been cold checking buildings, but I did have a warm patrol car to ride in and a warm home waiting for me at the end of the night.

I've never had to dig through dumpsters in the middle of a freezing night and nail up cardboard just to keep my family warm. It's funny, whenever I start to complain about things, the Lord shows me just how really blessed I am. I still complain sometimes, but then the Lord sets me straight.

WE WERE ABLE TO HELP THEM

FIRE FIGHTERS HAVE A TOUGH job—no question about it. Personally, I would rather search for an armed suspect in a building than to rush into one engulfed in flames. There's something about getting burned that just doesn't sit too well with me. On Tuesday, March 26, 1985, I got to experience firsthand just how dangerous a fire can be.

Officer Jon Shultz and I were covering Districts Seven and Eight on the night shift. We were patrolling McGehee Road around 3:30 in the morning when we smelled smoke in the area.

It wasn't cold enough outside for anyone to need a fireplace, and the late hour immediately raised our suspicions, so we began riding through the area trying to locate the source of the smoke. We drove slowly down Fisk Road until we saw a haze of smoke hovering like a dirty ghost over the street. As we drove toward the haze, I noticed an orange glow above the house in its midst. Thick black smoke billowed and boiled from the eaves at either end of the roof. Jon got on the radio quickly and advised the dispatcher of the address and requested fire units.

I bolted from the car and ran to the side door under the carport. I beat loudly on the door with my five-cell flashlight. The wooden storm door was locked, so I broke out the slats to get to the side door. I attempted to force the side door, but smoke quickly began to pool beneath the carport ceiling burning my eyes and filling my lungs with its burning taste. After a few moments, I had to run back into the clear air of the front yard before I passed out. After a few gasps of fresh air, I ran to the front door and began to beat on the door, still trying to rouse any sleeping occupants who may have been inside. I wasn't sure if the house was occupied since there was no car in the driveway, but I couldn't take the chance. I tried several times to kick open the front door, but it was just too sturdy.

"Stand back!" Jon yelled. In the darkness I saw him run at full speed toward the front door and launch a flying side-kick against it. His hundred and sixty or so pounds on his six-foot-one inch frame was enough to burst like a battering ram through the door. Jon disappeared through the doorway into a thick black smoke. A few moments later, eyes still burning, I ran up to the door looking for him. All I could see was his soot-covered hand extending back toward me. I grabbed his hand and dragged him out into the yard. He was coughing, gagging and spewing up snot, but otherwise he seemed okay.

"Man! I saw you fly through the door and then you were gone!" I exclaimed.

"I didn't think the door would fly open like that," he said with some surprise. "I thought I was a goner until you pulled me out." I sensed the relief in his voice.

I then ran around to the left side of the house, grabbed the top of the chain link fence and hopped over. I wanted to try to go through the back door but as I hit the ground I saw the back door was fully engulfed in flames. I thought that was strange, but I just hopped back over the fence. I saw a window air conditioner and figured it was probably mounted in a bedroom window, so I punched my fist through the plastic accordion fillers between the sides of the unit and the window frame. My hand went inside, and I felt powerful heat from the flames in the room before quickly withdrawing my hand.

I went back around to the front of the house as the first fire truck pulled up. I ran to the supervisor on the truck. "We tried to get inside to see if anyone was home," I told him. "There are no cars here, so I don't think anyone's home." I had to pause to catch my breath. "We kicked the front door open, trying to get in. The back door is fully engulfed in flames."

"Okay, thanks. We got it now," he told me. His men went to work quickly hooking up hoses and assaulting the fire like a finely tuned machine.

Several additional fire units arrived, and we watched the fire fighters enter through the front door to battle the flames. The fire fighters were only in the house about thirty seconds when one of them attempted to run out of the house. He tripped and fell in the threshold of the doorway. He was screaming. The sound was muffled by the mask of his breathing apparatus, more commonly called a SCOT Pack, but I could tell something was wrong.

I had been to enough fires to know that something was not right because fire fighters don't come screaming out of burning houses. Jon and I ran up to the door when I heard a second fire fighter fall on top of the first, also screaming. Before we could cover the distance of the small yard, a third fire fighter had fallen on top of his comrades. Jon and I grabbed the guy on top of the pile by the air tank on his back and rolled him out of the door into the yard.

We then grabbed the second one and rolled him into the yard. The bottom fire fighter who had tried to get out first began to crawl out. We grabbed him also and pulled him out into the yard. Later, one of them told us that as they were crawling through the house, a stream of flames had shot up between their legs as they moved cautiously down the hallway. All of them received minor burns to their legs.

The next night, as we were waiting for roll call, one of the arson investigators from the fire department came down to the roll call room. I just happened to meet him at the bottom of the stairs. "Hey, how's it going tonight?" I asked.

"Great!" he replied. I saw him check my name tag.

"Who are you looking for?" I asked.

"You, as a matter of fact," he said.

"Really?" I replied. "What'd I do?"

"You were at the fire last night on Fisk Road, weren't you?" he asked.

"Yes sir, I was."

"It's going to be an arson case," he said.

"Arson?" I said. "Really?" I was surprised.

"The house was burglarized, and the suspect poured gasoline throughout the house and set it on fire," he said. "The suspect broke in through the back door and when he left, set the fire."

"That explains why the back door was on fire when I jumped over the fence," I said.

"What caused the fire fighters to come running out of the front door?" I asked.

"The suspect poured gas all through the house and when they were crawling down the hall, it caught on fire and the flames ran between their legs," he explained.

"That makes sense," I said. "Because I'd never seen firemen run out of a house screaming like that. They piled up in the door and my partner and I had to pull them out."

"I need to get a statement from you about what you saw."

"Okay. Let's go into the break room," I said and pointed the way.

I recounted the events of the incident in as much detail as I could recall and he recorded my statement. Afterward, he left. It never crossed my mind during the whole affair that the fire could be arson. I was more concerned about just getting everyone out of the house. I never did hear what happened with the investigation, but whenever I drove down Fisk Road afterward I was taken back to the night of the fire. Fire fighters and paramedics are always helping others, including police officers, and it seems the most we do in return is to direct traffic at a fire. So that night when those three fire fighters fell in the doorway, we were able to help them.

Thanks for the Phone Call

EARLY ON THE MORNING OF Saturday, August 10, 1985, while riding in District Five on third shift patrol, Officer Patrick Murphy and I responded to investigate a call from an employee of City Ambulance Company on Chestnut Street near Ann Street. The employee, who was an ambulance paramedic, had gone in to the small gas station on the corner next door to their building to buy something and noticed a woman crying in the back room of the business. He thought she might be in some sort of trouble and wanted the police to check on her.

As we drove toward Ann Street, I remember that Patrick asked me what I thought the problem might be.

"Probably a boyfriend-girlfriend thing," I replied. "But you never know. As soon as you think you've got it figured out, it'll be something else. So never assume anything."

I'd only been on the street since June of 1983, and I was still learning that I hadn't seen everything. Even though officers may call something routine in police work, there really is no such thing. The day any police officer falls into that trap, someone usually gets hurt.

Patrick was still a rookie officer on probation. The training and probation period began upon graduation from the police academy and lasted one year. I was substituting for his regular training officer, who had taken some time off, so this was our first time working together.

His identical twin brother, Kevin, was to join the department about a year later. I'm glad police officers wear name tags because I could never tell them apart. I'm not a hundred percent sure even today which is which.

Once we arrived, the ambulance medic waved us down.

"The white female was behind the counter in a back room crying," the medic told us. "The clerk is her boyfriend or husband or something. I think he has been beating on her because she's crying really bad. When I asked him if she was okay, he got really pissed and told me to mind my own business."

He walked back toward his office but turned toward us before we left. "Y'all be careful. I think the guy is crazy!" he shouted.

We entered the store cautiously and approached the male clerk standing silently behind the counter.

"Hey, how's it going?" I asked.

"Fine," he replied. His tone was sharp and blunt.

"Everything okay here?" I continued in a calm voice.

"Yeah, everything's fine. Why?"

"We got a call of a female crying, and we wanted to make sure everything was okay."

"There's no one here but me and, like I said, everything is *fine!*"

Patrick moved up and continued to question the guy. I moved to where I could get a better view behind the counter into the back room. I saw a young woman sitting on a plastic milk crate. Her eyes were red and puffy, and her face was splotchy. Tears streaked down her cheeks. When she looked up and saw me she put her hands together as if to pray and pleaded silently to me. She never said a word but I read her lips and heard her cry for help.

"Who's the young lady in the back room?" I asked the man.

He looked at me angrily. "That's my wife!" he said, spitting out the words. "Why?"

"She looks upset and she's been crying." I quickly replied.

The man looked to Patrick and me but didn't respond.

"Stay up front with him," I told Patrick. "I want to talk to her in the back room just a sec."

"You can't talk to my wife unless I say you can!" the man shouted at me.

"Sir, you need to calm down," Patrick told him firmly.

I walked into the back room keeping a cautious eye on the man.

I was careful to speak softly so the man couldn't hear. "Are you okay?"

"No!" She replied in a hoarse whisper. She was obviously terrified. "Please, please take me home!"

"Where do you live?" I asked.

"I live just up the road on Bradley Drive," she whispered. "I'm scared of him, and I think he's going to hurt me!"

"Okay," I said. "We'll take you home."

She walked out of the room with me. The terror she felt from the man's presence was tangible and etched into her face as we approached him.

"We're going to take her home," I told the man.

"You're not taking her anywhere!" he shouted. He stepped aggressively toward us.

The woman threw her arms up in front of her face defensively. She flinched with each word he spoke and moved quickly toward the door.

I stood between the man and his wife jutting my finger toward him. "You need to calm down, right now!" I said with every ounce of authority I could muster.

As soon as he moved toward us, Patrick stepped next to me adding to the barrier between the man and his wife. Patrick's demeanor told the husband clearly that he wasn't going to get to his wife or me without getting past him first.

Patrick hadn't been a cop very long, but he didn't hesitate for a moment to respond when the man became aggressive. When you ride with new officers you never know how they will react in stressful situations, especially potential confrontations.

The academy puts as much stress on trainees as they can to prepare them for physical combat, but the real test is when the young officer actually comes face to face with someone who really wants to hurt him. Officer Murphy rose to the challenge and was ready for the fight.

"We're going to take her home," I told the man. "When you get home you both can talk about whatever the problem is. This will give you a chance to calm down."

"I'll be home in a little while," he shouted angrily past Patrick at the woman. "I'll deal with you when I get home."

We escorted her to our patrol car, all the while keeping an eye on him to make sure he didn't follow us.

We loaded up and pulled onto Ann Street headed toward her house.

"What time does he get off work?" I asked.

"Seven," she replied.

I glance at my watch and saw that it was about 5:30. That gave her about an hour and a half. It would be daylight soon.

I heard her sobbing softly in the back seat. "He is so jealous when other men talk to me," she said. "He thinks they all want to sleep with me. I told him that he has nothing to be jealous about."

She got quiet for a moment. After a while she began speaking again. More softly and deliberate this time. "He said he was going to prostitute me out of the store," she said. Her voice seemed to convey the untold humiliation he had heaped upon her. "He says he was going to let men have sex with me in the back room."

"Why do you stay with him?" I asked her.

"He's not a bad guy," she replied. "Most of the time treats me good."

I can't remember how many times in the course of my police career I've heard a victim of domestic violence say the same thing.

We pulled up in front of her house. I saw that it had a large bay window. I don't really know why I remembered that detail, except maybe in the back of my mind I was thinking we might have to come back to the house later on another call. I made the mental note.

"Are you going to be okay?" I asked.

"Yeah," she said. "I'll be fine. Thanks for bringing me home."

"You've got an hour and a half before he gets off," I said. "If there's somewhere else you want to go, you've got time."

"No," she said. "I'll be fine."

Our shift ended an hour later. I got off, went home and got some sleep.

At about 3:30 that afternoon the desk sergeant called me at home and asked me if I had gone to a gas station on Ann Street and gave a young lady a ride home that morning.

I quickly recounted the incident to him

"This lady's husband has been calling all day and wants to know where you and Murphy live," the sergeant said. "He has called about four times already. When I told him we didn't give out that information he wanted to know what route you took to work every night, and if it was the same route. What did y'all do?"

"What's his problem?" I said. "We just took her home because she was upset."

"I don't know," the sergeant replied. "But he's been bothering the clerks down here all day long."

"Well, I don't know what his problem is," I said. "He was mad at us for taking her home, but he'll just have to get over that."

"Well, all right, I'll let you get back to sleep. Sorry for having to wake you up," the sergeant said. "Y'all be careful coming in tonight."

I hung up the phone. *Man, that guy must really be mad to call in so many times*, I thought to myself. I was good and awake by then, so I just got up.

About three hours later the desk sergeant called again.

"Steve, the guy's wife called just a little while ago," he said. "She told us not to send you and Murphy to her house tonight. I asked her why not and she told us that at around ten-thirty her husband was going to call in a disturbance at their house on Bradley Drive, hoping that you and Murphy respond. She said that when you two walk up, he's going to shoot you both in the front yard from inside the house, through the bay window. She told us that he has his deer rifle leaning against the wall by the window."

"Are you kidding me?" I asked. I felt a little shocked at this point. "Man, he must *really* be mad."

"You might want to take a different way to work tonight just to be on the safe side," the sergeant said. "We're checking with the warrant clerk to see if we can get a warrant for harassing communications for calling the desk so many times. Also," he added, "A second shift patrol supervisor and two patrol units are headed to that address to see if there's anything to the story."

"Alright, I appreciate the call, and I'll take a different route tonight," I said. "Thanks for the heads up on this guy."

"Okay," he added. "Be *careful*."

Like most people, I'm a creature of habit. Making myself drive another route to work took a little effort, so I left the house about fifteen minutes early. I was also curious about what had happened when the other patrol units arrived at the guy's house.

As I walked into the patrol assembly room, I saw Patrick and asked him if the desk had called him as well. He had received the same warning. About that time Lieutenant Russell Lindsey, the shift commander, called both of us into his office.

"Close the door and sit down," he said. "Let's talk about this call you went on this morning."

I just knew we were in trouble. The only time the shift commander ever called you into the office and closed the door was when you'd done something wrong. I tried to recall any mistakes we might have made, but I couldn't think of any.

"Did you give a white female a ride home from a gas station on Ann Street this morning?" he asked.

"Yes sir, we did," I replied. "We took her to her house on Bradley Drive."

"Well, the woman's husband is Chuck Blake.*" Lindsey said. "He's a mental case. I dealt with him years ago. He killed a guy on a construction site with a metal rod from a bulldozer about fifteen years ago and has been in prison."

Patrick and I just looked at each other.

"He's dangerous," Lindsey continued. "So we're going to pull you both out of five and put you somewhere else tonight in case he makes a bogus call and tries to carry out his threat."

"I understand, sir," I replied. "Where are you putting us?"

"Steve, I'm putting you in fourteen with Bishop, and I am putting Murphy with Sides in three."

I understood why he was moving us, but I also felt a sense of disappointment. It was almost as if we were letting the bad guy win by giving in to his intimidation. After all, we were police officers, and we knew the dangers of the job. We'd seen this man

---

* Name changed to protect the psychotic

face to face and knew what he looked like. If there were a call to his house or anywhere else, we could easily identify him and respond appropriately to any threat.

I figured the lieutenant moved us because, being young officers, he figured we'd ride by intentionally just to see what the guy might do. And being young officers, I can't say we wouldn't have done just that.

The work sheets are made up a day or two in advance, anytime a last minute change is made and two officers are split up, the other officers on the shift would know something was up. Once Patrick and I went into the lieutenant's office and closed the door, and the sergeant made the reassignments on the work sheet, we quickly became the hot topic among the other officers on the shift. Each officer, I'm sure, had his own theory as to what mortal sin we'd committed.

Once roll call began, however, Lieutenant Lindsey explained the situation to everyone. Afterward, as we headed out to our cars, the other officers began to pick at us a little.

"What did y'all do to piss the guy off so much to want to kill you?" one of them asked.

"Man, it sucks to be you," another added.

"I'm not sure I want to ride with you," one joked.

But that's all part of the camaraderie of being in law enforcement. Behind the jokes and kidding, I felt a genuine sense of concern from my fellow officers. I knew without a doubt that any one of them would rush to my aid even at the risk of his own life if the situation arose.

I've had many death threats in my career, but never has anyone gone to so much trouble to try and find where I live. The guy was never charged with anything because he never actually threatened either one of us directly.

After that night, I never heard anything more about him. I always assumed that the visit from the supervisor and second shift officers earlier in the day gave the guy a new outlook on things. But if I ever do get the chance to speak to the young lady who warned us about her strangely psychotic husband, I would like to say, "Thanks for the phone call!"

BE NICE

MONTGOMERY, ALABAMA IS HOME TO two major military bases; Maxwell Air Force Base and its annex, formerly known as Gunter Air Force Base. With military personnel constantly transferring in and out of these bases, I've had the opportunity to meet people from all over. Most of the soldiers and airmen I've met are very nice and show great respect for police officers; likely due to the structured military life and the similarity in training we both received. I do, however, recall a few rare occasions when I've encountered someone under the impression that military status entitled him to preferential treatment.

On September 9, 1985, my partner, Officer Terry Cullen, and I were working the midnight shift driving down Air Base Boulevard near Maxwell AFB when a vehicle flew past us on the right. Air Base Boulevard is a wide, four-lane thoroughfare that ends at the main gate of the air base. Terry and I were traveling at the speed limit when the vehicle passed us at least ten miles an hour faster. We caught up to the speeder, lit up the strobes, and stopped him with a quick blast of the siren. I walked up to the driver's window and saw that the man behind the wheel wore an Air Force uniform.

"Good evening, sir," I said politely. "I need to see your driver's license, please."

"Do you know who I am?" he replied. His tone was harsh and demanding.

"No, sir," I said calmly. "But if you give me your driver's license I'll know."

He handed me the license, and I glanced at the name. "Mr. Hendrix, the reason I stopped you...," I began.

"That's *Colonel* Charles Hendrix,[*] United States Air Force!" he said, interrupting me. "And you do *not* know who you are dealing with!"

"Well, sir," I said, mustering my own evident authority. "I'm *Corporal* Stephen Smith of the Montgomery Police Department, and I *do* know who I am dealing with because *I* have *your* driver's license."

"Let me tell you something, Corporal," he said, "I am a big man on the base and I can have your job!" His anger was evident in his tone.

"Sir, let me explain something to you," I let my tone convey the authority I knew I commanded in this situation. "All outside the base belongs to me. All inside the base belongs to you. And currently, you are *outside* the base."

The colonel sat quietly for several seconds thinking about what I'd said.

I have never been in the military and I didn't know how a colonel speaks to a military police officer, but I was *not* a military police officer.

He dropped his head slightly. "I am so sorry, Corporal. I truly am," he began slowly and much more humbly than before. "I forgot where I was. I just want to apologize for my actions and how I talked to you."

I warned him about his driving, reminded him of the speed limit, and told him to slow down. He assured me he would drive more safely in the future.

I let him go with just a verbal warning.

I have told this story to other military officers who've said that a few high-ranking officers will try to intimidate enlisted military policemen this way. Some think they can do the same with civilian police officers. The fact is that even high-ranking military officers can get in trouble with the base commander for off-base traffic violations. Disrespect toward the civilian authority is tolerated even less. I guess once he found out I wasn't intimidated by his rank, he decided to rethink his attitude.

Very few of the military personnel I've met in my professional

---

[*] The name was changed to protect the guilty

capacity have ever been rude or disrespectful. I've found that most are courteous to a fault and greatly appreciate what police officers do. But if you are in the military and were to be stopped by me for a traffic violation, if you do feel the need to tell me your name *and* rank... be nice.

THE MAN WHO WOULD BE CHIEF

OVEMBER 9, 1985, WAS JUST another Saturday night in the big
city. My partner, Officer Tom Wright, and I were riding twelve
on third shift patrol. At that time, one of the more popular clubs on
the west side was the Talk of the Town Club on Caffey Drive in the
northwest corner of that district. Cars lined the street for blocks on
the weekend as people flocked to the crowded night spot. The club
also had a reputation as being a trouble spot. Club overcrowding,
drugs and gambling were frequent problems there.

The crack cocaine epidemic was still a year or two away, so
the primary drug bought and sold on the street at that time was
marijuana. The drug dealers who frequented Talk of the Town
usually conducted business between the numerous parked cars. The
most popular vice, however, was gambling. Guys would kneel on a
brick and concrete porch that stood about three to four feet higher
than the surrounding parking lot. The gamblers rolled dice and bet
money on each throw, which was referred to as "rollin' the bones."
To combat these problems, we spent a lot of time cruising by the club
when things were busiest on the lookout for any criminal activity.

On this particular night, our supervisor, Sergeant Arthur Baylor,
had seen several young men loitering around the parked cars and
had called us over to ride by and see what they were doing. As we
cruised down Caffey Drive, we saw Sergeant Baylor's car parked in
front of the club. We pulled up and saw him standing on the porch,
looking out across the parking lot. We parked some distance away,
got out, and began walking toward the club.

As I approached the club I saw a young man sitting behind
the wheel of one of the cars parked directly in front of the club. I
approached the passenger side of the car from behind, unseen by the

driver, as Tom walked around the back toward the driver's side. I stood behind the passenger side door, in the driver's blind spot, to see what the guy was up to.

I watched closely as he leaned to his right and reached down with his right arm toward the glove compartment. His movements were slow and deliberate, and all the while his gaze was steadily focused on Sergeant Baylor standing on the porch directly above him to his right.

I glanced toward the sergeant, but he wasn't looking in our direction. When I looked back, I saw the subject slowly raising his right arm up in the direction of Sergeant Baylor. I leaned on the car and stood up on my tiptoes to get a better look at his hand. In it was a small, silver pistol.

I immediately drew my own sidearm, a .357 magnum revolver. The Tex Shoemaker holster that held my weapon made a very distinctive snap when a weapon was drawn from it. This immediately summoned my partner's attention.

I threw open the passenger door with my left hand and thrust my pistol against the man's right temple.

"Drop it or die!" I ordered sternly.

He had the gun up to dashboard level and froze perfectly still when he felt the muzzle of my pistol suddenly planted firmly against his skull. He glanced toward me out of the corner of his eye then dropped the pistol on the floorboard. It landed with a dull thud.

"What is it?" Tom shouted.

"Code eight!" I replied just loud enough for him to hear, referring to the radio code for someone with a firearm.

Tom pulled the guy from the driver's side and handcuffed him. I retrieved the pistol, which turned out to be a .22 caliber Derringer. After seeing Tom yank the guy from the car, Sergeant Baylor quickly approached us.

"S.Z., what have you got?" he asked me, calling me as many did at that time by my initials.

"This guy was pointing a gun at you while you were on the porch!" I replied. "I don't know what he thought he was doing. Surely he wasn't going to try and shoot you through the windshield."

"I wasn't gonna shoot nobody!" the man shouted.

"You had the gun, and you were pointing at my sergeant," I snapped. "That's *all* I need to know!"

"I appreciate you watching my back, S. Z.!" Baylor said. A broad smile crossed his face.

We arrested the man and charged him for carrying the pistol without a permit and placed him into the city jail.

Little did I know that many years later Baylor would become Montgomery's Chief of Police. I recount this story often when I see him and remind him that I saved his life. He says he doesn't remember it, but I have it in my field notes.

I don't know if the guy was really going to try and shoot him through the windshield. The passenger window was up and I don't think the small caliber bullet would have penetrated the thick glass. But now when I tell the story, I always say that I saved the life of the man who would be chief.

THE DETAIL

FOR ANY OFFICER WHO WORKED the midnight shift with the Montgomery Police Department at any time between 1980 and 2000, it was the most dreaded of all details. Seeing your name on the upcoming schedule swept you with trepidation at the upcoming tour of absolute boredom in your near future. This was known as the Mayor's Detail or simply "The Detail" to those of us misfortunate enough to draw this unenviable duty.

First, a little background about the mayor of Montgomery during those years. Emory Folmar is a unique individual, both as a person and as a mayor. He was a meticulous, demanding leader whose principle as mayor was, "People don't do what you *expect*; they do what you *inspect*."

He lived strictly by that creed, and kept his hand on virtually every aspect of city government—particularly the police department. He appointed officers who supported him and shared his views to positions of power within the department, and ruled everything and everyone with a heavy, inexorable hand.

His presence was felt in every department of the city government as well as the city itself. As strong-willed and forceful as he was, he naturally made a lot of enemies. A few of those enemies took out their frustration by making death threats against the mayor. One individual who was never identified even shot out the window of the mayor's car late one night as it sat parked in front of his Allendale Road residence.

The result of these threats was that the mayor appointed certain officers, known as the "aides," who accompanied the mayor in plain clothes wherever he went. These officers served as both drivers and bodyguards for the mayor as he went about his day-to-day duties.

At night while the mayor and his wife slept, the duty of watching his house fell on the unfortunate midnight shift officer whose name came up in the rotation. This duty consisted of sitting in a black, unmarked police car in the driveway of the residence directly across the street from the mayor's house. The unit was expected to arrive precisely at 10 p.m. and leave absolutely no earlier than 7 a.m. the following morning. The cardinal rule was that the officer watching the house would never leave the post for any reason, and was never to be caught sleeping. Punishment for either offense would be both swift and severe.

Originally, the entire detail fell on one officer each night, but after a few years of catching officers dozing during that nine-hour stretch, the supervisors got permission to split the detail into two shifts and put two officers per night on the detail. The first officer would arrive at ten and be relieved by the second officer at 2:30 a.m. The first officer would then swap out with his relief and ride with the other officer's partner for the remainder of the shift. If you were lucky, it fell on you no more than once every month.

Bathroom breaks were a hassle because you had to call the district unit over to drop off an officer so you could hitch a ride to a nearby gas station. The trick was to make sure you went before the detail and try to hold out until your shift was done.

To let the supervisors know you were still awake, you were required to check in on the radio every thirty minutes at the top and bottom of the hour. The detail unit number was 333, so a typical check-in sounded something like, "3-33, 10-21.

10-21 was the code for any radio traffic for this unit. The dispatcher would then respond with 10-22, which means, no radio traffic for this unit. There was never any radio traffic for this unit.

The second half of the detail was by far the worst. While everyone else got off at 6:30, you had to stay the extra half hour. The hardest part of the second half was when the sun came up. This was when sleepiness plagued you most. The one good thing about the detail was that you earned one hour overtime for coming in early, or staying late. But ask any officer who ever sat the detail, and they would've gladly given up the hour of overtime to avoid the detail.

Monday through Friday, when you sat the second half of the detail, you had to make sure you were especially alert starting around 4:30 a.m. This was when Mayor Folmar would be preparing to leave his house. Around 5:30, he would get in his car and pull up to the end of driveway. He would look left, then right, blow the horn and wave to you from across the street. He would then pull out of the driveway, turning left toward his office.

If you didn't wave back, he assumed you were asleep and you would be called into the supervisor's office that night, that is, if the patrol division commander didn't call you at home sooner. No matter what your excuse for not waving, it wasn't good enough. There was no excuse. Either way, it wasn't pretty.

Whenever I had to sit the detail—especially the second half, I would stay up the day before, and go to bed later than usual so I'd have more rest to stay awake all night. In the winter, I would take a dose of Nyquil to help me sleep all day before I got up to go to work that night.

The detail car was an old, worn-out patrol car that had been painted flat black to better camouflage it in the darkness. The detail was intended to be a closely guarded secret from regular citizens. One of the many rules was that the detail unit was never to reveal its location on the radio to alert the many citizens who monitored police radio traffic on scanners. That rule stayed in place many years after the presence of the detail car became common knowledge.

The car we used had close to 100,000 miles on it when it was reassigned to the detail and was on its last leg. It wasn't always easy to keep it running. When it frequently broke down and had to be limped in or towed to the shop, the supervisors would jump on us for mistreating it.

"It doesn't have *that* many miles on it to break down so often," was a typical cry from the supervisors.

We would try to explain that even though we didn't put a lot of miles on the car, the engine ran almost constantly to power the air conditioner in the summer or to provide heat in the winter. Ultimately, the endless hours of idling took their toll on the beleaguered car.

I was on third shift patrol from June of 1983 through November

1985. This was long before DVD players, lap top computers, I-Pods and Gameboys. So the trunk of the car was filled with the world's largest collection of gossip magazines and tabloids. I don't think the supervisors even knew about them. Contained in a large plastic garbage bag was a year's worth of the *National Enquirer, The Globe,* and *Star* magazine. You could actually kill about an hour just straightening them in preparation for reading them. I knew more about alien sightings, Elvis sightings and alien Elvis sightings, than any one person should ever have to know.

On the way to the detail, officers would stop to buy a drink and get a snack. Also, whoever had the detail at the first of the week would buy the latest edition of one of the trash magazines.

The detail car didn't have an AM-FM radio installed in the dashboard, so you had to bring your own. Then one night an officer brought a boom box and caused us to lose that privilege. I had a small transistor radio I kept in my briefcase, so if a supervisor drove up on me, I simply closed the lid to my brief case to conceal it. My usual practice was to get out of the car and meet him before he walked up to the car.

We were allowed to read as long as the light was kept low and couldn't be seen outside the vehicle. Then one night an officer brought a lamp clamped to the steering wheel that was too bright and cost us that privilege as well. To circumvent this rule, I taped a field interview card with a narrow slit over the lens of my flashlight that gave me just enough light to read by.

During the summer months, I would sit on the hood and listen to the police radio until I got so bored or sleepy and had to do something else to stay awake. During the winter, however, staying awake was a much tougher proposition. Sitting in a warm car with the heater running full blast while the temperature outside dropped into the low twenties could be quite relaxing. During the second half of the detail, I would set the alarm on my digital watch to beep every thirty minutes then attach it to the left epaulet on my uniform near my ear in case I fell asleep. It was just loud enough to rouse me in case I dozed off.

Allendale Road was a quiet street in a ritzy, upper-class neighborhood. Not much happened late at night. However, there were occasions when people drove down the street looking to get into mischief. One thing we encountered from time to time, usually during that period in the fall when college fraternities were initiating new pledges, was a group of students as part of a pledge challenge or scavenger hunt would try to steal the wooden address sign that hung from a pole in the mayor's front yard. The sign bore the name "Folmar" and the address of 2124.

The joke on these pledges, usually from out of town, was that they were unaware that a police officer watched the house all night from a blacked-out car parked in the shadows across the street.

You could usually tell when this was about to take place, because a car with two or three young men in it would drive by at least twice to locate the sign. On the third pass the car would slow down and someone would get out and attempt to abscond with the sign. After the second drive by of any vehicle, I would get out of the car and stand in the shadows to wait and see what was going to happen next.

On one particular night, I observed a Ford Pinto drive by slowly. I watched the occupants, who looked like a group of gullible fraternity pledges, as they neared the sign and began pointing at it before moving on. They made two passes as they assessed their target. On the third pass, I watched them approach, then stepped out in the middle of the street with my pistol drawn on the vehicle. They got to within about thirty feet before they saw me. The driver panicked and jammed on the emergency brake, bringing the Pinto and its petrified occupants to a screeching halt.

I walked up to the driver's window and asked everyone for identification. After checking the young men for warrants, I explained that their buddies had set them up for failure. I also explained that as I stood there talking to them, their friends were all back at the fraternity house laughing hysterically at their predicament.

I also told the young pledges that it was wise for them not to return, and they assured me that it wouldn't happen again. I was very serious and acted completely official with them the whole time, like the typical no nonsense television cop. But after they drove off, still terrified but wiser in the ways of the world, I just laughed.

I always enjoyed helping with these initiations.

Some time later the officers on my shift got chewed out at roll call because an officer sitting the detail left his post to investigate something suspicious he saw a couple of houses down from the mayor. I'm sure our sergeant received implicit instructions from the captain to make certain that the mayor's house was *never* left unprotected.

"What if something happened to the mayor while you're distracted doing something else!" the sergeant yelled as we stood silently in formation. "You are only responsible for one house on that street and *that* is the mayor's house! You are not concerned about what happens in any other yard but the mayor's!"

As fate would have it, I had the second half of the mayor's detail that night. I relieved the first-half officer at the usual 2:30 and was there for about thirty minutes when a car pulled up about three houses down. An adult woman and two teenage boys got out holding several rolls of toilet paper. They walked toward the yard next to the mayor's and began to roll the trees.

With the words of the sergeant still echoing in my head, I walked over to the three and asked them for identification. I asked whose yard they were rolling and they said it was a friend of her son and his friend. After getting their information I started back to my vehicle. They asked if they could still roll their friend's yard.

"I am only responsible for one house on this street and that is this one," I said pointing toward the mayor's house. "As long as you don't go into this yard, you can do what you want to."

They thanked me and assured me they wouldn't get into the mayor's yard, and continued rolling. I went back to my vehicle. After getting off that morning, I got a call from the desk sergeant.

"You fell asleep on the detail last night, didn't you Steve?"

"No, actually I had a pretty easy time staying awake last night. Why do you ask?" I knew where this was going.

"The house next door to the mayor got rolled last night," he said.

"Yes, I know," I replied. "I watched them do it. It was a lady and two teenage boys."

"You watched them do it?" he said in disbelief. "Why did you let them do that?"

"We were told by the sergeant at roll call last night that we were only responsible for the mayor's house and no other house on the street. So, since they were not in the mayor's yard I did not stop them. I got their names and went back to my vehicle, just like we were told to do."

"Okay, but you may hear about it tonight at work," he warned.

"That's okay. I was just doing what I was told by the sergeant."

I never heard anything from the supervisors, but several of my fellow officers asked me about it.

"Man, you got guts for lettin' them do that," one of them said.

"I was just doin' what the sergeant told us, and nothin' more," became my official reply.

One of the complaints we got from the people who lived in the house where we parked was that the big cedar tree next to the driveway was turning brown. Apparently, some of the officers were urinating on the cedar tree instead of calling for a bathroom break. This was most apparent during the summer months. Had that been my house, I wouldn't have complained. That was a small price to pay for free police protection in your driveway 365 nights a year.

None of the officers liked the duty but we did the job. But where you had some who didn't take the job seriously, one officer in particular took it very seriously. A supervisor told me of one particular evening he went by to check on a young officer sitting the detail for the first time. Whenever a supervisor drove up, you were supposed to go to his vehicle and speak to him.

When the officer didn't get out, the supervisor walked up to his car, thinking he was asleep. When he looked in the detail car, the officer wasn't there.

"Hey, Sarge. Psst, Sarge! Over here," a voice whispered loudly from behind him.

The sergeant looked over toward where he'd heard the voice, but didn't see anything.

"Up here, Sarge," came the same whispering voice.

The young officer had climbed up a large tree and was watching the house. He told the sergeant that if someone tried to take him out that he wouldn't be in the car and could get the jump on them.

The sergeant immediately ordered the young officer down from the tree. Knowing this officer personally, I was not at all surprised when the sergeant told the story.

For the most part, the detail was extremely boring and rarely did anything happen. You would hope for a vehicle pursuit, business robbery or shooting to give you something to listen to, anything to keep you awake.

The radio traffic you wanted to hear the most was when the relief unit called the dispatcher and said, "Show us en route to relieve the detail."

My Days as a Motorman

RIDING MOTORCYCLES IS A LOT of fun. It's a great way to see the country. But riding for fun and for work are two totally different things. After spending my first two years as a police officer on third shift patrol, I was ready for a change. I put in for a transfer to the Traffic Division to be a motor officer. My thinking at the time was that since riding a motorcycle is a lot of fun, why not have a little fun while working?

It sounded good in theory.

I received word that I was being transferred to traffic and would begin motorcycle training on Monday, November 22, 1985. I had ridden a motorcycle a couple of times but nothing as big as the police bikes used by our department, so I borrowed a civilian bike from a friend to familiarize myself with riding in traffic. His motorcycle was somewhat smaller than a police motor, but I figured I needed to start small and work my way up.

Basically I hadn't ridden much, but the motor instructor, Sergeant T.D. Jones, later told me I'd be easier to train because he wouldn't have to force me to break any bad habits. Officers Joe Walker, Russell Pierce and I were to begin our training that Monday morning.

I picked up Joe at his apartment around 6 a.m. and drove to the city lot where we met Russell and Sergeant Jones at the motor shed. He'd selected three of the older motorcycles for us to use as trainers. Since I'd never been on a motorcycle that large and powerful, Sergeant Jones called another motor officer to ride it up to Patterson Field parking lot where our training would begin. Once there, he had me ride slowly around in the parking lot a few times to get familiar with the balance and power of the bike.

After about twenty minutes of riding through the parking lot and getting comfortable with the turning, acceleration, and braking, he pointed to a painted mark on the pavement and had us all practice turning and running over the same spot over and over. This exercise laid the groundwork for teaching us to maneuver in tight areas at slow speed.

Later in the day we had to stop on a two-by-four board then accelerate smoothly without throwing the board from under the rear tire. The training was not as hard as I had imagined, but that was only the first day.

The next day we warmed up again with some lazy turns through the parking lot before taking the motors onto the roadway and getting the feel of moving through traffic. I didn't have much experience in that area, so it was a little unnerving. I was more comfortable in the relative safety of an enclosed car rather than riding a motorcycle where your protection from hazards and the elements are minimal at best.

Part of our training took us to Garrett Coliseum at "the barns," where animals were stored during rodeos and other livestock shows, to become familiar with off-road riding. We played 'follow the leader' trailing closely behind Sergeant Jones as he weaved through various obstacles. I managed to follow him up and down grassy slopes, across dirt driveways, and down narrow sidewalks between the safety rails.

We then rode inside the cattle stalls, each about ten feet wide, in the livestock barns and moved from stall to stall making tight turns. I was able to do this—most of the time. On one of these outings, I was the third in line. Sergeant Jones was leading us, riding about 25 to 30 miles per hour followed by Joe and me. Russell brought up the rear.

Between one set of barns, someone had spread sand to fill in ruts made by cattle and horse trailers. The sand was several inches deep, and as we rode through, the front tire of my motor began to wobble. I hit a deep rut, and the front tire dug in and stopped the bike in an instant catapulting me over the windshield. I landed on my back and lay there for a few seconds.

As I was getting up, Sergeant Jones, Joe, and Russell raced over to check on me. I got up slowly to make sure I wasn't injured.

Fortunately, I was okay.

Joe picked up my bike. I hopped back on it—none the worse for wear—and we continued our training.

The motorcycle skills course used by the police department was set up in the five-acre parking lot of Patterson Field where we began the tough part of the training. The course consisted of a number of obstacles set up with orange cones that force the rider to maneuver through them in a certain manner to demonstrate riding proficiency and control.

These obstacles have descriptive names like the Iron Cross, the Keyhole, and the Brake and Escape, and each one challenges the rider to maintain precise control over balance, turning, acceleration, and braking while navigating its passageway.

As the training progressed, I began to sense deep inside that this wasn't what I wanted to do with my career. I slowly mastered the required skills, but being a motor officer wasn't what I thought it would be.

Later in the week, I met with Major Roger Owens, the commander of the Traffic Division, and told him that although I appreciated the opportunity he'd given me, my heart just wasn't in it.

"I feel like I'm preventing an accident before it ever occurs," I told him.

He said I'd made a wise decision, and that most other officers would be too proud to quit before having an accident.

He told me that I could come back and try again whenever I wanted. Then he asked me if I wanted to try working as an accident investigator.

I told him I'd give it a shot.

I began working day shift in Accident Investigation. The supervisor, Sergeant Barry Tolbert, told the dispatcher on the first day to give me all the traffic accidents involving injury, which are always more difficult and time-consuming than your average fender-bender.

I'm not sure if he didn't want me working there because I'd only lasted a week in motor training, or if he were just challenging my resolve to stay in the Traffic Division. Either way, I never quite felt at home in Traffic. Joe and Russell each completed their training and went on to serve for several years as motor officers.

Accident investigators do nothing but investigate accidents, and I began to miss patrol duty. I ended up staying in A.I. for about a week before transferring back to the Patrol Division, this time on second shift, on December 6th.

Looking back on the whole thing, some people may think I just quit because it was hard and the hazards for a motor officer, in my opinion, far outweighed the rewards.

But I have to look at the big picture. My subsequent transfer to second shift patrol exposed me to a different facet of police work and sparked my interest in processing crime scenes. After spending almost three years on second shift patrol, I transferred to the Evidence Technician bureau on September 29, 1989.

I look back on my journey to see where this obstacle fit into God's plan for me. The twists and turns at this point in my career meandered like the tight turns of the Iron Cross and eventually led to my calling in crime scene investigation.

I can honestly credit it all to my days as a motorman.

THE NEKKID GUY

BEING A POLICE CADET EARLY in my career assigned to the detective division enabled me to get to know a lot of the investigators with the Montgomery Police Department. After becoming a patrol officer, I would often check with investigators and see who was wanted and gather the latest intelligence on where they might be hiding.

On Thursday, January 23, 1986, I went upstairs to the robbery-homicide office and spoke with Investigator Bob Davis to see who he was currently looking for. He told me he was looking for Teryl Mason*for a murder that happened in Montgomery County. He told me he went by the street name of "Bullet."

His name had come up several times during the death investigation of Charlie Williams in the Davenport community that occurred on October 15, 1985. Mr. Williams had operated a grocery store and bar in the community for forty years. Bob said that "Bullet" got into a fight at a bar and killed a guy with a broken pool cue. Bob also advised that the police department currently held a robbery and theft of property warrants on him. I made a note of it and went to roll call.

On Monday, February 3, 1986, my partner, Officer Cliff LaBarge, and I were riding in eleven on second shift patrol. District Eleven is in the center part of town and was always very active. One of the duties on second shift patrol was to serve misdemeanor warrants. That day we had about six warrants to attempt to serve. While Cliff drove, I read the affidavit attached to each warrant out loud. Anyone who signs a warrant against another person must write out the precise details of the offense in a sworn affidavit, and that

---

*   Name changed to protect the naked

becomes the basis upon which the warrant for arrest is issued by a magistrate.

The things people do to each other are just amazing. I would read the affidavit exactly as it was written. Grammar, spelling and punctuation were often as comical as some of the facts of the case. The saddest thing was when you read an affidavit and it was full of spelling errors and you find out it was written by a school teacher or guidance counselor.

As I was reading the last affidavit the woman had written about how someone had threatened her and damaged her property. She wrote at the very end, "...this information was given to me by my friend Teryl Mason." I looked at Cliff and said, "Teryl Mason! Bob Davis is looking for him! He's wanted for murder."

I called Bob at the office and asked if Teryl Mason was still wanted by us and he said he was. We gave him the address of 3770 Norman Bridge Road. Bob told us that he would get with us later on that night to try and serve the warrant. I was excited about trying to capture him. The apartment complex was not in our district but the supervisors would allow us to go and help make the arrest since we came up with the information.

We waited all night to try to serve the warrant but the investigators were busy with other cases going on in the city. Around ten that evening, Bob called and said he would meet us at the Normandale Shopping Center on Norman Bridge Road. We got our game plan together and decided who would go to the front door and who would go to the back door.

We went to the apartment and Bob and I knocked on the door while Cliff and Investigator Pat Downing went to the back. A woman answered the door. She was wearing a bathrobe, and it was obvious that she had been asleep. Bob asked her where Teryl Mason was and she said he was upstairs in bed.

Bob and I headed cautiously up the stairs. We entered the bedroom where a naked man slept soundly in the bed. I walked around the bed and positioned myself between the man and the window overlooking the courtyard. On the floor lay a steak knife. I kicked it under the bed.

Bob awakened the man and told him we needed to talk to him. He looked over at me then crawled out of bed toward the door.

"I need to put on my robe," the man said. He put on a red robe and as he pulled it over his shoulders he pushed past Bob and bolted downstairs.

I immediately took off running down the stairs and out the front door. I saw him running toward the back of the apartment complex with the red robe flowing in the breeze like a cape. He ran about thirty yards before he came out of the robe. I managed to grab my radio as I ran. "2-11," I yelled into it. "I'm in foot pursuit of Teryl Mason, black male!"

"10-4," the dispatcher responded. "Do you have a description?"

"He's wearing no clothes and has a bandage on his right bicep!" I muttered as I ran.

"10-4," she replied. I could tell she was fighting not to laugh as she asked, "Which way is he running?"

"The subject is running west through the apartments!"

"Attention all units," the dispatcher began to announce on the air, "2-11 is in foot pursuit of black male, Teryl Mason, last seen running west from the apartments."

Cliff and Pat were standing behind the apartments talking about Alabama football thinking the subject would not be in the apartment. They had been watching our flashlights through the window when all of a sudden they heard me on the radio saying I was in foot pursuit. They both looked at each other and said, "Did he say foot pursuit?"

Cliff looked to his left and saw a naked guy running with a bathrobe trailing behind him. Cliff immediately gave chase and Pat ran to his unmarked detective car.

Lieutenant Terry Ward, our supervisor, chimed in on the radio, "2-25, Teryl Mason is wanted by the county for murder."

The dispatcher's voice then lost its humorous tone, "10-4," she said in earnest. "Attention, all units, the Teryl Mason subject is wanted for murder by the county."

I continued to chase the subject through the apartment complex and into a concrete drainage ditch. I slid into the ditch and tried to grab him, but because he was naked and all sweaty, he slipped loose and continued running.

To be honest, I was not too crazy about trying to tackle a naked man. This is not a normal thing most guys like to do. The concrete walls were too steep to climb out and all he could do was run. As I chased after him I was trying to be cautious about the green slime that grows on the bottom of concrete ditches. As a kid, I grew up exploring similar ditches and this green slimy growth is slicker than snot and you will lose your footing in a heartbeat. As I continued my pursuit after him I used a technique I did not learn in the police academy. I threw a 'kag' on him and knocked him to the ground, hard on his chest.

Growing up playing backyard football, if you were chasing someone, and you couldn't catch them, you could throw your leg forward and grabbed the guy's ankle with the top of your foot and trip him while running. We called this a 'kag'.

At the time I did not know where Cliff was but later I found out that he had crossed the ditch behind me and was running along the top of the ditch without using his flashlight. He later told me he saw me fall not knowing I used a tactic from my childhood when I threw the 'kag'.

He popped up immediately after the fall and took off again. I continued to chase him in the ditch but he was pulling away from me. My ballistic vest had soaked up water like a sponge when we fell and felt like it weighed twenty pounds now. He attempted to climb out of the ditch, but then continued to run. Cliff would later recount that the pathway next to the ditch was becoming more narrow due to the chain link fences and he had to turn on his flashlight. Mason saw the light and continued to run in the ditch.

I chased Mason about a quarter of a mile before he was able to climb out of the ditch in the 300 block of Lynwood Drive, in the next neighborhood approximately a half-mile away. He climbed over several fences thinking he had lost us, all the while Cliff was following him over each fence and through the backyards. Cliff told me he could hear the acceleration of a car as he approached the last fence. Mason was still unaware that Cliff was close behind him and laid down on the ground in the shadows and appeared to be exhausted. Cliff pulled out his flashlight and was prepared to throw it at him in case he got up to run again but since Mason was unaware of my partner's presence Cliff did'nt have to.

Mason saw Cliff running up to him and jumped up to continue his attempt at freedom. As he ran across the last backyard toward the gate and freedom, Pat suddenly appeared out of the darkness and both Cliff and Pat tackled him into the chain link fence. They hit him so hard that the gate was torn down in several pieces. Pat handcuffed Mason despite his continued efforts to flee. When they stood Mason up he tried to bolt again and Cliff stepped back and rolled his ankle. His ankle popped loudly three different times as he fell backwards. Cliff screamed in pain, "Pat! I just broke my ankle!"

I managed to climb out of the ditch and ran up to where I saw a black and white unit with it's blue lights illuminating the quiet neighborhood. The suspect was already in custody when I heard Cliff's voice of obvious pain. Cliff was on the ground in pain but I did not know what had happened. I could hear sirens in the distance coming in our direction when I radioed in *'officer down'*. Immediately, Pat advised the dispatcher that it was only an ankle injury and wasn't serious.

The suspect was taken to police headquarters and I was told later that he was met by a small contingent of my fellow officers from the shift. They'd heard the chase on the radio and wanted to see what the guy looked like. He was taken up to the jail through the sally port. This is an enclosed area that had roll-up doors on both ends that you could drive your patrol car into and close both doors when you had a high risk prisoner, those who are prone to escape, in a wheelchair or in this case, "buck naked."

I drove our police cruiser to the emergency room so I could be checked out. Cliff was taken by ambulance. While chasing the subject I cut my knee and got glass embedded in it. I found out later that when I put the 'kag' on the suspect, he fell and tore off part of his upper lip and scraped all the skin off the top of his feet. I called home and my dad brought me a change of clothes to police headquarters since mine were soaked with nasty, stagnant ditch water. The smell wasn't as bad since it was February, but I've been in ditches in the heat of the summer, and the water would smell like sewage.

When I took the cover off my body armor, I found bits of rock and glass embedded in it. If I had that much debris in my clothes then I can only imagine what Mason had in his naked body. I was off the next two days and was able to rest my injuries.

Cliff was on light duty for about four weeks with an ankle injury, assigned to the back desk. We never went to court on the arrest, and I never found out what happened in the case. Cliff later transferred to the Detective Division where he worked as an investigator in robbery-homicide. A year or so later, he left the department to work for the U.S. Marshal Service.

You just never know what you will encounter when you go to serve a warrant on someone. You are taught in the academy that no call is routine, and this one certainly wasn't.

This was the one and only time I ever had to chase a naked guy. I got a tape of the radio traffic from dispatch and played it for a few of my friends.

Lewis Grizzard, a popular southern storyteller and comedian, spoke of the difference between "naked" and "nekkid." He said that if you were not wearing any clothes you were naked. However, if you're not wearing any clothes and were up to something, then you were "nekkid." In this case, I have to say that Teryl Mason was "nekkid." And for a year or two at parties I often heard, "Hey, Steve, tell the story about the "nekkid" guy!!

Police Capture Nude Man, Quiz Him in County Slaying

By BRUCE RITCHIE
Advertiser Staff Writer

Montgomery police questioned Tuesday a 29-year-old man they captured in the Normandale area late Monday night to determine if he knows anything about the recent slaying of a county resident.

████████ of 3770 Norman Bridge Road was captured after he ran nude from police through a drainage sewer.

He was questioned by detectives in the Montgomery County Sheriff's Department as part of an investigation into the death of Charlie Williams, who was found beaten to death in the Davenport community on Oct. 15, 1985.

Bruce Huggins, a sheriff's department investigator, said ████ name was mentioned by several people interviewed during the department's investigation into the slaying and ████ was being questioned to learn what he may know about the death.

The sheriff's department issued an advisory in December asking law enforcement officials to apprehend ████, but no warrant has been signed against him in connection with the murder, Huggins said.

Police have charged ████ with robbery and theft in connection with the robbery of a Montgomery man about one month ago, according to Lt. Larry Armstead, a police spokesman.

Police patrol units and detectives arrived at ████ apartment at about 10 p.m. Monday to arrest him, but he evaded police by escaping from the apartment while wearing only an overcoat, Armstead said.

████ shed the coat and ran nude through streets in the Normandale area and a storm sewer but was captured in front of a residence on Lynwood Drive.

████ allegedly assaulted the two arresting officers in front of the house and was charged with escape in connection with the arrest, Armstead said.

Armstead said one officer was treated at Baptist Medical Center for a sprained ankle and the other was treated for abrasions and cuts. Lewis was being held late Tuesday in the city jail on $30,500 bond and for more questioning by the sheriff's department, according to a jail spokesman.

The sheriff's department has made no charges in the death of the 73-year-old Williams, whose body was found in the grocery store and bar he operated for about 40 years.

February 4, 1986 – Newspaper article of murder suspect capture (Courtesy of Alabama Journal)

"The Bomb Gag Lives On"

AFTER SEPTEMBER **11, 2001,** THE world changed when it came to the nation's security and how police handled certain calls for service, but back in 1986 things were different. Standard procedure on any bomb threat was pretty simple. The responding patrol unit would notify the dispatcher about thirty seconds before arrival at the scene and shut off their radio to prevent any radio transmission from accidentally setting off a remote controlled device.

The fire department would dispatch a fire truck to park nearby, usually at the outer most part of the parking lot. After the police evacuated the building, officers and the manager or owner of the business would conduct a search of the building for anything suspicious. To be honest, we never took bomb threats that seriously before 9-11. Things like that just didn't happen.

On Sunday, March 30, 1986, Officer Ed McCloud and I were riding in District Five. Around 4:00 in the afternoon we responded on a dispatch call to U.S. Haircutters on the Atlanta Highway at the Eastmont Shopping Center. Someone called in a bomb threat. This seemed odd to me since the business was not open on Sunday. We followed proper procedure and met the manager at the door. A pumper truck from the fire department parked at the outer edge of the parking lot near the Atlanta Highway. We entered the business and explained to the manager about procedure and asked her if she saw anything that looked out of place or if anyone suspicious had been in the building. She didn't recall anything to indicate someone would have done so.

Ed and I also looked around for anything that looked like a bomb. I kept an eye out for the basic stereotypical bomb, a bundle of dynamite sticks with a clock attached, or a big black ball with a fizzling fuse sticking out of it. Like I said before, I really did not take bomb threats serious in 1986 because I never really expected to find one.

As we searched the business we didn't find any bombs, but I saw Ed handling a brown paper bag.

"What are you doin'?" I asked him.

He looked around, motioned with his head for me to come toward him. "C'mere, a second," he whispered. He held the bag up to me and said in an excited tone, "Listen to this!"

I leaned in and listened to the bag and I heard ticking. Just like the bombs you see in the movies. "What is that?" I asked. He unrolled the top of the bag and I looked inside and he had placed an egg timer inside the bag. I wondered where he got the egg timer. I looked around and saw one at every chair. They are used to time perms.

Ed has a good sense of humor, but I never knew him to pull practical jokes. This was only the second time we had ridden together, so I guess he felt comfortable enough around me to pull a few practical jokes.

About the time I heard the ticking, Sergeant Margaret Faulkner walked up to us. "What have you got there?" she asked.

I was about to tell her what was in the bag, when Ed interrupted me. "Ah! Listen to this!" He held out the bag toward her.

She leaned in and listened. "Oh, my gosh!" she cried in disbelief.

Margaret had just recently been promoted. She had been a detective, but her promotion to supervisor had landed her back in patrol. I know she was just getting familiar with patrol techniques again, but I'm sure an actual bomb isn't what she expected when she got to work that day.

"Okay," she said, letting go a deep breath. "What do we do now?"

I looked at Ed expecting him to let her in on the gag. Instead he got a serious look on his face. He opened the bag slowly and looked in. A slight smile crossed his face. "I think I can diffuse it," he said.

Now I'm thinking to myself, *Diffuse it! Man, he's really pushing this to the limit.*

This was out of character for Ed, or at least I thought it was. I guess I was seeing a side of Ed I never had before.

I figured Sergeant Faulkner must have assumed that Ed had some sort of formal training in the Military with bombs or explosives. I could tell that she was nervous. "If you think you can, then do it." Her voice was in a whisper as if any loud sounds might set it off. I just waited to see how far Ed was going to go with the gag.

He slowly and very carefully pulled out the egg timer from the bag. As it emerged, Sergeant Faulkner's gaze was transfixed on Ed's hands and their dangerous cargo. At the moment the timer came into view, Ed quickly spun the dial to zero causing the little bell to go 'ding.' He smiled and looked at both of us, pleased with his joke.

The sergeant was not the least bit amused. She pointed an angry finger at us. "You two are written up!" She then stormed toward the door.

Margaret is a pleasant woman with a strong Christian faith in God. I'd never seen her angry before. I know that even Christian people get mad and find themselves in bad moods because I can get very angry at times. I'd just never seen that side of her before.

She turned to address me just as she reached the door. "You are the senior officer, and you know better," she said angrily. "Both of you see me when you get in tonight!" She immediately burst out the door and disappeared.

The manager stood by and witnessed the whole thing. "I thought it was kinda funny myself," she said. "I like seeing police officers with a sense of humor."

Well, at least three of us thought it was funny. I notified the dispatcher that everything was okay at the business and we returned to our regular duties.

"Man, are we in trouble now," I told Ed. "I just knew at any moment you were going to tell the sergeant it was a joke before you opened the bag."

"I didn't know she was going to come to the call," Ed said.

After patrolling for about an hour or so, Lieutenant Les Brown, the second shift patrol supervisor, asked us to meet him at the shopping center at Perry Hill Road and Harrison Road.

"Oh, no, things are fixin' to get worse now," I said. "The sergeant has told the lieutenant and now we're gonna really get it. It's bad enough we're going to get written up, but now the lieutenant is going to chew us out," I lamented. "Great, just great!"

When we arrived Lieutenant Brown was already in the parking lot. We pulled up to his car, driver's door to driver's door.

"What's up, Lieutenant?" I asked, hoping to lighten the moment.

He looked down at some paperwork in his lap and took a moment to respond. His tone was stern. "That whole thing at the hair cutting place with the bomb and all," he began. "Y'all need to be a little more professional when you are on calls."

"Yes, sir," we both responded.

"And quit screwing around with the new sergeant," he said. "Consider this your verbal reprimand."

"Yes, sir," I said. I couldn't keep the smile off my face.

He responded with a smile of his own. "Y'all stay out of trouble and do some work." He then drove off.

"Whew! Man, are we lucky. I thought we were really going to get it," I said. "The next time you want to pull a bomb gag, how about letting me know first."

Nothing else was said about the bomb stunt that night.

A couple of years later Margaret left the department and took a job with the FBI and I didn't see her for a while. After she graduated the FBI academy, she was assigned to the regional field office in Hawaii. I saw her a year or so later when she came to visit friends in Montgomery.

About nine years later, she was reassigned to the Montgomery office and I saw her fairly regularly at Cops for Christ meetings. We talked about the bomb incident, and she remembers the call but doesn't remember getting angry with Ed and me. She told me she remembers that radios were being used in the area and that was not proper procedure.

I told her that I recalled her reaction because I was on the receiving end. Ed later transferred to the police academy and I eventually transferred to the Evidence Technician's office. I taught fingerprint theory to the new recruits at the police academy. I would tell this story to them and the recruits always got a big kick out of it. Most people who knew Ed found it hard to believe he would pull that kind of practical joke.

On one particular morning I was telling this story to a new academy class when Ed stepped in just long enough to throw a paper bag at me as I stood in front of the class. He closed the door quickly behind him. I picked up the bag and inside was an egg timer, turned on. I pulled out the egg timer and turned it off. It went 'ding.' The class laughed hysterically.

"Police work is serious business!" I said to the amused class. I held up the bag, "The bomb gag lives on."

ANOTHER MAN ALMOST
LOST HIS LIFE

SOMETIMES EVEN THE SIMPLEST CALLS can turn bad in a hurry because one big mouth in the crowd wants to be the 'big man' in front of his buddies. Saturday, September 6, 1986, my partner and I encountered just such an individual.

Officer Jerroll Richardson had been with the department nine months. At 29, he was older and more mature than most of the other rookie officers. He and I were on second shift patrol riding in District Three, in the northern part of the city. Around 10:30 that night, we responded to a disturbance call at the Zippy Mart on Forbes Road. The clerk at the store gave us a description of a young black man wearing a light colored tee shirt and a pair of blue flowered jam shorts who'd been in the store earlier with several other men. The guy in the jam shorts had attempted to steal a can of meat but had been stopped by the security guard before fleeing the store with his pals into the night.

We left the store and resumed our patrol down on Forbes Road. As we drove past Brookview Drive, we saw several young black men standing in the curve beside two parked cars, one of whom matched the description of the suspect from the store. The men were calmly talking beneath the harsh glare of the streetlight.

We got out of the car and approached the men. Jerroll questioned the suspect in the blue flowered shorts about being at the Zippy Mart. The man and his friends, of course, denied being there.

It was then that another man in a blue shirt boldly stepped up and told his buddy, "You don't have to tell them a f**kin' thing!"

My partner looked the man square in the eyes. "If *you* weren't there, *you* need to be quiet," Jerroll said with absolute authority.

Jerroll turned his attention back to the man in the flowered shorts and told him that there had been a problem at the store and that he fit the description of the suspect given by the clerk. "Just stay away from the store," he calmly ordered.

At this point, the confrontation should have ended. The guy could have simply replied, "Okay, we'll stay away from the store." Then we would have left and got back to more important things. But, this is where stupidity kicks in. Some people just don't know to leave well enough alone and shut up.

The man in the blue shirt had a point to make—even at his own peril. "We don't have to tell you a go★★★mn f★★kin' thing!" he shouted in defiance.

At this point, we'd both had enough of his mouth. Jerroll looked at the guy and told him he was under arrest for disorderly conduct. I handcuffed him and led him to the car, where I opened the rear passenger door and told him to have a seat. He just stood there without saying a word.

I repeated the order, but he continued to ignore me. As I attempted to push him into the car he began to struggle against me and pull away. Suddenly the other four men surrounded us and grabbed their friend attempting to pull him away from me. As I hung onto him another man joined the fray and grabbed our prisoner. At some point in the struggle, our big-mouthed prisoner was pulled up against my partner, who then bit Jerroll hard on the right shoulder.

The melee was fully engaged at this time with everyone pushing and pulling in a frantic tug-of-war over the handcuffed man. With a free hand, I managed to grab my hand-held radio. "2-0-3! Brookview and Forbes! We need *back-up!*" I screamed into it.

I drew my baton, but before I could strike anyone, the man in the white tee shirt and blue flowered jam shorts jumped on me. I threw him off and tried to push him away with my outstretched baton, which I held tightly gripped at both ends. He also grabbed the baton with both hands, his fists just inside mine. As we struggled for the baton, he managed to pin me up against the front of our car and press the baton firmly against my throat.

I realized then that this guy wasn't just trying to help his friend; he was trying to kill me. I made up my mind in that instant I wasn't going to die that way. I twisted the baton quickly to the left to break his grip, got leverage on him, then struggled to pin *him* against the car. He fell in front of the car however as I swung the baton to hit him.

During the fight, I lost sight of my partner, but I could hear the sweet music of yelping sirens as the other units rushed quickly to our aid. As I attempted to strike my attacker, he crawled away, desperately trying to regain his footing. Officer John Mann and his partner, Unit 302, then appeared suddenly, turning the corner sideways, tires squalling, and rubber screeching against asphalt as they hurtled toward us. John had flipped off the siren as he approached to better surprise the men we were fighting.

However, as the cavalry appeared, the men fled like startled cockroaches into the darkness. Several other units arrived in quick succession, and we were finally able to grab a breath and seat our prisoner in the car.

Another unit took Jerroll to the hospital, while John and his partner transported our prisoner to jail. The man in the jam shorts refused to give his name, so along with the warrants I signed on him for disorderly conduct and resisting arrest, I added another for concealing identity.

The regrettable fact remains that the whole incident was totally unnecessary. All of it started over the fact that these idiots tried to steal a can of meat. Five grown men with nothing better to do on a Saturday night, not to mention the cowardly attack on two police officers.

Ironically enough, when our back-up arrived and evened the odds, they simply deserted their friend for the safety of the shadows. Because of this little stunt, a police officer simply doing his job had to go to the hospital with a severe bite wound. Jerroll was released to regular duty the next day, but his shoulder remained sore for about two weeks.

I'm haunted by what happened that night. I continue to second guess myself and have always felt as if I could've handled things differently. I feel guilty about Jerroll's injury and, even though he reassured me on several occasions it wasn't my fault, I've always felt responsible.

Growing up, I never got into many fights. I got along with pretty much everyone, but this incident profoundly affected how I handled physical confrontations from then on. After all I knew about the Todd Road Incident, the impact of that brutal assault never hit home until that night. That's not to say that the circumstances on Todd Road were the same—far from it. It was the simple fact that we were attacked by a pack of enraged thugs intent on our destruction that brought it to mind.

Nearly everyone who truly wants to avoid arrest will fight to get away, yet it's uncommon for someone to fight a police officer with the intent to harm or even kill him. Being shot at is one thing, I've had that happen to me, but to have someone try to kill me face to face is a whole different deal.

What the guy who jumped me apparently never realized was that if I hadn't been able to twist my baton loose from his grip, fearing for my life I would have drawn my pistol and shot him dead. Because one big mouth in the crowd had to show off and couldn't keep his mouth shut, another man almost lost his life.

I Wish I Had Shot Him

ON THURSDAY, NOVEMBER **6, 1986,** I was partnered with Officer Scott Weatherson in District Ten on second shift. Scott was a good officer and not afraid to speak his mind. He was also a serious body builder and has the physique to prove it. In the gym, his motto is, "If you're gonna be a bear, be a grizzly. Be the biggest bear in the forest."

That afternoon had been unusually busy. Around 4:30, Officers Tony Simmons and J.D. Happney in a neighboring district responded to a fight call at the Chevron station on the South Boulevard at Court Street.

Scott and I responded as their back up.

This business had become a regular hangout for thugs and drug dealers, and calls of this nature were coming in on a regular basis. Scott and I arrived at the same time as the other unit, but we couldn't see a fight anywhere.

As we prepared to leave, an elderly couple pulled up to us and said that there was a fight taking place on Court Street about two blocks away and that one of those involved was holding something to the other person's throat.

As we drove up the street, followed by Tony and J.D. in the other unit, two other men flagged us down as we neared Southmont Street pointing toward a fight between two men.

As we pulled to the corner and bailed from the car, we saw a young black man in his early twenties sitting on the chest of an elderly white man, apparently in his sixties. The younger man was using an old, rusty knife to saw at the throat of the older man, who was wounded and bleeding badly.

All of us drew our weapons and ordered the young man to drop the knife and to get off of the older man. He looked at us as if he didn't understand, then looked back at his helpless victim on the ground bleeding profusely from his throat wound.

He resumed his attack on the older man with the knife, and again we ordered him to stop, drop the weapon and get on the ground. We steadily approached him, all four of our pistols aimed directly at him. As we drew nearer, the young man abruptly ceased his assault, jumped off the man, threw down the knife, and laid face-down on the ground.

Tony immediately jumped on the guy and handcuffed him. Scott retrieved the knife and placed it on the hood of our car for safekeeping, then rushed to the victim's aid. While we waited on the paramedics, Scott determined that the older man's throat was badly cut, but it didn't appear that the windpipe had been severed.

The medics arrived and transported the older man to the hospital. Scott and I transported the handcuffed attacker to headquarters and took him upstairs to the investigators. While on the way to headquarters we had asked the young man a few questions.

"What would you have done if we hadn't driven up?" I asked him.

"I was going to slit his throat and stick him in the bushes," he replied.

The elderly victim survived the assault. We later learned that he was Allen Morton, who had lived on Southmont Drive since 1955. He had been out on his daily walk in the neighborhood when he was attacked. Mr. Morton was known in Montgomery as "the Bookmobile man" from his many years of driving the Bookmobile for the local public library.

I don't remember him personally, but I do remember getting books from the bookmobile during the summer as a kid.

Mr. Morton's attacker was Jonathan Reed,* twenty-three-years old. He had been admitted to the psychiatric ward of Jackson Hospital on October 27 and was released the day before the assault on Mr. Morton.

On December 11, Nina M. Kruger of Tallahassee, Florida, wrote a very nice letter to the editor of the *Alabama Journal,* Montgomery's

---

*   Name changed to protect the criminally deranged

afternoon newspaper, commending and thanking us for our quick action. She also expressed gratitude to the paramedics and hospital staff who worked on Mr. Morton.

I ran the scenario through my mind over and over for weeks after the incident. I questioned myself as to the reason I didn't immediately fire at the deranged man while he continued his assault on the victim. The only reason I can see why I didn't shoot him was because I was concerned I might have accidentally hit the older man.

I heard it said by several people familiar with the incident, "If it had been me, I would have shot him!"

My answer to them is, "Well, you weren't there."

You really don't know how you'd react until it happens to you. It was comforting to know that there were three other officers there who also held their fire, two of whom more experienced than I.

Everything worked out and Mr. Morton lived, but it still haunted me for months. It may not be the Christian thing to say about the disturbed young man, but there are some days when I wish I had shot him.

Man charged in throat slashing

A Montgomery man charged with cutting the throat of a 77-year-old Southmont Drive man Thursday was released from a hospital psychiatric ward less than 24 hours before the incident, police said.

Twenty-three-year-old ████████████ of 32 W. Clover Lane, was charged with attempted murder Thursday.

He was being held at 8 a.m. today in the County Jail in lieu of $125,000 bond.

Allen Morton, of 71 Southmont Drive, was in the intensive care unit at St. Margaret's Hospital this morning following surgery.

His condition was not available, a hospital spokesman said.

Morton was attacked Thursday afternoon at the intersection of South Court Street and Southmont Drive by a man wielding a butcher knife, said police reports.

Sgt. Tommi Hord, the Montgomery Police Department's public information officer, said two officers drove into the intersection by chance while the man was on Morton cutting his throat.

████████ was admitted for treatment at Jackson Hospital's psychiatric ward Oct. 27 and was released at 7 p.m. Wednesday, Hord said.

An official at Jackson Hospital would not confirm at noon whether Hunter had been treated there.

November 7, 1986 – Newspaper article of throat
slashing (Courtesy of Alabama Journal)

TENDERONIES

SATURDAY, JANUARY 24, 1987, WAS a warm, sunny day for that time of year. I was riding in District Three with Officer Mike Ilczyszyn, an intense man whose northern accent told anyone right away that he wasn't an Alabama native.

Mike had a dry sense of humor that you knew and understood after you got to know him. Mike had spent a great deal of his life in the Marine Corps and rising to the rank of major in the reserves. He is a squared away marine and serious man who was accustomed to giving orders and having them immediately obeyed. This was directly opposite from the way most people respond to authority on the street.

We would respond to calls to homes or businesses and have to give advice about the problems and personal conflicts faced by various people. As is often the case, most people chose to ignore what we told them to do. This irritated Mike to no end.

On several occasions I told Mike, "These people were fighting long before we became police officers. They'll be fighting as long as we're police officers, and they will be fighting long after we're gone."

"Yeah, yeah," he always replied.

On this particular afternoon the citizens were active in the city. During the winter months or during long rainy periods, people tended to get "cabin fever." An occasional warm day drove them out in the open and usually meant more calls for the police. That Saturday turned out to be one of those days.

Around 4:30 in the afternoon, we were patrolling in the 300 block of Randolph Street, approaching Decatur Street. Tenderonies, a local nightspot, is located on the corner and is one of several clubs that have occupied that building over the years. As we approached the club we observed two black men who appeared to be in their late fifties arguing in the middle of the street. Both were thin, wore worn clothing, and appeared to be drunk.

We saw one of the men pick up a small log a little more than a foot long from a pile of wood in the grass. The log was obviously heavy by the way the man struggled to lift it, trying with all his might to heave it toward the other man. He made several attempts to lift and heave the log, but managed to pitch the log only a foot or two on each attempt. The other man stood about three feet away from his attacker and seemed unfazed by the threat of being pummeled by the cumbersome log. He was far too busy giving the struggling drunk an earful of his opinion.

A crowd from the club quickly gathered outside to enjoy the show. The people in the crowd laughed and jeered at the two old guys and their feeble attempt at a fight. As we pulled up to the men, I grabbed one of the drunks and put him against the front quarter panel of our patrol car. Mike grabbed the other guy and braced him against the front of the car. I stood at the corner of the car separating them. Mike walked toward the gathered crowd and tried to disperse them. He held his wooden baton in his hand and barked at the crowd.

"Get back inside the club!" he yelled.

The crowd, realizing that the entertainment was over, began to file slowly back into the club. As Mike patrolled down the sidewalk everyone went inside. I was trying to get the names of the two men to see if they had warrants. We really did not want to put them in jail if we didn't have to because of how busy I knew we'd be later on that night.

As I asked both men questions, they renewed their argument. Suddenly the man to my right dove across the hood of the car and grabbed the other man by the shirt trying to choke him. The second man backed away and dragged the first one right on top of him as they fell to the ground. They tangled up like two cats in an alley.

Mike was somewhere on the other side of the club, still clearing the crowd. I was able to separate the two men and stood them back against the car. I looked back and saw several subjects peering out of the club at the same time Mike rounded the corner. The club door opened to the outside and one of the patrons had his face half way out of the door watching the two scrapping drunks and me. Mike walked up from behind the door and saw it partially opened, but didn't see the man peering out behind it.

Mike walked up and kicked the door shut as hard as he could. The force of the kick slammed the door against the guy's head and knocked him out. As the man lay motionless, face down in the doorway, someone inside grabbed him by the feet and slowly dragged him back into the club. The door closed and didn't open again until after we left.

During all the commotion, the dispatcher had tried several times to call us on the radio to check on us, but neither Mike nor I heard her call. As we handcuffed the two men, a couple of patrol units came speeding to our location. Mike and I were somewhat surprised to see them.

One of the officers bailed from the car and ran up to me. "Are you guys alright?" he asked.

"Yeah, we're okay," I replied. "What's goin' on?"

"They've been trying to raise y'all on the radio."

"Really?"

The officer let the dispatcher know that we were okay. Our supervisor had us to switch to channel three to find out why we didn't answer the radio, and I explained about the crowd and the two guys fighting. We arrested both men for being drunk in public. Later, I gave our supervisor a little more detail about what happened.

Watching two old drunk guys fight was pretty entertaining. With the exception of the guy with the severe headache, the crowd seemed to enjoy it too.

We put both men in jail to sleep it off. These guys were what police call "old school." They didn't fight with guns or knives; they used their fists—or the occasional log.

A few years later, Mike was reassigned as an instructor at the police academy. On the occasions when I taught my evidence class there, I was always sure to include the story of Tenderonies.

Herb

ONE OF THE MORE INTERESTING things about being a police officer is that occasionally you get to meet famous people. Athletes, actors and political figures aren't exempt from problems with the law either as victims or suspects. Sooner or later, even the rich and famous will encounter a police officer. On a more pleasant note, celebrities will often go out of their way to greet police officers and mention a relative or friend in law enforcement, though usually they just want to show appreciation for the job we do.

April 26, 1987 had been a quiet Sunday night. My partner, M. O. Johnson and I were riding in District Twelve which is the neighborhoods north of the Western Boulevard and east of I-65. There aren't any restaurants open on Sunday nights in this district so we decided to have dinner at the Madison Hotel. The city had just hosted the George Lindsey Celebrity Golf Tournament the day before. George Lindsey, who played Goober Pyle on *The Andy Griffith Show*, was born in Jasper, Alabama, two hours north of Montgomery. Between 1971 and 1988, he hosted an annual golf tournament and variety show in Montgomery featuring many Hollywood celebrities that raised over a million dollars for the Special Olympics. Mr. Lindsey and nearly all the featured celebrities who were guests in the hotel were usually gone by the following day.

Just as our dinner arrived, I picked up the ketchup bottle and was attempting to pour some next to my fries. As is often the case with a particular brand of very thick ketchup, it refused to pour out quickly enough for me. I placed the cap back on the bottle and while holding the bottle in my left hand, flung the bottle quickly down beside the table to force all the ketchup to the top. I had done this in the past and it would make the ketchup pour more quickly. Just as I whipped the bottle down beside the table, the actor Frank Bonner walked up to us.

Frank Bonner played Herb Tarlek on the popular television show *WKRP in Cincinnati* that aired on CBS from 1978 to 1982. I'd been a fan of the show and recognized him immediately. He'd played in the tournament that weekend and had decided to stay in Montgomery another day. As he walked up to our table and stuck out his right hand and asked, "Gentleman, how are you doing this evening?"

"Just fine, sir, and you?" I replied shaking his hand.

"Just fine," he said. "You fellas having a quiet night?"

"So far, so good." I said.

We exchanged some light conversation where he mentioned that a close relative was a police officer in some other city. I don't recall exactly who or where he said, but he told us that he had great respect for law enforcement officers.

"Thank you very much," I told him. "We appreciate that."

"I'll let you guys get back to your meal," he said. "I just wanted to say thank you for doing what you do." He shook hands with both of us again.

"Well, thank you again, sir," I said.

He flashed his signature Herb Tarlek grin, turned and walked away.

I looked at my partner. "Do you know who that was?" I asked him. "That was Herb Tarlek from *WKRP in Cincinnati*!"

It was at that time I remembered that I had the ketchup bottle in my left hand. I had held it beside the table the whole time, not realizing that I'd been holding it upside down below the edge of the table where it couldn't be seen. As I raised it I saw that the cap was gone and bottle was empty. I looked down on the floor. A thick, brilliant red pool of ketchup lay beneath the table. Somewhere beneath the gooey pile was the cap.

Fortunately, the puddle was near the wall where there wasn't much traffic and not visible to anyone standing next to the table. When the waitress came back to the table to ask if we needed anything, I just looked at her as if nothing had happened.

"Could I have another bottle of ketchup?" I held up the bottle. "This one is empty."

A minute later she brought me another bottle. We finished our meal, paid and left. I know it was wrong to just leave the mess on the floor under the table. I felt pretty stupid about doing it and I really didn't want to tell the waitress how I did it. I left a larger than normal tip to make up for her having to clean it up and also to ease my guilt of making such a big mess. It was stupid and I admit it.

Later, I told my fellow officers and friends how we'd met Herb Tarlek from *WKRP* at the Madison Hotel. But it was quite a while before I added the detail about the ketchup during our encounter with Herb.

April 1987 – Nancy introduces me at her bridal shower

I Was There That Day

Tuesday, February 2, 1988, was another historic day in Montgomery, Alabama. This was nothing new for Montgomery, the city nationally known both as the Capital of the Confederacy as well as the birthplace of the civil rights movement. Once again the city became a flashpoint of racial and social conflict.

Thomas Reed, the President of the Alabama chapter of the N.A.A.C.P. (National Association for the Advancement of Colored People) had pledged to take down the confederate battle flag that flew over the dome of the state capitol building as it had since Governor George Wallace ordered it placed there in April of 1963. The black community, led by Reed, Alvin Holmes, and an assortment of so-called black leaders declared the flag a symbol of racism and wanted it removed from the capitol. Then governor Guy Hunt refused to remove the flag and ordered the State Capitol Police to arrest anyone who tried to take it down.

Anytime Holmes or his colleagues heard that they couldn't do something, they used the conflict to promote themselves in the media, regardless of how ignorant it made them appear. Holmes was also quick to utter his catchphrase in the press when he didn't get his way, "I'm filin' a lawsuit!"

Thomas Reed publicly stated that he would climb to the top of the capital and remove the flag himself at noon on February 2nd. I believe he picked noon because all the state employees would be out for lunch and could stand around and watch the show. I don't know if he thought this would bolster support for him and his cause or not, but we had to be prepared for anything.

I was on the riot squad from second shift patrol. We were trained to handle large, unruly crowds. We practiced every three months preparing for the worst, but hoped that the conflict would resolve itself somehow.

Second shift and third shift patrol each trained its own riot platoon. Each platoon consisted of four squads of twelve officers totaling forty-eight officers per platoon. A corporal led each squad, and a lieutenant and a sergeant led each platoon. Both platoons together comprised a riot company led by a captain. Each officer in the company wore class-B duty uniforms during any deployment with combat boots, duty belts with sidearm, and a four-foot oak riot stick. We carried a gas mask on our left side in a canvas bag in case tear gas was used on the crowd, and black helmets with pull down shatter-resistant face shields.

We met at police headquarters at 9:30 a.m. and was on stand-by in case we were needed. In all the years I spent on the riot squad on both second and third shift patrol, I had never confronted a large angry crowd. If we weren't working at the Christmas parade keeping kids from running out in front of the floats, we usually sat down at the Civic Center all day eating poorly-made ham sandwiches on city overtime.

At the time of this incident, the capitol building was in the midst of a complete restoration. It was closed to the public and surrounded by an eight-foot chain link fence. Most of the instigators, including Reed, were elderly, over-weight and certainly in no shape to climb a small fence, much less one eight foot high. Even if any of them had managed to get past the fence, they still faced the daunting task of scaling the dome of the capitol that stood over a hundred feet from the ground. It was fairly obvious to anyone that the feat was impossible for anyone other than an experienced climber in good physical condition. However, my attitude toward their protest and their effort to scale the building was, let 'em try.

It was my day off, but I was glad to make the overtime. I was on the schedule to work security at Eastdale Mall that evening, so I knew I was going to be making time and a half. After about an hour of waiting, a supervisor told us that members of the Ku Klux Klan and other white supremacists were gathering on Monroe Street near North Union Street waving Confederate flags in support of the Confederate flag. A group of black protesters, some bearing African flags, were across the street from them showing support for Reed and his group. Both groups hurled racial insults at each other, and I knew this was turning into something ugly.

At approximately 11:00 a.m., we boarded buses and rode to the parking lot of Cramton Bowl a few blocks east of the capitol to wait because the situation was beginning to escalate. The crowds on both side of the issue were growing, and the media was having a field day. Media representatives from all over the state, and several more from out of state, were ready to record history.

A little before noon we moved from Cramton Bowl to Monroe Street to begin controlling the swelling crowd. We were let out of the buses at Monroe Street and Decatur Street and formed into a unified company. We began marching in formation east on Monroe Street between the Ku Klux Klan and the black agitators.

Suddenly I heard on the police radio, "North Union Street—shots fired!"

I said to myself, "Here we go." I pulled down the face shield of my helmet preparing for the worst.

I had no idea what was happening beyond my immediate surroundings, but I knew that we were in the middle of the action. As we marched between the two hostile crowds, adrenaline pumped through me and seemed to sharpen my senses. A photographer stood in front of the squad snapping photos of us as we marched. As we approached him, it was apparent he wasn't going to move, hoping I guess that we would march around him and let him snap a few pictures from inside the platoon's ranks. He obviously didn't understand the strength of our resolve to remain in tight formation as we marched.

Officer Dale Warke, the first officer to pass him, pushed him gently with the butt of his riot stick and it caused him to fall backwards. He caught himself with his left hand and as he rocked back to a squatting position and prepared to take another photo, I bumped him with the butt of my riot stick and he fell hard on his butt. Since he was off balance already, it didn't take much to push him back. The platoon marched steadfastly on as he scrambled to get off the ground and out of the way.

It wasn't the right or polite thing to do, but the adrenaline was pumping, and the stress level was off the meter. I just got caught up in the moment.

As we marched pass the agitators, Lieutenant Les Brown, our platoon commander, gave the order for us to form a line down Monroe Street and around onto North Union Street. I still wondered about the shooting I heard on the radio. I thought for a moment that I must have misunderstood. Later, I found out that the shooting had happened on North Union Circle in the Trenholm Court housing project, three blocks north of our location, but it was completely unrelated with the events at the capitol.

I was standing on North Union Street at Monroe Street where a large crowd had gathered on the sidewalk to watch the show. I didn't know at the time but I was standing at the point where Thomas Reed would attempt to climb the fence. It turned out I had the best seat in the house.

The crowd there wasn't hostile at all. The fact that we were dead serious, holding four-foot sticks and wearing shielded helmets might have quelled any notion anyone had about breaching the peace that day. Intimidation can be an important tool when used properly.

The crowd where I stood seemed content to stay and watch the show.

"You don't have to worry about us crossing the line," one man said. "We're just here to see what's going to happen."

"We're not here to cause problems, just to see the show," I heard a lady say.

Lieutenant Brown walked back and forth behind us. "Be alert!" he ordered. "Maintain your positions."

I could see that he had a live tear gas grenade in each of his back pockets. This was the real deal and I was in the middle of it.

Mr. Reed finally walked out of the State House across Union Street, followed closely by two State Capitol police officers. He walked up to the fence and reached up as high as he could to grasp the chain link. He made a half-hearted effort to pull himself up by kicking his feet against the fence. There were a few snickers from the crowd at first, followed by outright laughter as he did his poor impression of a man climbing a fence.

After a few moments of the charade, the two officers with him ended the pitiful attempt. They pulled him gently from the fence. I wonder how long he would have gone on with his act had the officers not put an end to it. Reed could no more have scaled the fence than he could have jumped to the moon, but they all made a big show of it. He was arrested without incident, just as he'd planned. He and his thirteen colleagues were placed in custody and put aboard a Blue Bird school bus and taken to jail. They hung a sign out the window and began to sing "We Shall Overcome." When the bus drove away, the crowd calmly dispersed like smoke on a windy day.

Nothing serious or truly dramatic took place, but once again, Montgomery headlined the national news that day as a hotbed of racism and injustice as if it were somehow still the 1950's.

I worked until 2:00 that afternoon, filled out my overtime, and then went to my extra job at the mall. To sum it up, it was just a big bunch of nothing, and a lot of taxpayers money was wasted.

Following a legal battle, Judge Shashy ordered Governor Hunt to remove the flag on April 22, 1993, over five years after the protest began. The Governor ordered the flag moved south across Washington Avenue to the First White House of the Confederacy.

Whether the flag flies on top of the capitol building or not makes no difference to me. Montgomery was the Capital of the Confederacy during the Civil War. I personally think the flag should fly over the capitol building because it's a part of our history. It has its place beneath both the state flag of Alabama and the flag of the United States, but a judge made the final decision and that's that. I've never lost any sleep over it.

Alvin and his gang won that battle, but what did they really win? The flag itself never harmed anyone, and removing it didn't solve anything. I witnessed a little history, and even though not that many people know or even care, I was there that day.

But Some Folks are Just Not that Sharp

THROUGH MY YEARS OF BEING a police officer, I've been asked to do an array of things. Many of them fell within the scope of my job description, but police officers have a broad scope of duties. Every once in a while someone would ask me to do something that appeared to be simple but the results would turn out completely unexpected. Some folks just don't think when they ask the police to do things for them.

On Sunday, February 14, 1988, I was riding in District Eight with Officer A.D. Williams. His first name was Andre, but I called him A.D.

Around 1:45 in the morning we were talking to Detective Jamie Reynolds of the Juvenile Division in the Sam's Warehouse parking lot on Carmichael Road at the Eastern Boulevard. We had a mutual friend, Danny Cheek, riding with him as an observer and they were looking for something interesting to do. Whenever you have an observer riding with you, you want to show them some interesting aspect of police work, like an arrest, disturbance, traffic stop, something that the general public thinks a police officer does every day. Most people don't realize that we spend most of our time just patrolling, waiting for something to happen.

We'd been talking for about fifteen minutes when Jamie said, "It's been slow all night. Go get into something so Danny can see something."

"Sure, no problem," I said. "We'll just go find somebody and put them in jail so Danny can see real police work," I said half-jokingly.

About that time a subject walked up to us and said, "I'm sorry to bother y'all, but I locked my keys in my car and I was hoping y'all could unlock my car."

"Where are you parked?" I asked.

"In the Cuco's parking lot over there." He pointed toward the business on the far end of an adjacent parking lot.

"Head over to your car and we'll be there in just a minute."

I looked at Danny sitting in the passenger side of Jamie's unmarked Chevrolet Caprice and said sarcastically, "You want to see us open up a locked vehicle? That's *real* police work. It could be dangerous. I trained in the academy for weeks to learn this skill."

"Nah, it's gettin' late," Jamie said. "I think we'll just head in. I think y'all can handle it."

Jamie drove off and we went over to the guy's car parked at Cuco's, next to the East Boulevard.

I retrieved the slim-jim from above my head, which was wedged behind the plastic trim of the headliner. The slim-jim is a flat strip of stainless steel with a handle on one end and notches cut out on the other end used to slide down beside the glass inside a locked car door. The tool can manipulate the locking mechanism and unlock the door. With a little practice, most older cars can be unlocked in less than a minute

My partner had the owner sign a wavier stating that there was a possibility that the tool could cause internal damage to the vehicle's door and that by signing the waiver, the police department wouldn't be held responsible for any damage.

As I started to work on the door, I noticed a drug pipe on the console of the vehicle with a brown substance inside. I had seen these pipes many times in the past and I knew what it was as soon as I saw it. As I continued to work on the door I looked more carefully in the vehicle and saw a postal clip with a weight on it used to weigh single envelopes, but very common for small independent drug dealers to weigh small amounts of marijuana.

As I popped open the door lock, I opened the driver's door two or three inches, the owner quickly tried to slip between me and the door.

"Thanks! I really appreciate it," he said quickly.

"Hold on there, Buddy," I said, pushing him back away from the door. I spun him around and put him on the car and my partner instantly reacted and grabbed hold of the man.

"Hang on to him, A.D., for just a second," I ordered.

A.D. took him around to the back of the car and had him spread his hands out on the trunk. I retrieved the pipe and smelled it. It had the distinct odor of burnt marijuana. I asked the guy if he had any marijuana in the vehicle. He hesitated for a moment, shook his head as he lowered it.

"Yeah, it's in the glove box," he said.

I retrieved a clear plastic bag containing marijuana that I later weighed at 2.5 grams. A.D. placed handcuffs on the subject and we transported him to the Vice and Narcotics office. After my partner radioed in that we were transporting a prisoner, Jamie called me and asked what we had. I told him he should have hung around for the unlocking of the car and that the subject had marijuana in the vehicle.

"The guy had marijuana in the car and asked you to unlock it for him?" I could hear the amazement in his voice.

"Yeah, pretty much," I said. "Not the brightest bulb on the Christmas tree. I'll tell you all the details later."

"That's 10-4."

Sometimes I just wonder what people are thinking. If I had locked my keys in my car and had drugs in it, I would never ask the police to unlock my car, no matter how far away I was from home. I would come up with another plan, but some folks just aren't that sharp.

"Hey, Gran'daddy!"

FROM TIME TO TIME I would make an arrest that made me wonder, "Was it really that easy?"

On Sunday, May 15, 1988, Officer Gerald Tippins and I were riding in District One. We came on duty at 2:30 that afternoon, and it had been quiet all evening. Around 6:45, we were on routine patrol in the Trenholm Court housing projects when we drove past a group of men standing around talking. I observed an older man in the group resting his right elbow on the top of a vehicle. In his hand he was swinging a small zip-lock baggie that contained something white.

I had to do a double-take to realize what I'd seen.

When the man saw us, he dropped the baggie, turned back toward his buddies and kept talking as if nothing had happened.

"Did you see that?" I asked Gerald in disbelief. "He had a drug baggie in his hand!"

I stopped the car and walked over with Gerald to the group of men. Lying on the ground next to the man was the clear plastic zip-lock baggie partially filled with a fine white powder.

I was surprised that none of the men ran or at least tried to walk away. The man with the baggie may have chosen not to run because he was fifty-three-years old. Most people arrested for drug possession range in age from their late teens to their early thirties.

I picked up the baggie, placed the man under arrest and transported him to the narcotics office, where the powder tested positive for cocaine. We filled out the appropriate paperwork then got back to work.

The arrest was just too easy.

On October 26, 1988, Gerald and I were subpoenaed to Circuit

Court to testify in the case. I couldn't believe the man was actually going to fight the charge. Of course, I wondered what a jury thinks when they hear a case like that; a person waving a small baggie of cocaine as the police drive by. It just seemed too unbelievable.

We had been there about two hours, a jury had been seated, and we were preparing to begin the trial when the judge announced we would take a ten-minute break. He said that an elementary school class was on a field trip and that they were being brought to our courtroom to observe an actual trial.

Many elementary schools schedule a law enforcement week and have speakers come to their schools and speak to the students about good citizenship. I have spoken at schools in the past where the administrators want the police officer to emphasize the evils of drugs, alcohol, gangs and peer pressure. I think it is good that the kids get to see actual trials of those people who refuse to hear the message.

The youngsters walked quietly into the courtroom in a single file. They looked to be in the fourth grade. As they each sat down, one of the little girls looked over at the defendant. Instantly recognizing him, she waved and yelled, "Hey, Gran'daddy!"

"Oh, no!" I said to myself. Of all the courtrooms these kids could have come into, they had to come into this one. Even though the defendant was on trial for drugs, I felt sorry for him because his granddaughter had to see him in court. I was just glad he was not wearing jail clothes and belly chains.

We took another ten-minute break so the kids could be led from our courtroom to another. Another class was escorted into our courtroom and stayed until the first break. The defense attorney made a big show about how I testified that the suspect was waving the bag of cocaine as we drove by. I just told the truth, and the suspect was found guilty. He was sentenced to three years suspended sentence and three years probation.

I have told the story many times about how you just never know whom you'll see in court at any given time. I'll never forget that precious little girl walking in and just as innocent as she could be, saying, "Hey Gran'daddy!"

THE TWILIGHT ZONE

ONDAY, MAY 23, 1988, AROUND 4:00 in the afternoon, Officer Gerald Tippins and I were riding the downtown district. Dexter Avenue is the main street in downtown Montgomery, and the focal point for a lot of history in the South. The state capitol building sits at the top of Dexter Avenue and is where Jefferson Davis was sworn in as the first president of the Confederacy. Martin Luther King Jr. preached at Dexter Avenue Baptist Church, and the first electric trolley cars in the United States, nicknamed the Lightning Route, began running in 1886 on tracks down the middle of this street.

A lot of things have happened on Dexter Avenue, but nothing as strange as what happened to us. Gerald and I responded to a call to the S.H. Kress department store on a suspicious person. It was not uncommon to get calls like this to the stores downtown. People would often ride the bus downtown then wander from store to store and would eventually sit down and cool off in one of the air-conditioned stores.

When we arrived, a clerk met us at the door. She said the man smelled like he'd been drinking and appeared to be lost. She took us to the back office where he'd been taken. The man told us his name was Kevin Harold.*

We asked him a few questions, and we learned that he was forty-nine years old and was from Wewahitchka, Florida. He told us that he'd been living on the streets for the last couple of days. I smelled cheap booze on his breath along with the pungent odor of someone who hadn't bathed in several days.

Gerald recorded all his personal information and ran a warrant check on the radio while I talked to him. He didn't have any family

---

* Name changed to protect those in another dimension

in town and he seemed confused. Besides confusion, I could tell that he sensed that something else wasn't quite right.

I asked him how he got to Montgomery. He replied that he had ridden the bus into town. I asked him where he came from, and he said that he just got back from overseas.

The more we talked, the more he opened up and began to tell us about himself. He talked about being in the war and how he was glad to be back home. He spoke of the war and his buddies still over there fighting as if the war was still going on.

Gerald and I became a bit confused. At the time, the United States wasn't involved in any long-term military conflict anywhere.

"What war are you talking about?" I asked finally.

He looked me square in the eye. "Vietnam," he replied.

I sat there for a few seconds without saying a word. I was trying to decide if he was just making it up or if he was just completely mental. He did not seem crazy as far as I could tell.

Gerald answered the dispatcher on the radio then told me that the warrant check on the guy was negative.

I continued to talk to him. I knew something wasn't right, but could not quite put my finger on it. I don't really know why I thought about this but for some reason I wondered for a moment if he knew what day it was.

"What's today's date?" I asked him.

"May 13, 1968," he replied.

I looked at him completely puzzled. "What did you say the date was?"

"May 13th," he said. "I know this because I left Vietnam fours day ago—and that was on the ninth."

"And what year is it again?" I asked to make sure I heard him correctly.

"1968," he replied.

Gerald and I glanced at each other, both of us slightly bewildered. I was trying to figure out if the guy was putting us on. The man's demeanor indicated to me that he was completely serious and believed everything he was telling us.

Once I was convinced that the guy was on the level, the debate for me began. How do you tell a person that he had lost twenty years of his life? I thought to myself, he's not going to believe me if I tell him what year it really is. And how do you convince a person he is living twenty years in the future?

I sat at the desk in the small office, and he sat in a chair next to the desk facing me. I looked up on the cork bulletin board over the desk and saw a calendar hanging there, among several other papers. I took down the calendar and before I showed it to him.

"Sir, I don't really know how to tell you this," I began. "But it's not 1968; it's 1988."

He looked at me blankly for a moment. "Why do you want to tell me something like that, officer?" he asked.

"Sir, I'm not trying to be mean, but it wouldn't be right to not tell you the truth," I said. "My partner and I are only trying to help you."

I held up the calendar and showed him it was May, then pointed to the year at the top of the page where "1988" was printed in bold, red ink.

"You see, sir, it really is 1988."

He stared at the calendar and had a look on his face that is hard to describe. It was a look of shock, disbelief and wonder. I felt like he needed a little more convincing. So I pointed toward Gerald, who is black.

"Do you think they would let this man be a police officer in Montgomery, Alabama, if it were 1968?"

He looked at Gerald, who nodded politely at him. The man slumped down in the chair as if someone had let the air out of him.

"No, I guess not," he said.

We sat there for about a minute or so with him, and I could see the man soaking in the reality of the situation. I wasn't exactly sure how he would react to the news.

After a few moments, he stood up. "Well, I guess I need to move on now," he said slowly. There was also a profound, undeniable sadness in his voice.

"Where're you going to go, sir?" I asked.

"I guess I'll try to get back to Florida."

I didn't know what else to do for him. I guess if it happened again today, I'd contact the Department of Veterans Affairs to see if anything could be done for him. This may be a common occurrence among war veterans with which I'm unfamiliar, but I can't imagine how I'd feel if I lost twenty years of my life in an instant.

The man thanked us for helping him and he said he'd be okay. He left the store walking down Dexter Avenue and into history. That was the last we saw of him.

"That's so sad about him," the store manager said afterward. "What will happen to him?"

"I don't really know, to be honest with you," I said. "But there is nothing else we can do for him."

From time to time I've wondered whatever happened to the man lost in time. The S.H. Kress store is gone now, and it's just one of those hard to believe stories. It's one of those stories best told with music playing in the background. The only appropriate music would be the theme from "The Twilight Zone."

1988 – Second shift patrol

It's Not Always Easy, But It's Worth It.

POOR PARENTING IS THE CAUSE of a lot of problems police officers have in their day to day duties. A child having to raise themselves or their younger siblings is a very sad thing. I've met kids who do this and do their best. Some, for their age, even do a pretty good job. But sometimes you run across a situation that is more than just sad. Tragic is the word that comes to mind. Scary is the word that describes the night of June 10, 1988.

On this particular Friday night, around 11:50 p.m., my partner, Officer Gerald Tippins, and I were riding in District One patrolling in the area of High Street and South Jackson Street. The Top Flight Disco was located in this block of High Street and on Friday and Saturday nights cars lined the street into the wee hours of the morning. There were numerous thefts from vehicles over the past several weekends and we were patrolling heavily in the area in an attempt to catch the suspects.

As I drove our marked unit west on High Street, we observed a kid taking a gas can from the back of a pickup. As my partner exited our vehicle the suspect ran east. My partner pursued him on foot and caught him approximately one block away on Watts Street. I met my partner with the patrol vehicle and we took the suspect to his home in the 500 block of Watts Street. He was ten years old and lived in Tulane Court Housing Project. I'm not exactly sure when the Tulane Projects were built but the builder used the old red brick that most of the older projects were built with back in the fifties and sixties.

As we walked to the door of the apartment, I was expecting to talk to parents, release him back to their custody, fill out a Youth Form and be back on patrol. This should have taken about ten minutes, but when we opened the front door I knew we were going to be there much longer. I stood there in disbelief as I saw an eleven-year-old boy running down a flight of stairs chasing a seven-year-old boy with a can of bug spray. The eleven-year-old was spraying bug spray as he ran. The seven-year-old was running holding a ten-inch butcher knife. Both boys ran down the stairs from my left to right and through the living room into the kitchen screaming and laughing. There was a two-year-old, three-year-old and a four-year-old sitting on the couch watching.

Gerald grabbed the butcher knife. I grabbed the bug spray and we sat everyone down on the couch. There were a total of six kids alone. I asked the nine-year-old where their mother was.

"She's at the club," he replied.

"What club did she go to?" I asked.

"I don't know," he said. "Just the club."

"Who watchin' y'all while she's at the club?" I asked.

"Nobody," one replied.

"Nobody!" I said. I couldn't believe what I was hearing. "Nobody is watching y'all while she is gone? How long has she been gone?"

"I don't know. Maybe since about six or so."

I looked at Gerald. "Go ahead and notify Juvenile and have them come out here."

While we waited on a Juvenile detective to arrive, we talked to the kids to find out how they were doing. They told us that they'd not eaten since breakfast. The two-year-old was holding a half-eaten wiener in her hand when we arrived, so I assumed they found something to eat after their mother left.

While talking to the ten-year-old, we found out that he was playing with his father's shotgun when he was seven-years-old and had accidentally killed his five-year-old brother.

It took about twenty minutes for a Juvenile detective to arrive and during that short period of time we talked to the kids, we were amazed that they had not been seriously injured or killed. This was not the first time they had been left home alone for long periods of time. A Juvenile detective arrived, we briefed him on what we had, turned the kids over to him and we left. He later turned them over to a neighbor.

Often I have wondered just how many other kids are left alone every day to fend for themselves, without parental supervision. I *really* don't want to know the answer to this question. It scares me to think about it.

You hear stories about kids being injured and people ask, "Where were the parents?" My usual answer is, "There ain't no tellin'. There are people in this world who should never be allowed to have children, much less raise them."

I didn't have children then. I do now, and I can't imagine leaving them home alone at such a young age for any length of time. Children are precious gifts from God and some people treat them like they are pets; feed them when they're hungry, then leave them to take care of themselves.

I don't know whatever happened to the kids. I hope they are okay. I can only hope that their mother was charged with child neglect and the kids were placed with a responsible relative. More than likely she got a reprimand from a juvenile court judge who had more serious cases to worry about. I imagine that the Department of Human Resources (DHR) got involved somehow and made some attempt to correct the mother's behavior.

If you have kids, then be responsible enough to raise them. I love my kids, and I thank the Lord for them. Children need you to be there for them. Raising children, it's not always easy, but they are worth it.

JUST ANOTHER DAY IN DISTRICT ONE

NDEPENDENCE DAY IS WHAT I consider one of the two most dangerous days of the year for police officers. New Year's Eve is the other. Some people feel the need to shoot guns instead of fireworks to celebrate the holiday. The police department receives more than a hundred code 7 (shootings in progress) calls on these two days. Most are fireworks but a lot of them are actual shots being fired.

My regular partner had taken the Monday holiday off, so on July 4, 1988, Officer Derek K. Jones was my partner. Everyone called him D.K. D.K. and I had never been partners before but I knew him from the shift and from just being around him I saw he had a great sense of humor.

I was assigned to District One and once we left headquarters after roll call, we were in my district. Since it was a holiday all the businesses downtown were closed. Whenever there is Monday holiday, such as Independence Day, it gives everyone an extra day to consume alcoholic beverages. Alcohol, guns and high temperatures sometimes make for a very busy shift. The high was expected to be 85 degrees that day.

D.K. and I had been on patrol for about an hour when around 3:30 p.m. we were dispatched to the CSX Railroad yard on Waters Street on a trespassing call. The dispatcher advised us that three transients were found on one of the boxcars and were in the custody of CSX Railroad investigators. Most of these investigators are either retired or former police officers, and I knew the investigators who had called.

District One was my assigned beat and encompassed all the

downtown Montgomery area. I often had to deal with homeless transients who camped out in the railroad yards near the river waiting to hitch a ride on the next freight train. We received this sort of call about once or twice a month. It was a fairly routine matter to show up, arrest the trespassers, and transport them to jail. We never knew exactly from where these guys blew in, but the one thing we did know was that they didn't bathe very often, especially during the summer.

The overpowering smell of a sweaty transient can make you heave your lunch. After just the few minutes it took to transport one to headquarters, it would take a whole day and a can of air freshener to get the smell out of your car. That was usually followed by a night of riding around with the windows down in an attempt to remove their "essence" from the back seat.

When we arrived at the CSX security office, three disheveled men sat despondently outside on the steps of the building. This was not a good sign, considering they were usually detained in the office. I had told D.K. that if they were sitting outside, that meant they were *really* ripe. Very often the transients kept opened cans of Vienna sausages or tuna or whatever they'd eaten for lunch in their pockets and wanted to save for later. These odors combined with the fragrance of unwashed armpit and rancid sweat to form a blend of new and vicious aromas.

As my partner and I got out of our vehicle, we spoke with the CSX security investigators and exchanged pleasantries for a few minutes. We then handcuffed the three men and sat them in the back of our car. One of the subjects was so nasty he actually had flies buzzing around him like Pigpen in the Peanuts comic strip.

Two of the men got into the back seat with no problem, but in a group there always seems to be one guy who wants to be difficult. The third man sat down in the back seat on the passenger side but refused to put his right leg in the car. "Sir, put your leg in the car" I asked calmly.

"You put it in," he said defiantly and without looking at me.

"Put your leg in the car," I said again with a little anger in my voice.

"You put it in," he said again as he looked at his buddies.

Now believe it or not, this is something many people do who are being arrested. For some reason, I guess they think that if they don't put their leg in the car then they won't go to jail. In my younger, less experienced, days I would push and pull on the leg often to the amusement of the person being arrested. However, after a couple of tries, I could usually get the leg in and close the door.

Well, I'd been with the police department for quite some time and had learned a few things. One of these was that there was an easy way to handle things and a hard way. Trying to put the leg in the car by hand was the hard way. This also let the prisoner feel like he was getting the best of you. Now the easy way was to tell the subject only once to put his leg in the car then slam the car door on it.

Taking into consideration it was a hot day and these guys were especially rank, I wasn't at all amused by his stubborn protest. I pulled out my wooden baton and struck the right leg several times as hard as I could. "Put your leg in the car!" I ordered.

After wailing on the leg for a little while, I slammed the door on his leg... several times, but every time the door hit his leg, it just bounced back. D.K. and I swapped looks of disbelief. He did not even flinch as I hit him with my baton and slammed the door. As I continued to whack the leg with my baton and repeatedly slammed the door, I ordered him to move his leg, I heard a voice come from inside the car. "Excuse me, Officer. It's not real," the man said softly.

The statement didn't register and certainly had no effect on my brutal assault on the defiant leg. The man in the middle seat sitting next to my stubborn friend spoke again, somewhat louder this time. "Excuse me officer. It's not real, Officer. It's a fake!"

I stopped for a moment. "What are you talking about?"

"The leg's not real. It's a prosthetic leg," he said calmly.

I pulled up the man's pant leg and saw that the leg was in fact made out of some kind of plastic polymer substance or whatever it is artificial limbs are made. I also noticed that the leg had about a dozen dents from my baton and about six well-defined crease marks from the slamming door.

Without further ado, I lifted the leg and shoved it onto the floorboard. D.K. chuckled in amazement after seeing the leg.

The owner of the leg yelled. "You're gonna' buy me a new leg!"

I slammed the door shut.

The CSX investigators got a real kick out of what had happened. D.K. really didn't know what to think as he stood there laughing in disbelief. I got back into my car and told the railroad investigators to meet us downtown and sign their warrants.

As I backed the car to turn around, the bumper struck a water spigot sticking up from the ground. It snapped off cleanly and it erupted in a towering spray of water like a geyser. I thought to myself, *this is not going to be a good day.*

"We oughta get them out and let them take a shower," D.K. said in a tongue in cheek smiling. Thinking about the statements I was going to have to write and possibly a private property accident report, I was not amused at the moment. I looked at D.K. and just snapped back, "Shut up!" He just laughed. I apologized to the CSX supervisor and he assured me, "It happens all the time. Don't worry about it." After we transported the three men to jail, we broke out the Windex and cleaned the back seat, sprayed it with air freshener, and rode with the windows down for the rest of the shift. Just another day in District One.

I'm Smarter than the Average Drunk

WHEN I TELL FRIENDS ABOUT my experiences as a police officer, I often see a look of disbelief. They know I'm not lying, but as I tell the story they may wonder if I'm embellishing the tale just a bit. I have often wished that a friend or relative could ride with me to see for themselves the strange things I've seen, the unusual people I've met, and the peculiar situations police officers face every day.

On Saturday, August 13, 1988, I got my wish. One of my closest friends, Eddy Luckie, whom I've known since high school, was working at WMCF, the local Christian television station. He was the sound man for their live nightly television show. The police chief was trying to improve media relations by allowing reporters with television cameras to ride with patrol units. I asked my supervisors if Eddy could ride with me on patrol one evening. When I was asked why he wanted to ride, I explained that other television stations were being allowed to ride and I thought the local Christian television station should be allowed also. He ran the request up the chain of command and got it approved.

"At least if a Christian TV station rides, they will not misrepresent us like some of the others have," my lieutenant said. "Any video footage he shoots must be viewed by the department before it's shown on TV."

"That's not a problem at all," I quickly answered.

Eddy was the sound man for the television station, not a reporter and would not be shooting any video. I never said he was a reporter, I just said he worked for the television station and wanted to ride.

Another station taping footage of a police unit had aired a small

136

portion of an incident out of context that put the department in an unfavorable light. Had the entire incident been shown, the actions of the officers involved would have been more justifiable. The news media naturally will air the most shocking piece of footage to draw more viewers, and the reporters usually couldn't care less whether or not the officers are treated fairly. More often than not the media will side with the person who confronted or fought the police and caused the problem in the first place.

I introduced Eddy to the supervisors before roll call and they briefed him and me on what was expected of him as an observer. After the brief meeting, my supervisor asked me to hang around a second while Eddy went out in the roll call room. He looked at me and said, "Don't get him killed tonight, okay, Steve," he said in a semi-joking, semi-serious manner.

"I won't, sir," I assured him.

I showed Eddy the various clipboards of lookouts, incident / offense reports and memo's and procedures for checking out equipment for the shift. After roll call we hit the streets. Officer Perry Bullard was my partner that night. We were assigned to District Eleven.

Around 4:30 in the afternoon, we were dispatched to East 2nd Street in Oak Park on a code 22 (subject drunk). Dispatch advised us that the subject was drinking and being loud. We arrived at the address and the subject was sitting on the front porch. As we walked up to the porch, we could see numerous beer cans scattered about at his feet and knew he had had quite a bit to drink. He was not being loud but his speech was slurred and it was obvious he was extremely inebriated.

"How you doin' this evening?" I asked with a smile.

"I'm doin' jus fine, ossifer! How you!" he said in his drunken, slurred speech.

"I'm doin' good. But not as good as you, I can see," I replied with a humorous tone.

"Who's that guy?" he asked, pointing at Eddy.

"He's J. Edger Hoover," I told him.

"How you doin', Mr. Hoover?" he asked.

"I'm doin' fine," Eddy answered, looking at me and then him.

"What can I do for y'all this fine day?" he said slowly and deliberately. It was a good thing he was sitting because I believe he would have fallen off the porch trying to stand and talk.

"We got a call that you are drunk and being loud."

"That's not true, ossifer. I'm drunk, but I ain't being loud. But, that's okay, cause I can be drunk on my own property and you cain't do nothin' bout it," he said in a confident but defiant tone.

"Well, this is true." I said. "Do you think you can go inside so you won't disturb your neighbors?"

"Nope! I tol' ya, I ain't bein' loud and I'm on my own property. So I'm jus' gonna sit here and drink beer and you can jus' git off my property. I know the law."

"Now don't be disrespectful," I warned. "You're the one that's drunk and I will put you in jail if you keep on."

"I'm on my own property and I can git as drunk as I wanna and you cain't do nothin' bout it."

The thing about it was he was right. As long as he stayed on his own property he could get as drunk as he wanted and we could do nothing about it. The only way I could put him in jail is if he were to threaten me or get so loud to be heard by the neighbors. But he would have to do this in my presence. The only other thing would be for the neighbors to sign a warrant for being loud. Citizens are not too eager to sign warrants on neighbors so this was not going to happen. He apparently knew enough about the law dealing with alcoholic beverages that he did not cross the line. We asked him to keep it down and he told us to leave his property.

We got back in our vehicle and left. "That guys funny!" Eddy said.

"Yeah, he's a hoot alright." I replied. "But we will be back, I can promise you that." Drunks can be funny, but sometimes they can be a pain in the butt.

I explained to Eddy the laws of public intoxication, disorderly conduct and harassment and how being on his own property was not considered to be in the public. I told him if only he would walk into the street, then we could put him in jail for public intoxication.

About an hour and a half later we got called back to the same address and by now our drunken friend had probably consumed several more "brew skees." On the way to the call, Perry and I knew we were going to have the same problem with the guy again. As long as he is on his own property, we could not do anything to him. Then we came up with a plan.

We arrived in front of his house and he had not moved from his chair. "What do y'all want?" he hollered. Perry pointed his finger at him and said, "Hey, c'mere!" motioning his finger for him to come to us. In a surprising move, he stood up and staggered across his yard to us. Perry was standing in the road and the guy walked right up to him. "What cha want?" he asked.

"You're under arrest," Perry told him.

"You cain't arrest me, I'm on my own property.

"No, you're not. You're standing in the street and that is the public," Perry told him as he grabbed him by the wrist and spun him, placing his arm behind his back.

"What am I under arrest for!" he asked, as he was being put in the back seat of the car. Once he was secured on the passenger side, I sat next to him on the driver's side. While en route to jail he asked, "What are you chargin' me with?"

"Rape and pillaging", I said in an aggravated tone.

"I ain't raped and pillaged nobody! You better let me go, I know people down at the jail."

We walked him to the back door of police headquarters and Eddy and I took him upstairs to the jail. Perry went straight to the Warrants Clerk's office to sign the warrant for public intoxication. As we topped the stairs we turned toward the large metal jail door. A corrections officer was coming out and held the door for us. As we walked in the corrections officer called our drunken friend by name. "See! I tol ya I knew people down here." After booking him, I took Eddy down to the warrant clerk's office and showed him where we signed warrants and the procedures involved. Eddy commented several times how funny he thought the guy was. "Yeah, usually you get one of two kinds of drunks. They are either funny or violent. Fortunately he was a funny drunk, but I could see him turning violent if you pushed his button."

We joked and laughed about the guy and how drunk he was. Sometimes you can just tell who the problem people are going to be when you arrive on a scene. With the amount of beer he was drinking and his defiant attitude, I knew we would be back. But with us being sober and him being drunk, I told Eddy, "He may know the law, but I'm smarter than the average drunk."

I Did Not Want That
to Happen Again

August 15, 1988, started out like any other Monday. My partner, Officer Gerald Tippins, and I were working the downtown district. At that time we were working ten hour shifts from 4:00 p.m. till 2:00 a.m. The downtown area is usually busy until around 7:00 p.m. when everyone has gone home from work. After that it's quiet except maybe for the weekend nights in the fall when the local high schools play football at Cramton Bowl.

But this was Monday, and nothing happens on Monday. It was the first of the week and everyone couldn't wait to get home. With the exception of a few alarm calls and a theft or two, Gerald and I really didn't have much to do.

Around 12:30 a.m., the dispatcher came on the radio to advise units in the area of the Beeline Package Store on the corner of Madison Avenue and South Jackson Street to be on the lookout for a black man wearing a blue shirt and multi-colored shorts who had just stolen a pack of cigarettes. He'd last been seen running toward the Trenholm Court housing project on North Union Circle a couple of blocks away. This was in our district, so we headed straight for Trenholm Court.

We cruised slowly through the 600 block of North Union Circle under the harsh glare of the street lights and observed four or five young black men kneeling in a circle gambling with a pair of dice— known on the street as "rolling the bones." With our cigarette thief nowhere in sight, we decided to ease up on them and try to make an arrest for the illegal gambling. We got fairly close until one of them spotted us and they all took off running in all directions like quail flushed from tall grass. One of the men ran a couple of steps and then crouched down behind a car attempting to hide from us. Gerald got out of the car, ran straight toward him, and apprehended him without any trouble. I walked over to the spot where we had first seen the men and found the dice lying on the ground.

Usually when people gamble like this they often abandon the dice and the money as well. They do this because they've learned over the years that without any evidence in their possession, it's extremely difficult to get a conviction for simple gambling in the municipal court. The officer's testimony is seldom enough to convince the court of guilt without the hard evidence from the crime.

Gerald arrested the man on the gambling charge and walked him in cuffs back to our car. Not an exceptionally large man, James Reed* was thirty-three, stood 5' 6", and weighed about 190 pounds. He was also very drunk and reeked of cheap wine. He had a ten-dollar bill from the dice game clinched tightly in his left fist and refused to release it. Gerald attempted to sit James in the backseat when he suddenly pushed against both of us and fell to the ground. He began kicking at both of us striking me once in the shin.

"Get the f**k off me!" James shouted.

A common tactic for someone being arrested in a housing project is to draw a crowd by yelling, "They're beatin' me" or "Police brutality!" And since the police aren't exactly popular or welcome in most housing projects, other residents will often intervene to help a prisoner escape, usually without any clue as to why the officers are making the arrest.

As James yelled, his sister, Vicky Reed,**suddenly emerged from a nearby apartment, ran over toward us and launched herself onto my partner's back.

"You god*amn as*hole, leave my brother the f*ck alone!" she screamed.

Vicky was thirty, only stood about 5' 5", but weighed in at a hefty 200 pounds. I have little doubt that Gerald knew she was on him.

A large crowd quickly gathered, and I figured I had only one

---

* Name changed to protect the guilty

** Name changed to protect the guilty

good chance to call for backup before the crowd overtook us. I knew if I could get out our location on the radio, it wouldn't matter if I skipped the formality of leading with my unit number. Any type of distress call from a police unit always summons the cavalry.

"North Union Circle—get us some back up!" I yelled quickly into the radio.

Vicky had grabbed James' clothing trying to pull him back out of the car. In the confusion, James managed to give Vicky the ten-dollar bill, who in turn handed it off to a young girl about seven.

"RUN!" Vicky screamed at the girl.

I attempted to grab the little girl as she took off, thinking James may have passed on narcotics as well as the money, when a third sister arrived and attacked me. Lillian,* about the same height as Vicky, but about 10 pounds bulkier, grabbed me by the shirt and spun me around. Gerald and I had managed to get James into the back seat of our car and were trying to keep him there while fighting with Vicky. Gerald took off after the little girl while I fought with Lillian.

During the melee, a crowd of about seventy or so angry people had gathered around us. Some of them began throwing bottles, rocks, sticks and anything else they could get their hands on, but I heard sirens in the distance and knew help was on the way.

I was trying to take Lillian into custody when I saw someone from the crowd open the back door of the patrol car and let James out. He ran at me and I tackled him. Gerald had caught up to the little girl and retrieved the evidence before returning to help me. James and Vicky both attacked him again.

"Get your god**mn hand off my daughter!" Vicky screamed.

Gerald threw her to the ground and jumped on her back. I had my handcuffs in my hand when I tackled James, and while lying on my back, I rolled over and snapped one of the cuffs on Vicky's wrist while she was on her hands and knees.

"I got one cuff on her, Gerald!" I yelled.

Lillian helped James to his feet, and he immediately began kicking Gerald and me. I struck him once in the knee and once in the head with my baton to subdue him. I got up, dropped my baton

---

*   Name changed to protect the guilty

and grabbed him by the throat with my right hand. I pushed him back toward the car when suddenly Lillian grabbed my left hand and pulled. My wedding ring slipped off my finger into her hand. She looked at it for a moment then spiked it like a football into the asphalt. I'd only been married just over a year and I was determined not to lose that ring.

I cannot believe what happened next.

"*HOLD IT!*" I yelled over all the commotion.

Everyone froze as if someone had pressed the 'pause' button on the remote.

The crowd and all the combatants waited patiently as I picked up the ring and slid it into my pocket.

I then grabbed James by the throat, the pause button was released, and the fight was back on. I renewed my effort to push him back toward the patrol car. Other units began arriving on the scene. I heard a multitude of tires screech against asphalt followed by the reassuring clinking of flashlights against metal as our backup units ran from their cars toward us.

The group of agitators who'd been throwing rocks and bottles immediately vanished like ghosts into the darkness leaving only James, Vicky and the little girl.

I seated James in the back seat of my car while another officer seated Vicky in a different unit. The little girl was Vicky's daughter. We didn't charge the child since, even though it was wrong, she was only doing what her mother told her.

Gerald and I charged James with gambling and resisting arrest. I charged Vicky with harassment and interfering with an officer. Vicky hadn't been drinking, but a breath test showed James' alcohol level to be 0.194 percent, twice the level of what the law considered drunk at the time. Everyone involved suffered minor cuts, scrapes and bruises.

Several weeks later the cases were heard in the municipal court. James pled guilty to his charges. Vicky fought the charges, but after hearing all the testimony in the case the judge found her guilty as well.

What started out as just an average Monday quickly became a dangerous incident. James was facing only the gambling charge, which amounted to a small fine and no jail time. The ensuing fracas that resulted from his sister's efforts to free him got them both tossed in the slammer.

To me, the most amazing thing about the whole incident was how everyone stopped fighting for that brief moment when I retrieved my ring from the ground. Afterward, I stopped wearing my ring on duty. I was afraid that I might not be lucky enough to have everyone stop for me if I lost it again. Another distraction like that could have been extremely hazardous. Stopping to pick up my ring endangered my partner and me, and I did not want that to happen again.

SOME PEOPLE ARE JUST STUPID

SOMETIMES PEOPLE ARE JUST PLAIN stupid. That may not sound very nice, but I believe that everyone knows or has dealt with someone who acted in such a way that leaves no other explanation.

On Wednesday, October 5, 1988, Officer Larry Watson and I were riding in District Ten on second shift patrol. Around 3:45 that afternoon we were traveling down McGehee Road toward Montgomery Mall and saw a late model maroon Chevrolet Chevette run the red light on McGehee Road at Oxford Drive.

Traffic was bumper to bumper from the flood of traffic leaving Jeff Davis High School. We stopped the vehicle near the intersection of McGhee Road and Fieldcrest Drive, and I walked up to the driver's window and asked the woman behind the wheel for her license. She made the usual excuses you hear when a person doesn't have a license.

"I'm just going down the road a little ways," she said. "I must have left it at home."

"Ma'am, do you really have one or is it suspended or revoked?" I asked her. "I'm going to check on the radio and they are going to tell me in just a minute."

Her tone changed at that point. "Oh! Jus' cuz I don't have a driver's license with me you just assume that it's suspended, huh?" she said sarcastically.

"Yes, ma'am, that is what I usually think until I check with dispatch."

Then the guy sitting in the passenger seat next to her, who turned out to be her boyfriend, leaned over toward her side of the car and said to me, loudly, "You need to shut the f*ck up and leave her alone."

"Sir, I was not talkin' to you, so you need to just sit there and be quiet." I told him.

"No!" he replied in a calm but defiant tone. "You need to just shut the f★★k up and let us go before I kick your a★s."

I was taken a little by surprise. My first thought was that the guy was drunk enough to give him *stupid courage*, but I didn't smell any alcohol coming from the car.

I just stood there for a moment. "Ma'am, I'll be back in just a second."

I walked around the back end of the Chevette to the passenger side of the car. As I was walking up to the window I saw him turn to his right, smile and lock the door.

"They think I'm stupid," I heard him tell his girlfriend. "I just locked the door."

Even though the door was now locked, the window was rolled all the way down. I walked up to the open window while he looked confidently forward and laughed as if he had completely outwitted everyone.

I calmly pulled up the lock on the door. He glanced at it for a moment.

"Ohhh SH★T!" was all he managed to say.

I threw open the door. Larry and I grabbed the man, snatched him out of the car and threw him to the ground. There was a slight down grade on the shoulder so he tumbled about six or seven feet after hitting the grass. He landed face down. He struggled against us when we grabbed him, but it didn't take long to get him cuffed.

He was only about five-six and weighed around 125 pounds, but he talked like he was seven feet tall. He continued to spew a string of profanities as we placed him in the back seat of our patrol car, still talking all his big talk. The entire time we wrestled with the guy, his girlfriend screamed at us from the car to leave him alone, although she never bothered to get out of the car.

After he was secured in our car, I walked back to the driver's window where the woman sat. "Now, do you have a driver's license or not?" I asked.

"No, sir, I don't." she said, this time with a little more respect.

I wrote her two tickets for the red light and for driving without a license then sent her on her way. We took her beleaguered boyfriend to jail and charged him with disorderly conduct.

While filling out the arrest report we learned that he worked as a cook at the Waffle House on the Troy Highway. I sent out a memo to warn the other patrol units who ate there of the incident in case they might not want this guy cooking their food.

Movie legend Forrest Gump once said, "Stupid is as stupid does." This quote seems to sum up the actions of this one misguided soul whose mouth got him into more trouble than he could handle. Had the man been drunk, I could almost rationalize what he did, but as far as we could tell, he was stone, cold sober.

I have only one explanation—some people are just stupid.

THE GUY WHO BEAT UP JESUS

SOMETIMES A SITUATION HITS CLOSE to home. This is one of those stories. On Thursday, October 6, 1988, my partner, Officer Larry Watson, and I were riding District Ten. Larry is older than me, a quiet man who works out regularly and has a toned, muscular build. He was a recent graduate of the police academy, and I was his training officer.

District Ten is a quiet area of town, composed of mostly middle-class neighborhoods with the exception of the business district that runs along the Southern Boulevard. This area includs Baptist Medical Center. Several churches are located in the area including my own, Woodley Baptist Church on Antoinette Drive.

Around 9:15 that evening, we responded to the Meadhaven clinic next to Baptist Medical Center on a disturbance call involving a patient. Meadhaven is a psychiatric medical facility where people with a drug addiction or mental illness receive treatment. The dispatcher told us that a patient had broken out the windows of a car in the parking lot before fleeing on foot. We were given the description of a white male, age nineteen, wearing white flannel pants, no shirt, wearing one tennis shoe.

After arriving on the scene, a Meadhaven staff member informed us that the man's wife had brought the patient in for treatment. He'd been smoking marijuana and taking Robitussin for three days and had become extremely violent. She had driven him to the front door of the facility, but when he got out he took a crutch from the hospital and broke out all the windows of their car. That's when he ran off into the neighborhood.

My partner got the necessary information to complete the report.

After she signed it, we parked in the back parking lot of the hospital to complete the report.

While Larry completed the report, I listened to the radio and took a moment to relax. The dispatcher then sent a unit from a neighboring district to Woodley Baptist Church at 3920 Antoinette Drive to investigate a possible trespasser. She stated that the music minister had gone into the church and confronted someone inside. She added that the trespasser had locked himself inside the church.

Woodley Baptist Church was just three blocks away, so I notified the dispatcher that we were responding to the call. I raced the three blocks toward the church before screeching to a halt in the parking lot. I jumped from the car and checked the front door of the church. It was locked.

Mike Anderson, the music and youth minister ran quickly from across the street to meet us. I was the youth deacon for the church and worked with Mike teaching the Junior High Sunday School class.

I asked Mike what was going on, and he told me that he was returning from a citywide deacons meeting and had gone inside the church to do some work. He said that when he went inside he locked the door behind him, but when he turned on the lights he saw a guy sitting on the hallway floor. I asked Mike exactly where the subject was sitting. He told me the man was near the phone in the hallway. This was approximately thirty to forty feet beyond the locked door where we stood.

Now, the proper procedure in a situation like this is to secure the building and wait for a K-9 unit to show up and search the building with his dog. Any other time I would have done this. But this was *my* church, and I felt personally violated.

It was bad enough that the man had broken into a church. But this was the place where I worshipped with the people who felt like family to me, and that brought the crime too close to home. I acted quickly and let proper police procedure give way to my own rendition of a building search.

Mike unlocked the door and I went in looking for the suspect. I turned on the light and walked toward the phone. The suspect had taken the counter where the phone sat and spun it around to use as a barricade to block anyone from seeing him from the entrance. As I approached the counter, my partner was walking about three steps behind me.

"Hey!" I called out to the suspect.

He stood up, looked at me. "What the f★ck do you want?" he yelled.

He was dirty and disheveled and smelled like he was about a week away from his last bath. I could almost hear my mother say that he looked like something the cat spit up.

"This is my church and you don't use *that* kind of language in *my* church!" I yelled back at him.

"I'm Jesus Christ, and this is my f★ckin' church, and I'll worship as I please," he ranted like a madman. "And if you don't like it you can get the f★ck out!"

I ran at the suspect, grabbed him by the neck, and threw him up against the wall. He hit the wall with his head and fell to the floor. I jumped on him and we struggled until I got the handcuffs on him. I was so outraged and pumped with adrenaline that I was able to do all this before my partner knew what happened. We had patrolled by the church several times during our shift, so he knew this was my church and that my Christian faith was very important to me.

He later told me he knew I had everything under control and when the suspect cussed me in the church, he knew it wasn't going to be pretty for him.

After I handcuffed the man, Mike opened the door, and I grabbed the deranged man by the back of the pants with my right hand and his left arm with my left hand and led him out the door at a quick pace before tossing him onto the hood of the patrol car. The guy was about five ten and weighed a hundred thirty pounds, but with all the adrenaline pumping through me, I tossed him around like he was weightless.

As I threw him onto the hood of the car, some of the other deacons of the church pulled into the parking lot in the two church vans. I could see them all looking in our direction to see what was happening.

I placed the man in the back seat of the patrol car and was finally able to calm down. While Larry watched our prisoner, I advised dispatch that the suspect was in custody and that no other units were needed.

Mike and I walked through the church and found where the man had broken the glass on the front door and unlocked it. Mike appeared to be in shock and couldn't believe what had happened. He told me that when he confronted the man and spoke briefly with him, the deranged man had asked for a Christian lawyer and a Christian reporter. Mike told him that he knew some and used that excuse to leave the church and call for help. All Mike wanted to do was get out of the church and away from the crazed man.

I asked Mike several questions for the report, but he was having difficulty answering. After Mike signed the report, I asked Tom Wilbanks, the chairman of deacons, to drive Mike down to police headquarters to sign the trespassing warrant.

When Larry and I transported the prisoner to headquarters I rode in the back seat with him and filled out the arrest report. The prisoner sat on the passenger side, and I sat behind Larry. To fill out the report, I asked the man all the standard questions: name, address, date of birth, etc., but I saw out of the corner of my eye he was squirming in his seat. When prisoners moved around too much, it made me nervous. As I was about to ask him where he worked, I looked at him and I noticed that he had slipped his handcuffed wrists down below his buttocks and stepped back through them bringing his hands in front of him. Then he reared back and was about to hit me with both his cuffed hands. Before he could move, I dropped my pen and punched him squarely in the face with everything I had. My clenched fist connected solidly with his mouth. I felt his teeth crunch like gravel beneath my knuckles.

His head snapped back, and blood spattered onto the window. He rolled onto his side and attempted to kick me. I jumped on top of him and struck two more solid, bone-crunching blows to the head. This stunned him enough so that I could order him to step back through his cuffed arms and get his hands back behind him.

As he was stepping through the handcuffs, I remained on top of him. My partner slowly and carefully pulled the patrol vehicle over on Hall Street at Carter Hill Road. After putting the car in park, he leaned over the back seat.

"Do you need any help?" he asked. His tone was almost facetious.

I could tell by the way he so calmly pulled over and asked that he knew I needed no help with this guy. I was very angry but completely in control of the situation.

After I got the man a little more compliant, Larry eased back into traffic and got us to headquarters. When we arrived, the prisoner looked a little more banged up than when we'd found him, so we called for the paramedics and a supervisor to meet us there. The medics checked him out, and other than a few bumps and bruises, the man had no permanent physical injuries.

Larry took the prisoner up to the jail, and it fell to me to inform the lieutenant about the arrest. He thought that we'd gone looking for the man after he broke out the window of the car. Once I explained what happened, he told us to write a statement on the man's injury and get it to him.

I was standing at the back door of police headquarters eating a bag of corn chips and drinking a Coke when Mike and Tom walked up. Mike's eyes were still as big as saucers. Tom told me that Mike hadn't said much on the ride down. I led Mike to the warrant clerk's office and got an affidavit for him to fill out. We stepped into the empty courtroom, and I told Mike just to write down in detail what happened after he went into the church. He sat there for several seconds then looked at me.

"I can't think right now," he said.

I took the affidavit and wrote down what Mike had told me earlier and had him read it.

"Is this what happened, Mike?"

He read it carefully. "Yes," he replied.

"Just sign here, and I will give it to the warrant clerk."

While we were waiting on Mike to finish signing all the paper work, I told Tom about how the guy tried to hit me in the car and tried to fight with me. I told him about him smoking marijuana and taking Robitussin for three days. Tom happened to be a pharmacist and understood what that combination of drugs could produce in a person.

"Wow, he was really strung out," he said.

Tom told me that while they were getting ready to come down to police headquarters that one of the deacons complained to him about how I had treated the man.

"I don't think it is very Christian-like the way he is treating that guy," the deacon had said to Tom.

"What did you say?" I asked.

"I told him that he did not have all the facts, and that I have known Steve for years and that if he was handling him that way, then it needed to be done."

"And what did he say after that?" I asked.

"The other deacons agreed with me and got onto him and he let it go. The other deacons defended you and your actions, so don't worry about it."

The next afternoon I went by the church to see how Mike was doing. I saw the pastor, Paul Balducci.

"I understand you had an interesting night last night," Brother Paul said as I walked into his office.

"Yeah, just a little bit."

"So, what happened?" he asked.

I told him the story and how the prisoner took a swing at me and how we fought in the car. I told Brother Paul that I had to "witness" to him. He said that was great.

"Yeah, I had to beat the devil out of him," I added.

He paused for a second and then chuckled. I'm not really sure he appreciated the humor of the joke. It was at this time Anne Reynolds, who was a member of the church and a friend of mine, came into the office. She walked up smiling.

"So, I hear you beat up Jesus last night," she said.

"Yeah, something like that."

So I recounted the story to her and the other ladies in the office. After telling the story again, Mike walked in looking like he was still in shock. He told the story from his point of view, and I told him about fighting the guy in the back seat.

"Tom didn't mention that, but then again he could have," he said. "I don't remember too much about what happened after he cussed you and you grabbed him."

By Sunday morning, several people had heard about what

happened, and I had to recount the episode a few more times. Brother Paul told the congregation about how the man broke into the church and that Mike had walked in on him. I was expecting him to tell every detail about my fight with the man.

"After Mike walked in on him, he then went across the street and called the police," Brother Paul told the congregation. "The police came and took the guy away and everything was okay."

That was all he said about the incident.

Looking back, I certainly didn't handle the situation as I should have. I should've waited on the K-9 unit to search the building then let another officer who wasn't emotionally involved take custody of the man.

Sometimes you just get caught up in the moment. I took the violation of my church personally, but I should have used common sense. Everything worked out, and we never had to go to court and testify against the man. Evidently he pled guilty to the charge.

For several years afterward, however, whenever someone new came to a church fellowship, Anne Reynolds always introduced me as the guy who beat up Jesus.

Suspenseful Wait

By Jay Sailors/Staff

Montgomery police and a Taft Street resident wait in front of a west Montgomery house where a man suspected of armed robbery was believed to be barricaded in the attic Thursday afternoon. Officers surrounded a house at 1907 Taft St. after the Tennece Oil Co. at 654 Fairview Ave, was robbed about 1:40 p.m., police Lt. Robert Hankins said. The suspect, armed with a blue-steel revolver, fled toward Taft and Malvern streets with an undisclosed amount of money, Lt. Hankins said. No arrests had been made as of Thursday night.

January 13, 1989 – Newspaper article from Fairview Ave robbery. Officers surround a house where the suspect reportedly was hiding. (l to r) Officer Arlene Walker, me, home owner (sitting) Officer Derrick Shonk (Courtesy of Alabama Journal)

Police circle house; suspect still at large

Hasty Hudson, left, gets help from Steve Smith

By Janet Jimmerson
and Allan Freedman
Journal staff writers

Montgomery police surrounded a Taft Street house Thursday after a report that a service station robbery suspect was hiding there.

The suspect, believed to have hit a Tenneco Oil station that has been robbed three times in as many months, apparently never was in the house.

According to police records, a man armed with a blue steel, long-barrel revolver took an undisclosed amount of money from the Tenneco station at 654 Fairview Ave. at 1:45 p.m. Thursday.

Lt. Robert Hankins, a police spokesman, said witnesses told police the suspect ran into a house at 1907 Taft St. after fleeing the station. Officers surrounded the home, but they found no sign of the man.

"Apparently, he just ran in between houses," Lt. Hankins said.

A search of the area and the house failed to locate the man or the money, the spokesman said. However, police continued patrolling the neighborhood.

A description of the suspect has not been released.

Lt. Hankins said a woman who lives in the house surrounded by police was pulled behind police lines Thursday while officers tried to determine whether the suspect was inside.

Police were notified earlier this week of a robbery at the same station by someone armed with a small handgun.

According to police records, a clerk said somone with a black handgun entered the station at 3:30 a.m. Tuesday and demanded money. The suspect escaped with an undisclosed amount of money.

In December, police arrested a man in connection with a November robbery at the station. ████████, 33, of 1604 Well St. was charged with first-degree robbery in connection with a Nov. 27 robbery.

Police stake out back of the house near a shed

*January 13, 1989 – Newspaper article from Fairview Ave robbery. I assist
Cpl Hasty Hudson of the SWAT (Strike Force) Team into his ballistic
gear before he enters house. Second photo (l to r) me, Officer Derrick
Shonk and Officer Robert Green (Courtesy of Alabama Journal)*

*January 13, 1989 – Officer Robert Green and
I search a shed for a robbery suspect.*

Another Perspective of the Legal System

POLICE OFFICERS RESPOND TO ALARM calls 24 hours a day. Well over ninety percent of these calls prove to be false alarms, but every once in a while, an alarm pays off and alerts the police to an actual burglary. The problem is that after you've answered so many false alarms, some officers become complacent and just assume that it's *just another false alarm*. As a veteran officer I knew better, but I will admit that there were times when I assumed that the alarm was false and let my guard down for a moment.

That is until Friday, July 28, 1989.

My partner, Officer Kevin Brightwell, and I were riding in District Fourteen one evening about 9:00 when we received an alarm call at Rollins Auto Repair on the Mobile Highway near the Western Boulevard. The business sat off the roadway and was hidden behind another building. We approached the business with our headlights off then got out of the car quietly. Since I was a training officer, I have to make sure I always followed proper procedure so as not to teach a rookie officer any bad habits.

A station wagon with wood-grain paneled sides sat parked across the gravel driveway from the building. That didn't seem unusually suspicious because it was a garage. I walked past the first door toward the corner of the building. Kevin stopped and checked it to see if it was locked. As I rounded the corner I saw that the roll up door used to drive vehicles inside the building was pushed in. About the time I realized that the door had been pushed in, I saw a flashlight beam shining out through the hole in the door. Before I could get on the radio and advise the dispatcher of a possible burglary in progress, a man crawled out and ran toward the woods behind the building.

"Kevin!" I shouted. "We got a subject running!"

Kevin played baseball for Auburn University of Montgomery and was a very fast runner. He immediately took off after the suspect. I paused just long enough to advise the dispatcher on the radio. It is hard to understand an officer running and talking on the radio at the same time, so I wanted to make sure the other units in the area knew what we had.

"Two-fourteen, code four in progress!" I said into the radio. "We have a suspect running from the back of the building east into the wooded area. My partner is in foot pursuit!"

After notifying dispatch, I took off after Kevin. We chased the man into the woods to a bridge that crossed a deep gully. I could hear splashing in the creek below, and I knew the suspect hadn't crossed the bridge. We both slid down the embankment into the water. The embankment was steep and covered with briers. We both got cut up pretty bad and tore our uniforms. I did not realize just how many cuts I had until several hours later when I took a shower.

The water was almost knee deep and we ran south following the sound of splashing. After about ten seconds I grabbed Kevin by the uniform shirt. "Hold it, Hold it!" I said in a hoarse whisper.

"What is it?" he asked.

"I don't hear splashing. He has gotten out of the creek."

We started looking above us with our flashlights to see if we could locate the suspect. The gully was about twenty to thirty feet deep. The sides were lined with large rocks. I shined my flashlight up to my right and saw the suspect holding on to a small tree, looking down at us.

"Don't move!" I yelled up at him.

He just stood on the edge of the gully and stared down at us and did not even flinch. He could have easily run into the woods and by the time we made it to the top he would have been long gone.

Kevin and I began to climb toward the suspect. He held onto the tree and started kicking at us in an attempt to knock us back into the creek.

"Grab him and hang on, Kevin, so I can get to him!" I said.

Kevin grabbed his shoe as he tried to kick us for the fifth or sixth time. I climbed over Kevin and stood up in front of him. As he swung his left fist at me in a round motion, I leaned back and he missed. I hit him on the left side of his head with my flashlight. He then swung at me with his right fist in the same round motion and I leaned back and he missed again. I then struck him on the front of his head with my flashlight. He staggered for a moment and then fell to the ground.

Once we handcuffed the man, we had to get him down the embankment, through the creek and back up the other side while he was handcuffed and woozy. After getting him to the other side of the creek, two motor officers found us in the woods and were able to get him out of the gully. They walked him across the bridge and back to the business and called the paramedics to check out his injuries.

He had a gash on the front of his head, and by the time we made it out of the gully it was bandaged. The wood grain station wagon parked beside the fence belonged to the suspect. He had rammed the roll up door with the front of the car and pushed it in just enough to created an opening through which he entered the building. The suspect was taken to the hospital for further treatment. Kevin and I went to headquarters to start the paperwork.

The suspect was charged with Burglary and Theft and placed into the Montgomery County Jail. This was not his first run in with the law. He had a parole board hearing on August 9th and his parole was revoked. We gave testimony against him in District Court on August 14th.

On January 27, 1989, he stood trial on the burglary and felony theft charges. The District Attorney tried the case, Kevin and I both testified against him. The suspect was supposed to testify after lunch but decided not to show up.

He was found guilty.

In October of 1989 I transferred to the Evidence Technician section. I had begun a new chapter in my police career. I had been in patrol for six years and now those days were behind me.

On November 11, 1990, I walked into the office and before

I could say anything Corporal Tommy Shanks said, "Boy, you're being sued."

The guys in the office were always messing with each other so I didn't take him seriously.

As I walked over to my desk, I asked, "What do mean, being sued? I just walked into the office. I haven't had time to do anything to anybody yet."

"You got a registered letter on your desk," he said. "You only get registered letters when you're being sued." He was laughing. "You're being sued."

Police officers have a macabre sense of humor sometimes. On my desk was a registered letter addressed to Officer S.Z. Smith, Montgomery City Jail.

"This is not for me," I said. "This is for somebody in the city jail. I don't work and never have worked in the city jail," I was joking, of course, but it was true.

I was being sued for the first time in my career. I was always told that if you never got complaints, or you were never sued at least once in your career then, you haven't done anything. I guess I had arrived now. I was really being sued.

Charles Scott,* the man Kevin Brightwell and I had caught burglarizing Rollins Auto Repair over a year earlier, had filed a lawsuit against us in federal court. Scott was alleging excessive force, police brutality, and a violation of his constitutional rights, and was suing me for $150,000. He was seeking the same amount from Kevin for a grand total of $300,000. Mr. Scott stated in his affidavit that was filed from Ventress Correctional Facility in Clayton, Alabama.

Here is an excerpt from his affidavit as it was typed:

"On the nite of July 28, 1989 or thereabouts, the plaintiff was involved in an accident whereby he ran his automobile into the Rollins Auto Repair Building. He tried to crank his car and move from the building to access the damage that he had done and while he as doing such, the squad car from the Montgomery City Police and the policemen in the car called out that they were policemen. It was extremely dark and because he was black and the Montgomery City Police officer had a history of beating

---

*   Name changed

and killing black males in such a position. He got out of the car and ran…. He ran behind the Auto Repair shop and approached a bridge approximate 50 feet tall and jumped off of it trying to allude the pursuit of the Officers. When he landed, he had jumped from such a height THAT HIS LEGS JAMMED IN A DRIED UP STREAM. He struggled to pull his self to the embankment with his hands and when he was lying on the Embankment the two Officers of the Montgomery Police Department who were Officers, S.Z. Smith And K.G. Brightwell sought upon him and began to beat him with their metal flashlights trying to get him to confess to trying to break and enter the Rollins Auto Repair Shoppe…All while the beating occurred, he could not move his legs because they had been injured from the high leap, He never resisted the arrest or attack and never assaulted any one of them with his leg or hands as was testified to by the officer in his criminal trial…."

On March 29, 1993, Kevin and I met with attorney Andy Birchfield in reference to the lawsuit. It had been three years since we were notified that we were being sued. After telling our attorney what really happened that night, I asked Mr. Birchfield why we were just now giving statements. He said Mr. Scott filed his lawsuit right after he was incarcerated.

"After he got out we never heard from him and assumed it had been dropped," Birchfield said. "It wasn't until he got arrested in the county for the same charge and sent back to prison that he started up the suit again."

"So you can just file a lawsuit in prison at taxpayer's expense, then wait around to go to court and if you get out then you can just forget about it. Then get arrested for the same charge, go back to prison and pickup where you left off?" I asked in disgust.

"That's pretty much the way it works."

"That's such a waste of time. You would think once you're released and you did not follow up on your suit in a certain amount of time, then the courts would drop it."

"Yes, that would be the logical thing, but it doesn't work that way."

"What if he wants to settle out of court for a lesser amount?" I asked. "The city has done that before to save money. After all, his story is a complete lie and he tried to kick us down the embankment."

"The city is not going to settle. We are going to fight this one." Mr. Birchfield said with confidence.

October 25, 1993, four years and three months after the original arrest of Charles Scott, my partner and I testified in federal court. I had to miss my brother-in-law's wedding the previous Saturday in Arkansas because I needed to be ready for this trial Monday morning. I was supposed to be one of the groomsmen, but because a felon breaks the law, gets caught and then claims police brutality, I had to miss out on a family event. I know that it is just part of the job but it still didn't sit well, especially when you've done nothing wrong.

Mr. Scott, in his infinite wisdom, decided to not use the court appointed attorney, but to represent himself. The court went through the process of picking a jury to hear the case. I had never been the defendant in a jury trial so it felt strange.

I asked our attorney, "Okay, what's the worst possible thing that could happen to us? Let's say we are found guilty of all charges. What's the worst thing that can happen to us?"

"First of all, we are not going to lose this case. He has a weak case," Birchfield said.

"I understand what you are saying, but let's just say things don't go as we hope and we are found guilty. Is there any possibility that we can go to prison?"

"No, you won't go to prison. The absolute worst thing that can happen is the city will have to pay the money he is suing for."

"Whew, that's a relief! I can relax a little now." I said.

The judge was patient with Mr. Scott and walked him through the process of questioning the witnesses. Mr. Scott testified first and told his story. His story was not even close to the truth. He testified how I beat him and that he had lost all his hearing in his left ear and had ringing in his right ear. He showed the jury the scar on the front of his head and how it took thirteen stitches to sew it up.

"They should have been able to arrest a five-feet ten-inch person who weighed only one hundred and sixty pounds," he said.

When our attorney asked on cross-examination why he ran, Scott replied that he was scared.

Mr. Scott questioned me regarding the police brutality allegation. He testified that I beat him.

I testified that I only struck him twice.

"You beat me with that flashlight!" he said raising his voice.

"I struck you twice," I replied calmly.

"You beat me and you know you beat me!"

"You swung at me and I struck you," I said. "You swung at me again and I struck you again. I only struck you twice."

"You beat me and you know it!" he continued in his raised voice.

"I think we covered that Mr. Scott. Let's move on," the judge said.

The trial was convened for the day and we were to be back in court at 9:00 the following morning. The judge told the jury that they were not to talk about the case.

Tuesday, October 26, was the second day of the trial.

Kevin testified how I saw the suspect crawl out of the building and he chased him into the woods. He stated during the trial that he saw the suspect running and *commenced* to chase him. After he was done testifying, both sides rested and we took a break. Kevin said he could not believe that he had really said *commenced* in federal court.

The jury was out less than an hour and we were called back into the courtroom. The bailiff told the defendants to rise.

I looked at Mr. Scott unconsciously assuming he was still "the defendant."

Our attorney nudged me and said, "That's you."

He pushed out his chair to stand. Kevin and I, along with our attorney, stood and faced the jury. The judge asked the jury if they had reached a verdict. The foreman said they had.

The foreman announced that the jury had found Kevin and me not guilty on all three counts.

We were both relieved, but at the same time, humbled because I had never been on trial before. Even though we were just doing our job, it's irritating to think that someone can just accuse you of wrongdoing and you have to go through all the grief of a trial when they know good and well they are lying. I guess if I had to find a positive in the whole thing it would be that I got to experience testifying in federal court. I had never been the defendant in a trial so that gave me another perspective of the legal system.

A Perfect Christian Gentleman

ENFORCING LAWS IS NEVER EASY. Going strictly by the book is seldom practical because most criminals know and exploit the loopholes and gray areas in the law. This is where you have to be creative and think outside the box.

One of our most annoying problems was dealing with people who loitered in apartment complexes in lower-income neighborhoods. Apartment managers and tenants who lived in these areas didn't want people hanging around outside the buildings. People who stood around with nothing constructive to do made the tenants nervous.

Normally, if a person had that much time on his hands he was looking for something to get into. You also have the street pharmaceutical reps—more commonly known as drug dealers. They conducted business by standing on the corners and selling their poison. The police have always told tenants and management that if they want the problem solved they would have to enforce the no-loitering policy.

Some people are naturally lazy and expect the police to do this for them. What they fail to understand is that apartment complexes are private property, and the police can't enforce loitering laws on private property if the property owner isn't willing to press charges.

When nothing gets done and the problem gets worse, the tenants and other citizens start to complain. The officers then catch heat from their supervisors, the city council, or even the mayor. Then you have to come up with a creative idea to solve the problem.

The complaint cycle runs something like this: one citizen will call his city councilman about the rampant drug dealing, prostitution, loitering, people shooting guns, or whatever. The councilman then calls the mayor's office and wants to know why the police department doesn't do something about the problem. This is the first time the mayor has heard about the problem, of course, so he calls the chief and tells him to have someone check into it. The chief then passes it on to the major of the patrol division, who then passes it to the captain, where it continues downhill past the sergeant and lands in the lap of the officer who rides that district.

"This complaint came straight from the mayor's office," the sergeant tells the officer. "Do whatever it takes to take care of the problem,"

"Yes, sir," the officer replies.

Then we're back to square one. How do you take care of a problem where people aren't willing to help themselves? To add to our dilemma, the department didn't want us to chase people unless we had a charge.

"It's not against the law to run from the police," we were told time and time again. "Just because a person runs, doesn't give you the right to chase them."

Common sense tells you that if a person runs from the police, they're probably guilty of something, or they *think* they're guilty. My experience has been that the vast majority of people who run from the police are holding drugs, guns, or have warrants.

They don't run without a reason.

Recently the U.S. Supreme Court finally ruled that if a person recognizes a law enforcement officer and runs away, the officer has the right to pursue that person and investigate their reason for fleeing.

This is where you have to be a little clever and think outside the box. I had a similar problem in the Windwood Apartments (pronounced Windy-wood for some strange reason) on the Mobile Highway. I guess if you lived there you could call it what you wanted. We had older teenagers and young adults hanging out around the buildings up to no good. The management and tenants wanted something done about it, but they refused to sign warrants against any of the offenders. I often wondered what exactly it was they wanted me to do.

Thursday, August 17, 1989 my partner was Officer Mike Britton.

Mike is a very educated Christian family man. If you asked him, he'd tell you that he was a Christian first, then a family man. He was also a U.S. Marine. He is very articulate and knows the value of an education. He is in very good physical condition, lean and strong and could run like a deer. Mike was absolutely one of the fastest men I ever met.

During roll call we got the complaints from the sergeant of all the loitering in Windwood apartments. We were told to do something about it.

I always drove and Mike rode shotgun because he was so much faster than I was. He sat where he could bail out of the car quickly and run someone down if need be.

On this particular day we pulled into the Windwood Apartments and saw a group of about five or six young black guys hanging out in front of one of the apartments. We pulled up and got out to talk to them when one of them suddenly took off running. Usually the runner was the one holding the drugs. As soon as he took off, Mike took off like a shot after him. I stood there not moving and continued talking to the other men.

"Ain't you gonna go chase him, too?" one of them asked.

"No, there's no need," I said confidently. "My partner will catch him."

Within about two minutes, Mike returned leading the man by the arm. The young man was heaving trying to catch his breath. Mike had barely broken a sweat.

Mike was in such good shape and ran so fast that he actually taunted the young man as he chased him until he got ready to burst forward and catch him.

When I was in my best shape, I couldn't talk while chasing a person. I wasn't much for conversation following a chase either.

When we had everyone back together, I checked everyone for warrants. Oddly enough, the guy who ran was the only one with warrants, for unpaid traffic tickets. We arrested him, but we told him and all his friends that he was going to jail for running from the police. We lied and told them that a new law had been passed making it illegal to run from an officer. For the rest of that evening, no one hung out at the complex.

The next day we went back to the Windwood. A new group of about five young black guys were there hanging on the corner of one of the buildings. We pulled up to talk to them and a guy took off running.

Mike took off after him.

I remained as I had the day before talking with the other guys and ran warrant checks on everyone. A minute or two later Mike brought the runner back, and lo and behold he had warrants on him for tickets. We replayed the drama from the day before and arrested him. Again, we told him and his friends that he was under arrest for running from the police. We explained the new "law" was to discourage loitering and drug sales.

The third day we drove straight out to the Windwood apartments and again we saw a third group of young black guys hanging out by one of the buildings. And as with the two previous days, one of the guys ran and Mike quickly retrieved him. This particular guy fell as Mike chased him, but Mike was running so fast that he tried to jump over the guy and stepped on his back. When he brought the guy back, Mike showed me the large shoe print on the back of the guy's white t-shirt.

We ran a warrant check on the guy, and yes, he had warrants on him also. We told these guys like the rest that he was under arrest for running from the police.

The fourth day we went straight to the Windwood apartments. As we pulled into the complex we saw a group of people standing outside a building. "Well, here we go again. Some people just don't get it," I said.

As we pulled up, we got out of our car expecting one or more of this new crowd to run. To our amazement, no one did. They all started walking away slowly.

"We're not runnin' officers, we're walkin," one of them said. "We're not runnin, we're walkin."

"Well, alright, y'all need to quit hanging out around these buildings," I said.

"Okay, officer. We're leaving now."

Mike and I got lucky that all the guys who'd run had warrants on them. We couldn't have solved the problem if no one had run from us. Just giving them a warning wouldn't have taken care of the problem. The management would never have signed a warrant on those who were trespassing for fear of repercussions, so we had to be creative and use our bit of luck to solve *their* problem for them.

Mike and I rode as partners for three weeks before I transferred to the Evidence Technician Bureau. I really enjoyed riding with him. If you didn't know him, he came across as a somewhat quiet, always serious person. Spend time with him, however, and you'd find that he has a great sense of humor. One of the things I remember about Mike is he had this dialog where he did imitations of the crew members of the *U.S.S. Enterprise* from the television show *Star Trek*. He did dead-on imitations of Scotty, Captain Kirk and Spock.

Captain Kirk would cry out in his velvety, overly-inflected voice, "Scotty, I need more power!"

"Aye, Captain. I'm givin' her all she's got," Scotty replied in his familiar Scottish brogue.

"Don't give me excuses, Scotty; give me... more *power!*" Kirk demanded.

"Aye, Captain. I canna give 'er what I don't 'ave Capt'n."

"Spock," Kirk ordered. "Kill Scotty!"

"That would not be logical, Captain," the Vulcan replied in his steady, monotone voice.

I'm not a fan of *Star Trek*. I've seen maybe a few episodes, but Mike's rendition would invariably crack me up. He often did his impressions when I least expected them. When you first meet Mike you certainly don't expect this kind of humor from him, but as you get to know him it slowly emerges with hilarious consequences. I enjoyed our time together, immensely.

Mike stayed with the police department for several years before being hired on with the Alabama State Troopers. I still see him from time to time. He always asks me how Mrs. Smith and the family are doing. My wife and Mike are roughly the same age, but he stills calls her Mrs. Smith out of respect. He then will ask me how things are with the church.

I have a lot of respect for Mike. He's a perfect Christian gentleman.

I Know I've Never Met Them

ON FRIDAY, SEPTEMBER **22, 1989** I was transferred to the Evidence Technician Bureau. At that time we were called "Evidence Techs" or "ET's." Today they are referred to as Crime Scene Investigators or CSI's. Back then, however, not too many people knew what a Crime Scene Investigator was, much less what they did.

I really didn't know what the job entailed, but I knew they took photographs and videos. My hobby was photography, so I thought it would be a great job. The Evidence Technician's office was at the old morgue about two blocks from police headquarters. For many years, all of the autopsies were done there until the Department of Forensic Sciences opened up a newer, more modern facility across town.

Before becoming the morgue, the old building served as the jail for the Montgomery Police Department until the Public Affairs building and the new jail was built in 1966. Hank Williams, Martin Luther King, and Rosa Parks were some of the more notable guests who spent time at the old jail. It was renovated and remodeled into office space after 1966, but you can still see the old bars of the jail in the storage rooms. The upstairs is used for storage and still has the cells adorned with their own rusty iron bars.

I found out that being an Evidence Tech was a lot more complicated and detailed than I imagined. I knew it was a specialized field, and I figured it would help me later in my career or after I retired. I didn't know at the time how much being an Evidence Tech would impact my life. With this new job, I'd found my calling in police work.

One of the things I liked about being an evidence tech is that I got to go to all the really interesting calls. October 10, 1989, provided me with my first taste of what was to come.

My training officer was Corporal Jere Knox. Our homicide investigators were working a death investigation that was a potential murder case. Jere (pronounced Jerry) and I had to go to Bozeman Cemetery to exhume the body of Lillian Thomas,* an elderly woman dead nearly a year from what was originally assumed to be natural causes. An investigation had turned up evidence that a Hospice nurse may have murdered her.

Exhumations were something you saw only in movies and on television. I never imagined that I would actually attend one. Jere and I, along with a couple of inmates from the jail to do the dirty work, met with employees from a local funeral home with a backhoe at the cemetery. Jere and I took several photos of the gravesite before the backhoe operator dug into the earth and worked his way toward Mrs. Thomas' remains. Everything in crime scene work has to be documented with photos. So I took photos at various stages of the exhumation.

Once they reached the concrete vault that housed the casket, I took photos both before and after it was opened. When the lid to the vault was lifted off with a chain attached to the backhoe, I noticed that the top of the casket had scrape marks on the top of it. At first I didn't understand what caused the top of the casket to be damaged until we removed it from the vault. After lifting the casket out, I could see about five inches of water in the bottom of the vault and several pieces of paper the size of playing cards in the water. The small paper squares did resemble playing cards because of the designs on them, but upon closer examination I found them to be stickers from the sides of the casket loosened by the water in the vault.

It appeared that a watertight vault was actually not so watertight. During a heavy rain, the vault would fill up with water and float the casket up to the top of the vault. The floating casket would then scrape against the underside of the concrete vault lid.

The funeral director must have thought that since the vault was flooded, then the casket may have flooded as well. He told one of the inmates to knock a couple of holes in the bottom of the casket with

---

* Name changed to protect the innocent

the sharp end of the pick to drain out any water inside. The inmate then made two quick jabs at the underside of the casket, and a thick fluid began to pour out onto the freshly upturned soil. The inmate quickly covered his mouth and nose with his hand. He dropped the pick and ran about thirty feet away, bent over at the waist and began returning his jail breakfast to the earth.

I didn't realize what was wrong until I got a whiff of the fluid. The casket had remained sealed and watertight, but the bottom of the casket had filled with various bodily fluids as Mrs. Thomas decomposed. The odor was horrific!

After the casket drained and the rest of us recovered from the blinding stench of the fluid spill, we loaded the casket into the van from the funeral home and transported it to the newly opened morgue near the Auburn University at Montgomery campus. I was told the pathologists and those who are experts in the field had designed this new facility.

The building was considered state of the art. The body intake was in the rear of the building, and we followed the van. There were two entrances at the back door. One door was for "decomps," or bodies dead several days or more with the characteristic strong, unpleasant odor. The other door was for the less pungent guests who were more recently deceased. The decomp door lead directly into a refrigerated room where the body could be quickly cooled to reduce the odor.

The casket was offloaded and placed on the ground until a special dolly was brought out to carry it inside. I'd never been to the new morgue, so I had no idea what to expect. Jere and I went inside and changed into disposable coveralls to observe the autopsy. I couldn't help noticing the foul putrid smell that was in the building. *How in the world could a person stand working in such a smell?* I wondered.

Jere and I photographed the various stages of the autopsy. The pathologists were checking to see if a certain gland was enlarged as a result of a particular poison to determine if the cause of death was natural or homicide. After more than an hour, we were done and shed the coveralls.

Phil Holland, a former Montgomery Police Officer who left to work as an investigator for the Alabama Department of Forensic

Sciences, gave us a tour of the morgue and offices. It was Phil's job I took when he left the department.

I noticed the putrid smell all through the building, so I asked him how he stood the smell. He said that the rest of the building didn't usually smell like that.

After the tour I was ready for some fresh air, so we stepped outside. As we were standing outside talking we started looking at the design of the building. It was then I noticed a major flaw. Apparently no one noticed that the air conditioner intake fans were placed immediately adjacent to the rear intake doors. When we removed the casket from the van, we placed it on the ground next to the intake vents. Since the holes were knocked in the bottom of the casket and some remaining fluid still seeped from the holes, all of the sickening odor was drawn into the building by the powerful fans of the ventilation system. All of the administrative employees in the building got nauseous and had to go home for the day.

That was the one and only time I attended an exhumation. As interesting as it was, I think I'd rather have seen an exhumation of someone buried a century or more. I'd like the experience of looking back in time. I've seen television shows where they've exhumed bodies buried two or three centuries to determine identity or cause of death. That just seems utterly fascinating to me.

I guess with me personally, exhuming someone dead for a year versus one hundred years makes me feel like enough time has gone by where I know I've never met them.

I Kicked out Five People
and Arrested One

FOOTBALL IS KING IN THE state of Alabama. When you are born in this state one of the earliest decisions you make as a child is to which school you will pledge your lifelong allegiance: The Alabama Crimson Tide or the Auburn Tigers. It's a fact, and everyone who lives in Alabama knows it.

No matter what anybody tells you, Alabama-Auburn is the biggest football rivalry in the country. This game is talked about three hundred sixty four days a year and then played on that long-awaited Saturday. The winner of the Iron Bowl owns the bragging rights for a whole year.

For many years this game was played at Legion Field in Birmingham. Over the years both schools expanded their stadiums to the point where each could host the thousands of fans who made the annual pilgrimage. On December 2, 1989, the University of Alabama football team traveled to Jordan-Hare Stadium to take on the Auburn Tigers. This was the inaugural game for Alabama to play Auburn on their home field.

During the week before the game, both coaches and several of the players had received death threats and game officials wanted the security beefed up for this game. The Montgomery Police Department was one of several agencies Auburn University asked to help with security.

Sergeant Richard Foster, my supervisor in the Evidence Technician section, asked if any of us wanted to work this detail. Corporal Tommy Shanks and I both volunteered. Tommy was a veteran of the Evidence Technician division. He was one of the first to be assigned to the unit when it was created. It was originally called the Identification Section or "I.D." section for short. Richard Foster had been in the section for more than ten years and had been promoted to sergeant and was left in that position as the supervisor.

We had to be in Auburn at the stadium by 10 a.m. to be briefed and to get our assignments before kick-off. I was hoping that I would be assigned inside so I could at least see some of the game. We met at police headquarters at 7:00 that morning and boarded the police department bus, a large school bus painted black and white, the same type of bus I rode to school for ten of my twelve years of school.

Auburn is a forty-five minute to an hour drive from Montgomery, but since we were on the bus and traffic was going to be heavy we left early. It was cool that morning and was expected to be bitterly cold by the end of the game.

We boarded the bus and sat mostly two to a seat. We pulled out and hit I-85 northbound for the game that some were calling the game of the century. The bus was divided equally between Tide fans and Tiger fans, each of us bragging how badly the game would turn out for the other team. We all swapped a few Alabama-Auburn jokes and planned to have a great day.

Just as we were leaving the county, traffic slowed down to a crawl then stopped altogether as thousands of cars jammed the interstate. I was beginning to wonder if we would even make it to the game on time. Fans were driving by us with their cars painted up and they were hollering out the window, "ROLL TIDE" or "WAR EAGLE!"

I sat in the back of the bus with several investigators, one of whom was Shannon Fontaine. He worked late night detective car and has a great sense of humor. His claim to fame was his dead-on imitation of Mayor Emory Folmar. I think he sounded more like Mayor Folmar than Folmar himself. He liked doing the imitation but never wanted Mayor Folmar to know he was imitating him. He didn't really know how the mayor would take it.

We noticed how slow the bus was traveling and how everybody was passing us, so we talked Shannon into getting on the radio and calling the supervisors in the patrol car in front of the bus. We were going to use channel three to talk to each other during the ballgame detail. Channel one was the main channel used by dispatch to send out calls. Channel three was used for special details such as football games and other similar events.

Lieutenant J.B. Tolbert, Lieutenant Terry Ward, and Sergeant Foster were riding in the patrol car leading the bus. We were far enough out of town that no other units could hear the radio traffic. After quieting everyone on the bus, Shannon, doing one of his best Folmar imitations, called to them by using the Mayor's call number—100.

"This is one hundred to the patrol unit on the interstate in front of the police bus."

There was a long pause, then Lieutenant Ward answered. "Go ahead one hundred."

"We are not out there on the boo-lee-vard. Turn on them blue lights and get this bus through traffic."

You could hear the snickering throughout the bus. Everyone was trying not to laugh.

"Yes sir. We will take care of that, sir," Lieutenant Ward replied.

Everyone on the bus just burst out laughing. Shannon did a few more lines of the Mayor, but not on the radio. The supervisors in the car ahead were sharp enough to catch on and never did turn on the blue lights, but we figured they wouldn't.

We finally made it to the stadium and off-loaded. Corporal Mary Neilson and I were trying to find a vendor selling programs. Mary is an Auburn fan, and I am an Alabama fan, but we both wanted to keep one as a souvenir because it was the first game in Jordan-Hare Stadium. People were buying them up by the box load.

Mary and I were assigned to one of the gates with a couple of stadium officials to check people for alcohol before they entered the game. Mainly we were to look in the inside coat pockets for alcohol containers. We had two large yellow fifty-gallon plastic drums to hold the confiscated liquor. By the time the game started, both drums were overflowing with liquor bottles, whiskey flasks, and beer cans. Even though we confiscated that many bottles, many more still got into the game.

I was assigned to the West side in front of one of the tunnels about half way up in the stands. There was a stiff breeze blowing through the tunnel and as the night went on it turned cold.

Alabama was leading 10 - 7 at half time. At the beginning of the second half, the liquor being consumed in the stadium was beginning to affect some of the fans. I started watching the crowd in the section below me and I could see that certain people were becoming more rowdy than others and becoming obnoxious. I suspected that they had been successful in smuggling in alcohol and had become intoxicated. As I watched I could see that they would look around and then pull out a bottle and take a drink and then conceal it again.

I spotted a man take a drink from a bottle and I went to the end of the row and asked him to come out to the aisle. When I found the alcohol I escorted him out of the game.

"I can't believe you are making me leave the game!" he said. "I paid two hundred dollars for these tickets!"

"You knew that having alcohol was against the rules," I replied as we made our way to the gate.

"Can I get back in the game?" he asked.

"No," I said. "Once you are kicked out you are out for good. You should have thought about that before you brought in the alcohol."

After I returned back to my post, several people in that section thanked me for putting him out. As I stood there, other people in the stands would get my attention and then point out others drinking. I would smile and watch them until I witnessed them take a drink. Then I would politely escort them out.

By the end of the third quarter, the alcohol was beginning to fuel more aggressive behavior. One man started a fight near my post and I had to wade into the crowd to physically take him out. As we got in the aisle, he was on the step above me and I was trying to push him up to the top. He was about six-one, but seemed much taller on the higher step. He grabbed my coat and was about to push me down the steps when a Lee County Sheriff's Deputy grabbed him by the back of the coat and abruptly pulled him to the ground.

Apparently the deputy had seen the fight and came over to assist me. I never saw the deputy until the drunken man hit the concrete. I was then able to handcuff the man and walk him up to the top of the steps. The crowd around us cheered and applauded as we took him away. He left the other fans with a few choice words as we walked away.

I took him to a holding cell beneath the stands, which was a chain link enclosure with a top that more closely resembled a cage. I got all his information and placed him in with several other fans already confined there. After signing a warrant on the man for disorderly conduct, I noticed the time and made my way down onto the field. We'd been told to move onto the playing field when the play clock showed five minutes left in the game to prevent the crowd from rushing the field.

It was exciting to see the game from field level, but it isn't a very good place to watch the game. You can't see the opposite end of the field and the air is much colder, I guess because the grass was damp.

As I walked around the field I noticed that the ground was littered with small empty black and gray plastic film containers. I was surprised at how many people hung around the field after the ballgame. They would ask us to get them various things from the field. One guy asked Shannon Fontaine for some grass from the end zone that had white paint from the word Tigers. The guy said he would pay him for it, so Shannon picked up one of the film containers, pulled some of the grass with white paint on it, filled the container and gave it to the guy.

What some fans will do to own a piece of history.

After the stadium cleared, we loaded back on the bus and headed to Montgomery. I had taken a chill from standing in the wind from the tunnel. I could tell I was running fever and having chills. On the way back, we didn't move much faster. It seemed slower to me because I was sick.

Somewhere between Auburn and Montgomery we saw a young man about nineteen or twenty years old, walking down the interstate in the darkness and we stopped to pick him up. The temperature had plunged by this time and the man wasn't wearing a coat. Tommy Shanks was driving the bus and his dark blue trench coat wasn't marked with any police patches, so you couldn't see his uniform underneath.

Tommy opened the door and asked the guy if he wanted a ride.

"Yeah, thanks," the young man replied. He bounded onto the bus in two quick steps, grabbed the pole next to the door, swung around and sat down in the first seat. The bus was dark and he did not pay attention to any of the other passengers.

"Why are you walking?" Tommy asked him. "Did your car break down?"

"No, my girlfriend kicked me out of the car," the young man replied. "She said I was drunk and was getting on her nerves. So she kicked me out."

"Where do you live?" Tommy asked.

"Tuscaloosa," he replied. "I'm a student at Alabama."

"How are you goin' to get back?"

"I don't know but I have an aunt that lives in Montgomery and if I can get there I can stay with her," he said. "Man, did I get lucky you guys came by. I was afraid the police would pick me up and I would go to jail. Man, did I get lucky!" He seemed relieved.

Tommy looked back at the guy and smiled. "Well, you are not as lucky as you think," he said. "Turn around."

As he turned around, Tommy turned on the interior light and about half of the officers in unison shouted, "You have the right to remain silent!"

The guy just dropped his head and slowly turned around in his seat. He bent over and put his face in his hands and just sat there. After a minute or so, Tommy laughed and told him that he wasn't going to jail and that one of the officers would take him to his aunt's house. He seemed relieved but was still nervous about being drunk on a bus full of police officers. Corporal John Gallups took the guy to his aunt's, and we all got a good laugh out of the whole thing.

Alabama had lost the game 30-20, and I ended up missing five days of work from the flu. I made one hundred and twenty dollars from working the game but it cost me at least that much being sick.

On January 9, 1990, I went to the Auburn Municipal Court to testify on the disorderly conduct arrest. The guy had to drive all the way from Cocoa Beach, Florida, to appear in court. He pled guilty.

Even though my team lost and I got the flu, I still enjoyed being a part of history. I can tell everyone that I attended the first Alabama-Auburn game played at Jordan–Hare Stadium.

And, oh yeah, I kicked out five people and arrested one.

A Contradiction in Terms

DEATH CASES WERE NEVER PLEASANT. I think it is especially tragic when a person dies and the family and friends who loved that person remain to suffer the loss. In my career, I responded to a great many deaths. The causes were varied: natural, homicide, traffic fatalities and accidental deaths, but of all of these, the saddest were suicides. For whatever reason, someone decided that life wasn't worth living and elected to end it. This may have seemed like an easy way out for them, but it was traumatic for those left behind.

Sunday, May 6, 1990, I had less than an hour before I got off duty at midnight. I was in the office wrapping up paperwork on some other cases when I heard a patrol unit dispatched to an address in the Chisholm Community on a Code 6 (subject shot).

"Great!" I said out loud. "This will be at least three more hours of work."

As I listened to the radio traffic, I was hoping that it was actually a suicide and not a homicide because suicides are much easier cases to work. With a suicide, the perpetrator and the victim are one in the same, and since the perpetrator is deceased, the case is not as difficult to solve. Don't get me wrong, every suicide is investigated carefully to make sure it is not a murder, but some suicides are obvious of what happened.

You take photographs and a video of the scene, but comparatively speaking, there is usually little evidence to collect; the weapon of choice, whether it is a gun, pill bottles or maybe a rope, belt or sheet used to hang themselves, and a suicide note if the victim wrote one. The other thing you hope for is that the victim's body is found soon after death and hasn't had too much time to decompose.

The patrol unit's job was to arrive and access the situation, then advise their supervisor and the robbery-homicide supervisor, which on this particular night was Lieutenant D.T. Marshall.

Most everyone called him "D.T." He was a street-wise lieutenant who seemed to know every criminal on the street personally. He was divorced and lived only for the job, spending most of his free time out on the street pursuing leads on a number of cases until three or four in the morning. D.T. worked his way up through the ranks, spending most of his career as a detective, so he knew intimately how to handle a criminal investigation.

The patrol unit arrived on the scene and notified dispatch that the victim was dead from a single shotgun wound.

After hearing the radio traffic, my office phone rang.

"Smitty," D.T. said. "Did you copy that radio traffic?"

"I copied it, Lieutenant," I replied. "I'll be en route."

"Thanks, Smitty. Danny's en route and will meet you there," he said, referring to Corporal Danny Carmichael, another homicide detective.

I passed the paramedics leaving as I pulled up to the house. I approached the officer keeping the crime scene log and gave him my name and unit number. Rookie officers are usually assigned to stand outside the house and keep a log of everyone who enters and leaves the scene, noting the times of arrival and departure. New guys don't always recognize the investigators, so I always made sure I let them know who I am. Some officers and investigators often forget what it was like to be new and not know everybody and just want to walk past the new guy. I figured he had enough to do without having to worry about me being rude to him.

I walked in with camera in hand and asked the senior officer where the victim was.

He gave the standard answer, "Down the hall to the left, you can't miss him."

A shotgun blast to the head is always messy, and I prepared myself mentally to see the victim. I'd seen quite a few suicides in my career, but the initial shock is the worst. I walked to the end of the hall and in the last bedroom on the left was the victim.

He was lying on his back with the shotgun on the floor next to him. The scene appeared typical of a shotgun suicide. In most suicides where a rifle or shotgun is used, the victim will place the gun under their chin or in their mouth then pull the trigger with either his toe or some type of tool. The blast will normally cause the back of the head to explode outward spraying blood, bone, hair and brains all over the ceiling, walls and floor. The head and face will usually flatten out to resemble a Hollywood special effects mask.

This one, however, was not like any I'd seen before. The victim had used bird shot instead of a larger pellet size, and the force of the blast into the mouth had caused the explosive discharge to expel out his ears rather than blowing out the back of the skull. There were fine particles of brain and blood spatter on both walls to either side of him. His head was still intact but fractured, like a boiled egg that has the shell cracked before being peeled.

Shotgun and rifle shots to the head are normally very messy, but in this case the clean up would be minimal. After taking photographs and shooting a video of the scene, the Alabama Department of Forensic Sciences (DFS) was called to collect the body. While they were en route I bagged the hands separately in paper bags to preserve any gunshot residue for examination during autopsy.

Before DFS was called, we found out that the victim was a sergeant on active duty with the U.S. Air Force. This meant that OSI (Office of Special Investigations) would also have to be called to conduct their own investigation. We held off calling DFS until the OSI investigators arrived and finished their initial investigation. This usually consisted of looking over the scene, making a few notes, then, asking for a copy of my photos, video and paperwork.

Two OSI investigators arrived about forty-five minutes later. D.T. met them at the front door and I went back to the victim. I was standing in the room across from the victim and D.T. led the two men to the bedroom doorway. He introduced us, and I began to detail the scene to them.

As I finished pointing out the specifics of the scene, one of the investigators rubbed his chin and said, "Hmm, that's odd."

I immediately looked over the scene again trying to see if I missed something. D.T., Danny and I had been there for more than an hour and hadn't noticed anything out of the ordinary. I looked around again and then looked at the investigator with what had to have been a perplexed expression. "What's wrong?" I asked. "What did I miss?"

"How did he tape up his other hand after he taped up the first one?" he asked, in a serious, puzzled tone.

I looked at his hands that I had bagged up earlier, looked at D.T., then both of us burst into laughter. The OSI investigators apparently failed to see the humor in it and looked at us like we had lost our minds.

After a few moments, our raucous laughter subsided into amused chuckling. D.T. looked at the two men. "My man did that," he said as he walked back down the hall toward the living room.

"I bagged his hands to preserve any gunshot residue," I explained.

"Oh, okay. I see." The investigator said.

I am not sure if he really understood why I did it or if he was just sleep deprived, being that it was close to three-thirty in the morning. They asked if they could get copies of the photos, video and paperwork and I told them I would take care of it. As they were leaving, Danny advised dispatch to contact DFS and have them en route.

We sat down in the living room and watched the rodeo on television. Danny knows horses and rodeos and was explaining what the riders were doing right and wrong on each ride and the scoring process. I had never had anyone explain what the judges were looking for so it was interesting.

D.T. had me call dispatch and find out which Forensic Investigator was coming to the scene and I was told it would be Carl Murdock. Carl was a short, black man who had worked for the DFS since before the city got its own morgue in 1978. He was a very comical character and a prankster with a great sense of humor. He often smoked a cigar down to a stub then chewed on it in the corner of his mouth. If you worked robbery-homicide in Montgomery, you knew Carl Murdock well. He and D.T. had known each other for years and they were notorious for pulling pranks on each other. With these two guys, nothing was off limits.

When D.T. found out that Carl was coming, his face lit up. "Hey, Smitty," he said. "Go find me a white bed sheet."

"What are you goin' to do, Lieutenant?" I asked.

"Just go find me a sheet and you will see." I went and got a sheet out of the linen closet and brought it to him. "Let me know when you see him drive up." We continued to watch the rodeo but I was preoccupied with watching the living room window, looking for headlights. As soon as I saw him pull up I told D.T., "I think he's here."

"Cut the front porch light out and let me get into the bushes," D.T. said, smiling.

I cut the light out and he hid in the large shrubs just outside the front door and pulled the sheet over his head. Carl came up to the door with clipboard in hand and his cigar stub lodged in the corner of his mouth. I stood in the front doorway. As Carl walked onto the stoop, D.T. jumped out of the bushes and grabbed him from behind and shouted, "I got you now!"

Carl had a startled look on his face. D.T. pulled the sheet off his head.

"D★★N IT, D.T.!" Carl said. "You trying to give me a heart attack?"

We all laughed and Carl walked in and D.T. followed as he rolled up the sheet. I hadn't been around Carl enough to know how he would react but he took the prank in stride as if he was not even surprised that it was pulled on him.

"What you got, D.T., that you dragged me out in the middle of the night?" Carl said, getting back to business.

We all walked back to the bedroom, with Carl and D.T. still making verbal jabs back and forth at each like two old army buddies. After taking a few photographs, and filling out his paperwork, I followed Carl out to his large, white, state-issued station wagon and helped him unload the stretcher.

We loaded the victim on the stretcher and as we were wheeling him out to the car, we told Carl about what the OSI investigators had said about the bagged hands.

He laughed and shook his head. I told him it was an example of "military intelligence," a contradiction in terms.

Woman shot while hanging wash in project

By Don Morse
Journal staff writer

Montgomery's 17th slaying victim of 1990 apparently was hit by a bullet intended for someone else, and is the daughter of a woman stabbed to death last year, police said today.

█████████████████████████ was hanging laundry in a back yard of the Trenholm Court housing project Wednesday night when she was hit in the head by a bullet apparently fired by a juvenile shooting at another juvenile, police and fire department officials said.

Police are seeking one of the juveniles, intending to charge him with murder, said Lt. Robert Hankins, a Montgomery Police Department spokesman.

The shooting occurred about 9:50 p.m. Wednesday, Lt. Hankins said.

Trenholm Court is a low-income housing project near the corner of Ripley and Columbus streets. However, police listed Ms. ████████'s address as the Tray-lor Road.

Montgomery firemedics arrived at 9:52 p.m. when they

pronounced Ms. ████████ dead, said Scott Spradley, a firemedic.

The bullet struck her in the side of the head, the firemedic said.

On July 23, 1989, Ms. ████████'s mother, ████████████ died of multiple stab wounds in the same housing project.

Shortly after the 1989 slaying, ████████████'s body was dumped under a parking canopy at the Montgomery Police Department by a man who allegedly witnessed the stabbing but didn't want to be involved, a Montgomery homicide detective said at the time.

Later, the man who left the body at police headquarters was arrested in connection with the slaying, Lt. Hankins said today.

The slaying of Ms. ████████ is Montgomery's 17th of the year but only its second in the last two months, police said.

During the first four months of 1990, someone was killed an average of every nine days. Since May 19, however, when Roderick ████ was killed in the heart of Montgomery's black district, there have been only two slayings — or one every 34 days.

Police investigate shooting death of 24-year-old Montgomery woman

POLICE OFFICER OF THE QUARTER

A ROUND AUGUST OF **1990,** OUR church bought a brand new grand piano, and I was helping several other members move it up onto the church platform. The piano was extremely heavy, and it was all we could do to move it without causing any damage. It had a shiny deep-black finish and the last thing we wanted to do was scratch it.

As we carefully maneuvered it toward the platform, the piano began to fall toward me. One of the guys on my side had moved around to give me some help, but when he moved, the extra weight fell on me. I didn't want the piano to fall, so I caught it with my left hand—bearing the piano's full weight. I saved the piano, but all that extra weight pulled something in my shoulder.

We managed to get the piano placed without scratching it. I didn't think too much about the pain in my shoulder at the time— just assuming that I had pulled a muscle and it would heal on its own in a couple of days. As time went on, however, the pain got worse. Several days later I went to an orthopedic surgeon. He told me that I had torn some ligaments in the shoulder and needed surgery to repair the damage.

I had arthroscopic surgery in the early part of November. After a few days, I was in rehab to rebuild the strength in my shoulder.

By early December I was going to rehab on Mondays, Wednesdays and Fridays in the morning before work. I was working as an Evidence Technician and was able to do my job with very little assistance.

On Monday, December 17, 1990, I had been going to rehab at Health South on the Southern Boulevard for several weeks. As I was leaving at 11:45 that morning, I heard radio traffic that patrol units were searching for two suspects involved in a burglary in the area of

Byrne Drive. Health South was located in the same neighborhood. Even though I was off-duty and out of uniform, I couldn't resist heading toward the area to help look for the suspects.

As I drove down Audubon Drive toward Berkley Drive, I saw two young men who fit the description run across a front yard on Berkley Drive and jump the fence into one of the back yards. I notified dispatch on my car radio, drew my Beretta 9mm pistol, and jumped out of the car. I saw one of the suspects climb over the fence and crawl behind some bushes next to a house. I walked up to the suspect and ordered him out at gunpoint. I told him to lie face down on the ground then I sat on his back to hold him down because I didn't have any handcuffs with me.

I pulled out my wallet and identified myself as a police officer. A woman came out of a house across the street and saw me sitting on the suspect and told me to let him go or she was going to call the police.

"Call 9-1-1!" I yelled at her since I didn't have a hand-held radio.

I forgot that I was in civilian clothes when I got out looking for the suspects. I was wearing a light blue tee shirt with a shark logo on the front and denim pants. My vehicle was a solid black Chevrolet Caprice with no police markings.

After about three minutes, a black and white patrol unit pulled up and saw me with the suspect and took the guy into custody. I then left and went home, took a shower and reported to work at 3 p.m. I informed my supervisor, Sergeant Richard Foster, about the arrest and typed out a statement for the investigators. I found out later that the young man I apprehended and his accomplice had burglarized the residence at 801 Byrne Drive.

Sergeant Foster wrote up a commendation and forwarded it to Major Mobley, the detective division commander, and he put me in for Police Officer of the Month. On January 31, 1991, I was awarded Police Officer of the Month. On March 31, 1991, I was awarded Police Officer of the Quarter, by Mayor Emory Folmar at the City Council meeting. Nancy called my parents and they drove down from Birmingham as a surprise to see me receive the award. I was surprised and pleased that they were able to see that.

I had no idea that when I left rehab that day that I would end up receiving an award just for doing my job. Sergeant Foster told me that my days of chasing bad guys were supposed to be over since I was an Evidence Technician and no longer a patrolman. But I just couldn't resist getting in a chase when a couple of bad guys were running from the police.

I guess it's just in my blood.

When someone is awarded Police Officer of the Quarter it comes with a check for $300, which is really nice. Unfortunately, I'd received a speeding ticket from the Florida Highway Patrol in February of 1991, while driving to a school in Orlando and had to use $112 of the money to pay the ticket. I didn't receive Police Officer of the Year for 1991, but I was very proud to have been chosen as Police Officer of the Quarter.

April 1991 – Receiving the Police Officer of the Quarter Award from the Civitan Club in Montgomery, Ala, with my wife Nancy

WHAT LIFE THROWS AT THEM

I BELIEVE THAT ANYONE WHO WORKS in the ministry should be exposed to the real world from time to time. What I mean is that if someone works in a church surrounded by Christian people day in and day out they may lose sight of what a world steeped in sin actually looks like. On Sunday you have a church full of Christian people, or those who say they are Christians. They don't have to work in the secular world on an everyday basis. On the other side of the coin, police officers see the real world and see people at their worst. As a Christian police officer, it's been a challenge being a Christian example and dealing with people who don't know Jesus and that are as lost as Easter eggs. I think that anyone in the ministry should periodically ride with a police officer or a paramedic unit and see what is happening in the real world. A minister who works with young people needs to be especially familiar with the worldly things that distract kids from Christ.

When I was in high school there were no cell phones and crack cocaine wasn't a problem. AIDS was completely unknown, and the only thing we were taught in schools was how too avoid venereal disease.

Friday, August 2, 1991, Mike Anderson, the youth minister of my church (Woodley Baptist Church) accompanied me on a ride-a-long one evening. I was working as an Evidence Technician on the evening shift from 3:00 to midnight and was able to ride anywhere in the city.

On my off days, I worked on the R.O.T. (Retake Our Turf) team. This was a high-profile zero-tolerance drug interdiction unit that targeted the street dealers who operated in the housing projects and other high drug areas. I was actually able to take Mike to the high drug areas and show him how drug dealers operate and sell their product. Crack cocaine was and still is a huge problem in Montgomery, as well as the rest of the country.

About 4:30 that afternoon I drove by one of the areas where a lot of crack cocaine was bought and sold, Riverside Heights Housing Projects. I drove down Bell Street and showed Mike what it looked like from the outside.

"They sell crack on Gunter Street between Riverside Drive and Pill Street." I told him. We turned on Eugene Street from Bell Street and then left on Riverside Drive and stopped.

"Okay, this is what's gonna happen," I said. "I'm gonna turn onto Gunter and then you'll see two or three subjects standing in the road. They're the ones sellin' crack. I'm gonna gun the engine and run up on them and stop. Once they realize I'm the police, they'll take off runnin' and some of them will throw down the dope."

I pulled up to the corner, stopped and looked at Mike and said, "You ready?"

"I guess so," he said hesitantly.

I turned the corner and saw three young men standing at the driver's side of a beige Buick Skylark. I gunned the engine, sped toward them, then stopped quickly in front of them. The subjects threw the small, clear plastic bags of crack in the air and ran. The driver of the Skylark took off while looking at me in the mirror, sideswiping a parked car. He squealed the tires as he sped around the corner on Rouse Street.

"Get the dope. Get the dope!" I yelled at Mike.

I jumped out of the car and Mike followed. We both were gathering up the small bags of crack when Mike trotted back to the car. I finished picking up the drugs and went back to the car.

"Why did you go back to the car?" I asked.

"I looked around and realized that we were the only two white people in the projects and we were picking up drugs. I didn't feel comfortable so I went back to the car," he said.

I guess I have been doing this so long that it did not bother me. I am always aware of what is around me but I had a job to do also. I drove around the corner and found the Skylark abandoned in the middle of the street. I ran the tag but it didn't come back stolen. I called for an Accident Investigation unit and told them what happened.

The vehicle was towed and the owner would have to explain who was driving and why they left it abandoned in the road. More than likely the owner of the car was the parent or grandparent of someone buying drugs. The owner would be contacted and would have no idea of how it got there and the driver will make up some kind of story about what happened and deny ever trying to buy dope.

Mike and I recovered 3.5 grams of crack cocaine and 1.5 grams of marijuana. I impounded the drugs as found property and it was eventually destroyed. Mike told me later that he did not believe the part about when I would drive around the corner that the subjects would toss the drugs and run. He said it gave him a new insight on the drug problem in Montgomery and how he had no idea it was sold so openly and in broad daylight.

Being a police officer is a tough job. Being a Christian police officer is an even tougher job. Being exposed to the evils of everyday and seeing the worst in people can take its toll on you. I think the only reason I have been able to maintain my convictions and sanity is that I surround myself with strong Christian people. I'm a youth Sunday School teacher and I am aware of what is happening in my city.

If you are a Christian police officer, you need to take your youth minister on a ride-a-long. The experience will help them minister to their youth and make him a more knowledgeable youth minister. The youth are our future and they need to be prepared to deal with what life throws at them.

WHAT AN EVIDENCE
TECHNICIAN DOES

PASTORS SPEND A GREAT DEAL of their time guiding, working with and caring for their church members, yet sometimes a dose of reality is just what is needed to broaden that pastor's horizons. Even the shepherd should know what's happening in the world today, or even in his own hometown.

On Saturday, August 3, 1991, I took my pastor, Gary Aldridge, on a ride-a-long. At the time I was working as an evidence technician collecting evidence and photographing crime scenes. The youth minister, Mike Anderson, had gone with me to work the night before. Mike was exposed to some things he'd never seen before and probably never could have imagined. Saturday was my pastor's night. I didn't know what was in store for us, but I was pretty sure it would be a little different and not anything he expected.

I picked him up at his home at about 2:30 that afternoon and took him to my office. I showed him around the lab and explained some of the things we did to process all the evidence collected at the scene of major crimes. He seemed fascinated at the things we did to manage and preserve evidence and some of our techniques for bringing out evidence unseen with the naked eye.

We got our first call that day about 4:30. It was a child abuse case on North Burbank Drive. Oddly enough, this particular call was less than a half mile from my own home.

A young boy, about seven years old, had been beaten with a folded television cable. The responding officers noticed that the child had horseshoe shaped bruises all over his back from several earlier beatings. I took several photographs of the child's injuries for the Juvenile investigator working the case. Gary was appalled at what he saw.

After we left the house, he seemed troubled by what he'd seen. "How could a person beat a child like that?" he asked.

"I don't know, but I see it *way* too much," I replied.

"Do you see a lot of this abuse?" he asked in disbelief.

"Unfortunately, yes, I do," I said.

As we headed back into town, we heard dispatch send a unit on a possible suicide attempt on the Bell Street overpass that spanned Interstate 65. The dispatcher reported to the responding units that there was a young man clinging to the outside of the chain link fence on the guardrail threatening to jump into traffic on the interstate below.

We listened by radio as the officers responded and positioned themselves to attempt a rescue. Officers on the interstate below had stopped traffic, and other officers on the overpass were trying to talk to the despondent man back over the fence.

We arrived in the area, and I tried to drive as close as possible to the man's position from another overpass about a hundred feet away at the Herron Street exit. I had my camera ready in case the man released his grip and fell to the pavement about forty feet below. I watched as a couple of patrol officers who were talking to him suddenly grabbed his clothes through the fence and held on until another officer climbed out onto the bridge and secured the man safely to the fence with a leather K-9 leash. The fire department came and raised a ladder from a truck and brought him and the officers restraining him safely down.

After leaving there, Gary and I went to get something to eat. Gary asked questions about the calls I went on and how they affected me. It seemed during the course of our conversation that he was counseling me as a pastor would normally do someone who had witnessed trauma of some kind. But that was okay because he was my pastor and that was his job. Other times he was curious about all I did. At one point he asked, "Is this a *normal* day?"

"No, not really," I replied. "It's actually been kind of slow."

After dinner we rode around a little, and I showed him some of the sights of the city, those most tourists weren't interested in seeing.

I showed him where I took Mike the day before and watched as a young man tossed a bag of drugs running from the police and crashed his car trying to get away.

About 7:00 that evening, dispatch sent a unit to Interstate 85 on a suspicious subject walking along the shoulder of the highway talking to himself. He was described as wearing a blue sweat suit. I thought this would be an interesting call, so I drove down the interstate and located the man. We reached him before the dispatched unit, so I got out with the subject. He was an older black man wearing a dirty blue sweat suit and smoking a cigar. He had the words, "I AM GOD" written on the front of his shirt with a black marker.

I talked to him for about five minutes and then let him go on his way. As we got back into the car Gary commented on the encounter. "I didn't know God smoked a cigar," he said.

After leaving the man on the interstate we drove back into town and heard over the radio that a patrol officer was chasing a young man nearby suspected of possessing narcotics. As we turned onto Jackson Street from High Street, I said, "This guy's gonna run through the cut."

"What's 'the cut'"?

"It's the path between the apartment buildings that goes from Watts Street to Jackson Street. It crosses Key Street, and that's where we're goin,'" I explained.

It was dark by then, so I turned off my lights and turned on Key Street and parked. I pointed to my right and told Gary, "The guy will be running from there and will cross the street and run through there," I said pointing to my left.

"No way is that going to happen." Gary replied, as if he didn't have any faith in my experience.

"When he runs by, I'm not going to chase him since you're in the car," I said. "I can't leave you alone. If he was wanted for something more serious like robbery or murder then I'd try to catch him."

About fifteen seconds later, a young man exploded in full stride from between the buildings just as I had predicted. He ran across the street right in front of us and continued at full speed quickly disappearing again into the darkness.

"Criminals tend to be creatures of habit." I told him. "They do whatever works for them."

I heard on the radio that other officers out on nearby Jackson Street also familiar with this escape route caught him shortly thereafter climbing over a fence.

About 10:30, I was called to West Street and 4th Street in the Oak Park community where someone had been shot. After we arrived I was told that the victim had died on the way to the hospital. I took the necessary photos at the scene and enlisted Gary's help to take notes on my photographs as I dictated them. I would later regret this decision because his hand writing was horrible. It closely resembled the scribbling of a nervous doctor on a hastily-written prescription.

We left 4th Street and went straight to the Emergency Room, where the victim, Richard Scott,* had been taken. Richard was fairly well known to the police department. He'd often been in trouble and was a career criminal. I overheard a comment made by one of the officers at the hospital. "He deserved what he got," the officer said.

His partner added, "Couldn't have happened to a better guy."

Gary was surprised by all the comments. "Does everyone really know this guy?"

"Yeah, he's one of those guys who's always doing something to somebody."

"Did you know him?" Gary asked.

"Yeah, I was familiar with him," I replied. "Can't say that I ever met him, but I've heard his name on the radio a couple of times and he has been wanted a couple of times. I gotta go in and take a few photos of him," I said. "Are you up to this?"

"I'll be okay." Gary replied.

I pulled the curtain back and approached the bed. Richard was naked except for the sheet draped over him. He still had the ventilation tube sticking out of his mouth placed there by the paramedics at the scene as they tried desperately to save him. I pulled the sheet back and photographed the small black hole in his chest left by the bullet that ended his life. Gary made a few notes and we left.

---

*   Name changed

"Not much dignity left to a person when they're just laid out on a table with no clothes on," Gary commented.

"No," I replied. "Not too much."

While we were still at the emergency room, another gunshot victim came in. The night was turning out to be busy. Someone had shot Charles Reed* in the back, but his injury wasn't serious. I took some photos of his wound as well.

"I don't suppose you know this guy?" Gary asked.

"No, I'm not familiar with him."

We left the emergency room about one that morning. I went back to the office to make a few notes and to pick up some more film. I secured the evidence from the last two calls and decided it was time to take Gary home. I knew that he usually went to bed between 9:00 and 10:00 p.m. and it was approaching 3:00 in the morning. He also had to preach the next day. After dropping him off, I went back to the office to finish some paperwork so I could go home. I got home around 5:00.

The night was a little busier than normal, but then again, what exactly *is* normal for an evidence technician? Gary and Mike saw just a small sample of what I've experienced over the years combing crime scenes for evidence and photographing every tragedy imaginable. I think the ride-a-longs accomplished the goal I intended and gave them a peek at what went on in Montgomery.

Gary spoke briefly about his experience that night to the congregation. I don't really remember too much about the sermon that followed. I had to be there at 9:00 to teach my Sunday School class, so I only got three hours sleep that night. It was worth it though; both Gary and Mike got a whole new perspective of what police officers do each day, and saw first-hand what an evidence technician does.

---

*   Name also changed

THAT IN ITSELF IS AN EXTREMELY SCARY THOUGHT

THERE WERE MANY TIMES IN my career when I responded to a call and asked myself, "What was he thinking?" I've seen some stupid things, met some dim-witted fools, and encountered some extremely lucky people. On one particular day I answered a call and got to do all three at once.

On Sunday, April 5, 1992, I was working on second shift as an Evidence Technician when I was dispatched to the Pecan Grove neighborhood on an explosion that had injured someone. When I arrived I learned that a young man had been mixing up some homemade explosives in a shed in his back yard when the mixture suddenly detonated.

An arson investigator with the fire department was on the scene along with the State Fire Marshall. Several patrol units and a couple of homicide detectives were present. I grabbed my 35mm Pentax camera from the trunk of my car and walked around behind the house where the shed was located. As I walked through the gate of the chain-link fence I saw everyone standing at the door of a large metal storage building. I could see no obvious sign of a fire or an explosion, and I began to wonder why I'd been called. My presence was usually required where a serious injury or death had taken place.

As I approached the crowd of officials, I spoke to one of the detectives. He informed me there was an explosion inside the shed and he needed some photos of the scene. I was expecting bent and twisted metal and from what I could see there was no sign of an explosion at all.

"What exactly happened?" I asked.

"This guy was mixing some type of homemade explosive inside the shed and it blew up on him. He was injured pretty badly," the detective said. "He's on his way to the ER. I just need some photos of inside the shed and the Skoal cans he was using."

"Skoal can?" The smokeless tobacco held in a small pinch behind the lip comes in a small green plastic can about three inches in diameter.

"Yeah, this guy was mixing up some kind of homemade explosive in these Skoal cans with his fingers and it blew up on him."

"Are you serious?" I was having a hard time believing this.

"It blew most of his fingers off," he replied. He was dead serious.

I made my way through the crowd and saw Ed Paulk, one of the State Fire Marshall investigators inside the building. Ed was a former auto-theft investigator with our department.

"Hey Ed, whatcha got here?" I asked.

"Hey Steve, how are things?" he replied, reaching out to shake my hand. "It's amazing we have anything, if you want to know the truth," he said. "Usually, in these types of cases, there is nothing but a burned spot and not much evidence to work with."

"What was he doing?"

"He was mixing some type of explosive in these little cans you see here." He pointed to the work bench. As long as it stays moist, it's stable. Once it starts to dry, it becomes very unstable," Ed explained. "It looks like he was mixing this stuff up and must have set it down for a minute, and when he went to stir it up again, it exploded. He was stirring it with his fingers and blew them all off."

"He was using his *fingers* to stir this stuff?" I asked. I wonder sometimes how some people live as long as they do. "What an idiot!" I exclaimed.

I looked over the bench to see what I needed to photograph. I noticed a severed finger mixed in with all the other items scattered about on its surface. I photographed the Skoal cans and then the lone finger. As I looked more closely I started finding more fingers scattered in the debris. As I recall, there wasn't much blood present resulting from the multiple amputation.

I went back to my car and got a zip-lock bag to contain the detached digits. I ended up collecting about eight fingers.

"What am I suppose to do with this bag of fingers?" I asked Ed.

"I don't know," he replied. "That's a new one on me."

I decided I'd take them to the emergency room and give them to the doctor treating the young man. I'm sure he'd know what to do with them, but first I needed to finish taking my photos.

"We'll take care of the other evidence, Steve," Ed told me.

As I was leaving Major Vic Hicks, the commander of the detective division met me coming up the driveway.

"Hey, Steve," he said with a smile, "Whatcha got?"

I held up the bag. "Finger food," I said.

This was just another example of my often macabre sense of humor; and yes, it did seem funny at the time.

"What is that?" he asked.

"These are the guy's fingers that got blown off in the explosion," I told him.

"Oh, no, I meant what kind of scene do you have?" He asked. "Not what's in the bag?"

"Oh, my bad, sir," I corrected. "Not much of an explosion. Ed Paulk said it's rare to have an explosion and still have this much of a scene."

"What are you planning on doing with those things?" he asked.

"I'm taking them to the hospital to give to the doctor," I said. "I've never had a case like this before. Not sure what I'm supposed to do. I wouldn't think you would take them to the morgue."

I went to the hospital and asked to speak to the doctor treating the young man. After a few minutes, the doctor stepped out and greeted me.

"What can you do with these?" I asked him, holding up the bag of fingers.

"Well, I don't know," he said. "They can't be reattached, so I guess I'll have to dispose of them."

He took the bag from me and disappeared back into the treatment area.

I don't know if the young man's neighbors realize how fortunate they were that the explosion wasn't anymore powerful than it was. If he'd had more of the mixture it could have destroyed the house, or half the block, depending on the amount of explosive he decided to mix. The young man was fortunate he didn't lose his life.

I never learned if there were any children living at the residence, but that could have easily turned into a disaster if a child had taken any of the mixture out of the shed, or to school.

That in itself is an extremely scary thought.

It's a Tough Job, But Somebody's Gotta Do It

"**O**FFICER DOWN! OFFICER DOWN!"

Hearing these words on the radio will make any police officer's heart screech to a halt. Of all the calls for help a police officer is likely to hear, that one is the most terrifying. Double Zero is the universal radio code for "officer needs help." When this signal goes out, any law enforcement officer within earshot will drop everything and fly to his fellow officer's aid, just as he would expect his colleagues to do for him. The additional message of "officer down" tells you that a brother officer already lies wounded.

The worst call of all is when a citizen gets on a police radio. Terror evident in a voice unfamiliar with codes or radio jargon, the plea for help is unmistakable.

"Dispatch?" the voice begins reluctantly. "You've got two officers that have been involved in an accident."

If we're lucky, the good Samaritan knows his exact location and can provide enough detail to assist the injured officers. Sometimes they're shaken and unfamiliar with their surroundings. The stress takes its toll on even seasoned officers in the same situation. When the citizen is trying to guide help to the downed officer, we know immediately that the officer cannot speak for himself. Everyone assumes the worst. This is what the call was on Friday, April 24, 1992.

Officers Jack Clark and Scott Bowers were motor officers riding as partners that night on their way home around 10:30 p.m. after completing their shift. They were traveling east through the intersection of Atlanta Highway and Eastern Boulevard at close to

50 miles per hour when a vehicle turned suddenly into their path from the left. They were riding side by side, with Jack on the left and Scott on the right. Scott was able to dodge quickly to the right and avoid a straight on collision, but the vehicle struck him in the left leg and knocked him off the motorcycle spinning like a rag doll through the air. Jack had no where to go but straight into the side of the vehicle. He struck the vehicle with his face and flipped over the car flying a good distance like a missile arcing through the night sky before landing hard on the pavement on the other side of the intersection.

I was working as an Evidence Technician and when the call went out I immediately jumped into my vehicle and headed that way. Whenever a motor officer was involved in an accident I had to take photographs. A citizen had retrieved one of the police radios from one of the fallen officers and called it in. Fortunately that citizen was a retired Montgomery fireman. Being a retired firefighter, he knew his streets and was able to give the exact location of the accident. Moments later, Jack's feeble, disoriented voice came over the radio requesting an ambulance for his partner, apparently unaware of his own injuries.

I listened intently as the other units arrived on the scene to check on the condition of the officers. The first units on the scene advised that they were conscious and talking. I was able to breathe a sigh of relief. When you have a motorcycle-verses-car accident, the car always wins.

As I topped the crest of the hill on Atlanta Highway at Watson Circle, I could see the intersection was lit up with a light-show of red and blue lights from police cars, fire trucks, and paramedics already on the scene. I weaved my way in as close to the accident as I could. I was able to maneuver my vehicle into the middle of the intersection in front of a black and white unit with blue lights. Both Jack and Scott were already on their way to the hospital by ambulance when I arrived.

I took my overall photos of the scene from all directions, then moved in and took the closer shots of the vehicle involved in the accident and each motorcycle. I took photos of where the officers had fallen and the bloody bandages on the ground. There is just something about seeing the blood of a fellow officer on the ground that makes me feel uneasy.

Seeing blood does not bother me, but when I know that blood was spilled by a fellow officer, particularly someone I know, I feel it deep inside. Their injuries, though bad, didn't turn out to be life-threatening; nonetheless I don't like seeing a friend's blood on the street.

As I continued to take my photos, I took close up shots of the vehicle tag numbers, damage and the inside of the vehicle that caused the accident. Interior shots can establish the presence of alcohol or drugs involved at the time of the accident. As I photographed the damage to the car, I saw what looked like a small piece of meat embedded in the twisted metal. It turned out to be part of Jack's nose where he hit the side of the car. Jack's nose was so shattered the doctor described it as *being like "corn flakes."* When the doctor was asked how many stitches it took to repair his nose, the doctor said he lost count.

Two accident investigators and a supervisor worked the scene with me. There is a lot more paperwork for the accident investigators when an officer is involved. It doubles when there are injuries. And then you add a second injured officer and the paperwork begins to mount up. As far as my paperwork goes, it is the same, but it's the amount of photographs taken that increases for me. I also have to notify my supervisor since an officer was injured.

We were trying to hurry and get the scene photographed and marked because a storm was brewing and moving in fast. The wind had picked up and I always get a strange feeling when a storm is coming. The investigators were marking the scene with orange paint so the intersection could be cleared. They would come back later and do measurements.

While standing at the rear of my vehicle you could hear the gentle tapping of ice falling on the metal of the cars at the scene. And before we knew what hit us the bottom fell out. The wind was blowing so hard that the marble size hail was blowing in sideways. Thinking quickly, I opened the trunk of my Chevrolet Caprice. I and the other two investigators held the trunk lid open to shield us from the pelting ice. The wind was blowing so hard, that it took two of us to keep the trunk lid up. The hail storm lasted about five minutes, and as suddenly as it started, it stopped. No rain followed, so when the hail stopped, everything was quiet. The street was covered with small balls of ice which melted in a matter of minutes. By the time we left the scene you could not even tell there ever was a hail storm.

Jack spent three days in the hospital with a shattered nose. The doctor molded it the best he could with what he had left to work with. Scott spent about five days in the hospital with head injuries and a knee injury. He has had about three or four surgeries on his knee since the accident.

Police work is dangerous and riding a police motorcycle adds to that risk. Any motor officer will tell you, "It's not if you're going have an accident, but when." The only question is how bad. I know a lot of current and former officers who have ridden motorcycles and they all have had accidents. They also suffer from everything from arthritis, achy joints to bad backs. They also have scars from road rash to reconstructive surgeries from the accidents. It's one of those jobs you just have to love it to do it.

Riding a motorcycle for pleasure and riding as a job is two entirely different things. But to the guys who ride day in and day out in the extreme heat and the extreme cold, you can have it. It's a tough job, but somebody's gotta do it.

EXPERIENCE OR LUCK

FRIDAY, MAY 29, 1992, WAS a warm night with a lot of activities happening in the city. The local high schools were graduating their seniors and everyone seemed busy. I was working as an Evidence Technician that evening and knew that anything could happen. Around 6:00 that evening, two postal inspectors had attempted to serve a federal warrant on Andrew Graham.* He'd eluded them from the area of the apartments on Montgomery Street, but they'd received information that he was in the area.

The inspectors, along with officers from our department, searched the area for several hours but were unable to locate him. He had time to get a ride or hide in the area. One by one the patrol units and detectives got back in service and left the area. We knew that Andrew hung out in the area and eventually would return. It was just a matter of time.

I wasn't busy at the time and decided to stake out the apartment building and wait for him. I was in a black Chevrolet Caprice and found a dark spot in some bushes and trees to conceal my car. I turned off my lights and kept the radio turned down low. It was 8:30 and I was prepared to sit and wait for at least an hour.

It was warm and I had the window down. I had only been sitting there for about thirty minutes when I saw a white male sneaking around the apartments across the street from me. He was looking around very nervously as if he did not want to be seen. He walked cautiously across the street, right in front of my car. He kept looking to his left, but never toward his right. Had he looked to his right, he might have seen me in the car. Then he did something I had only seen in the movies. He began to creep slowly in front of me with his

***

*   Not his real name

elbows up and taking high slow steps. The same thing people do in the movies or cartoons when they are deliberately trying to be quiet sneaking up on people or tiptoeing by a sleeping dog. I got tickled watching him. In a quiet low voice I called in that I had a visual on the suspect that was wanted by the Postal Inspectors. I advised the units that he was walking toward Clayton Street from Montgomery Street. As he passed me he started walking faster so I believed he must have thought I was in the car. I let him get far enough away to exit. I had taken the interior light out so I would not be lit up when I opened the door. Most all police officers have done this to their vehicles, especially those who work at night.

I started to run toward him, trying to get as close as I could before he looked back. He saw me and took off running. I chased him behind a house where he disappeared through some hedges. I knew K-9 was close so I stopped and backed off. I did not want my scent near the bushes. When the K-9 officer arrived I showed him the area by pointing out where he went into the bushes with the beam of my flashlight.

The K-9 unit trailed the suspect to the next house, to the crawl space beneath the house. Several uniformed officers and I surrounded the house to wait and to see if the suspect was under there. The dog went under the house and we heard a lot of barking, growling and hollering. Then a male subject came crawling out with that look on his face when you are startled awake. He turned out to be a transient who was sleeping and was not the right subject. Then a woman came scurrying out screaming. A moment later, a third male subject came out and I said, "That's him!" He was arrested immediately and taken back to a waiting patrol car.

He was taken upstairs of police headquarters, to the Detective Division, and placed in the interview room and the Postal Inspectors were notified. Lieutenant D.T. Marshall, supervisor of the Robbery / Homicide division said, "In case no one told you, that was a great job, Smitty." I related to him and the other detectives how he came sneaking in front of me like people do in movies. "What an idiot!" was the common reaction they gave. If he had waited another thirty to forty-five minutes I would not have been sitting there and he would have gotten away.

Police work is part skill, part anticipating what the bad guys will do and part luck. Part of me sitting there was from experience knowing that sooner or later he would return back to the area he was familiar with. People are creatures of habit and like to be in their comfort zone. Part of it was luck, guessing the right time-frame that he might return. I have sat on stake-outs with no results and then you get lucky as in what happened that night.

Sometimes I don't know which is better, experience or luck.

Solving Crime with Science

A S AN EVIDENCE TECHNICIAN, I worked a lot of crime scenes. I've had some very interesting cases, but not all of them involved crime scenes. On Monday, June 29, 1992, I was working second shift. The police department ran a full crew of detectives on day and evening shifts but from 11 p.m. till 7 a.m. there were only two detectives working. They usually rode together and were commonly referred to as "the late car."

The late car handled all major felony cases during the night and then turned them over to other detectives in the morning. Usually these detectives worked this shift from about eighteen months to two years before being moved up to the evening shift. One of the detectives would work crimes against persons cases; robberies, assaults, rapes, etc., while the other handled property cases like burglaries, thefts, and the like.

Detective Shannon Fontaine was the property detective working late car during this tour. He and I are good friends, and he is a Christian who was open with his Christian beliefs. He has a great sense of humor and a quick wit. He always kept me laughing, and I enjoyed working cases with him. One evening about 11:30, he called my office and asked if I had any expertise in looking at fingerprints.

"What exactly do you mean, expertise in looking at fingerprints?" I asked.

"Patrol has brought in a guy who says he is one person but his girlfriend says he is another," he said. "His girlfriend got mad at him, like women will sometimes do, and called the police and says he is wanted by the police in Florida. He's got his brother's birth certificate and has an Alabama driver's license made under his

211

brother's name and has been using it as his own. I have a copy of the NCIC printout, and he looks just like the picture. I have the Henry classification on the printout but I don't understand it."

NCIC stands for National Crime Information Center. It is the national computer system used by all law enforcement agencies to broadcast lookouts for wanted subjects, stolen cars, and anything else suitable for nationwide broadcast.

The Henry classification for fingerprints is the system used to arrange the same type patterns of fingerprints together and the ridge count within the fingerprint. The ridges are the little lines in your fingerprint.

"Do you know how to look at a set of prints and compare them to the Henry classification on the printout?" Fontaine asked.

"Funny you should ask that," I replied with some sense of excitement. "I just had a class at the academy last week and I ought to be able to do that. I'll be up there in a few minutes."

I got my FBI fingerprint book out of the cabinet and quickly reviewed how to read and compare the classifications. I also gave some thought to convincing our suspect that I was a fingerprint expert. Often a bluff of this sort will persuade a suspect to admit to something if he thinks an "expert" has been called in on the case.

So I took off my gun belt with all my equipment and badge, got a white lab coat from the office and, along with my fingerprint glass and two fingerprint pointers, I headed up to Detective Fontaine's office.

I walked into the office and saw the suspect sitting in a chair next to Detective Fontaine's desk. His left wrist was handcuffed to the chair. Fontaine signaled for me to step in the hall so we could talk. He showed me the printout and the photo of the suspect.

"His girlfriend says that this is him," Fontaine explained. "But he and his brother look just alike." He then stepped back from me and looked me over, up and down. He smiled. "Nice lab coat."

"I'm going for the fingerprint examiner look," I replied. "I just need some thick black rimmed glasses with white tape in the middle to complete the effect."

We both walked in and he gave me the fingerprint card with the suspect's fingerprints he had just taken. I sat down at his desk and began to look at the card and started counting ridges out loud so the subject could hear me. He was sitting only two feet away, and I could tell he was watching me very intently. After about a good minute, I leaned back in the chair and looked at the subject with disgust. I grinned and tossed the fingerprint card at the subject and stated, "It's him! No doubt."

The subject just dropped his head and did not say a word. Fontaine looked at the subject and said, "So, how about it, Chuck?* Just tell the truth. You've been busted out by your girlfriend and now the fingerprint man."

The subject looked up slowly, but with hesitation, replied, "Okay! Okay! It's me. You got me."

Fontaine looked at the suspect. "If you're going to live a life of crime, don't make your girlfriend mad," he said. "Women will dime you out every time."

Fontaine filled out an arrest report and I told him I would be back in a minute to help transport the suspect to the Montgomery County Detention Facility. I went back to my office, hung up my lab coat and put on my gun belt and badge. I returned to Detective Fontaine's office and we walked the suspect down to Fontaine's unmarked vehicle. While riding over to the Detention Facility, Fontaine asked the suspect, "Why didn't you just admit that it was you, instead of us having to waste all that time trying to prove who you were. Your girlfriend had already ratted you out and we had your fingerprints."

The man thought for a second, then slowly confessed, "I've been stopped several times in different cities but it's always been at night. None of the other departments had a fingerprint guy working, so they always let me go. I never expected you to have a nighttime fingerprint guy working this late."

I wanted to just bust out laughing. I had just completed a weeklong class, but I was by no means an expert. Fontaine looked in the rear view mirror and made eye contact with me but said nothing. He just grinned.

As we pulled up to the jail, Fontaine looked at me. "You gotta' love it when a plan comes together," he said. "Solving crime with science."

★   Not his real name

Shooting at the Police

FRIDAY, SEPTEMBER **10, 1993,** BEGAN uneventfully. I had worked my regular day-shift hours as an Evidence Technician. I got off at 4:00 that afternoon then went home to have supper. I returned to the Narcotics office to work extra duty on the R.O.T. (Retake Our Turf) truck, a drug interdiction detail that targeted street-level drug dealers. I arrived around 7:30 that evening. We were scheduled to hit the streets at 8:00.

Riding on the truck with me that night were Sergeant Lester Webb, an instructor at the Police Academy; Sergeant Bill Jamison and Corporal Ed Rogers, both narcotics detectives; Officers Steve Johnson and Hillary Castleberry, both assigned to the patrol division.

The team left the office at 8:00 and turned left onto Highland Avenue patrolling through the Tulane Court Housing project. We stopped a young man on Yougene Street and spoke with him for a few minutes. While talking to the man we heard a single gunshot nearby that seemed to come from somewhere west of our location. We left the man and drove west toward Watts Street off Highland Avenue. Three or four more shots rang out as we rode slowly passed the apartments. The shots sounded like they were coming from a medium to large caliber handgun.

Sergeant Webb was driving the truck and stopped on Watts Street. Corporal Rogers, Officer Castleberry and I jumped off the back of the truck. Sergeant Jamison got out from inside the vehicle and led the way as we moved swiftly in the direction of the gunshots. Corporal Ed Rogers trailed him by a couple of steps and offset to his left. I trailed Ed by a couple of steps and slightly to his left. Castleberry followed me at about the same distance and angle. We were moving in what was called an echelon.

We observed a young man at the far end of the broad alley between the apartment buildings, next to the street, with his back to us. I remember he was wearing a turquoise-blue colored shirt. He had a handgun in his left hand. As we approached him silently, he fired a single shot toward the ground away from his body.

"HALT! POLICE! DROP THE GUN!" Sergeant Jamison ordered.

The man turned completely around to his right and fired a shot at us. Sergeant Jamison answered with three shots of his own as he moved steadily toward the man. I wanted to fire but there were large steel poles used for clotheslines in front of me. These poles were four inches in diameter and Ed was just to my right. I was afraid that one of my shots might ricochet off a pole and hit Ed in the back. I couldn't take that chance. No other officers fired at the suspect because none of us had a clear line of fire.

The man turned and ran to his left through the housing project. Castleberry and I ran to our left trying to parallel his movement between the buildings. We ran across Smythe Curve and lost sight of him. We questioned several people in the area to see if anyone had seen him.

We saw a female lying in the parking lot with blood on the pavement. I assumed she might have been shot, but since there was a group of officers already assisting her, we continued looking for the armed suspect. Castleberry and I continued to question the people standing around to see if they had seen the suspect and to get a possible direction of travel.

One of the people we talked to told us that they saw a man fitting the description running north on Hall Street. We spotted the man fitting the description wearing a turquoise-blue shirt and stopped him. After talking to him for about a minute, we determined that he wasn't the shooter. We told him to take off the shirt so he would not be stopped again since there were a lot of police in the area looking for our suspect.

We crossed Hall Street and began walking slowly between the buildings when I spotted Detective Randy Markham, one of our undercover officers, walking by himself. He'd heard the radio traffic and came to assist in the search. He told us he had been on the east side of Hall Street immediately after the shooting but didn't see the suspect cross the street.

About twenty minutes had passed since the shooting and the housing complex was now crowding with people who'd come outside to see what all the commotion was. We figured the suspect had gotten into a vehicle and left the scene. He either escaped in his own vehicle or had caught a ride with someone, lying low in the seat to get out of the area unseen. This is a common tactic with criminals fleeing the scene of a crime.

We went back to the parking lot at the corner of Hall Street and Highland Avenue. The paramedics were on the scene treating the female. Sergeant Webb asked us to help keep the crowd back from the scene while the medics worked on her.

I went back to where the R.O.T. truck was parked and met with Sergeant Bill Morris from second shift patrol. We retraced our steps before and during the shooting. We found the three casings fired from Sgt Jamison's gun and the first one was already marked with Sergeant Morris' hat. I marked the other two with my leather gloves. Lieutenant D. T. Marshall, the robbery-homicide supervisor, arrived and I walked him through the scene of the shooting pointing out the shell casings.

Evidence Technician Howie Dave Kenney arrived shortly thereafter, and I did the same for him. Since I was an Evidence Technician and had worked many police-involved shootings, I knew what he would be looking to photograph and collect from the crime scene. As I walked back toward where the woman was shot, I located a fragment of a copper jacket and pointed it out for Corporal Derrick Cunningham, another evidence technician on the scene.

As I stood back at the scene and watched the crowd, Captain Mike Coker, the assistant division commander of the Detective Division, and one of my bosses, arrived on the scene. He had already been advised who had been involved in the shooting and when he walked up to me he smiled. "You're not going to be able to work this one, Steve," he said.

"Well, if you say so, Sir," I replied. I smiled thinking on some level that I was getting out of extra work. Somehow, I think working the scene and collecting evidence would have been easier.

Evidence Technicians weren't normally involved in shootings. We usually arrived on the scene after the fact. I also knew that since someone had been shot and that a police officer had fired his weapon we would have to go to the ABI (Alabama Bureau of Investigation) office to give statements.

This turned out to be a long night.

We left the Narcotics office at 8:00 p.m. and by 8:20, we'd already been involved in a police shooting.

We arrived at the ABI office around 9:30 and were placed in separate rooms as we waited to be interviewed. I bought a Coke and began to review in my mind exactly what had taken place.

At 1:20 a.m., Corporal Anthony Burton with the ABI interviewed me and took my statement. I went over the details step by step. I also drew a map of the area and showed him the directions that Officer Castleberry and I took before, during and after the shooting. We finally finished up at around 2:30 in the morning.

I found out the next day that the gunshot victim was twenty-three-year-old Stacy Kelly.* She was walking with her mother, her two and three-year-old sons when one of the rounds fired that night struck her in the leg. She was also nine-months pregnant. Another round grazed her two-year-old son on the buttocks. He was treated by paramedics on the scene for a minor injury.

A twenty-three-year old man was arrested the following Sunday and charged with attempted assault first degree for firing his weapon at us. He was later found guilty of the assault against the officers and sentenced to fifteen years in prison. He had several previous arrests on his criminal record.

Stacy Kelly, to no one's surprise, subsequently filed a lawsuit against the City of Montgomery and Sergeant Jamison for excessive force and violation of her right to due process, assault and battery, negligence and wantonness. All of us there that night had to give depositions in the case. I was deposed by Ms. Kelly's attorney, Dan W. Taliaferro of the firm of Copeland, Franco, Screws and Gill.

---

* Name changed to protect the legally misguided

George B. Azar with the firm Azar and Azar defended the allegations against Sergeant Jamison and city.

On May 12, 1995, a U.S. Circuit Court judge dismissed Ms. Kelly's case against the City of Montgomery and Sergeant Jamison. The judge also cleared the city of any liability in his ruling.

It really was no surprise that Ms. Kelly sued the city and the officer who fired the shots. When something like this happens, it all seems to be about how much money the victim and her attorney can get. After all, the city has plenty of money, so why not sue them?

A police officer must sometimes make a split second decision to defend himself or someone else with deadly force. When things don't go as they think they should, people always seem to want some undeserved compensation from the city and the officer who made the decision.

No one could say for sure who fired the shot that struck Ms. Kelly, since the bullet was not removed. So why didn't she and her attorney go after the suspect? After all, it was he who started the whole series of events in the first place by firing a gun in the projects then later shooting at the police.

Police, man exchange gunfire; female bystander hit

■ **Victim:** Area residents said the woman apparently was shot in the leg and was pregnant

By Liam T.A. Ford
ADVERTISER STAFF WRITER

A woman was shot Friday night during an exchange of gunfire between police and a man who shot at police patrolling the Tulane Court area, a police spokesman said.

Area residents said the woman apparently was shot in the leg and was pregnant.

The shooting started when a man shot at police patrolling the Tulane Court housing project about 8:30 p.m., said Sgt. M.S. Ward, a police spokesman. A member of the Montgomery Police Department's Retake Our Turf Team, a narcotics unit, returned the man's fire, Sgt. Ward said.

A woman who was standing behind Hair Studio One at 1225 Highland Ave. was shot during the exchange of gunfire, Sgt. Ward said. The woman, whose name and age police did not release, was taken to Baptist Medical Center. A nursing supervisor at Baptist said he could not release the woman's condition, but a police officer on the scene told members of the woman's family

that she would survive.

About 8:45 p.m., an ambulance took the woman from the scene. She appeared pregnant, and several area residents who claimed to know her later said she was.

The man who shot at police escaped on foot, Sgt. Ward said. He did not know in which direction the man fled.

It was unknown whether the woman was hit by police or by the man who shot at the officers on patrol, Sgt. Ward said.

The Alabama Bureau of Investigation is investigating the incident and its findings will be presented to a Montgomery County grand jury, Sgt. Ward said.

A woman who lives in Tulane Court said she was pulling her late model Buick out of her parking space on Hall Street when she heard several shots.

Please turn to **FIRE, 2B**

FIRE

from page 1B

"As I got in the car, I heard shots, pow, pow, pow, pow," said Grace Burnett.

She turned into the parking lot behind Hair Studio One and came upon the woman, lying on the ground, Ms. Burnett said.

"We saw the young lady holding her son's hand," she said. "We were the first people to pull up."

A friend of Ms. Burnett's held the injured woman's head and tried to make certain she was all right, Ms. Burnett said.

A man an area resident referred to as the wounded woman's brother described the exchange of fire to police as he stood about 50 feet from Ms. Burnett's Buick.

The Buick was parked just north of a large pool of blood in the business's parking lot.

Ms. Burnett had been on the way to pick up an acquaintance from work, but police, who still were photographing the scene and combing it for clues, would not allow her to move her car. Instead, a police captain said he would dispatch a patrol unit to pick up Ms. Burnett's acquaintance.

About 15 minutes after the shooting, a large crowd had gathered near the parking lot at the south end of Tulane Court. Police ordered them off as officers cordoned off two parking lots in Tulane Court, the Hair Studio One parking lot and the entire alley that runs parallel to Highland Avenue between Hall Street and Smythe Curve.

September 11, 1993 – Newspaper article of ROT Team police shooting in Tulane Court (Courtesy of Montgomery Advertiser)

*May 16, 1995 – Newspaper article dismissing the law
suit against the city in the ROT Team shooting.*

An Exciting Evening and Good Conversation

SOMEONE WHO WORKS IN LAW enforcement long enough will work every shift around the clock and every day of the week at some point with every combination of off-days. On Monday, October 11, 1993, I was working day shift and had Sundays and Mondays off. These were fairly good days to have off. I had Sundays to go to church and Mondays to run errands and evenings to go to the movies or out to dinner. The stores and theaters weren't very crowded on Mondays. On this particular night, my wife, Nancy, and I were on our way to dinner, and then a movie. This was our date night.

Around 6:00 that evening, we were driving down the Eastern Boulevard, slowing down in heavy traffic in front of McClendon's Furniture store. I saw the blue strobes of a patrol unit flashing on the side of the road ahead of us and assumed it was a minor traffic accident. Then I saw movement to my left and noticed a police officer on foot chasing a young man across the parking lot. They were running from the direction of the parked patrol unit.

"That officer's in foot pursuit!" I yelled to Nancy.

I turned quickly onto the service road entrance and sped across the parking lot of McClendon's Furniture store to get ahead of the young man fleeing from the officer. I was driving my wife's dark blue Chevy Nova, but it didn't have much get up and go. I recognized the pursuing officer as Charles Athey.

He caught up to the young man and managed to grab his shirt, but was struggling to take him into custody. I screeched up to where they were fighting between two parked cars, and the young man was fighting desperately to escape. I didn't know why Charles had

221

been chasing the man, but that didn't really matter to me. An officer needed assistance, and I was there to help.

I jumped out of the car and ran to the officer. "Athey!" I shouted. "I'm Corporal Smith, First Shift Evidence Tech!"

He looked up and his expression told me that he was glad that help had arrived.

I jumped in and grabbed the suspect's left arm. "Let's take him to the ground," I said.

Both of us forced the young man face down to the ground, and I pulled his left arm behind him. Charles forced the right arm back. I barely knew Charles and we had never worked together, but through our training, we both knew exactly what to do and were able to subdue the suspect as if we'd been working together for years.

"He shoved my partner when we tried to arrest him," Charles explained as he handcuffed the man. "I think he twisted his ankle." Charles wrestled the man to his feet. "I appreciate the help. Where did you come from?"

"My wife and I were on our way to dinner and I saw you chasin' this guy and I pulled in to cut him off when I saw you grab 'em," I explained. "You got him, or do you need me to walk back with you?"

"No, I'm okay. Thanks again for the help," he said. He gave me a satisfied smile and heaved for a moment to catch his breath.

"No problem," I said. I got back in the car with my wife.

"Wow! That was exciting!" Nancy said. "What was he chasing him for?"

"They went to arrest him and he pushed his partner and took off running. He either had drugs or he has warrants on him," I explained.

It was in the confines of the car's interior that I noticed that I'd brought something unexpected back with me. "Whew!" I exclaimed. "Now I smell like that guy! He was all sweaty and now I got his stink on me. I'll ride with the window down for a minute and air out."

We went on to the restaurant and then to the movies. Nancy was impressed by how I'd reacted and knew exactly what to do. I explained that training dictates response and that you'll invariably react in the manner that you're trained. She wanted to know if I had ever had to chase down a suspect like that. I told her that I had done it several times and I had also assisted other officers in subduing subjects the way I did that night.

When I returned to work Tuesday I read on the daily SIR (serious incident report) that Officer John McCall was Charles' partner that night and he had sprained his ankle when he attempted to arrest the subject for drugs after stopping him for an expired tag. McCall's injury occurred during the initial foot pursuit before Charles took off after him.

Charles charged the twenty-one-year-old man with possession of crack cocaine and resisting arrest. Officer McCall spent ten days on the desk with the injury.

I don't usually get involved in off-duty arrests, especially when I am out with my family, but in this particular case I just reacted like I had been trained and came to the aid of a fellow officer.

My wife seemed impressed and it made for an exciting evening and good conversation.

"There's No Eleven
on the Phone!"

I LOVE TALKING TO KIDS ABOUT being a police officer and what we really do. Television and movies never show the real truth about the job. Being a police officer is more than shootouts and car chases. Talking to kids gives me a chance to shine a little light on what's it like to be a real cop.

Friday October 29, 1993, I was asked to speak to a group of four and five-year-olds at Woodley Baptist Church. This was my home church, so I knew a few of the kids in the group. The topic of my discussion was: What Police Officers Do; Safety and 911.

I was in uniform, so I started off by showing them all the equipment on my belt. I let them play with the handcuffs, the radio, the mace and my flashlight. I showed them my gun, without taking it out of the holster of course. "A gun is not something to play with and I never take it out of the holster unless someone's life is in danger," I told them.

I covered the basics; catching bad guys, writing tickets, and the importance of wearing a seat belt in the car. This was usually where a few of the kids told on their parents.

"My daddy speeds really fast and Mommy gets mad at him and tells him you're going too fast," a smiling little boy said.

"My mommy never wears her seatbelt," a little girl said.

"Why not?" I asked.

"Mommy says it wrinkles her clothes."

"My mommy never lets us ride in the car unless we got our seatbelt on," another little girl said proudly.

Then I gave my standard speech about general safety, being

safe at home, not talking to strangers, not wandering off from their parents in the store, not playing with guns or knives, and refusing all that candy from those ever-present strangers.

The last thing I talked about was 911. I asked them how many knew their home phone numbers by heart. A few did, but most had no clue. I then asked them if they knew their parents' first names. Some did, but other assumed it was simply "Mommy and Daddy."

I asked them what the emergency number was in case they ever needed to call the police or the paramedics. One or two did, but most didn't. I then started talking about calling nine-eleven. I talked for several minutes about how important it was and how everyone needs to know that number in case a parent got hurt and needed help.

Then one of the little boys raised his hand and said, "Officer, there's no eleven on the phone!" he said. "How can I call 9-11?"

I just stood there for a couple of seconds with my mouth hanging open in surprise. I realized that he had a point. So I corrected myself. "You are absolutely right. There is no eleven on the phone. Thanks for pointing that out."

I looked at all the kids and at the teacher in the room and told them all, "You call 9-1-1."

Kids are sharper than we think, and sometimes we can learn from them. We say we listen and pay attention to kids, but do we really? Whether you do or don't listen is up to you. To this day I have always remembered when I was told, "There's no eleven on the phone!"

Nope, Not A Thing

IN THE EARLY **1990'S THE** home computer had become all the rage. Computers weren't just for the office anymore. People were buying them for their personal use. Those who really knew about computers could order one, have it custom built, and shipped to their home. I wasn't one of those guys who knew enough to custom order one, but one of the guys in my office was.

Howard David Kenney was one of the Evidence Technicians, or as they are known now, Crime Scene Investigators. He was knowledgeable with computers and had ordered one the month before and it was finally due to arrive.

Howie Dave, as I called him, has a great sense of humor and loved a good practical joke. We were always pulling some kind of joke on each other, so we both had to be on our toes all the time. I don't know exactly when this practical joke took place but it was such a good one I had to write about it.

Around April or May of 1994, Howie Dave came into work telling us that his new computer had been delivered and he couldn't wait until he got home to put it together.

It was about 7:00 one evening when Howie Dave called me at the office. I was working second shift from three to midnight, and Howie Dave was working days from seven to four. He'd left a little early that day to begin assembling his new toy. He told me he had everything assembled and needed me to fax him something so he could check the fax machine.

Well, I had read an article about six months prior in Reader's Digest about great practical jokes and one of the jokes was about a person who needed something faxed and his friend faxed a blank sheet of paper. I thought to myself that if I ever had the chance to use this as a practical joke, I would.

When Howie Dave called and asked me to fax him something from the office, I could hardly contain myself. I told him I would fax him a photo sheet because it had a lot of lines that were vertical and horizontal and had writing at the top of the report.

Instead, I faxed a blank sheet of paper.

Howie Dave called a few minutes later, "Did you fax it yet?"

"Yes," I replied. "I faxed a photo sheet. Didn't you get it?"

"I got a fax," he said, "But it came out blank."

"Make some adjustments and I'll fax it to you again." I hurried with excitement to the copier and tore the Photo Sheet into a circle the best I could and then taped the center of the sheet to a blank sheet of paper. I then made a copy of it and faxed the copy to him.

Shortly, he called again. "I'm now getting the center part, but the outsides are blank."

While trying to keep from laughing, I told him, "Just make a few more adjustments and I'll fax it to you again." By this time I was laughing out loud. I was the only one in the office so no one heard me, but I could not help myself. I took the original copy and laid a blank piece of paper on top of it at an angle. I ran a copy of that and faxed it to him.

He called again. "Now, I'm getting most of the report but it's slanted."

"Okay. I think you're getting close," I said. "Make a couple more adjustments and I'll fax you another copy."

"That's okay," he said. I could hear the disgust in his voice. "I'll just return the fax machine and get my money back."

"Hold on! I think you've about got it. I'll fax you one more. Make a few more adjustments and see what happens." By this time, I was laughing so hard my sides were hurting. I was wishing someone else were there to see this. As I walked back to the copy machine, I was trying to think of one more fax to send him.

I took the same report and ran a copy of it. Then I took the original and moved it about an eighth of an inch at an angle and put the first copy back in the copy tray. When the second copy came out it was a double image of the report and made it look blurred. I then took the original and moved it another eighth of an inch and ran a third copy on the sheet that had been copied twice before. The image looked like three reports on one. I faxed the blurred copy to him and it did not take long for him to call the office again.

"Now I got the whole report but it's blurred! I'm just gonna take it back to the store in the morning."

Trying not to laugh, I asked. "Are you sure you don't want me to fax you one more copy?"

"No. I'll just get my money back on the fax machine," he said. "This is what happens when you order an expensive computer and buy a cheap fax at Sam's. I'll see you in the morning."

I thought to myself, *Man, that was too easy. Tomorrow is going to be funny.* The next morning I was working day shift when Howie Dave came in I was sitting at my desk. I asked him how the new computer was working out.

"It works great except for the fax," he said. "As soon as Sam's opens, I'm going to take it back."

Looking concerned, trying not to laugh, I asked, "Did you bring the copies in?"

He handed them to me. "Yeah, look at these," he said with disappointment still in his voice.

I acted as if I was studying them, a serious look on my face. "So what's wrong with them? They look okay to me." Total disbelief covered his face. He snapped back, "Are you kidding? Look at them!"

As I swiveled away from him in my chair towards my desk, I pulled the original copies of the faxes out of my desk drawer. Twirling back to him, I held them up in the air for him to see. "They look just like the originals to me!"

Howie Dave's mouth just dropped open and he started laughing, "That was a good one. You really got me on that one!" As he continued to laugh he asked, "So there's nothing wrong with my fax machine?"

Finally able to share my laughter, I answered, "Nope, not a thing."

Police seek dye-splattered robber

■ The Cloverdale branch of First Alabama Bank was robbed at 10:20 a.m. by a man police have linked to other heists.

By CARLA CROWDER
Staff Writer

Police and FBI investigators combed the city Monday for a man wanted in connection with a morning bank robbery and two other recent bank heists.

First Alabama Bank, 416 Cloverdale Road, near the intersection of Norman Bridge Road, buzzing with shoppers, merchants and mechanics, was robbed at 10:20 a.m., police said.

"We knew it's the same person who robbed Union Bank and we believe he robbed a Dothan bank," said Gerald Shockley, chief of the Montgomery FBI office.

Union Bank on Mount Meigs Road was robbed Oct. 23. In Dothan, a First Alabama Bank was robbed Oct. 16, investigators said.

After the Monday holdup, police found dye packs and money the man dropped as he fled on foot, Agent Shockley said.

So, the suspect could be splotched with red dye, police said.

"We don't believe he got much money, so he'll probably rob again," Agent Shockley said.

In Monday's robbery at the Cloverdale Branch of First Alabama Bank, the man walked into the bank, pointed a handgun at one teller and fled toward an alley with a bag of cash, said Capt. V.H. Hicks, commander of the Montgomery Police Department's detective division.

Police refused to further detail what happened inside the bank.

Bank security cameras photographed the robber.

Police believe a red dye pack exploded, possibly marking the robber and whatever cash he retrieved, Capt. Hicks said.

The red dye pack, a tool for finding bank robbers, looks like a stack of bills, but contains dye the teller sets to explode within 15 to 20 seconds, Capt. Hicks said.

"When it explodes, the dye goes everywhere," the detective said, marking money and sometimes the person carrying the money.

No one was injured in the holdup.

Montgomery police and FBI officials are jointly investigating the bank robbery and had made no arrests Monday.

They were searching for a black man, 5 feet 3 inches tall, wearing a striped golf shirt and navy blue Chicago White Sox cap, police said.

The bank on Cloverdale Road is flanked by two service stations. Employees at both the

Please see DYE, 2B

Montgomery Police Department Evidence Technician Steve Smith, right, and Officer Kathy Fleming dust for fingerprints at the front door of the bank.
BY PATRICIA VIKLIKIAN

November 3, 1993 – Newspaper article from bank robbery of First Alabama Bank on Cloverdale Road. Officer Kathy Fleming watches as I process the door for fingerprints.

"It's All My Fault!"

SUICIDE IS SOMETHING I DON'T understand, other than maybe a disease or condition that inflicts constant excruciating pain. But I still don't believe it's the only option. Taking your own life should never be an option. To kill oneself over losing a girlfriend or disappointing a parent with bad grades is simply impossible for me to fathom. Life is too precious and too short to end it voluntarily for any reason.

I examined many suicides over the years, and most were pretty much the same. The most common methods I saw were self-inflicted gunshots, drug overdoses, carbon monoxide poisoning, and hanging, but sometimes these despondent people come up with some creative ways to end their lives.

Tuesday, June 28, 1994, I was called to an address in the Chisholm Community to work a suicide resulting from a method I'd never seen. A thirty-year-old woman had covered her head with a plastic garbage bag then taped it around her neck. As with any scene, I tried to figure out how the event itself unfolded as I photograph it. So as I took shots of the scene I thought how awful it was to suffocate like that. *What kept her from tearing the bag from her face when she got to where she could not breathe?* I wondered. Your will to live is normally more powerful than your will to die. As I continued taking photos, I saw several open medicine bottles on the night stand beside the bed.

"Oh, okay," I said out loud to myself. "She passed out from the pills."

The patrol officer in the bedroom looked at me and asked, "Are you talking to me?"

"No, I'm just talking to myself." I answered before turning back to the matter at hand. "But, then, she would have to time the placing of the bag over her head just right to pass out before her will to survive kicked in and she tore off the bag."

Investigators discuss crime scenes with each other to figure out exactly what happened, and several different theories will be discussed before a conclusion is reached. Investigators will usually agree after all is said and done, but their opinions do differ from time to time. An autopsy or toxicology screen is sometimes needed to determine the true cause of death.

Another patrol officer and I, along with my supervisor, were all looking at the scene and discussing how this woman managed to take her own life. After I had taken my photographs and recorded a video of the scene, we waited for the Department of Forensic Sciences to arrive to take their photos before the victim is removed from the scene.

I carefully peeled off the duct tape from the plastic around her neck, and as I was removing the tape I could tell that there was something else inside the bag, a can of bug spray. It appeared that she had taped the bug spray in the plastic bag and sprayed it to poison herself as she suffocated.

A combination of pills, bug spray and the bag over her head finally killed her. I have never heard of anyone doing this. I could not even begin to tell you if she felt any pain, but I have thought about her from time to time. I don't think I'll ever understand the reason people kill themselves because I guess I've never hurt so bad or been in so much pain physically or emotionally to consider it. As far as I'm concerned, there's always a better way to deal with whatever is causing thoughts of self-destruction. I wish she could have talked to someone and received some help.

I do know that other people hurt whenever someone dies. The family and friends who survive the victim often ask if there is anything they could have done to prevent it. What's sad is that when I worked a suicide and heard a person in the other room say, "I should have known something was wrong, I wish they would have talked to me. I had no idea. It's all my fault!"

February 10, 1993 – Newspaper article of the shooting of Lt. Jeff Grimsley. Investigator J. R. Ward and I look for casings from shots fired at Lt. Grimsley's patrol vehicle by police after it was stolen by the suspect. J.R. Ward would be shot and killed in the line of duty on October 3, 1994 (Courtesy of Montgomery Advertiser)

Man drags, robs deputy U.S. marshal

■ Ordeal: The robber overpowered Pam Harding and pushed her to the ground, a police spokesman said

By Carla Crowder
ADVERTISER STAFF WRITER

A deputy U.S. marshal was dragged to the ground and robbed Wednesday when a man grabbed her briefcase outside the Federal Courthouse in downtown Montgomery.

The robber made off with the agent's handgun, several rounds of ammunition and her credentials during the 2 p.m. attack.

The victim, Deputy U.S. Marshal Pam Harding, was getting out of her car in a side parking lot of the Federal Courthouse on Lee Street when the man snatched her bag, a satchel-type briefcase, said U.S. Marshal Walter Bamberg.

The robber overpowered her and pushed her to the ground, said Capt. Wyatt Gantt, a Montgomery police spokesman.

"She's got abrasions on her hands and feet from the fall," he said.

She chased him on foot until she lost him, Marshal Bamberg said.

Dozens of Montgomery police and six to eight deputy marshals, converged on the area off Clayton and Goldthwaite streets and searched for suspects into the evening.

ANDY HAILS
Police Cpl. S.Z. Smith recovers Deputy U.S. Marshal Pam Harding's belongings from a lot on Holcombe Street.

there on Holcombe Street. Detectives collected the items in evidence bags.

Magazine carriers, all empty, also were found in the woods.

"The fact that he acquired federal credentials and a weapon makes the robbery a federal offense," Marshal Bamberg said. "It would be an assault on a federal agent."

The deputy marshal got a good look at the man as he grabbed her bag. Also, police are questioning a witness who knows the suspect, Capt. Gantt said.

> *"The fact that he acquired federal credentials and a weapon makes the robbery a federal offense."*
>
> **— Walter Bamberg**
> U.S. MARSHAL

August 12, 1993 – Newspaper article of the robbery of U.S. Marshall Pam Harding

MARK MILLER/STAFF

Montgomery police videotape the scene Wednesday night on Mount Vernon Road. ▮▮▮▮▮▮▮▮▮▮▮▮▮▮▮ **had lived there since 1946, and a couple of break-ins weren't going to drive the 85-year-old landlord away.**

February 4, 1994 – Newspaper article of homicide on Mount Vernon Road. Cpl Rick Huett and I video scene. (Courtesy of Montgomery Advertiser)

THE LOSS OF A FELLOW OFFICER

MONDAY, OCTOBER 3, **1994,** WAS cool and overcast. An intermittent sprinkling of rain kept the air damp and the mood dreary. It was one of those days that begged you to stay inside. I was working as a first shift Evidence Technician and had just finished photographing the retirement tea of Corporal Frank Michaud at police headquarters. One of our many duties, along with working crime scenes, was to photograph retirements, promotions and academy graduations. We served as staff photographers for the department. After leaving the retirement tea I stopped at Wendy's and brought my lunch back to the office. I did not want to be out in the weather anymore than I had to.

After lunch, I began to search an old jail inmate registry I had gotten from upstairs in the old jail, which had been largely abandoned after the new jail opened and had slowly evolved into a storage area for old records. I was searching for the country singer Hank Williams' name. Williams had grown up in Montgomery during the 1930's and 1940's and had been arrested a couple of times before he became a star.

Danny Smith, the latent fingerprint examiner, and I were trying to find a photograph or booking number to coincide with some old negatives that had been found recently in the basement. While exploring the dirt-floor basement, another evidence technician and I had discovered several file cabinets of crime scene evidence and mug shot negatives. Along with old equipment and the file cabinets, we also found an old wooden box painted red. Written in large white letters on the side of the box was the word *Explosives*. We had an explosives officer remove it before we did anymore exploring.

Just after 1 p.m., as I was reading through the book of handwritten entries, I heard a Code 3 (robbery call) go out over the radio. Two black males armed with a pistol had just robbed the Riverside Food and Meat Mart on Bell Street and were last seen running from the rear of the store. Patrol units were en-route and I got up and headed toward the door. I had hoped for a slow day that would keep me in the office, but I was the only Evidence Technician working day shift so I knew I had to go. Corporal Rick Huett, the senior Evidence Technician, had taken off that day.

"I'm headed to the Code 3. We can look for ole' Hank later," I told Danny as I walked out.

As I turned onto Columbus Street from North Ripley Street I heard Unit 131, Sergeant J.R. Ward of First Shift Patrol, on the radio advising that he had two subjects fitting the description of the suspects running down Greyhound Street toward the railroad tracks.

Greyhound Street is located some distance away from the business beyond a broad expanse of several sets of parallel railroad tracks. He added to the description that one subject was wearing blue pants and a white shirt and that the second subject was wearing a black shirt and white pants. I continued down Columbus Street behind the Civic Center and turned onto Bell Street. As I crossed the bridge over Interstate 85, Sgt. Ward called in again in a panicked voice, "131, I've been *shot!*"

A mixture of emotions jolted through me. I was suddenly overwhelmed with both concern and horror. *This can't be happening,* I thought to myself. I immediately turned left off Bell Street onto Oak Street and stopped at a small turn-off spot where I could see the railroad tracks. I looked for the suspects for what seemed about a minute but didn't see anyone. A Montgomery County Sheriff's unit pulled up and asked what was going on. He told me that he'd seen all the black-and-whites running full emergency. I explained quickly that an officer had been shot and that the suspects were last seen on the railroad tracks. He told me he would relay that information to the county dispatcher and that the Sheriff's deputies in the area would assist anyway they could.

I drove to the dead end of Greyhound Street and got out on foot with Corporal Mike Bush of the Accident Investigation Unit, who was already there. I advised the dispatcher of my location and told her that Corporal Bush and I would be in the area searching for the suspects. Mike and I walked down the embankment and waded through high weeds toward the tracks. Once on the tracks we could see several hundred yards in both directions.

I observed a black male walking toward us about 200 yards away, coming out from behind a parked railroad car. The suspect was wearing long, dark-colored pants and carrying what looked to be a white T-shirt in his left hand. I grabbed for my radio to notify the dispatcher and realized that in my haste of exiting the car, I must have dropped it.

"I've lost my radio," I said.

"Then don't leave my side," Mike ordered. Another officer later located the radio on the ground where I had dropped it next to my car.

The suspect looked in our direction and then began to walk away, crossing over several sets of railroad tracks. Once he stepped onto the middle set of tracks, the same set we were walking on, he took off running. I drew my weapon from my holster and pointed it at him and said, "Let's shoot him!"

Without hesitation, Mike said, "Okay!"

I knew that a 200-yard shot was nearly impossible with the handgun I carried, but a fellow officer had been shot, my emotions were running high, and I was *not* going to let this suspect get away. I figured I could shoot toward him and watch where the bullets hit the gravel then continue shooting and walk the rounds up until I hit him. As I started to pull the trigger, something made me pause. "Hold it," I said calmly. "J.R. said there were two suspects. This guy might not be the shooter."

We holstered our weapons and took off running on the uneven rocks of the railroad tracks after the suspect. We ran for a couple of hundred yards then lost sight of him. Once we got to the last location we'd seen him, we began searching the wooded area near the Boy's Club on Crenshaw Street to see if he was possibly lying down in the weeds. We walked down May Street and then began to backtrack on the railroad tracks, still searching the wooded area. Mike and I had split up about ten yards apart but remained within sight of each other. He had turned down his radio and we got very quiet to see if we could hear him moving in the weeds.

While Mike's radio was turned down during our search, the dispatcher began calling me. With the volume down, neither Mike nor I ever heard her call. After several attempts to raise me, other units in the area became concerned that I, too, may have become another victim of the shooter.

Suddenly, I heard movement in the thick under brush and I pointed my weapon in the direction of the sound and heard a familiar voice calling my name. "Steve! They're trying to raise you on the radio!" Lieutenant Frank Mitchell, who had been one of my instructors at the police academy, emerged from the woods and said, "They have been trying to raise you for about five minutes."

"I lost my radio somewhere. Let me see yours."

I called in to dispatch and was advised by Lieutenant Gene Miller, the Evidence Technician supervisor, to be en-route to 431 Loring Street, the scene of the shooting. I had to run back to my car that was now about a mile away and then go to the office to get the video camera. I arrived at the crime scene at 1:57 p.m.

I had to park several car lengths away on the very narrow street. As I walked up with my 35mm camera toward the scene, Lieutenant Miller met me halfway. "How is J.R. doing, Lieutenant?" I asked.

He had a sickened look on his face and said in a quiet voice, "He's dead."

"He can't be! He called in that he had been shot. He can't be dead!" I answered in complete disbelief.

The entire time I was searching for the suspect, I just somehow convinced myself that J.R. had only been wounded. For some reason I assumed he had been shot in the leg and that he would be okay. I have no idea why I thought this, because nothing was said on the radio about it. The human mind does some strange things and we don't always know why we think the things we do.

I think that it may have been the Lord's will that I lost my radio, because if I had known that while chasing the suspect J.R. had been killed, I may have started shooting at the suspect who, in fact, turned out later to be the accomplice and not the actual shooter.

I stood there for several moments and just stared at the scene in front of me. When Lieutenant Miller walked away, I became very emotional to the point that I wanted to cry. I had known J.R. for several years and we had even been partnered together on third shift patrol a couple of times. Now I had to work his murder scene. Police officers from the same department should never have to work the murder of fellow officers, especially fellow officers who are friends.

"No!" I said softly to myself. "You can't break down now. You've got to work this scene and figure out who did this. You can cry later. "Lord, give me the strength to work this case and to do my very best," I prayed. "Give me the wisdom and knowledge that I need to do the job. Lord, make me strong."

I felt strength and peace come over me and the emotions went away, and I was focused and began to take photos of the scene. Major Vic Hicks, the commander of the Investigative Division, told me to hold off on the photos for just a minute until an ABI (Alabama Bureau of Investigation) investigator arrived.

"Did J.R. shoot the guy?" I asked eagerly, hoping on some level that J.R. had at least wounded his killer and involved the ABI.

"We don't know, but he did get off some rounds," Major Hicks said.

In any police shooting it is standard procedure that if an officer is involved in a shooting and a civilian is shot; the ABI will work the case to minimize any prejudice that might favor a fellow officer within the same department. When officers fire their weapons but no one is hit, the police department will then work the investigation. In this particular case, we weren't sure if the suspect had been hit or not.

At first, I was told that an ABI investigator would work the case and that I would assist. But before we could start working the scene, Major Hicks had another meeting with the ABI supervisors. They concluded I would work the scene and that the ABI investigator would assist me. I think the reason they decided to defer to me was that I had more experience working murder scenes than the ABI investigator on the scene. In my opinion, Rick Huett of our department would have been the better Evidence Tech to work the case. He was more experienced than me by two years. But he was off that day, so the duty fell on me. This was the toughest case that I would ever have to work as an Evidence Tech.

While I was working the scene on Loring Street, the suspect Mike and I had chased on the tracks was captured nearby in the Riverside Heights housing project on Bell Street. The shooter was still at large.

We determined that J.R. had fired six rounds from his Beretta 9mm pistol, but we weren't able to determine if any of the rounds had struck the shooter. I took a number of photos of the crime scene and then shot several minutes of video. Photos and a video were always made at murder scenes. I then collected all the evidence we could locate. After processing the scene on Loring Street, I came to the conclusion that J.R. had been ambushed. J.R.'s black-and-white patrol vehicle was parked on the left side of the narrow street, and I believe that after briefly spotting the robbery suspect, he got out of his car and walked in front of it to look across a vacant lot toward Greyhound Street. Two other vehicles were parked on the right side of the street just behind his vehicle.

I believe the suspect was hiding between the parked cars, and when J.R. walked into the open in front of his vehicle the suspect opened fire on him. From the angle of where the projectile went into his lower left side, I think the suspect fired the first shot and missed with that projectile embedding itself between the storm door and wood door of 431 Loring Street. J.R. then instinctively bent forward and down in a defensive posture to return fire on the suspect, but a second round from the shooter struck him in the side of his chest just below his left arm. There is a narrow gap between the front and rear Kevlar panels of his body armor at that point that allowed the bullet to penetrate his torso and lodge in his heart.

J.R. died almost instantly, but it must have been the adrenaline that enabled him to fire off those six rounds and to make that last frantic call for help on the radio. The medical examiner said later that if J.R. had been on the operating table when he had been shot that he still could not have been saved.

As much as I wanted to be looking for the second suspect, I had a job to do. Several law enforcement agencies were looking for the suspect and I knew that my job was just as important as theirs.

After working the scene on Loring Street I went to the Riverside Food and Meat Mart on Bell Street and began to process the scene of the robbery. After photographing the scene and dusting for fingerprints there, I went back to the office and processed the evidence from Loring Street. J.R.'s gun was on half–cock, and we wondered if maybe he and the shooter might have fought over the weapon before he was killed. Joe Saloom, the ballistics expert with the Alabama Department of Forensic Sciences, was on a duck-hunting trip in the northeast and was snowed in. Normally I would have taken the weapon to him to be examined, but since he was unavailable I called the ballistic expert at the Birmingham office.

I processed J.R.'s pistol, radio, gun belt, the money tray from the store's cash register, and six cans of beer from the business, all possibly touched by the suspects. I prepared the pistol, the fired shell casings and the recovered projectiles to be sent to Birmingham office of the Alabama Department of Forensic Sciences. Rick Huett would be in the next morning and would personally drive them there.

After doing all that I could do with the evidence, I went to the Detective office at 10 o'clock that night to assist in picking up any suspects. As I was walking by one of the offices, I saw a black male wearing jail clothes sitting in a chair next to the door. I looked at him and asked, "Aren't you the one I was chasin' on the railroad tracks today?"

"Yes, sir, that was me," he said without hesitation.

Immediately, Lieutenant D.T. Marshall, the commander of the Robbery-Homicide Bureau, pointed at the suspect then looked at one of the investigators and said, "Get him into an interview room and get his statement."

He then looked at me and said, "I need a statement from you about what *he* just said."

I found out later that when the suspect was brought in he had denied being on the tracks and being chased by the police. Apparently, he'd been caught off guard when I asked him. He answered without thinking and unintentionally told the truth.

Later on that night I went out with several other investigators and we searched various drug houses and followed up on tips that had been called in about the murder. I was out until the wee hours of the morning. Nancy, my wife, had heard about the shooting on the news and knew that I would be late getting in, if I even came home at all.

On Tuesday, October 4th, Rick Huett signed for and transported J.R.'s weapon and the other evidence to the Forensics office in Birmingham. I processed J.R.'s patrol vehicle for fingerprints. We were hoping that maybe the suspect might have touched it.

From the intense investigation that followed and the tips that citizens had called in, we identified Willie Arthur Stallworth as the prime suspect. The Violent Crimes Task Force and MPD investigators captured him later that day. I went to Lowndes County with the Violent Crimes Task Force and collected evidence from a house owned by Stallworth's brother.

Louis Lattimore was identified as the suspect whom Mike Bush and I had chased on the railroad tracks that fateful afternoon. I was sore for several days after that foot chase across the railroad tracks.

On Wednesday, October 5th, I went to Stallworth's house on Dallas Drive in Montgomery on a search warrant and took photographs inside the house. Later that day I went with investigators to Riverside Food and Meat Mart and videotaped Louis Lattimore showing us how he left the store after the robbery and the route he took toward Greyhound Street.

That evening, I went to White Chapel Funeral Home to the viewing of J.R.'s body. The line of visitors stretched out and around the building. I waited in line two hours to see him. The casket was closed with two police officers in dress blues standing rigidly at parade rest at either end of it.

On Thursday, October 6th, I went into work at noon to help video the funeral and the procession from the Church of the Ascension to Greenwood Cemetery. All of the evidence techs shot video or took photographs at the funeral. WCOV television in Montgomery, which aired a local police ride-along television show called "MPD," based on the syndicated "COPS" television series, wanted to put together a video for their show and for the Ward family. They needed some help with footage, so I videotaped the officers carrying J.R.'s casket into the church. I also shot video of the officers from various departments standing outside the church, along with the large turnout from the Montgomery Fire Department.

I left the church and headed toward Greenwood Cemetery to videotape the procession traveling down Highland Avenue and entering the gates of the cemetery. While driving past Highland Avenue Elementary, I saw school children lining the street with posters, and practicing holding their hands over their hearts to express their respect for the fallen officer. I began to tear up and felt like I had a lump in my throat the size of a grapefruit. I had never seen such respect displayed by children, and I was deeply moved. As I continued down Highland Avenue, I saw other people standing on the side of the road, also waiting to show their respect.

I parked my car out of sight just inside the gates and set up my personal video camera on a tripod. I wanted to have a long still shot of the procession coming down the street and entering the cemetery gates. I held one of the evidence tech's cameras and shot the sides of the police vehicles showing the numerous departments. I needed to make sure I got this shot right. After the procession stopped at the graveside and all the vehicles had either entered the gate or parked, I went to the backside of the cemetery off of Harrison Road. There were so many cars parked there I had to stand on the trunk of a patrol car to shoot video of the 21-gun salute.

The producer of "MPD" did a fantastic job with the editing together the tribute and used a lot of the video I shot in the episode. The only file footage WCOV had of J.R. from the "MPD" show was an investigation taped years earlier of a dead body found at a drained pond used by Jenkins Brick Company on North McDonough Street. J.R. was shown attempting to step into the mud to help load the body on the backboard, sinking into the mud. Later, the tape showed him taking his muddy shoes and socks off. During the video there was no dialogue, but J.R. was laughing. I was the Evidence Tech on the scene that day when it was taped and could be heard off camera humming stripper music while J.R. pulled off his muddy socks. The producer included it in the montage.

Garth Brooks' song, "The Dance" was played over the entire video when it was shown. To this day, it is hard to hear that song without becoming emotional with memories from that week.

By Thursday evening, the week's events had taken their toll on me both physically and emotionally. I was at home sitting on the edge of my bed changing clothes after working all day, and I was just plain tired. I had taken my gun belt off and turned off my radio when I leaned forward with my head in my hands. Nancy had not gotten home yet and I was just sitting there, not really thinking about anything. I sat there for less than a minute when the telephone rang. It was one my closest friends, Eddy Luckie.

"Hey. How are you doin'?" he asked.

"Oh, okay, I guess." I answered quietly.

"I just called to see how you were doin'. I know you've had a tough week and wanted to see how you were holdin' up."

"It's been a tough week, as you can imagine, but I am doin' okay." I answered.

"Several people asked about you last night at church. Several said when I talked to you to let you know that they were praying for you."

"Thanks man, I really appreciate it. It means a lot to know that y'all are thinking about me. I really appreciate the prayers. It has been a really tough week."

"I don't really know what we can do for you but if you need something just let me know." Eddy said.

"Pray for J.R.'s family and all the other officers at the P.D. It's been very tough for all of us."

"Okay, I guess we can do that," he said, in a tongue-in-cheek tone. "I'll talk at cha' later."

I don't know if it was the fact that all these people were praying for me, or the emotion of working a police officer's murder and then attending the funeral, or a combination of it all, but it was at that point it all came to a head. I began to cry. I guess it all built up inside me and I had asked the Lord to give me the strength to work the case and that I could cry later. I guess this was later.

It felt good to release all the emotional stress, and after about five minutes I was feeling much better. I felt a heavy burden lift from my shoulders. By the time Nancy got home she was not aware that anything had happened. This was only one of two times that I cried after the death of an officer.

On Tuesday, October 11th, I met with investigators with the Violent Crimes Task Force to collect some projectiles from 420 Loring Street. This house was caddy-corner across the street from the crime scene in front of 431 Loring Street, and these projectiles were thought to be the missing 9mm rounds from J.R.'s weapon.

I returned to the scene on Loring Street on October 20th, at around 5:50 p.m. to perform trajectory tests with a laser light, assisting Joe Saloom from Forensic Sciences. We were trying to determine the shooter's exact position when he fired the fatal shot. Measurements of the height and distance of the shooter's stance were taken at the scene.

While there, Joe told me how bad he felt that he couldn't be there the day J.R. was killed to assist in the initial investigation.

***

On Monday, September 25th, 1995, the trial began in the murder of Sergeant J.R. Ward. The trial lasted several days, and I testified on two different days. During the trial, I had to show the jury the evidence collected during the investigation including J.R.'s pistol and uniform shirt. It was very difficult holding up his shirt with the nameplate still on it. Seeing the blood and bullet holes up close as I held it up to describe it to the jury brought back all the emotions of that day.

After testifying about his shirt and weapon, it was much easier to testify about the other evidence. I was on the stand for about two hours. Court recessed at 5:10 p.m. I was scheduled to continue as the first witness the next morning starting at 9:15 a.m.

The defense had all night to go over my testimony before they questioned me the next day. I never liked for the defense to have this much time to review my testimony. This gives them a chance to break it down, bit by bit, before questioning me again.

Tuesday morning, September 26th, 1995, I took the stand about 9:30. My testimony went well. At one point in the trial the defense attorney got confused about the difference between a casing and a copper jacket. After I corrected him he finally admitted that we were talking about two different things. My confidence took a boost. I had no other problems testifying.

I have testified many times in court but never on the murder of a police officer. I wanted to be sure that I did not mess up, so I put a lot of pressure on myself.

On October 3rd, 1995, exactly one year and a few hours after the death of Sergeant James Russell Ward, the jury found Willie Arthur Stallworth guilty of capital murder.

The death of a police officer is a difficult thing to deal with. Knowing the officer makes it even tougher, but working the case and dealing with the evidence takes it toll on fellow officers.

I knew J.R. from my early days of riding on third shift patrol. Later, he transferred to the Investigative Division (now called the Detective Division) and worked in the Robbery-Homicide Bureau before his promotion to sergeant. I worked many cases with J.R. after I became an Evidence Tech, and invariably I enjoyed our collaborations. He had a great sense of humor. He was married and had a young son, and his wife, Judy, was pregnant with their second child at the time of his death. Working J.R.'s murder was tough on all of us involved. I guess people deal with the loss of a co-worker and a friend in different ways. I can only speak of how I dealt with it.

There is a poem I carry in my wallet called "Footprints in the Sand." It states that when life is going well there are two sets of footprints in the sand. This is when God is walking beside you. When times are tough, there is only one set of footprints in the sand. This is when God is carrying you. There have been several times in my career that God has had to carry me, and this was one of them.

I guess most people think that police officers investigate so many cases it doesn't affect them, and there is some truth to that. But there are a few cases that do cause us to lose sleep. With me it's the crimes against the truly innocent, children and the elderly, or those who cannot defend themselves that seem to affect me most. Then there are crimes against police officers, the very people who take the oath to defend and protect the innocent. They are taken from us and we not only have to deal with their death, but we have to keep our emotions in check as we gather evidence against those responsible. We have to make sure that we don't violate the suspect's rights while helping each other deal with the loss of a fellow officer.

PATRICIA MIKLIK/STAFF

Investigators look for clues in the trunk of the Chrysler where ▮▮▮▮▮▮▮▮▮▮▮ was found Wednesday night.

July 15, 1994 – Newspaper article of homicide (victim in trunk) in K-Mart parking lot. Sgt. H. D. Kenney, Inv S Cowart and me. (Courtesy of Montgomery Advertiser)

Body Part

THERE ARE STRANGE CALLS AND then there are *strange* calls. I was working as a second shift Evidence Technician on Saturday, December 24, 1994, with Officer Steve Campbell, who had recently transferred to the Evidence Technician section from the patrol division. I was still training Steve, a retired army drill sergeant starting his second career in law enforcement as many retired soldiers do. He'd been with our department for about two years.

You'd think that at Christmas time most people would settle for a little peace on Earth and goodwill toward men, but for several Christmases prior to this one, there had been a murder in Montgomery either on Christmas Eve or Christmas Day. We were just trying to be prepared. We had already filled out our overtime sheets and left blanks for the victim's name, time of offense and the address of the crime scene. The night was busy for our patrol units, and we'd already responded to one armed robbery at the Pace Car on the corner of South Perry Street and Arba Street.

Around 7:30 that evening, the dispatcher sent Unit 202 on a very strange call. They were dispatched to St. John Street to investigate a possible assault, but the dispatcher added that the complainant had located what was possibly an amputated body part.

Listening to the radio traffic and patrolling near that location, I paused when I heard that. "Did I hear that right, a cut off body part?" I asked Steve in disbelief. I was expecting to hear calls about someone shot or stabbed possibly leading to the homicide we all expected, but amputations are quite rare. Our curiosity got the better of us, so we notified the dispatcher we were close by and would respond to the call with the marked unit. We actually arrived first, so in the absence of any need for a back-up unit, we decided to handle the call ourselves and cancelled the other unit.

We knocked on the door, and a lady invited us in, telling us that she only called the police because she really didn't know what to do. "Follow me into the kitchen," she said, waving us in that direction.

We walked into the kitchen and introduced ourselves to a gentleman standing by the sink. He had a smirk on his face as we walked in.

"How are you doing?" I asked him.

He got a smile just short of laughter and said, "Oh, *I'm* doin' fine, but *somebody's* not doin' so good." He looked at the woman and said, "This is your house, you tell 'em."

"I don't know exactly how to tell you, or what to say," she said. It was obvious that something was making her very uncomfortable.

"Well, *somebody's* got to tell us something," I said, getting right to the point. "We got a call about a cut off body part. So, where's the body part?"

The woman silently pointed toward the sink, so I walked over and looked in. Lying next to the drain was a round flesh-colored object roughly the diameter and texture of a large butter bean. It had a small closed hole on one side. I stepped aside so Steve could see the mystery item. "What is it?" I asked the man.

"You tell me," he said. The amused grin never left his face.

"Well, I know what it *looks* like," I said.

"I know what it looks like too. But is it or isn't it?" he asked.

I looked at Steve. "I know what it looks like too," he said.

"Is anyone in the house missing *that* end of their body part?" I asked, choosing my words carefully, being considerate of the lady in the room. Steve was grinning at me as he watched me being polite with my words.

"I got mine, and as far as I know, everyone here—who's supposed to have one—has one. No one has complained about missing one yet," the man said, trying not to laugh.

I put on a pair of rubber gloves and picked up the mysterious organ and examined it. It had an opening on one side, and a piece of skin between a second opening. "What have you been cutting up in the sink?" I asked the woman.

"I cut up a turkey for Christmas dinner earlier this evening," she replied.

"I think it might be some type of organ from the turkey. We'll take it with us and run it by the twenty-four hour emergency animal clinic and have the vet on call examine it. I don't think it's human. I think if it were human the owner would have complained by now that it was missing," I assured them.

"I think if someone were missing *that*, we'd have already heard about it by now," Steve added.

"Well, we didn't know what to do, so we decided if anybody would know, the police would know, or at least what to do with it," he said.

"It's smart to call the police when you don't know what to do in a case like this. That's what we're here for," Steve told the woman.

I asked for a zip-lock bag and placed the mystery organ in the bag and left. We took it to the twenty-four hour emergency animal clinic on Spruce Curve and showed it to Dr. Matthews, who immediately identified it as a turkey heart. He showed me the three ventricles that turkey hearts have. I told him about the call and what everyone at the house thought it was.

The doctor laughed. "You would think someone would have missed it, or at least said something," he said.

"That's what we said!" I added.

Well, the night ended without any homicides in the city for the first time in several years. We worked Christmas day and all was quiet that day as well. I began to think that maybe there was a little room for peace on earth and goodwill toward men. I worked several more Christmases as an Evidence Technician, but I'll never forget about the night Steve and I spent Christmas Eve examining the cut off body part.

It Doesn't Get Any Easier

S UNDAY, JANUARY **22, 1995,** STARTED out like any other day. It was warm and the temperature was headed up into the 70's. Not necessarily normal weather for January but in Alabama you just never know. I was working as an Evidence Technician on day shift.

Sundays are usually quiet, and I was able to get a lot of paperwork done that morning. I took my lunch break at 9 a.m. so I could teach my Sunday school class. I taught my class from 9:00 to 9:45 and always let the dispatcher know to page me if I was needed. The majority of my calls on Sundays were traffic accidents. I was on call for any accident involving a city vehicle, a serious injury, or a fatality, but I had an agreement with the accident investigators that they would not call me during my Sunday school class unless it was absolutely necessary.

Lieutenant Ed York, the accident investigation supervisor, had told me on several occasions that his units would take care of all the other details at an accident scene during my teaching time and would take their time with things until I got back on the air. The accident investigators working on Sundays respected the fact that I used my lunch hour to teach, and I greatly appreciated it.

After I finished teaching, I left the church headed north on Narrow Lane Road toward the office. The radio had been unusually quiet that morning, even for a Sunday, when suddenly I heard the dispatcher send the paramedics and an ambulance to Woodley Road and Aladena Drive on a Code 25 (traffic accident). I could tell by her tone that it was serious. She then sent an accident investigator on the call adding that the accident involved a motorcycle. With each transmission the stress in her voice grew more pronounced. I'd heard dispatchers express the same emotion in the past when an officer was in trouble. As I pulled up to the intersection of Narrow Lane Road and Woodley Road, the dispatcher called Sergeant Paul Walker, the supervisor of the motor units, on the radio. Paul and I graduated from the same police academy class in 1983.

Dispatcher: "93!"

Walker: "93."

Dispatcher: "Did you copy the accident involving the motorcycle?" She snapped with that same voice of concern.

Walker: "That's 10-4."

Dispatcher: "You did copy it involved a motorcycle?"

At this point I suspected the worst. One of our motor officers had been involved in a traffic accident. I could tell by her tone that the information she was getting from the complaint clerks was not good. I immediately turned right on Woodley Road and quickly headed south toward the accident scene.

After a pause of a couple of seconds, Sergeant Walker called back to the dispatcher.

Walker: "Is this 25 involving one of *our* motor units?"

Dispatcher: "That's 10-4!" she snapped back, in a tone suggesting that he should have understood what she was implying.

Sometimes emotions get the better of us and we don't always understand what the other person is trying to say. Whether it is an officer talking to the dispatcher or the dispatcher talking to the officer, emotions can sometimes interfere with the message. Dispatchers worry about the officers to whom they dispatch calls every day and take it personally when one of *their* units is in trouble. Looking back on the call, if the dispatcher had said, "Attention any units in the area of Woodley Road. We have a report of a motor man down at Woodley and Aladena." Then all units would have known exactly what was going on and would have responded. Dispatchers have a tough job and I am not criticizing how she put the call out. She heard that one of her officers was in an accident and let her emotions get the best of her.

I was the second unit to arrive on the scene. Corporal Gino Howton, a first shift patrolman, was already there and was visibly shaken. I saw Officer Willie Pryor lying motionless on his back adjacent to a white Nissan sitting at an odd angle in the middle of the intersection. An off-duty nurse and some other civilians were performing CPR on him. The driver's side of the Nissan was heavily damaged from the impact. The twisted wreckage of Pryor's motorcycle was sitting inverted on the side of the road on its handlebars with its wheels thrust forlornly into the air. A carpet of debris littered the roadway with small parts that had exploded from the bike on impact.

As I ran back toward the trunk of my car for my camera, I called for Investigator Huey Thornton, who was a new Evidence Technician, to come to the scene. He had heard the call and was already en route. I also advised the dispatcher to call Lieutenant Gene Miller, the Evidence Technician supervisor and advise him. I took several photos of the overall scene right away because I knew that in a matter of minutes the scene would be full of medical personnel and police officers.

Paul passed me running toward Pryor as I was running to the trunk of my car. After I took the first couple of photos, I waited on Investigator Thornton to arrive on the scene. Paul came up to me and was very upset. He did not usually show emotion and was always the one joking around, but this time he grabbed me by the shoulders with both hands and said, "You have to work this scene right. It's one of my guys!"

Holding my camera in my left hand, I grabbed Paul by his shoulder with my right hand and looked him square in his eyes, and said in a calm but firm voice, "Paul! Paul! I got it under control! I'll take care of him, and I'll do it right. Go to the hospital and meet the family and be there for your men." Continuing in a calming voice, I said, "Paul, I'll take care of him. I'll do it up right."

He seemed to calm down and looked relieved, and in a quiet voice said, "Thanks, Steve."

As paramedics and other officers began to arrive on the scene, I looked over the evidence to see exactly what I had. I didn't want a key piece of evidence destroyed during all the confusion. I called the dispatcher and asked if she had gotten in touch with Lieutenant Miller, but she hadn't. She stated one of the complaint clerks had spoken with his son and they said he was out of town, but should be on his way home by now. I advised her to page him periodically until he called, and then, have him call me on the radio.

Investigator Thornton arrived on the scene, and I told him that he was going to work this case. I explained that I had just worked the death of a police officer, Sergeant J.R. Ward who was killed just three months earlier. I was not up to working another one this soon. I told him that I would assist him in working the accident. By this time the road was completely blocked on both ends of the street and I knew we would be there for quite a while.

Officer Willie H. Pryor made the ultimate sacrifice that day. He was trying to catch up with a violator when the driver of another vehicle pulled out in front of him. The investigation later determined that Officer Pryor had been traveling south on Woodley Road in pursuit of a speeding van when the other vehicle pulled out from a stop sign on Aladena Road directly into his path. Pryor attempted to lay the motorcycle on its side and slide into the other vehicle, but the full force of the huge 1300cc Yamaha Venture at top speed slammed into the driver's side door of the other vehicle causing Pryor to be thrown in front of the car. The left front wheel of the car then rolled over his head, killing him instantly.

I did not know him very well except to speak in the hallway. He had been involved in a police shooting several years earlier, and I was the evidence technician who worked the case. Even though I did not know him very well, it always hurts to lose a fellow officer.

It's always hard when someone you know is killed in a traffic accident. It's even harder when you know that person *and* you have to work the accident. Taking photos at a traffic fatality where the victim is a friend or a coworker makes it even more difficult. You have to put aside your personal feelings and do the job. Some people will tell you, *it's your job to do that — it's what we pay you for.* It is true, that is one of the things we get paid to do. I've had to do it several times, and it doesn't get any easier.

I Had No Clue What I Was Doing

FEBRUARY 12, 1995, SEEMED AT first like any other Sunday with the exception that Nancy, my wife, was nine months pregnant with our first child. With each passing day I became more and more uneasy. We were having a little girl, and the baby's room was ready and waiting with freshly painted pink walls and pastel accents. We'd even worked out a code for my pager in case she went into labor and I wasn't near a phone. If Nancy went into labor, she was to call my pager and punch in the number 2229, which is the word "baby" spelled on the telephone keypad.

I left for work that morning and headed to the office. Sundays were usually quiet, and I looked forward to relaxing a little and getting some paperwork done. Being a police officer was all about making sure the paperwork is done. On television, officers do so much in a day, but you never see them do one bit of paperwork. It must be nice. In the real world, however, officers do lots and lots of paperwork. Investigators do even more.

Officer Steve Campbell and I were working together in the Evidence Technician section that day, and we liked our Sundays to be slow. About 8:30 that morning a patrol unit responded to a dead body call on Carey Drive. Steve and I monitored the radio traffic to see what kind of death it was in case we were needed. A patrol unit could handle a natural death with a simple report, but any death where foul play was suspected required that we respond. The more we listened to the radio traffic the more it sounded like it wasn't going to be natural. The patrol unit finally radioed that it was, in fact, a homicide.

"So much for a quiet Sunday," I said. "Let's head that way."

We arrived at the apartment and asked the patrol unit outside what they had.

"A dead woman and a *lot* of blood," the patrolman responded.

We walked to the top of the stairs to the apartment and opened the door. The floor was covered from one end to the other with dried blood. It looked like someone had painted the floor red.

We found out that the victim's mother had arrived earlier that morning with two bags of groceries and had walked in to discover her grandchildren sitting on the couch. The kids were about two and three years old. The twenty-four-year old mother of the two children had been beaten and stabbed to death, but not before putting up a horrific fight. There were bloody handprints on the windows where she had banged on the glass trying to attract the attention of her neighbors. Blood even stained the ceiling.

The victim lay dead in one of the bedrooms. This was the bloodiest crime scene I'd ever seen, and these two children had witnessed it all.

Life is so unfair sometimes.

I called Sergeant Kenney, the evidence technician supervisor, and told him what we had. Steve and I began processing the scene. Since Steve was new to the evidence technician section, he worked the scene while I supervised and assisted. He started with photographs, then videotaped the entire apartment. During the taping, Major Hicks and Captain Coker wanted to come in and look over the scene. I had to tell them to wait a few minutes until we were done. The major was okay with the delay, but the captain wasn't as patient. He did, however, wait until we were done. I went over the scene with both of them then got back to work.

That afternoon, Sergeant Kenney and Officer Booth James came to the scene to assist. Sergeant Kenney stayed for about an hour then left for a meeting at police headquarters in reference to the murder. We had no idea who had committed the murder, so it was being worked as a "whodunit."

About six that evening Sergeant Kenney called me on the radio and had me switch to channel three, the unit-to-unit channel used by officers to exchange information.

"Four-ten to four-seventy-three," he called.

"Four-seventy-three is on. Go ahead," I replied.

"You need to be en route to your house. Your wife has gone into labor. You need to go home."

"TEN-FOUR! Guys, I gotta go," I shouted. "My wife's havin' a baby!"

I hurried to the front door trying to peel off the white Tyvek suit I was wearing over my clothing to prevent any evidence transfer. I was having a hard time getting out of the suit. Corporal Andy Brasington and his partner Officer Mark Fox were standing at the front door handling security of the scene. When I told them I had to go because my wife had gone into labor they both grabbed the back of the suit and ripped it down to the floor in one quick swoop.

I stepped out of the legs and hollered at the guys inside. "Take care of my stuff! I'll get it later!" I said. "I'm outta here!"

On the way home I called Nancy to see how she was doing. She said she was doing okay and that Sandra, her brother's wife, was with her. I told her that I was nasty from all the black fingerprint powder and I would have to take a shower. She said Sandra would drive her to the hospital and that I would meet her there.

I flew into the house, stripping off my dirty clothes as I ran, and jumped into the shower. I soaped up as quickly as I could. Wet black powder ended up all over the walls of the shower. I got dressed and headed to Baptist Medical Center.

I parked and went into the hospital quickly. I didn't run because I did not want to look like one of those out of control expectant fathers. I went to the third floor and found out what room Nancy was in. She was hooked up to all kinds of monitors. We stayed there until a little after nine. The doctor said it was false labor and she wouldn't be having a baby that night, so we went home.

I took a personal day Monday to be with Nancy. She had Braxton-Hicks, or false labor, contractions all day. The doctor had given her a stopwatch to wear around her neck to time them. My mom came down from Birmingham that afternoon to stay with us. She'd already made plans to stay with Nancy for a week when the baby was born and was keeping her calendar open around Nancy's due date of February 16th.

Tuesday February 14th, we got up about seven that morning. I hadn't slept much that night anxiously waiting to see if Nancy was going into labor. Nancy slept well, much better than I would have expected. The doctor had us come in at nine and she was put in a room. We got the last room on the delivery floor.

My mom drove herself to the hospital later on that morning. Nancy was in labor all day. My mom was amazed how well the epidural worked. After each contraction she'd say, "*Wooo*, that was a big one! Did you see that one!" pointing at the monitor as the line on the screen rose in response to the tension compressing her uterus, which, thanks to the anesthesia, Nancy couldn't feel.

"Unbelievable!" my mom told me in disbelief. "I was in labor with you for thirty-six hours and Nancy didn't even mess up her hair."

Stacy Reneé Smith was born at 4:10 p.m. and weighed seven pounds and eight ounces. She was 19 inches long. I didn't know at the time but my mom and my in-laws, Graham and Erlene Mullins, were listening at the door to hear when the baby arrived. My mom was hoping for a granddaughter and even though we had been told it was a girl she still wanted to make sure.

She grew up with four brothers and had three sons, so she didn't want to get her hopes up.

As she listened, the first thing she heard me say was, "Hello, little baby." Not "Hello, little girl." She didn't know for sure she had a new granddaughter until they were all allowed into the room.

I'd never held a baby before, so when I held Stacy for the first time I told her, "I was saving myself for you."

My dad was speaking at a seminar in Birmingham and had told everyone that when his grandbaby was born that he would have to leave. My mom called him and he was already on his way. She'd been giving him updates all day. He called around five and wanted us to wait before Stacy was taken to the nursery.

He wanted to hold his grandbaby.

We all took turns holding her as family and friends began to trickle in. Dad called at 5:45 and said he was at Carter Hill Road and Narrow Lane Road. A few minutes later he called and said he was in the parking lot. I was sitting in the glider of the room when I saw him round the corner.

He was grinning from ear to ear and walked straight to me with his arms out. "Let me hold my grandbaby," he said.

He was a very proud granddad.

Lieutenant Gene Miller, the evidence technician supervisor, came by with his wife. He told me that I had forgotten to call in on a sick day. It completely slipped my mind. Later on that night, after everyone was gone, Steve Campbell came by. He worked security in the emergency room and had slipped away for a minute.

Nine babies were born at the hospital that day, February 14th, Valentine's Day. Some were intentionally induced so they would be born on Valentine's Day, and some, like Stacy, came on their own. Our youth minister, Mike Anderson, and his wife had their fifth child. She was born several rooms down from us. What are the odds that the youth minister and one of the youth Sunday School teacher's wives would deliver babies on the same day and in the same hospital?

The next day, my mom asked me what I got Nancy for Valentine's Day.

"A new baby! You were there!" I responded.

"No," she quickly replied, with a smile and a chuckle. "She got *you* a new baby!"

"Well, to be honest, I really didn't think about it, with everything going on and all."

"You might want to get her some flowers to let her know you did not forget," she said.

"Valentine's Day has already passed," I said without thinking. "It's too late to get her something now."

"Boy! Don't make me whoop you!" she said with a grin. "Go get her some flowers!"

With all that was going on I guess I should have thought of that, but this was our first baby and I just flat out forgot. I went to the nearest florist and told the young lady I needed some roses for Valentine's Day.

She looked at me somewhat stunned and said, "Valentine's Day was yesterday."

"Yes, I know. She had a baby yesterday and I was a little busy and missed getting her flowers, so I thought I would get her some now."

"Oh, I see. Well, congratulations," she said with a smile. "How many would you like?"

"A dozen big ones will work."

I had to run some errands, so I had them delivered to surprise her. My mom told me later that she had answered the door when the flowers came. Nancy cried when she saw them.

Everyone who came by to visit us thought it was great that I remembered. I thought to myself, *What a wonderful husband I am*, and I never told them any different.

The murder of the young mother was later solved, and the suspect who brutally murdered her was arrested.

I took two weeks off to begin learning how to be a father. We received lots of visitors from work and church. It was exciting being a new dad, but I had no clue what I was doing.

January 16, 1996 – Evidence Technicians with Stacy at two years old, (l to r) Sgt H. D. "Howie Dave" Kenney, Cpl Steve Campbell, Inv Huey Thornton

LIFE IS JUST TOO SHORT

SUICIDE IS HARD TO UNDERSTAND. I find it hard to believe that life could be so bad that killing yourself is the only way to solve your problems. I'm not saying I'm better than someone who makes that choice, but the Lord has blessed me such that I've never had to contemplate that option. When you think about it, suicide doesn't just affect the person who ends their life, but everyone connected to him or her as well. Parents, spouses, family, friends and co-workers, it hits them hard. The most vulnerable are the children, especially the little ones.

Tuesday, May 9, 1995, I was working as a second shift Evidence Technician. Around 8:30 that evening I heard a patrol unit on the radio responding to a report of someone shot at an address in the Cloverdale Park community. The person who called the police reported that it appeared to be a suicide. A few minutes later the responding unit confirmed that the victim was dead, so I headed that way.

When I arrived, several patrol officers had the scene secured and investigators were inside the house taking notes. I walked to the front door with my Pentax 35mm camera in hand and gave my name and unit number to the rookie officer keeping the crime scene log.

I approached the investigator in charge. "What have we got?" I asked him.

"Female," he replied flatly. "Shot one time in the head with a twenty-two caliber pistol." He paused long enough to allow me to infer the obvious. "Self-inflicted."

I followed him to the back bedroom where a young woman lay dead. She lay restfully on her side wearing a simple white blouse and a black skirt. She was facing away from me toward the far wall, but I could see the small wound on her right temple—a small blister of blood. Oddly there was no tell-tale trickle of blood from the wound and no other blood anywhere near the body other than a small bloody cloth that lay on the bed near her head. A small revolver lay near her right hand, dropped by a hand that was dead before she fell.

I began to take photographs of the scene. "Who found her?" I asked the investigator.

"Her son found her first," he replied. "Her *three-year-old* son." As I was about to take another photo the investigator continued, "When patrol units arrived, her son was wiping the blood from his mother's face and head with that wet wash cloth."

I paused and slowly lowered my camera as I looked at her lying on the bed. I pictured the little boy there, scared and confused, probably thinking... *hoping* that she was just only asleep as he gently wiped the blood from his mother's face.

"Oh, man," I said quietly. "That's just terrible for a child to have to go through that." I then thought of Stacy, my own daughter just shy of three months old. How terrible it would be for her if she were one day put in the same situation.

I finished working the scene and collected all the evidence. I couldn't get that mental picture of the little boy out of my mind. I can only hope that as the little boy got older, he would somehow forget the terrible way his mother died.

I've worked many suicides and have seen the emotional devastation it takes on those left behind, but for a young child to go through that was just too much for me to comprehend. I hope that if anyone, particularly a young mother, ever reached a low spot in her life, so low that she would even think about suicide, she would think about the lives of her children and reach out to someone for help.

This was one of those calls that deeply affected my life. I have thought about that little boy many times over the years and it saddens me. Not so much that he had to experience what he did, because hopefully he won't remember it, but for what she put him through. Life is just too short.

Cpl. S.Z. Smith, a Montgomery Police Department accident investigator, photographs a Ford Maverick that was involved Wednesday in a four-car accident on the Birmingham Highway near Hunter Loop Road.

June 15, 1995 – Newspaper photo of traffic accident on Birmingham Hwy. Sgt H. D. Kenney, me, and Accident Investigator (Courtesy of Montgomery Advertiser)

UNDERCOVER

A S A MEMBER OF THE R.O.T. (Retake our Turf) Team, our main duty was to target street level drug dealers and arrest them. We would receive information from concerned citizens who called into the secret witness line or from other officers who received reliable information about the street dealers in their districts.

Drug dealers are creatures of habit and will sell where they can make the most money but at the same time evade or elude the police. Once the police become wise to the tactics of the dealers, the dealers adapt to those changes. We then have to change our own tactics in a never-ending game of cat-and-mouse.

On Thursday, June 22, 1995, I was working the R.O.T. overtime detail on my off day from 7 p.m. until 2 a.m. That night we decided to try something new to see if we could lure the dealers to us. Our normal routine was to sneak up on them in the dark wearing blacked-out uniforms in an unmarked truck painted flat black to blend in with the darkness. We figured, though, that if we could lure them to us it would save us a lot of running. Our tactic on this particular night was to attempt to buy drugs undercover. Brian Lamb, another officer on the detail, and I were chosen to be the buyers.

The Narcotics Bureau loaned us a black Toyota pickup that had been seized in a drug arrest to use for our ambush scheme. Brian and I were wearing our black fatigues, so we had to come up with some plain clothes. Some of the other narcotics officers had t-shirts and ball caps in their lockers, so Brian borrowed a blue Dodgers cap and some kind of Hawaiian shirt. I wore an Alabama cap with a blue t-shirt. We wouldn't have to get out of the truck, so we could still wear the BDU bottoms and our leather gear with sidearms.

Brian wore his Dodgers cap spun around backward. I tried to

wear mine that way, but the other guys said that I was too clean-cut to pull that off. They said I looked more believable with the cap facing forward. Brian drove, while I monitored the radio tucked quietly away in my lap in the passenger seat.

We drove through the areas where drugs were routinely sold. As we approached the areas where the dealers worked, I keyed the mike and quietly relayed our location and descriptions of each dealer as they approached us.

Lying in the back of the pickup were two other members of the R.O.T. Team. Once the dealer approached either window, whichever of us he approached would engage them in conversation about a drug purchase. As soon as we determined that the dealers were holding narcotics, the two officers in the back of the truck would jump out quickly and grab them. The other members of the R.O.T. Team were always a block away in the other truck waiting for us to call or for the suspects to run.

Our first attempt to buy drugs was on Amanda Circle. As Brian drove down the street, I described over the radio what we were observing. We made our way down toward the dead end of the street where we had made arrests before. As we approached the dead end, we saw several young men standing next to a vacant house on our right.

"Got a twenty?" I called out to them.

A crack rock sold for that amount and was commonly called a "twenty."

"Get outta here, white boys!" one of them shouted back.

"You ain't foolin' nobody, Five-O!" another man shouted.

'Five-O' was street slang for the police, likely adapted from the old television show set in Hawaii. I doubt if any of them were old enough to have seen it, but street slang has a funny way of taking things from the popular culture and adapting them into the subculture of the street.

Brian turned the truck around and left the neighborhood. I never realized how vulnerable we were sitting in the truck. Luring a drug dealer up to us was a little unnerving. Any one of them could have easily walked up with a gun to rob or to shoot us. To know that real undercover officers routinely did this wearing nothing more than street clothes gave me a new respect for them.

We then decided to drive to the Trenholm Court housing project, located around North Union Circle. We drove in from North Bainbridge Street and saw about ten young men standing around near the dead end of Randolph Street.

"Got a twenty?" I called out again to this group.

One of the subjects eagerly trotted up to my window. He was carrying a beer in one hand and a couple of bags of marijuana in the other. He was about nineteen years old, and as he leaned inside the truck, he must have spotted my radio.

"FIVE-O!" he yelled as he threw the beer in on me and bolted like a panicked deer in the opposite direction.

The two officers in the back of the truck, unseen by the young man, jumped out quickly and took off after him. The quicker of the two officers tackled the young dealer in the street and the young man responded with flying fists and feet. Arms and legs flailed as the two men fought. The second officer tried vainly to help his partner to subdue the crazed dealer.

The R.O.T. truck screeched up to the tangle of the two men, and the other officers piled on the wildly thrashing man until he could no longer overcome the sheer size of the opposing force.

Brian and I stayed in our truck hoping that the other dealer watching from the shadows didn't realize we were police officers.

The young man continued to struggle until a healthy coating of mace turned his full attention to the sensation of flames consuming his face. The nineteen-year-old man was arrested and charged with Unlawful Possession of Marijuana and spent the night in jail waiting for the burning skin of his face to cool off. The OC spray has a lingering effect.

I went home at the end of the night smelling like cheap beer.

This was the one and only time I bought drugs, or should I say *attempted* to buy drugs as an undercover officer. We didn't have any money to actually purchase the drugs. Our strategy was to locate those dealers in possession of the narcotics and remove them both from the street.

We returned to the narcotics office where Narcotics Investigator

Randy Markham told us we did a good job. He'd been monitoring our radio traffic and told me I gave good information as we pulled into the different drug areas. I had no idea he was listening. I thought it was just the other officers on the R.O.T. truck.

It was exciting, but at the same time, a little scary and unnerving going after the dealers this way. I don't know if real undercover officers ever get used to it, since I only did it that one time.

Illegal drugs are killing this country, and I have to commend those brave undercover officers who do this every day. It takes a lot of nerve to do it, but it's one of those jobs that must be done. But, I will never forget the night that I got to work... *undercover.*

Early 1990's — Crack cocaine evidence from arrest while riding the R.O.T (Retake Our Turf) Team.

Drug Activity

MOST DRUG DEALERS ARE NOCTURNAL, working mostly at night under the cover of darkness selling their poison, then sleeping till around noon or so, but detectives from the MPD narcotics office had received several complaints about certain dealers in town boldly working during the day.

Wednesday, April 3, 1996, was my regular off-day, but I had volunteered to work overtime on the ROT Team. ROT stood for Retake Our Turf and was a high-profile enforcement unit that targeted street dealers. We came in around seven or eight that morning to patrol the areas where the narcotics detectives had received those complaints.

Around 12:30 we made our way through the Trenholm Court Housing Project when we observed Omer James*, a young double amputee confined to a wheelchair we'd encountered before known to be frequently involved in criminal activity. Omer often sold marijuana and carried a gun. He lost both of his legs just above the knee in a traffic accident, but it never dampened his taste for crime. He was a tough cookie who could run on his stumps and would fight anyone in a heartbeat.

As we drove down North Bainbridge Street, we spotted him sitting in his wheelchair in front of the last building at the end of the street. We turned into the housing project and drove to the side of the building and jumped off the back of the truck. I walked around behind the building hoping to sneak up on him and catch him off guard in case he was armed. As I quickly rounded the building Omer's wheelchair was there, but he was gone. He had gone inside the apartment. I walked over to his chair and lying on the seat was

---

*   Not his real name

two flattened out bags of marijuana. I retrieved the bags and put them in my right leg pocket of my BDU pants. We knocked on the door but no one answered. We walked back to the truck and drove out and turned back on North Bainbridge Street. As we drove to the end of the street, Omer was again sitting in his wheelchair.

I walked over to him. "Where did you go, Omer?" I asked.

"No where," he replied.

"Where's the dope you left in your chair?"

"What dope?" he replied. "I ain't got no dope."

"When you saw us coming you jumped out of your chair and left two bags of marijuana." I told him. "You're under arrest, Omer."

"I ain't had no marijuana," he repeated as he jumped out of the wheelchair and started to run on the short stumps toward the apartment. Another officer and I grabbed him, handcuffed him then picked him up and carried him back to the truck. An endless string of profanity began to spill from his mouth as he twisted and turned, trying to break our grip on him.

Another officer lowered the tailgate of our blacked-out Suburban, and we placed him in the back, but before we could lift up the tailgate he charged us, trying to escape. I pushed him down and we quickly closed the tailgate, but he got up and charged toward the back of the truck before we could get the window up. I knocked him back toward the front of the truck and we got the window up, finally sealing him inside.

We transported him to the narcotics office to process him and then put him in jail. He cussed us from the time we arrested him until he was placed in the custody of the jail officers. Some people may think we were being cruel by arresting him or that I was a little heartless when I knocked him down after we put him in the back of the truck, but his handicap was deceiving. He was a drug dealer, a career criminal, and a dangerous man. I knew that if he'd had the chance, he would have done whatever it took to escape. Shortly thereafter when I made another arrest, I saw Omer working in the jail as an inmate. He was standing in a chair opening the jail door for officers as they brought in prisoners. We exchanged a glance. I could only smile.

That was the last I saw of him. I heard later that he had done some time in prison then had moved to another state. Some criminals do use their handicap as a reason to cover or justify their criminal activity. There are officers who tend to be lenient with the handicapped if they possibly can, and I can understand their thinking. I don't enjoy arresting anyone with a handicap, but if he is breaking the law then he is part of the problem. It may seem heartless or unchristian, but I look at criminals as criminals—especially drug dealers. The majority of *all* crimes are connected in some way to drug activity.

Early 1990's – Several members of the ROT Team (l to r) me, Cpl Bob Steelman, Cpl Brian Lamb, Inv Tom Leonard, undercover narcotics officer.

They Showered Me in Mace

RIDING ON THE **ROT** TEAM and chasing drug dealers was a lot of fun. I know it sounds crazy, but catching bad guys was our job and making overtime at time-and-a-half doing it made it even better. I enjoyed working on the ROT Team because it was a change of pace from my regular duty. I worked as an Evidence Technician during the day and worked the ROT Team after hours.

On Thursday, May 16, 1996, we were working from 6:00 till midnight. About an hour into the shift we were patrolling the area of North Decatur Street where a lot of drug activity had been reported when we saw several young men standing in the street. We stopped to talk with them and to conduct a little street interrogation. We patted them down for weapons, and I located a small bag of crack cocaine in the pocket of one young man. As soon as I retrieved the bag, the guy bolted and raced back into the neighborhood.

The other officers and I immediately took off after him, splitting up and chasing him over several fences. I ran down the sidewalk parallel to the backyards getting a glimpse of him as he crossed one backyard fence after another, waiting to see if he would turn toward the street. I saw Officer Steve Campbell attempt to tackle him but the suspect had about a foot or so in height on Steve and he just ran him over.

The young man hopped the fence into the next yard then ran beside the house out to the sidewalk. He turned suddenly and began running toward me. I had a fence on my right side and a car on my left. As he ran straight at me, I squared up with him like a linebacker on the football field. He lowered his shoulder and was preparing to run me over. At the last possible second, I stepped to my left and

271

tripped him with my leg. He fell hard on the sidewalk, and I jumped on his back immediately.

He got up anyway and started to run, dragging me down the sidewalk as I hung onto the back of his shirt. As he dragged me, I pulled myself up on his back and grabbed him in a head lock. He started punching me in my left rib cage so I started punching his face with my right fist.

I heard a woman cry out, "They fightin' for *real!*"

As we fought, we crashed into the side of an old wooden house, tearing off the asbestos siding. We both stood. I still had him in the head lock and was starting to get tired. Steve Campbell ran around the corner and tackled both of us at full speed, knocking us into a chain link fence. Steve hit us so hard that we tore the fence flat to the ground.

Sergeant Ed Rogers, commander of the ROT Team, and Sergeant Terry Reid ran up to assist.

"MACE HIM!" I yelled.

Immediately Rogers, Reid and Steve Campbell began spraying us both with mace.

I turned my head hoping not to get it in my face, but there was just too much flowing in my direction. They hosed us down like a Toyota at a church car wash. My face began to burn as if someone had torched my flesh.

I started coughing and gagging, so Steve pulled me away from the growing cloud of mace. He jumped on the young man with some help from Sergeant Rogers and got him handcuffed.

We transported the young man to the jail, rinsed the mace from his face and placed him in a holding cell. I washed off as much of the mace as I could before signing a warrant for possession of cocaine. Then I impounded the evidence.

I never went to court on that case in Montgomery, so I assumed he pled guilty. I was, however, subpoenaed to Enterprise, Alabama, to testify to how the suspect was arrested. He had outstanding warrants in Enterprise and had been hiding in Montgomery.

The next day my ribs were extremely sore and I went to Jackson Hospital to be checked out. It was Sergeant Rogers' off day, but since he was the commander of the ROT Team, he had to come into work and complete the paperwork on my injury.

I didn't want to call him in, but I was afraid I'd broken some ribs in the fall. It turned out that they were only bruised.

After that, Ed would ask me each week after we finished our tour on the ROT truck, "Steve, are you injured?" or "Steve, I'm going on vacation next week. You're not going to call me about being hurt, are you?"

I took all the kidding in stride. Ed and I have been friends for years and he knew that I wouldn't have called him at home on his off day if I didn't need to. Every so often when I see Steve Campbell or Terry Reid and we get to telling stories, I remind them of the day we tore down the fence... and they showered me in mace.

TOOTIE

THIS STORY HAPPENED ON TUESDAY night, October 1, 1996. The reason I say this is because it is one of Howie Dave Kenney's favorite stories. The actual story is not his favorite, it's the embellished version *he* likes to tell. Every time he tells it, the suspect gets younger and I get beat up worse. In some versions, I've even spent time in the hospital. It's kinda like the ol' fishing stories that fishermen tell; as time passes, the fish gets larger and the time to reel it in gets longer.

'Howie Dave' is my friend and at that time was known professionally as Sergeant Howard David Kenney of the Montgomery Police Department. He injured his hand while in patrol and was temporarily transferred to the Evidence Technician section where I worked.

In the statement he gave regarding the injury to his hand, he wrote, "I lost control of my finger." To this day I don't know exactly what that meant. After his finger healed, he remained assigned to the Evidence Technician Section.

When he first came to the bureau I called him 'Howie Dave.' As he climbed through the ranks, I added his rank to his name. Detective Howie Dave, and then Sergeant Howie Dave. Just before I retired, he became Lieutenant Howie Dave, commander of the Evidence Technician Bureau.

Well, as the *true* story goes, he and I, along with three other members of the R.O.T. team, were on patrol in the 600 block of Mildred Street, one block away from the police academy. We had complaints of a large amount of drug activity in the area from some of the law abiding citizens.

Around 8:30 p.m. we observed several young black men standing in the road, talking to another man seated behind the wheel of a car. Drug dealers often stand in the road to flag down cars to sell drugs to customers. On a busy night, cars can be lined four and five in a row waiting like hungry customers at a McDonald's drive-through.

The team members jumped from the truck and confronted all the young men surrounding the car. As we talked to them, we patted them all down checking for weapons. The young man I checked remained silent and stood motionless. Normally, when we stopped someone for questioning, we got standard questions about why we were harassing them or what right we had to interfere with their evening. This guy said zilch.

I continued to question him as I felt along his legs and waist for any telltale sign of a pistol or a knife. I asked his name and where he lived, but he never responded.

The longer he was silent the more suspicious I became. To me that meant only one thing, he had drugs in his mouth. I stood in front of him and told him to open his mouth. His eyes got big and I told him again to open his mouth. He opened his mouth just a little bit and I could see a clear plastic bag containing small white rocks, obviously crack cocaine.

He looked me square in the eyes, then shoved me in the chest with both of his hands and took off running.

"Assault on an officer!" I yelled "He's got drugs!" I began chasing him, and Sergeant Jamie Reynolds followed close behind us. I caught him, grabbed the back of his shirt and tried to tackle him but he was able to break away and avoid both Jamie and me. He ran around a house and crossed Mildred Street toward the Deluxe Social Saving Club a block away. I continued after him and he ducked behind another house into square open area unfamiliar to me in the darkness. As I turned the corner, I saw that the young man had simply vanished.

I slowed down to a trot and then I stopped suddenly. I was trying to maintain my balance and not fall. I realized I had run from a hillside adjoining a building and out onto the flat expanse of the roof of the Deluxe Social Savings Club.

The club was built into an embankment and had been there for as long as I could remember. Over the years leaves had fallen on top of it and it blended it with the adjoining embankment. The front of the club was about 15 feet high off the sidewalk below, and I had almost run off without realizing it.

I looked down and saw the suspect squatting, with his hand on the ground. The young man had made the leap and was recovering from the fall. He looked up at me, stood, then took off running toward Rosa Parks Drive. I radioed his direction of travel, and two of the R.O.T. team members headed over to the area. I don't know if he knew where he was and if he was trying to lure me off the roof, or if it caught him by surprise also. But, whatever the reason, he wanted to get away more than I wanted to catch him.

I walked back to where we first started chasing the subject and began to question the other subjects. "Who was that guy I was chasin'"? I roared at them. I was tired and had almost taken a 15-foot plunge, so I was a little perturbed. "Did y'all understand the question?" I asked. "Who was that guy I was chasin?"

One of the guys said, "Tootie."

"Tootie? What's his real name? I don't want hear some stupid street name!"

"I don't know his real name, jus' Tootie."

"Where does he stay?" I continued, using the street term for the location most people in the 'hood call home.

"On Jeff Davis," the man said.

"Where on Jeff Davis?" I asked.

"Don't know," he replied. "Just somewheres on Jeff Davis."

None of the young men were holding and a check for warrants proved negative as well. Tootie was the mule that night, and he got away, at least for the night. We left and resumed our patrol of the area. I was going to check the name "Tootie" in our computer database at a later time and try to find out his real name.

I told everyone how close I came to running off the building and we drove around to see just how high it was.

Howie Dave started in on me immediately. "He punked you out, Steve! You got abused!" he laughed. "He punked you!"

"I'll find out who he is," I replied. "He just got away tonight. But I will find out who he is."

The next day I began to look in the narcotics files and investigative computer for the name "Tootie." I couldn't find anything.

Several weeks went by and he was still not in custody. I was not concerned because I knew eventually he would be caught. During the weeks we were looking for him, Howie Dave would make a point to sit next to me in the R.O.T. truck *to protect me* from Tootie.

He would climb in the truck and tell me, "You look scared tonight, I'll protect you from Tootie." Another gem I often heard was, "If we get out with some subjects, you don't have to stay in the truck. You can stand close to me in case Tootie comes around."

Then the laughter would begin.

He loved to tell the story of how I was beat up by a little kid on Mildred Street. Usually the way it would get started was a group of officers would be standing around and I would walk up and Howie Dave would say, "Did you hear about the little kid that beat up Steve on the R.O.T. truck?"

The guys standing around would chime in, "What! No, he didn't tell us about that. So, what's the story?"

"You haven't heard the Tootie story?" Howie Dave would ask with excitement in his voice.

Then he would go into *his* version. Lieutenant Terry Reid and Sergeant Ed Rogers, the commander of the R.O.T. team also got in on the action and had their version of what happened that night. Their story was not as detailed or as graphic, but they liked to pick at me about that night too. Their story was not exactly true, but usually they did this to get Howie Dave cranked up.

Tootie's age would fluctuate somewhere from 7-years-old to an infant. Howie Dave's version of the story would go something like this: "We got out on Mildred Street and there were probably about ten big guys and one little kid standing in the street. Steve didn't want to get out at first, so I had to coax him out. He then jumped out and ran straight to the little kid, who was probably, maybe 6-years-old and not even five-foot tall.

"While we are talking to these other big guys, we heard this screaming that sounded like a little girl. I looked over and saw Steve lying in the middle of the street. This little kid was standing over him and Steve was saying, 'Don't hit me, again. Please don't hit me, again!' The kid then just ran off. I walked over to help Steve up and he was shaking, crying and wanted to go home."

Sometimes, he would tell the story that I was spinning in the road because the little kid hit me so hard I looked like I was break dancing. He would continue the story of how I was scared to get out of the truck and how I would ask him to protect me. The version of the story told would depend on the day and just how funny Howie Dave felt.

Usually after Howie Dave finished his tale, the person hearing the story would turn to me and ask something like, "You let a kid beat you up?"

"It's his story," I would reply. "You'll have to ask him. But according to Howie Dave, I guess so."

On Monday, November 4, Tootie's brother, Charles Thomas,* was arrested for possession of crack cocaine by another patrol officer. He later told the narcotics investigators that Tootie was his brother, James Thomas.** I found a photo of James to check, and sure enough it was him!

James had been arrested several times, and his last known address was on West Jeff Davis Avenue. All the times he had been arrested, his street name wasn't listed, so it never made it into our database. I also learned that he had eleven misdemeanor warrants on him. I signed another one on him for harassment.

Sergeant Rogers told me several days later that Tootie had been arrested and was working the door as a trustee in the city jail.

"Do you want to go and see him?" he asked. "I'll go with you, if you want me to," as if I were a scared little kid.

I went to the jail and saw him sitting in the chair by the door. One prisoner would sit in a chair and open the door whenever an officer would bring a prisoner in, or leave.

"Do you remember me?" I asked him.

"No," he replied.

"You don't remember pushing me and running from me on Mildred Street?"

"Nah, man," he said. "That wadn't me."

---

*   Not his real name

**   Not his real name

Regardless of what he told me, he would later plead guilty to the harassment charge.

Several years later, Tootie died, likely as a result of his business practices, but I can't say for sure.

Howie Dave, Terry and Ed would ask me from time to time where I was the day Tootie died.

I would tell them, "None of your business and don't ask so many questions." They still pick at me about Tootie. It's now become an inside joke between us. To this day, Howie Dave, whenever I come around, especially when I am around a new officer, or an officer from a different agency, he'll either say, "Have you heard about the little kid that beat up Steve, or, has Steve told you about Tootie?"

ROADSIDE SHOOTING

Sgt. H.D. Kenney and Cpl. Steve Smith mark shell casings and bloodstains Friday at the scene of a shooting off South Decatur Street. After a near accident in traffic, two cars pulled off the road and the driver of one of the cars was shot by a man in the other car. See story, Page 5D.

March 1997 – Newspaper article from shooting scene on Decatur St. Sgt H D Kenney takes notes as I collect evidence. (Courtesy of Montgomery Advertiser)

Basically, It's Just a Big Chess Game

ONE OF THE MOST FUN and exciting duties I had with the police department was working on the R.O.T. team. The acronym stood for Retake Our Turf. This was a zero tolerance drug unit that targeted street-level drug dealers and was initiated to combat the growing crack cocaine epidemic. Officers in the unit were volunteers from all over the department who worked overtime paid for by a federal grant. We dressed in black BDU's, a fatigue-style uniform similar to military combat attire.

We worked the detail with a specially customized black Chevy Suburban outfitted with an extended bumper on the rear of the vehicle with room for three officers to stand on and a bar across the top rear of the truck to hang on to. This enabled the officers to jump off the truck at a moment's notice and chase fleeing drug dealers, or to stealthily sneak up on street dealers without having to open and close the vehicle doors.

Other officers in the department often chided us by saying that R.O.T. stood for "Ride On The Truck" or "Ride On The Tailgate." Even though we had a lot of fun with the unit, there was an element of danger involved. Where there are drug dealers, there are also people with guns willing to use them. Drugs are big business, and any business must be protected, even if it's illegal.

On November 26, 1996, I was working on the R.O.T. team from six to midnight. I had requested and received permission for my younger brother, Shane, to ride with us as an observer. He and his family were down from Ohio for Thanksgiving. I drove down from spending the holiday at my parent's home in Birmingham to work so my brother could ride with us.

The commander of the R.O.T. team that night was Sergeant Ed Rogers, a calm easy-going man with a good sense of humor and not easily rattled. He was well respected by his peers. Ed and I were good friends who was just "Ed" to me off-duty but "Sergeant" at work as a sign of respect. Some supervisors I called by their rank because I respected the rank. Some I called by their rank because I respected the person who wore the rank. I deferred the courtesy to Ed both as a person and as a supervisor.

We had patrolled all the usual high drug areas but hadn't seen anyone dealing so far. It may have been that it was cold that night or that it was so close to Thanksgiving and most people were staying inside. We decided to do a walk-through in the Cedar Park housing project on the Mobile Highway.

Cedar Park was one of the government housing projects in the city that had a major drug problem. Two streets ran through the complex, Young Drive and Forte Lane. A walk-through was simply a stealthy foot patrol through the housing community using the darkness and shadows of the building to sneak up on the drug dealers.

We exited the vehicle on the Mobile Highway and entered the complex from behind Cook's Plaza walking in from the north and moving quietly and carefully from building to building. Sergeant Rogers, Lieutenant Terry Reid and my brother, waited on the opposite side of the highway at the old Jet Drive-in, an outdoor movie theater which had been closed down and abandoned for many years. The large outdoor movie screen still towered over the ghostly vacant rows of terraced parking and provided a great place to remain out of sight when conducting low-key police operations.

Sergeant Howard Kenney, Officer Sean Loughridge and I crept cautiously down Young Drive, dancing between the shadows from one building to the next. About twenty-five large apartment buildings comprised the entire complex. Ten to twelve of the buildings were lined up in a row like dominos standing on their side. As we made our way through, I walked down one end of the building, Kenney walked down the other end and Loughridge walked through the breezeways. Each building had two breezeways with a staircase connecting eight apartments on two floors.

As we came to the corner of each building we stopped and peeked around to see who was standing out between the buildings. As we came to the edge of the second building, we saw two young men standing in front of one of the breezeways. One of us, I don't remember who, observed one of the men pulling on the front of the sweat pants he wore trying to keep them up. It appeared to me that he had a gun in front of his pants and that the weight of the weapon was pulling them down. Whoever noticed it first radioed to the others that he appeared to have a gun in the front of his pants.

As we approached him, he spotted us and ran. At that same moment we heard gunshots near where he'd been standing. While he was running, he was pulling on the gun, trying to get it out of his pants.

We took off after him. "Shots fired, shots fired!" I shouted into the mike on my radio.

The young man fled through the breezeways of each building in succession. I was expecting him to turn and run to one end or the other of the building. He knew that one officer was behind him in the breezeways, but he may not have known that Kenney and I were on each end of the building running parallel with him.

After chasing him through three breezeways, Loughridge caught up to the man and tackled him.

He then asked us the standard question that all the people we chase and catch ask. "Why're you chasin' me, I ain't done nothin'?"

I gave him the standard reply. "If you ain't done nothin', then why are you running?"

This is when you get all kinds of excuses such as, "I was scared" or "I was just runnin' because I wanted to."

Officer Loughridge searched the subject but didn't find a gun. Sergeant Kenney and I backtracked his steps looking under stairs, in dark corners and in garbage cans trying to see where he might have tossed the gun, but we never found it. My guess was that he was able to pass it to someone else, or someone picked it up after he tossed it.

Sergeant Kenney and Officer Loughridge tried to identify the guy, but he gave us several different names, and of course, he didn't carry ID. While questioning the man, Sergeant Rogers, Lieutenant Reid and my brother, came screeching up in the black Suburban.

Ed got out quickly and ran to where we were standing. "Is everybody okay!" he seemed very excited.

"Everybody's fine. Just a little foot pursuit." I said calmly.

"Who was shootin'?" he asked.

"I don't know, Sergeant. We heard the shots and he started running and he was trying to get a gun out of his pants while we were chasin' him."

"So, none of you fired a shot?" he asked.

"No, sir," I said. "None of us fired shots."

"Steve," he said calmly. "Let me talk to you a second, please."

I walked over to him, and he put his arm around me. "You just about gave me a heart attack just then."

"What do you mean, Sergeant?" I was more than a little confused. "It was just a little foot pursuit."

He smiled. "When *we* are doing the shooting, its 'shots fired,'" he explained. "When the *bad guys* are doing the shooting, it's called a 'code seven.'" He was referring to the radio code for a shooting in progress.

I stepped back from Sergeant Rogers and returned his smile. "Oh, my bad, Sergeant," I said. "I wasn't thinking. I could see where that would make you a little nervous."

"That's all I need is to tell the captain that you were involved in a police shooting with your brother riding with us."

Since we didn't find the gun or any drugs on the guy, we cut him loose. I remember explaining to the young man that if you aren't guilty of a crime, you don't need to run from the police. I doubt it made much of an impact on him.

Some people run from the police because they have warrants on them, they're holding drugs, or they're doing something illegal. Often they run to lead us away from the guy who's holding the drugs. When we learn the criminal's tactics we adapt our tactics to catch them. The criminals then learn our new tactics and adapt theirs to try and stay a step ahead. In police work we are just trying to stay one move ahead of the bad guys.

Basically, it's just a big chess game.

September 1995 – ROT Team truck

Christmas 1996 – Christmas morning at my in-laws, Stacy at three years old and Nancy. I had to work on Christmas day.

The MPD Angel

ON THURSDAY, JULY 31, 1997, I had only been back in uniform six days after spending the previous eight years as an evidence technician. I'd felt the urge to get back on the streets again and had requested a transfer back to patrol. It had been a long time since I had ridden a district and answered calls, and I was having to re-learn all the duties of a Patrol Corporal again both in and out of the office.

One of those administrative duties was to run copies of the daily worksheet. These copies had to be run a certain way so when you flipped the page over vertically you could read the information on the back. Majors and Captains got a hand-delivered copy, the desk got the original and four copies for the dispatchers and payroll, and then you had to run a copy for each of the shift supervisors and corporals. If the copier was functioning properly and running well then it would be easy. But if someone called in sick, then it threw off the whole system. You would have to change the roster, round up all the copies, and run new ones.

On this particular day, I was walking up the stairs to the enormous copier at the back desk with Corporal Les Crumble to run the worksheets when I was stopped in the hallway by Lieutenant-Colonel Sandra Pierce-Hanna.

"Steve, you need to head over to Jackson Hospital and meet with Donna White's family," she said solemnly. "She's been involved in a serious car accident and is being transported to the E.R. right now."

Donna was a police officer with our department and a member of my church. Years earlier she had been one of my Sunday school students. She told me once that one of the reasons she became a police officer was because of some of the stories I told my Sunday School class when she was younger. She had worked as a police cadet before graduating the Montgomery Police Academy, December 12, 1996. She was the first female president of a class at the police academy. She had only been on the streets less than a year and had just come off training and probation.

"How bad is she hurt, Colonel?" I asked. I was stunned by the news.

"It sounds pretty bad." I could see in her face that she meant it. "You need to go on over there now and check on the family," she added. "I'll be there shortly."

The Lieutenant-Colonel knew Donna and I were good friends, so I gave Les the worksheets to run and headed downstairs to grab my hat and my cell phone and to let my supervisors know where I was going. I was assigned to ride with Corporal Crumble that day and hadn't been issued a patrol vehicle yet. I made it upstairs and was standing outside waiting on Les to finish and to give me a lift to the hospital. As I waited outside, I called our pastor, Gary Aldridge. The secretary told me he was in a meeting and couldn't be disturbed but that he would call me later. I relayed the news about Donna and asked that she send him to the hospital as soon as he could get there.

After what seemed like forever, Les came out the back door and he drove me to the hospital. As I walked toward the emergency entrance, I met Donna's mother, Peggy White. Everyone called her Miss Peggy. I took her by the arm and walked her down the ramp toward the emergency room doors. The paramedics were unloading Donna from the ambulance as we approached. Brother Gary was walking down the ramp from the ambulance exit and met us there.

We immediately went to the trauma room where they began to work on her. A nurse pulled the curtain and asked us to step out to the waiting room. She told us a doctor would be with us shortly. I could tell by the frantic way they were scrambling around Donna that her injuries were grave. I'd seen it many times before, but it's always a little different when it's someone you know and care about. Brother Gary led us to a private room adjacent to the emergency room and led us in prayer. Within about fifteen minutes, more of her family members began to arrive. Sergeant Mary Neilson arrived and she waved me out in the hallway. I excused myself to speak to her.

"Have you heard how she is doing yet?" Mary asked.

"No, not yet, but they just started working on her," I replied. "Let's go around to the trauma room and see if we can find out anything."

We walked around, and the curtain was standing open. The doctor, surrounded by his busy trauma team, was doing chest compressions on her. She was in full arrest and he was frantically trying to start her heart again.

We both just walked away. Mary looked at me, "That's not good," she said quietly.

"Let's just go see how the family's doing," I said. "We won't mention that to the family. Let's just let the doctors do their job." I tried to keep my voice from quivering.

Alabama State Trooper Tim Pullen, who was investigating the accident, arrived at the hospital and came to check on her injuries. I knew Tim from his years as an officer with our department before he moved on to work for the state.

I asked about the accident and Tim told me that she'd been ejected from the vehicle. Tim added that a former military medic had pulled up on the scene of the accident and had worked on her before the Montgomery Firemedics arrived. Donna was off duty and had been at the firing range doing some target practice. She decided to go get a few cold soft drinks for some of her classmates who were at the range shooting with her. When she entered traffic on the busy four-lane highway nearby, she pulled into the path of an SUV. It struck her on the driver's side near the back door of her little blue Mitsubishi, causing the front door to fly open and fling her from the car. She landed hard on the pavement hitting the back of her head.

Donna was in the trauma room for several hours before being taken to SICU. She was on a respirator and was unconscious. My superiors assigned me to the waiting room to assist the family with whatever they needed. I was given home and cell numbers from several majors, captains and concerned fellow employees with instructions to call if there was any change in her condition. Police officers, friends and family arrived and filled the waiting room. I answered the phone in the waiting room, took messages and ordered food and refreshments for the family. I was also making calls to anyone I could think of to let them know about the accident. Donna was never one to make a big show of things, and she would have been embarrassed at how many people were at the hospital so concerned about her.

On Friday, visitors were able to see her every three hours for just a few minutes. Most of her close friends didn't want to go see her alone, so I would walk into the room with them. The sight of Donna hooked up to so many machines as she lay there seemingly lifeless was hard for them to take. Leanne Kenerly and Janice Cardwell were two of her closest friends from the youth group at church and high school. They asked me to take them around to see her. They only wanted to see her through the large plate glass window. I commented that she was looking much better today.

"How can you say that?" Leanne asked. Her tone conveyed her disbelief. "She doesn't look good at all!" She struggled to fight back her tears.

I hugged her and said in a low, calming tone, "You didn't see her yesterday. She looks much better than yesterday."

Leanne and Janice both began to sob softly at the sight of their friend clinging perilously to life. They finally decided to go back to the waiting room. I'm not sure they really believed me. Maybe they thought I was just trying to make them both feel better, but she did look better. Thursday, she looked lifeless, and on Friday she looked more like she was just sleeping. When you have a brain injury, recovery is a slow process.

Saturday, Donna regained consciousness and was able to sit up slightly in bed. She wasn't able to fully comprehend what had happened or what was going on in the room. She was aware of people in the room but couldn't speak. The doctors and nurses told the family that she needed mental stimulation to help with her recovery.

Her sister, Deidre, and her mother were in the room when I arrived at the hospital. I was allowed to come and go as I pleased since I was assigned as an aide to the family. I didn't abuse the privilege and only went back during visiting hours. Deidre was asking Donna questions one after the other, but Donna continued to be agitated with her. She had to look up to see her sister and it seemed to be uncomfortable for her. Her doctor said she needed to sit up for a couple of hours a day, but she kept trying to swing her leg over toward the bed so she could lie back down. Sitting up seemed stressful, but it was what she needed at that time.

Even though she did not have all her faculties, she was sneaky. She indicated to her mother that she needed to go to the bathroom and wanted me to leave. Her mother explained that she had a catheter but she was still self-conscious about urinating while I was in the room. So I stepped out and closed the door almost completely. As soon as I walked out, Donna tried to stand up. She was stronger than her sister and her mother and they could not hold her down.

"Steve!" Miss Peggy cried.

I rushed in and immediately saw what she was doing and pushed her gently back down in the chair by both shoulders. That was just like Donna to try something like this. I then sat on the bed and began to talk to her. I asked her if she knew who I was and she nodded her head and mouthed the word 'Thang.' Donna and I called each other 'Thang' for reasons I cannot remember now. Once I was comfortable she knew who I was I started talking to her.

Donna's aunt, Nelda Edwards, from Atlanta, came into the room about this time and sat down next to me. I had gotten back from our church mission trip the month before and so I started telling them about the trip. We had gone to Ralston, Oklahoma, to build a fellowship hall onto an existing church. This was also the same town that the movie *Twister* was filmed. I talked to her for about an hour until visiting hours was over, then her family and I left the room.

Nelda and I went back to the waiting room and were visiting with the family. About ten minutes later, the nurse from SICU came and asked to speak to Nelda and me. We went out in the hallway and the nurse asked if we would come back and talk to Donna some more. When we asked why, the nurse explained that when we talked to her she seemed more stimulated and more relaxed than when other visitors saw her. It seemed that carrying on a regular conversation with her was much more productive than simply talking to her like an accident victim.

Donna could listen to us and not have to really think, but picture in her mind what I was telling her. Nelda and I visited Donna three to four times during the day and evening and I would ask her if I had told her about the mission trip. Her injury would have wiped all of it from her memory, and she would shake her head no. I would then tell her the same story again.

I felt sorry for Nelda, because she had to listen to the same story three to four times a day for four days. One time I asked her if she remembered us getting married and she had this surprised look on her face. I questioned her later if she remembered me asking her that but her memory of that had disappeared as well. Her memories seemed to come and go like ghosts in a haunted castle. She would often forget that she was even in the hospital.

Donna was moved to a private room and my special assignment to the family ended. She was on her way to recovery, but it was obvious that it wasn't going to be quick or easy. She was later moved to a rehabilitation clinic for several weeks of intense therapy. One day Miss Peggy called me and asked if I was planning on coming to visit Donna. I told her I was headed there as soon as I left headquarters. When I walked in Donna's room her face lit up and she said in a loud voice, "I can remember! I can remember everything! My memory is back!"

In the months following the accident, Donna seemed to be in what I called a funk. It was like she was not Donna. But, this was a different Donna. Then one day after several weeks, I came and saw that old sparkle in her eye once more. The swelling in her brain had gone and allowed it to return to its normal size. She was her old self again. She remembered me being her Sunday school teacher and that I was a police officer. She did not remember much about working for the police department but seemed to remember all that had happened before that.

Donna recovered most of her faculties in time, but was never able to return to regular duty. She suffered regular seizures as a result of her head injury and in time medication reduced the number of seizures to about once a month. She was assigned light duty and put on the desk before being transferred to the police academy doing administrative work.

Donna had memory lapses and couldn't remember some people from her past. After the accident she developed a love for writing poetry. She became very sensitive to the needs and feelings of others. She was always sending cards with poems she had written especially for them for that occasion. Myra Meeks, who was a secretary at the police department, named her 'The MPD Angel.'

I visited her often at her mother's house. If Miss Peggy had to run errands I would stay with Donna. Because of her injury, she would often try to leave and go walking, and we were afraid she wouldn't remember how to get back home. Because of her injury she would often become difficult to handle at home and was sometimes too much for Miss Peggy and Chad, Donna's nephew, who stayed with them.

Miss Peggy would tell her, "Are we goin' to have to call Steve over here?"

She usually settled down after that.

She also had a hard time remembering all the people with whom she worked. On one occasion Major Randy Dixon and Captain Larry Armstead called and wanted to come by for a visit. She asked that I stay because she couldn't remember who they were. I explained that they were the patrol commanders, but she still couldn't remember. I teased her a little and told her I was going to leave and let her figure it out for herself, but after a moment she knew I was kidding. I told her that when they came in I would shake hands with each man and call them by name so she would know who they were.

She was always afraid she would hurt someone's feelings if she forgot a name. She never wanted anyone to know that she had forgotten a name even though this was something beyond her control. People understood that she'd suffered a terrible blow to her ability to remember things, but she never quite understood that fact herself.

One of the things we talked about when she first joined the police department was the day we could ride together as partners. Unfortunately, that never happened. Donna worked five years with the department before taking a medical retirement on March 22,

2000. She had a full retirement tea at the police department and received everything that any other retiree would receive after twenty years of service.

She asked that I stand on the platform with her because she was still worried about forgetting names. She surprised me with a poem she wrote about me and read it at the retirement. I got very choked up and fought back the tears. I hugged her and a newspaper photographer took our picture and put it in the paper. She touched the lives of so many people in such a short time with her Christian walk. I am proud to call 'Thang' my friend, the MPD Angel.

This is the poem that Donna wrote for me.

Cpl. S. Z. Smith

You joined the Montgomery Police Department 20 years ago.
There were busy days and then days that were slow.
But you did not get into Law Enforcement to pass "time,"
The Lord uses you on the scene of crimes.
There is no telling how many lives you have reached out to,
Just as the quote goes..."What would Jesus Do?"
People are hurting and in great need, and usually
The first thing they do is call the police.
When the Lord sends a servant like you,
There is no telling the impact you make on lives
And what a great job that you do.
You also reach out to others in your work place-
Thank you for taking the time to start a
Monthly Cops for Christ.
That is all in honor of recognition of you.
The Lord is going to bless you greatly.
Thank you so much...Steve!

God Bless you.
I love you,
Donna 'Thang'

"For I know the plans I have for you," declares the Lord, "Plans to prosper you and not to harm you, plans to give you a hope and a future."

Jeremiah 29: 11-13

Donna's seizures became at times severe in the five years following the accident. There were several occasions where she would stop breathing during one of her episodes. Sadly for all of us, Donna went home to be with the Lord on Monday, May 13, 2002, the day after Mother's Day. Although I was officially retired, her mother asked Chief Wilson if I could wear a police uniform one more time for her funeral. Her request was granted and I served as one of her pallbearers and delivered the eulogy at her funeral.

On Thursday, May 16, 2002, Donna was buried with full police honors.

Police honor injured retiree

Todd Van Emst Staff

Officers paid tribute to the 24-year-old with honors and words of respect

By Kim Williams-Neil
Montgomery Advertiser

The Montgomery Police Department on Wednesday said goodbye to the "MPD Angel."

Officers and staff members gathered for a retirement tea in honor of Donna White, a 24-year-old officer who was seriously injured in a 1997 off-duty car accident.

White, who had only been on the job about seven months before the accident, never fully recovered from her injuries and decided to take a medical retirement. Tuesday was her last day

with the department.

"You just don't know the daily inspiration that child has brought to us," Myra Meeks, a police academy secretary, said as she wiped tears from her eyes Wednesday during the retirement tea. "You can't help but to love someone who loves life and shares that with you. She's our angel, our MPD angel," she said.

White came to the department in the early 1990s as a member of its cadet program. She had the encouragement of Cpl. Z. Stephen Smith, her former Sunday School teacher.

Smith had mixed emotions Wednesday about White's retirement.

"I'm glad for her because I

know the Lord has bigger, better plans for her, but I hate to see her go. She'll always have her police family, though," he said.

White attended the police academy in 1996. In December of that same year, she graduated as president of her police academy class.

White was off-duty and returning from a training session at the Montgomery firing range in July 1997 when a GMC Jimmy struck the driver's side door of her Mitsubishi Eclipse. The then firstshift patrol officer suffered critical head injuries and was in a coma for a week. She still suffers occasional seizures and is no longer allow-

Retiree Page 5B

"I'VE BEEN WATCHING YOU"

O N SUNDAY SEPTEMBER **14, 1997,** I was working as a patrol officer on the evening shift. I had transferred from the Evidence Technician section working crime scenes in July and was still adjusting to my new hours and new off days.

It was around 4:00 that afternoon when I responded to a call at the Number 1 Nails near Eastdale Mall. This beauty and nail salon is located in a small cluster of stores adjacent to the mall. The manager had called in to report a theft and an ensuing dispute with the alleged perpetrator.

When I arrived, I saw a young black couple talking to two white women. One of the white women appeared to be in her twenties, and the other slightly older. One of our K-9 units, Corporal Donnie Foster, pulled in behind me a few moments later as my back-up unit since I was riding solo that day.

"Who called the police?" I asked the small gathering.

The older of the two white women, who turned out to be the owner of the business, stepped forward and replied. "I did," she said. "My employee saw this young woman take some nail polish and put it in her purse." She indicated with her hand that the other white woman was her employee and that the young black woman was the alleged shoplifter.

"Is that true?" I asked the employee.

"Yes, officer," the younger woman replied. "This lady took some nail polish off the shelf and put it in her purse." Again she was indicating the young black woman who stood silently nearby. "Then she went to her car for a couple of minutes before she came back into the store."

"Now are you sure this is what you saw?" I asked. I wanted to be sure that the owner and employee both understood the seriousness of accusing someone of a theft.

"I'm sure that's what I saw," the younger woman said. "If that nail polish isn't in her purse, then she put it in her car when she walked out."

I noticed during my conversation with the two women that Donnie had pulled his car up close enough to hear what we were saying. That's common in police work so that the back-up officer can pick up on anything that may require him to intervene. As long as the situation remains peaceful, he could remain out of the way. If there were to be trouble or a violent confrontation, however, he and his partner, a one-hundred-twenty-five-pound German Shepherd, were ready to leap into action.

I walked over to the young black couple. They appeared to be nice people and were certainly cooperative. "Let me hear your side of the story," I asked.

"I did not steal any nail polish, officer," the woman said. "I just went to my car to get my checkbook."

"That's right, officer," the young man added. "We both work for the Board of Education. There would be no need for us to steal anything. We can certainly afford to pay for nail polish."

I always try to remain neutral in any conflict between people until I can determine who's lying and who's telling the truth. It's not my job to judge people, just to discern the truth and try to apply the law fairly.

"Do you mind if I look in your car for any nail polish?" I asked the young woman.

"I'd rather you didn't look in my car, officer," she replied. "I haven't done anything."

"Look," I said. "If you didn't take anything, you don't have anything to worry about. This is the only way to see who's telling the truth."

"Well, I guess so," she said. "Go ahead and look."

The young employee had told me what kind of nail polish it was, but being a guy I couldn't for the life of me remember what she said. I searched through the car as thoroughly as I could, but I didn't see any nail polish of any kind.

The young employee wasn't satisfied with that. "I know it has to be in there," she said. She seemed a bit agitated that I didn't find anything. "Can I look for it?" she asked me.

"Do you mind, ma'am?" I asked the woman.

"Go right ahead," she replied.

The employee spent a couple of minutes searching the car and could not find any fingernail polish.

I also searched the young woman's purse and didn't find it there either.

The young woman and her companion were obviously frustrated and insulted at the accusation, my presence there, and subsequent searches to which I subjected her. "Well I'm sorry, ma'am," I said. "I have to investigate every complaint, even if it's an honest mistake, and I appreciate your cooperation."

"We're also very sorry," the business owner added. I smoothed things over between everyone involved as best as I could before leaving the business. I got back in service on the radio and went back to patrolling my district. A few minutes later Donnie called me over the radio and asked me to meet him nearby on Wares Ferry Road. I made my way over to a parking lot near another small cluster of businesses and pulled up next to his car.

"What's going on?" I asked.

"Not too much," he replied calmly. "Just ridin' around with my dog."

"Do you ever let him drive?"

"Nah, he usually likes to nap on Sunday," he said. He paused for a moment and began to talk seriously. "I liked the way you handled that call," he began. "I liked the way you handled everyone out there."

"Well, I was just trying to figure out what had happened," I replied honestly. "And those folks didn't really seem like thieves to me."

He then got a somewhat somber look on his face but kept the friendly smile. "I've been watching you for about a year now and I want what you've got."

I was surprised with that statement and did not know what he was talking about. "What do you mean, what I've got?"

"The way you handle people," he said. "The way you handle things that happen and the way you handle working at this place."

I started thinking about what all I had done over the previous year. I knew in my own mind that I always tried to be professional and to temper all my actions with my Christian faith. "You just have something about you that's different than other officers," he continued. "And I want that."

I hesitated for a moment. "Do you mean me being a Christian?"

"Yeah, that," he said. "How can I become a Christian?"

"You have to ask Jesus to come into your life and admit that you are a sinner."

It was at this point that I began to get excited, and when I get excited talking about Jesus I tend to talk a lot, and fast. As Christians we're always taught that we are to witness for Christ. I always figured I would have to bring it up, but suddenly I had an opportunity to share with someone on how to become a Christian. *This is going to be a great day,* I thought to myself.

I glanced around quickly. "Meet me behind the building," I said.

As he followed me in his car, I was praying, "Thank you, Lord. Thank you, Lord! Please don't let me mess this up, Lord!"

I parked behind the building and got out of my car. Donnie pulled up directly behind me and got out. I stood by the driver's door of my car and as he walked up I put out my hand and shook his. I put my right hand on his left shoulder. "Repeat after me," I said.

Due to my excitement, I started out praying the Sinner's Prayer with a long first sentence, but then I realized that he was supposed to repeat what I said. After he repeated the first sentence, I spoke in shorter sentences. We went all the way through the prayer and, after the Amen, I looked at him and announced with a big smile, "You're in, dude!" I said. "You're a born again Christian!"

His face took on a glow I'd never seen before as if the weight of the world had been lifted from his shoulders. He had a look of relief and calm.

"Now you need to find a church that has solid Bible teaching," I said.

"I've been going to a church in Wetumpka for about the last year," he said. "I've also been reading the Bible every night when I get home from work."

"Well, I think you're on the right track," I said.

I didn't work the same district everyday, so I didn't see Donnie that often at work. On the occasions I did meet him afterward he would tell me what book of the Bible he was reading. He also mentioned that there was a preacher on television each night when he got off work that he enjoyed watching. I could tell though that he was beginning his walk with the Lord in earnest, and I continue to pray that he keep Jesus in his heart each day.

As a Christian, I never know who will be watching me. And from time to time, I get reminded that people watch what I do and listen to what I say. Some of the people with whom I have worked with over the years have told me how much they admire me for my convictions, and ask how I can live a Christian life and do what I do. I think this is always God's reminder that I am to live for Him everyday. I've been made aware of it in so many different ways, but Corporal Donnie Foster was the only one to actually say, "I've been watching you."

★★★

After reading this story, if you feel that your life is missing something or you feel you need Jesus Christ in your life, the bible says there is only one way to heaven. Jesus said in John 14:6; *"I am the way, the truth, and the life: no man cometh unto the Father, but by me."*

The bible tells us in the book of Romans, "That if you confess that Jesus is Lord and believe in your heart that God raised him from the dead, then you will be saved." If you want to become a Christian you must;

1. Admit you are a sinner.
2. Be willing to turn from sin (repent).
3. Believe that Jesus Christ died for you, was buried and rose from the dead.
4. Through prayer, invite Jesus into your life to become your personal Savior.

If you would like to ask Jesus into your heart but do not know how to pray, here is a prayer you can pray.

Dear Lord,
I am a sinner and I need forgiveness. I believe that Jesus died on the cross for my sins. I am now inviting Jesus into my life and my heart to be my personal Savior. I pray this prayer in his Holy name. Amen.

If you prayed this prayer and you have accepted Jesus Christ as your personal savior, congratulations, you are now a Christian. Now, you need to contact a local church in your area. Ask a Christian friend what church they attend and visit with them. Christians need to be around other Christians to grow in the Lord.

"You Played for the Bear!"

I N ALL MY YEARS AS a police officer, I found that most people I encountered on the job would lie to me. I really never understood this. I'm not just talking about criminals either; it was even law-abiding citizens in everyday situations. People lied even when there was no need for it. Instead of just telling the truth about where they were going or what they were doing, for whatever reason, they just made up a lie. I suppose there were certain things people just didn't want a cop to know about them, but I was always amazed by their creativity. Just when I thought I'd pretty much heard every story that could be told, someone would come up with something new, so it became kind of a game for me at some point to see who could surprise me with the tallest tale.

Sometime between September and October of 1997, I was on patrol in District Five. College football was all the talk on the sports radio shows and I would listen each afternoon to see what the latest gossip was about Alabama and Auburn. The Crimson Tide is my team but I also wanted to hear the latest on what was happening on the Plains.

Around 4:00, I was dispatched to Seton Haven nursing home on Wares Ferry Road near the Atlanta Highway on the report of a suspicious person sitting in a vehicle. Now usually on a call like this we'd find someone simply waiting to pick up an employee from work, so I really didn't expect anything unusual. As I pulled into the parking lot I saw a large green Chevy parked in one of the parking spaces near the entrance. A young man about twenty sat calmly behind the wheel. I approached the driver's window.

"Good afternoon," I said. "Can I ask what you're doing here, sir?"

"My car broke down and I am trying to see if I can get it started," he replied.

"Well, how did you wind up in this parking lot?"

"My car quit up the road a piece," he said. "And since the road was sloped downhill, I just coasted down until I could turn in here and park."

I thought it was odd that he could coast into the parking lot, then cross the entire lot to the entrance of the nursing home into a marked parking space. The more I talked to him, the more I sensed that maybe his mental faculties weren't what they should have been. He seemed a little immature to be as old as he was.

I asked him for his driver's license then ran a warrant check on him. I also checked the registration to see if he owned the car. I noticed the guy was big, about six-four and two hundred and sixty pounds or so. He was heavy but not really muscular or athletic in any way.

"Do you work or go to school?" I asked.

"I go to Florida State University," he said.

"What are you studying?"

"Pharmacy," he replied.

Now, my father is a retired pharmacist, and I happened to know how much education is required for that profession. To me, this guy didn't seem quite sharp enough to do such a thing.

"I also play football for Coach Bobby Bowden," he added, with some enthusiasm.

"Are you still playing now?" I asked.

"No," he replied. I could sense some disappointment in his voice. "I tore up my knee and I can't play anymore."

"How long did you play?"

"I played for two years, then I injured my knee." He then pulled up his shorts and showed me a long zipper-shaped scar on his left knee.

For some reason I just couldn't believe he was really a football player, especially at one of the premier programs in the country. He just didn't seem to have the demeanor or the confidence one would expect of a football player for a large university like Florida State.

He also didn't seem to have the intellect to be a pharmacy student. Something just wasn't right about him.

I explained that his presence was making some of the employees at the nursing home nervous, and I asked him where he lived. He gave me his address, and that matched what was on his driver's license. At least in that regard, he told me the truth.

His house was just a few miles down Wares Ferry Road, so I offered to take him home. He accepted but asked that I call his sister and tell her where his car would be and that he was getting a ride home.

I called the number he gave me and stepped away so he couldn't hear my conversation with his sister, a nurse at one of the local hospitals. When she answered, I told her who I was and explained about her brother's car and how I came to be there with him. Then, for some reason, I don't really know why, I guess I just had to know, I had one more question to ask.

"Ma'am," I began, "Does your brother play football at Florida State?"

There was a long pause on the other end.

Finally she spoke. "Is he telling *that* story again?" she asked. "No, Officer, he does *not* play football at Florida State and never has! He's a big Florida State fan, *and* a Bobby Bowden fan, and for some reason he tells people that, but he *never* has played for them. I'm really sorry about that. I really am."

"It's okay, ma'am," I assured her. "I just wanted to ask."

"Thank you," she said. "I'll have a talk with him when he gets home."

"Don't worry about it. It's no big deal," I said. "I'll be on the way with him in just a minute."

I got into my car, and he climbed in the front passenger seat. In just a moment we were headed down Wares Ferry Road toward his address. We'd traveled about a tenth of a mile when he spoke.

"You're a pretty big dude," he said. "You ever play football?"

Now I am only six foot and weighed one-ninety-five, but I guess with a gun belt and body armor on I seemed somewhat bigger. I thought this was my chance to get even for the whopper of a story he'd been telling me. "Yeah," I replied. "I played at Alabama."

"Wow, that's pretty cool," he said. I could tell he was impressed. "When did you play?"

"I played from 1980 to 83," I said. These were the last years that legendary football coach Paul "Bear" Bryant led the Crimson Tide just before he retired from coaching.

"You're pretty big and you look fast," he said. "I'll bet you were a linebacker."

"No, I was a quarterback," I replied. My imagination shifted into overdrive. "But I didn't get to play much because Steadman Shealy was the starter then, and I didn't get much time on the field."

He sat there for a minute and then I heard him gasp with excitement and he said in an excited whisper, "Oh, my gosh!" he said. "You played for the *Bear!*"

"Well, we called him Coach Bryant," I replied calmly.

"NO! You don't understand," he exclaimed. He was beside himself with excitement. "You played for *THE BEAR!* You played for the *man!* The greatest football coach ever and you played for him!"

I continued calmly, "Well, I hardly got to play much because the starting quarterback never got hurt, so I usually watched the games from the sidelines."

"Yeah, but still, you played for the Bear." Then he hesitated for a moment. "Can I shake the hand of the man who played for the Bear?" he asked.

I smiled. "Sure," I said.

After shaking my hand, he held up his hand before his face. "I shook the hand of the man who played for the Bear!" he said to himself.

I thought for a moment that he was going to give me the old "I'll-never-wash-this-hand-again speech," but he stopped short of that.

As we pulled up to his house, he thanked me for giving him a ride home and told me how honored he was to have ridden in the same car as someone who'd played under the great Bear Bryant. I was having a hard time trying not to laugh.

He was still shaking with excitement as he got out of the car.

"Can you wait right here for just a second?" he asked. "I'll be right back!"

He ran inside his house, and it reminded me of an excited seven-year-old boy eager to show off something special. After about two minutes he returned walking slowly. The disappointment was evident on his face. "I wanted to get a picture with you," he said. "But I can't find my camera."

"Well, maybe next time," I said, all the while thinking how glad I was that he couldn't find that camera. As I drove away, I started to laugh and shake my head. I only came up with a tall tale of my own to counter the whopper he was telling me. I had no idea he'd react the way he did and I didn't have the heart to tell him I made it up. I've told this story many times to people I know, and I'm always asked the same question, "What would you have done if he'd had his camera?"

I really don't know what I would have done. I guess I would have pretended I had an emergency or something and left there in a hurry. I would have had to cover up one lie with another. My mom and dad raised me not to lie and I've always tried to follow their teaching, but this was one of those times I just couldn't resist. Regardless of whether it was right or wrong to mislead him like I did, I'll never forget the excitement he showed and the look on his face as he exclaimed...

"You played for the *Bear!*"

River Region Chaplain Service

ON THE VERY FIRST DAY I attended the police academy in 1983, a very nice gentleman came into our classroom at one point and introduced himself as the police chaplain. This was one of only two times I ever saw or heard from this person, and to this day I couldn't tell you his name.

About five years later, Eddy Luckie, a longtime friend of mine from high school and church, was working as a sound technician for WMCF, the local Christian television station. The station aired a live show with a host who interviewed different guests each night, similar in format to *The Tonight Show*. Some of the guests would also sing and perform.

One particular night, Eddy was working in the sound booth when our own police chaplain was featured as a guest. I don't remember exactly, but he may have been the same chaplain who came to the police academy the first day I was there. Eddy asked the chaplain before the interview about the condition of Officer Mike Morand, who had suffered a near-fatal motorcycle accident about two weeks earlier.

The chaplain was unaware of the accident, so Eddy quickly briefed him about the accident and what he knew about Mike's period in a coma and his painfully slow recovery from a severe head injury. After the show, Eddy called me and asked if I knew who this guy was. I told Eddy that I didn't know him.

Mike had been in my academy class. Eddy and I both had visited Mike in the hospital on several occasions, and he thought it odd that our own police chaplain didn't know about the accident even though it had been on the local television news and in the newspaper several times since it happened. This really bothered me for years that we had a chaplain who had absolutely no connection to or interest in the department or its officers.

In late 1994, I had been talking with Ricky Creech of the Montgomery Baptist Association about the need for a real police chaplain for our department. I had also talked with Captain Wyatt Gantt, our media relations officer, about starting a chaplain program. Ricky Creech and I put together a program and presented it to Captain Gantt, who told us he would discuss the matter with Lieutenant Colonel Pierce-Hanna, the Deputy Chief of Police.

Months went by with no response.

On October 3, 1994, Sergeant J.R. Ward was shot while chasing two robbery suspects. J.R. managed to get on the radio one last time and notify the dispatcher that he had been shot. He died moments later. I remember screaming in the car while en route to his location, "THIS IS WHY WE NEED A POLICE CHAPLAIN!"

January 22, 1995, Officer Willie Pryor was killed in a police motorcycle accident on Woodley Road. In three months, two officers had been killed in the line of duty and we still did not have a police chaplain and I had not heard anything about the proposal I had given Captain Gantt.

In February, 1995, I received a copy of a memorandum addressed to Lt. Col. S.M. Pierce-Hanna from Captain Wyatt Gantt, dated September 12, 1994, and the subject was typed in all capital letters, "DEPARTMENTAL CHAPLAINCY PROGRAM." On the top right of the memo was a handwritten notation from the Deputy Chief, "Captain Gantt, The Chief and I agree. Let's give this program a shot. Have Steve proceed!"

At the bottom of the memo was another handwritten notation addressed to me from Captain Gantt, "Proceed with talking to Ricky about this. Let me know how I can help."

February of 1995, the Cops for Christ program had been going strong for three years and Firefighters for Christ had just been established by Captain Jeff Thompson of the Montgomery Fire Department. Officers were still grieving over the deaths of Sergeant Ward and Corporal Pryor, but both of these losses highlighted the need for a chaplain who could be exclusively available for officers who needed a minister and someone with whom to pray in an hour of need. Until then, local pastors had been kind enough to go to the hospital during a tragedy to comfort and minister to the families and officers.

Little did I know that the Lord was already working on the problem. Lieutenant Colonel Sandy Pierce-Hanna had been doing research on Police Chaplaincy programs around the country and had presented the idea to Chief John Wilson and Mayor Emory Folmar. Both seemed to like the idea but they needed more information. Lieutenant Colonel Pierce-Hanna called me to her office to discuss the idea. She wanted to establish a committee to discuss what would be needed to begin a program. I was chosen because of my involvement with Cops for Christ and she felt like I would be a good representative for the police department because I had no political agenda by being on the committee.

The first Interdenominational Police Chaplaincy Council Committee met on October 3, 1996. Members of the committee were: Neal Hughes, pastor of McGehee Road Baptist Church; Robert Finley, the executive director of the Alabama State Trooper's Association; Buddy McGohon, the director of missions for the Montgomery Baptist Association; Captain Billy Henderson with the Alabama State Troopers; Art Long, the associate pastor of Eastmont Baptist Church; Lieutenant Colonel Sandy Pierce-Hanna; and myself as founder of Cops for Christ.

Our first meeting lasted about an hour and was an introduction meeting. It began by discussing the need for the position of police chaplain and to work on the job description. We committed the chaplaincy program to prayer and asked the Lord for guidance in the right direction. Years later, I found out that Art Long had been hired as a police officer in 1980 with the intent that he would become the police chaplain. Unfortunately, the MPD was not ready for a chaplain at that time, and it never happened. So the Lord had a plan in the making long before I came to work for the police department.

June 7, 1996, the committee met with Debra Nowell with the Montgomery Baptist Association (MBA) Community Ministries for Chaplaincy Program for the Montgomery Police Department.

June 26, 1996, Debra Nowell attended the monthly Cops for Christ meeting and shared with us the progress of the plans for a chaplain for the police department. She told us that the MBA Church and Community Ministries Council had placed the beginning of a police chaplaincy program as a major goal of 1997 through their strategy planning efforts. She stated that, "We are hoping many of our churches will see the need, catch the vision, and support this ministry." This was very encouraging that the program was coming to fruition and soon we would have our first official police chaplain.

October 22, 1996, at 6:45 p.m. the Montgomery Baptist Association had its annual meeting at Ridgecrest Baptist Church. There were several speakers and singers and Captain Gantt and I were in a short skit about the starting of a new Police Chaplaincy Ministry. The more the MBA talked about the program the closer I knew the dream of having a police chaplain was coming true. The Lord was at work at the Montgomery Police Department.

June 2, 1997, after almost three years of planning, Kim Grueser, the Pastor of Valley Park Baptist Church, began his first official day as police chaplain. The program was funded by the Montgomery Baptist Association with donations from area churches. Ironically, on his first day as chaplain, as he sat in Lieutenant Colonel Pierce-Hanna's office, several officers were involved in a police shooting at Madison Avenue and North Ripley Street, just one block away from the police department. A disturbed young man had driven around waving a gun and firing it randomly out of the window as he sped through town. He had been followed by several patrol units, who were eventually able to stop his vehicle in heavy traffic. The officers then confronted him and were forced to shoot and kill him.

Chaplain Grueser and Lieutenant Colonel Pierce-Hanna walked to the scene and the new chaplain was able to not only comfort Officer Donnie Walker, who was injured slightly, but also an elderly couple who had witnessed the entire event. Chaplain Grueser recounted the events of that Monday afternoon.

"Baptism by fire," is how Lt. Col. Pierce-Hanna described my first minutes as chaplain for the Montgomery Police Department. Pierce-Hanna was the second-in-command to Police Chief John Wilson. She was a strong supporter of the ministry. I arrived at her office, for what

I assumed to be, an afternoon of polite introductions with the departmental leadership and a tour of the facilities. My first fifteen minutes of casual conversation in the Lieutenant-Colonel's office abruptly stopped when her law enforcement instincts propelled her to calmly announce, "Let's go."

Pierce-Hanna instantly responded to the call from the radio on the bookshelf behind her desk while I was still in mid-sentence about something neither of us would remember. A man speeds east on Madison Avenue, shooting indiscriminately while driving wild through the busy downtown district of the capital city during midday traffic. This had all the marks of a suicide-by-cop tragedy in the making. By the time we arrived on the scene the mayhem was subsiding with the out-of-control shooter in custody. My ministerial instincts propelled me to quickly identify an injured officer. He sat on the curb waiting medical treatment for a leg injury he got when he was knocked over by another officer's car in the confusing climactic moments of the chase. Nothing memorable was said by either of us as I knelt next to him. Maybe my presence would be reassuring, I thought. Soon, the arrival of the mayor, media and medical team meant it was time for me to move on. Sometimes ministry happens over long periods, sometimes in a moment. This was one of those moments."

Anything done for the Lord encounters obstacles. The chaplaincy ministry was no different. The administration did not fully support the program, but could not publicly appear to resist the ministry. Anything new seems to be met with resistance, especially if it involves any type of ministry. Rumors of the Chaplain trying to recruit people to come to his church spread throughout the police department. These rumors were completely false but as rumors go, people would rather believe the lie than find out the truth. Chaplain Grueser had recruited ten pastors from several different denominations to serve as volunteer chaplains.

Chaplain Grueser was venturing through uncharted territory with the chaplaincy program. He was putting in twenty to forty hours a week at police headquarters attending functions and getting to know the officers. Many of the officers were stand-offish and did not want to be around a chaplain. Some officers believed that religion and police work did not belong together. How wrong they were. Some officers were afraid that anything said to the chaplain would get back to supervisors and they would be in trouble. This was also a misnomer. I would take every opportunity to talk to the chaplain and introduce him to other officers whenever I saw him. He even went on a ride-a-long with me on patrol one night. The administration accepted the program in incremental stages. First, there was a period of cautious approval, then it transitioned into trust. This gave Chaplain Grueser greater access to minister to the officers in the department.

November 13, 1997, the police department held a news conference and announced the Police Chaplaincy Program and introduced Chaplain Kim Grueser as the official police chaplain for the Montgomery Police Department.

February 5, 1998, Chaplain Grueser and I were interviewed for the Montgomery Advertiser for an article that appeared in the February 7th issue. The article was on the Police Chaplaincy program and the Cops for Christ program. The program was now getting a lot of media attention and the officers were becoming more receptive of the chaplain.

February 24, 1999, the Montgomery Advertiser wrote an article about the seventh anniversary of the Cops for Christ and the fifth anniversary of the Firefighters for Christ program.

November 3, 1999, Bobby Bright beat out incumbent Mayor Emory Folmar and became our new mayor. During the election, I met Bobby Bright at a campaign function given by Beasley and Allen attorneys at the train shed on Waters Street. While my partner and I were eating, Bright sat down and talked with us. The subject of Cops for Christ came up and the Chaplaincy Program and he was very interested. He asked how many meetings Mayor Folmar had attended. When I told him "none", he said that if he was elected mayor he would be attending.

After the election, Chaplain Grueser set up an appointment with Mayor Bright to discuss making the Police Chaplain a full-time paid position. I was home on a sick day when the mayor called me at home to verify the appointment. To have the mayor call me at home was quite a shock. We met with him on December 13, 1999 at his office. He was very receptive to the idea of a full-time paid chaplain but would have to see what was in the budget. We would possibly have to wait until the following year for it to be put into the budget. I liked the idea of the chaplain being paid from the city budget but I did not want the entire salary paid from there. If there were ever serious budget cuts then I felt like the chaplain program would be one of the first to go. Currently the part-time position was being paid through the Montgomery Baptist Association from the Interdenominational Police Chaplaincy Program. This is funded by several different churches giving to the program.

August, 2000, Chaplain Kim Grueser resigned from Valley Park Baptist Church and took another position as pastor at the First Baptist Church in Pelham, Georgia. Because he was moving to Georgia he had to resign as our Police Chaplain. Even though the program appeared to be successful, it never really was accepted by the administration. The program needed to be revamped and looked at again. God had blessed us with a program, we just needed to improve on it, and so we went back to the drawing board.

We began meeting, taking an existing plan from the North American Mission Boards Chaplain program and re-wrote it line by line to fit the Montgomery Police Department. On April 17, 2001, we had the first draft of the new Chaplaincy Program with a job title and description. We then reviewed it and after a little more fine tuning we were ready to present it to Mayor Bright.

June 6, 2001, the Montgomery Advertiser wrote another story on the Cops for Christ program. I was interview by phone while on second shift patrol. I sat in the Wal-Mart parking lot on the East South Boulevard and conducted a twenty minute interview. In the interview I was asked about the search for a police chaplain. I told the reporter that all we wanted from the police department was a cell phone, pager and an office for the chaplain to be able to talk to officers in private. I told the reporter that we did not want any money from the city, whatsoever. We wanted the program to be financially supported by area churches. We were hoping to present the plan to the mayor in the next two or three weeks.

I did not know it during the interview but the reporter had also interviewed Pamela Summers, a staff attorney with the American Civil Liberties Union (A.C.L.U.). She said there could be a question of the constitutionality for taxpayers who may oppose public money being used for the program. She was quoted in the paper as saying, "I am not precisely certain if taxpayer funding is enough to render something unconstitutional, but they probably ought to think about that a little." I made a point to state in my interview that the program did not want to use taxpayer money but maybe that was not mentioned to the A.C.L.U. attorney. All I knew was that there were police departments and sheriff's offices all over the country that had chaplains and I did not think this would be a problem. I also knew that God was in control and that if He wanted the Montgomery Police Department to have a Chaplain's Program, then we would have one.

I truly believed that God wanted us to have a chaplain. I had to remember that we were not working on my time schedule but on God's. And God was in control. Sometimes I have to be reminded of this from time to time. The Inter-denominational Police Chaplaincy Committee continued to look at resumes and pray for the right person for the job. One of the committee members was a pastor from Bethel Baptist Church in Fort Deposit, Alabama named Eric Jackson. He had been a police officer with the Mobile, Alabama Police Department for four years before deciding that his calling was in the ministry. He quit the police department and attended the Southwestern Baptist Theological Seminary in Texas and graduated in 2000. After several meetings we decided that the best candidate was sitting in the room with us. Eric resigned from the committee and became a candidate for the job. God had provided us with the right person, right under our nose.

June 8, 2001, I was asked to be interviewed on a live call-in show at WVAS radio 90.7 FM. This is the radio station for Alabama State University in Montgomery, Alabama. The university is a historically black college. I was eagerly looking forward to talking about Cops for Christ and the Police Chaplaincy program. I had invited Corporal John Bowman to sit-in with me during the interview. I was retiring in September and he was taking over the program. The Cops for Christ program was in its ninth year.

The first caller asked about the program and said it was a great idea that there were Godly men and women with the police department. They knew that we were under a lot of stress and this was a great thing. The rest of the callers wanted to talk about racial profiling and how it was wrong. I tried several times to turn the program back to the Cops for Christ program but most of the callers did not want to talk about it. The interview lasted for an hour. It was a great experience.

April, 2001, Eric Jackson was hired and became the chaplain for the Montgomery Police Department. The Lord answered our prayers, as I knew He would, and brought us the right man for the job. Eric's experience as a police officer and now a minister made him the perfect fit. Many pastors decide they want to work as police chaplains, when in fact they just want to "play police." They like the idea of riding on patrol and the excitement of looking for criminals. Eric had already been a police officer and was led by God to the ministry.

September 7, 2001, the Montgomery Advertiser wrote a story about Eric, our new police chaplain. Since accepting the job in July, he was fitting in and relating well with the officers. The new revamped chaplaincy program was working better than ever. This by no means takes away from what Kim Grueser did as a police chaplain for two years. Kim came into a brand new program with his back against the wall. He was at a disadvantage because he had not been in law enforcement and did not relate to the officers as well as Eric. It has something to do with, *once-a-cop, always-a-cop* mentality. The original program was not embraced by the administration and I believe they were looking for a reason for it to fail.

As I look back over the years, I can see where God was there every step of the way. Even when it looked like the program was doomed to fail, God was putting the right people in the right place to carry out His plan. We must walk by faith and not by sight (2 Corinthians 5:7), when doing the Lord's work.

The Interdenominational Police Chaplaincy Program was established in 1996. In 2007, it became known as the River Region Chaplain Service.

SUPPORTING EACH OTHER WHILE SERVING THE PEOPLE

File photo

Steve Smith, right, leads the group in prayer during a lunch meeting of Cops for Christ and Firefighters for Christ at Young House Restaurant.

Cops for Christ seeks chaplain

Police officers share the burden of their duties with God and with each other

By Jannell McGrew
Montgomery Advertiser

They wear their badges with pride, and they believe in the Bible.

Cops for Christ has been a outlet for officers who want to join a support group for men and women who serve and protect.

More than a dozen Montgomery Police officers use the group as a forum to discuss issues they face at work. The religious group is currently looking for an official police department chaplain and are asking for the mayor to approve it.

The only thing we are asking for is a cell phone, a pager and an office the chaplain can have. We aren't asking for any money from the city whatsoever," said Cpl. S.Z. Smith of the Montgomery Police Department and co-founder of the group.

"I couldn't get through it without God. We all are human. It's good to get together with other Christians. It strengthens me. It's good to know the people I work with and be able to fellowship with them."
— Det. John Bowman

He said about five or six churches are on tap to help fund the endeavor and superiors are reviewing the drafted job description. The position is part-time, he said, and the pay would be about $15,000 a year.

"Hopefully, the mayor will get it within the next week or two," Smith said. "We take a lot home with us, and we have to remember the hurt, pain and sorrow. With the kind of work we do every day, we need someone to talk to."

Det. John Bowman, 26, is a crime scene detective for the Montgomery Police De-

"We take a lot home with us, and we have to remember the hurt, pain and sorrow."
— Cpl. S.Z. Smith

partment. He began coming to Cops for Christ gatherings as a cadet in 1994.

"I couldn't get through it without God. We all are human," Bowman said. "It's good to get together with other Christians. It strengthens me. It's good to know the people I work with and be able to fellowship with them."

Bowman said he also liked the idea of someday having a full-time chaplain.

Pamela Sumners, a staff attorney with the American Civil Liberties Union, said there could be a question of constitutionality for taxpay-

ers who may oppose using public money.

"I am not precisely certain if taxpayer funding is enough to render something unconstitutional," she said. "But they probably ought to think about that a little. If it's going to be sectarian or not, they probably need to make some effort to make it voluntary.

"If they could provide them (officers) with non-religious counselors, what's the purpose of setting up a chaplaincy, and that's a question the court might ask."

Smith said there "shouldn't be a problem" since the program won't be using public money.

"Even in the event we had budget cuts, the chaplain wouldn't be affected because there are no public monies being used," Smith said.

Sumners noted that in *Marsh vs. Chambers*, the Supreme Court ruled the Nebraska legislature was not violating the constitution when it opened its legislative session with a chaplain-led prayer.

June 6, 2001 – Newspaper article from our monthly Cops for Christ meeting. Pictured at table are Lt Darryl Sambor and Capt Jeff Thompson of the Montgomery Fire Dept and Det. John Bowman, Montgomery Police Dept. (Courtesy of Montgomery Advertiser)

317

Before He Makes a Threatening Phone Call

DOMESTIC VIOLENCE HAS ALWAYS BEEN a problem, but for years the police didn't have much power if the victim didn't want to sign a warrant. But O.J. Simpson's murder trial brought the problem to light and nearly every state enacted new laws to require the police to help those who were victims of this terrible crime.

On Saturday, April 25, 1998, Officer Rhett Hooper and I responded to a domestic violence call on Yarborough Street. The dispatcher advised us that the victim was receiving threatening phone calls from her boyfriend. We arrived at the residence and sat in the living room as the young woman told us about how her boyfriend had been calling her all day, about every ten or fifteen minutes. She said he had been accusing her of sleeping with other guys. She told us that he was just jealous whenever she talked to another man.

We hadn't been there more than a couple of minutes when the phone rang. "That's him callin' again," she said.

I answered the phone and a man on the other end of the phone began the conversation by saying, "Who the f★★k are you?"

"My name is Steve. Who are you?" I replied calmly.

"I'm Charles Blake,*who the hell are you?"

"I told you, I'm Steve and you are rude and I not talkin' to you no more." I hung up the phone.

"You shouldn't have done that," the woman said. "Now he is goin' to be really mad and come over here."

"Well, that will be good. Then we can take care of the problem when he gets here."

★   Name changed to protect the rude and abusive

The phone rang again and I answered and he shouted, "I'm comin' over and kickin' your ass, motherf★★ker!"

"Sir, why are you callin' and harrassin' this lady?" I asked.

"Who are you?" he asked. "Are you f★★kin' her?"

"No sir, I'm not."

I talked to the angry man for a few more minutes and he threatened several times to come over and kick my rear end. I tried several times to get him to come over to the house but each time he refused.

He continued to cuss me until I told him, "Okay, sir, I need to tell you that I'm Corporal Steve Smith, and I am a Montgomery Police Officer. I'm here because of all the threatening phone calls you made to your girlfriend."

He quickly changed his tone. "Hey, man, I don't have any problem with you," he said apologetically.

"You threatened me and I am going to sign a warrant on you for threatening me."

"I never threatened you, officer!"

"Yes, you did, sir, and you need to turn yourself in because I am on my way to sign a warrant on you."

I hung up on the guy, and told the woman that she needed to sign a warrant on him also for harassing communication. We left and I drove to headquarters and went to the warrant clerk's office and swore out a warrant. Since she told me his name and she told me his address I had all the information I needed.

Rhett could not believe I actually signed a warrant on him.

"It will make him think twice about who he threatens on the phone the next time he calls someone," I explained to my young inexperienced partner.

I found out from another officer that Charles was stopped the next day on the Birmingham Highway for a traffic violation. When the officer brought him down to police headquarters on the warrant I had signed and read the affidavit, his response was, "He really was a police officer!" he said. "If I had known, I never would have threatened him."

I never did go to court on the case so I assume he must have pled guilty to the charge. I thought it was pretty clever how I handled the call. I don't know if the woman ever signed a warrant. If I had to guess, I would say that she didn't. So many times police respond to domestic violence calls and the victims say they will sign a warrant but they never do. Unfortunately, some wait too late to do something about their situation. Maybe this guy will think twice before he makes a threatening phone call.

I Thought It Was Pretty Clever

FRIDAY MAY **1, 1998, I** was assigned a new partner. Officer Larry Maples wasn't too long out of the academy, and I was his second training officer. I was working District One at the time, and with any new partner I began to familiarize him with the district.

It always takes a couple of shifts together to get to know a new partner. Larry had attended Faulkner University where he was a star basketball player before becoming a police officer. He was also a squared away soldier who was serving in the U.S. Marine Corps Reserves. Larry was eager to learn, and I soon found out just how "gung ho" he was.

We were patrolling down Mobile Street near Mildred Street one afternoon when we observed a young man walking down the street. As I slowed down at the intersection and pulled up next to him, the man glanced over his left shoulder toward us then bolted like a scared rabbit.

Larry, without hesitation, jumped from the still moving patrol car and took off after him. Larry chased the man behind the buildings and through several back yards, jumping several fences. He caught the man several blocks away on Cobb Street. I was able to follow both of them in the car, catching glimpses of them as they dashed between houses.

Larry walked him back to the car, huffing loudly, still trying to catch his breath, and stated proudly, "I got him!"

"Great job," I said, indicating my approval.

After Larry placed him in the back seat, I asked, "What are you charging him with?"

"He ran, so I chased him," Larry explained.

"What did he do?" I asked.

"Well, he ran—*so* I chased him," he said, with a puzzled tone.

I had Larry get his identification and check him for warrants. The man had probably fled because he had drugs and had tossed them or *thought* he had an outstanding warrant. This is quite common in high crime areas. It turned out that the man didn't have any warrants, and we couldn't find any drugs.

We noted all his pertinent information on a field interview card and told him that if he weren't guilty of a crime there was no need to run. The young man was relieved not to be headed for jail. He apologized and told us of course, that he *wouldn't* do it again.

I explained to Larry that a police officer must be able to articulate the reason for pursuing someone before taking off after them. I'll admit that most folks who run from the police do so because they're guilty of something, but there are those who run because they're simply scared. I also recall a couple of occasions where officers were coaxed into chasing someone in the darkness just to be led into a wire clothesline that snared the officer across the neck causing a painful and embarrassing injury.

At first, Larry was understandably remorseful for chasing the man without a valid reason, until I explained that the man *did* have a reason. We only need to be able to justify why we initiated a pursuit.

Being that it was his first day with a new training officer, I think he felt kind of bad for what he thought was a mistake, even though I explained it was just part of the learning process. So I decided to try and ease the tension and take his mind off of it.

At the time, the Alabama Department of Public Safety was converting the state driver's license from the raised numbers credit card style license to the smooth style with the hologram on the front and the encrypted code on the back.

Because of the change, I got a bright idea for a little prank that I thought would add a little levity to the typical drudgery of the shift.

"Ya know," I started, "I can tell just by looking at a person driving a car if he has a driver's license or not."

Larry looked at me and said, "No way."

"Oh yeah, I can tell," I replied confidently. "Being the seasoned veteran that I am, you learn how to do this. Just stick with me, son, you'll see."

I couldn't really tell of course, but I thought I'd have a little fun with this young officer.

"Okay, prove it," he said. "Point out the next person you see driving with no license and we'll see."

We were sitting on Grady Street at South Holt Street and a couple of cars went by before I saw an untidy looking gentleman in an old junky car drive by. The car was dented up with a clothes hanger for an antenna.

"That guy," I said pointing out the car. "He doesn't have a driver's license."

"Okay, let's stop him and see," Larry said.

So we pulled the man over. I walked up to the driver's door and asked him for his license.

"I don't have one, Officer," he responded.

"Yeah, that's what I thought," I said.

"Why did you stop me, Officer?"

"Because you did not have a driver's license," I replied confidently.

"Yeah, but you didn't know that when you stopped me," he said. "Why'd you stop me before you knew I didn't have a driver's license?"

I hadn't thought what I would say if questioned about how I knew and quickly thought about how the state was changing the driver's license, then I noticed the ornament on the hood of my Ford police cruiser and how it looked like an old fashion radar antenna.

"The new licenses have a chip in them and our police cars are equipped with a sensor," I said. "And whenever a vehicle passes in front of us the sensor will beep. That's how we know if you have a license or not."

He paused for a second and looked at me, "I always wondered how y'all could tell that." He seemed amazed. "I promise I'll get one tomorrow. I've just been so busy I haven't had a chance," he assured me.

I'd heard that story many times before. No matter how old a

driver is they will use the excuse that, *"I've been so busy I just haven't had time to get one."*

My usual response is, "You have worked everyday since your sixteenth birthday and haven't had one free moment to go and get a license?"

Often the unlicensed driver would realize how stupid the excuse sounded, especially if that person was in his thirties or forties.

Since I actually couldn't write the man a ticket because I really didn't know if he had a driver's license, I told him I would let him off with a warning. He expressed his gratitude and went on his merry way.

"How do you come up with these crazy stories and keep a straight face when you tell them?" Larry asked afterward.

"It takes practice."

About three weeks later, Larry and I stopped at a store on Lower Wetumpka Road to get something to drink, and I went in with him.

"Excuse me, Officer," I heard a voice call from behind me. I turned around and saw a gentleman addressing me. "I've been looking for you, Sir," he said.

The man seemed familiar, but I couldn't place him at first. I spoke with so many people during the course of a day that after a couple of weeks it became difficult to recall everyone. He stuck his hand out and handed me his driver's license. I looked at it to see if it would jog my memory, but it didn't.

"You don't remember me," he said. "You stopped me on Holt Street. I didn't beep."

Now I was confused, and my mind was racing a mile a minute. *Didn't beep, didn't beep, what the heck does that mean?*

"You pulled me over because I didn't have a driver's license, and I wanted to show you that I got one now," he explained.

I suddenly remembered who he was. "Oh, that's great," I said. "Glad to see you got a driver's license."

"Yeah, so next time I drive passed you I'll beep, and you'll know I got my license," he said with great enthusiasm. "Well, I gotta go. I just wanted you to know I got my license. Go get some more folks drivin' with no license."

"Okay. I'll do that."

"What was that about?" Larry asked.

I reminded him of the traffic stop, and he got a laugh out of it.

"I can't believe we saw him again and he remembered me," I remarked in disbelief.

That was the one and only time I ever did that. I don't condone that sort of thing, I just got caught up in the moment, and I guess I really wanted to see if I could pick out someone driving with no driver's license. But I have to admit, it wasn't right, but I thought it was pretty clever.

Spring 1998 – Stacy and me before I leave for work

A Once in a Lifetime Call for Me

THURSDAY, MAY 14, 1998, SEEMED at first like any other day, but something happened to make it especially memorable for me. I think every police officer receives a once-in-a-lifetime call, and mine took place that day. Officer Larry Maples, and I were riding downtown in District One. We were leaving the parking lot of headquarters around five in the afternoon after making an arrest when the radio crackled to life with the dispatcher's voice.

"2-0-1!" she said. I could sense tension in her voice as she called our unit number.

Larry was finishing some paperwork in the passenger seat, so I grabbed the radio mike. "2-0-1, North Bainbridge and Columbus," I replied giving our location.

"Be en route to 3780 Day Street on a plane crash," she said.

"3780 Day Street, plane crash," I repeated to confirm that I'd heard the address correctly.

I knew this was serious, so I wanted our supervisor, Sergeant McQueen, to know that we'd be responding in a hurry. "Advise 2-3-3 we'll be running full emergency!" I radioed.

I flipped on the blue lights and siren and gunned the big Crown Vic west down Columbus toward Day street, immediately adjacent to Maxwell Air Force Base a couple of miles away.

"Did she say plane crash?" Larry asked over the wail and yelp of the siren.

"Yes, she did!" I yelled back. "And it must be pretty bad because that's next to Maxwell Air Force Base, and if a citizen had to call it in it must be a big crash!"

Major Armstead, the patrol division commander, came on

the radio. "Why is that unit running emergency?" he asked the dispatcher.

"They're en route to a plane crash!" she replied.

He hesitated for a moment as if to let the information sink in, "Uh, okay. That's ten-four."

Several other patrol and traffic units called in on the radio letting the dispatcher know they were also en route to the area to assist. Several units of the Montgomery Fire Department responded as well.

Larry and I sped cautiously down Day Street toward the 3700 block searching carefully ahead of us for any smoke or fire that would indicate a crash site, but nothing was obvious. I knew that the end of Maxwell's main aircraft runway sat about 100 yards north of Day Street separated by a grassy field and a chain link fence. I began to think maybe a plane had possibly overshot the runway and someone had called it in as a crash, but we saw nothing there.

As we pulled in front of the gate at the entrance to the base, Larry noticed that the military police officers were frantically waving us to the gate. I drove quickly. The MP's were directing cars away to clear a path for us. I spoke with the MP at the gate and asked for directions.

"Turn left at the traffic light, and follow it on around and you'll see it!" he shouted frantically.

I entered the base and continued to run full emergency toward the crash site.

I ran down a mental checklist wondering what type of aircraft I would see when we arrived. Nearly every type of military aircraft from huge, lumbering cargo planes to sleek, heavily armed fighter jets fly in and out of Maxwell on a routine basis. There are also several small private aircraft that use the base as well, so I prepared myself for anything.

We arrived at the Burger King on the base and saw the tail section of a small plane broken off from its fuselage lying on the edge of the parking lot. The forward section of the small military trainer sat in the middle of the parking lot crumpled like a broken toy against a black van. Leaking fuel from the aircraft had ignited and began to burn. The trainer was a two-seater used to instruct new pilots. The cockpit seemed fairly intact, and I couldn't see any victims right away. Bright orange fingers of fire licked furiously up both sides of the crushed fuselage, but the base fire department had already arrived and began to attack the flames.

I was the ranking MPD officer on the scene, so I took charge while I waited for one of my supervisors to arrive. I approached one of the military officers standing at the scene and asked if there were any injuries.

"There's a couple of people lying over there by those bushes," he said calmly pointing toward the Burger King.

He seemed lost somehow, as if he didn't really know what to do. Larry and I walked over to where some other base medical personnel stood. I identified Larry and myself and told him that we were there to assist in any way possible.

He identified himself as a captain and a flight surgeon, and told us that he appreciated all the help. He pointed to one person being worked on by two medics. "Their injuries appear to be serious but not life-threatening," the captain said. "The other appears to have only minor injuries." He pointed toward the restaurant. "There are more injuries over there."

I began to delegate duties to the officers arriving on the scene. I told Officers Maples, Jeff Davis and Mike McCord to go check on each victim and to update me on their conditions as soon as possible so I could advise Sergeant McQueen. I knew the sergeant was on his way to the scene, and I wanted everything secured and evaluated before he arrived.

Corporal Brian Lamb approached me and said that another captain had told him that he wanted our people off the base. The flight surgeon I'd spoken with earlier and the newly arrived captain to whom Corporal Lamb referred spoke briefly and their conversation had evolved into a heated disagreement. I stood some distance away and couldn't hear exactly what was being said, but the two men didn't see eye to eye on something.

I sensed, however, that the "something" was our presence on the base. Maxwell Air Force Base is a federal military facility and legally falls under the exclusive jurisdiction of the federal government and not the city of Montgomery. Technically speaking, MPD officers have no legal authority on the base, although we do have an agreement with the federal authority there to assist one another in times of disaster.

Sergeant McQueen arrived, and I updated him on what we knew so far. I told him about the captain who wanted us off the base.

The second captain had apparently won the argument with the flight surgeon and seemed determined as he approached us. "Sergeant," he began, "Your people need to leave the base *immediately*."

"We're only here because someone from the base called us," McQueen replied.

"I don't care who called you here," he said. "I want all your people off the base—*NOW*!"

Sergeant McQueen quickly turned and looked back at the MPD officers at the scene. "Let's go everybody," he shouted. "We're not wanted here!"

We found out later that when the crash occurred, one of the Maxwell MP's had called 911 and requested that the city police and fire department respond. The MP's seemed lost and unsure about securing a crime scene, which is how any aircraft accident, civilian or military, is usually handled.

I think the captain who ordered us off the base was embarrassed about how his people mishandled the response to the incident.

I'm not really sure if we should have responded to the accident. I've never been in the military, but I always thought a military base the size and importance of Maxwell would have its own 911 system or some emergency phone numbers for that sort of thing.

I was actually surprised that we were allowed onto the base and had immediate access to the crash site, considering how carefully the government and the military work to protect their secrets.

It was my one and only plane crash. Regardless of why we were called, it was still a once in a lifetime call for me.

"I'm a Trained Professional. Don't Try This at Home"

ONE OF THE GREAT THINGS about being a police officer is the interesting people you get to meet. There are some who work very hard every day; then there are those who've never done an honest day's work in their lives. There are some who are as good as gold and would give you the shirt off their back or their last dollar. Then there are those who are only alive because it's against the law to kill them. I know that doesn't sound very Christian, but the truth is the truth.

Then there are those people you meet who defy all explanation. In the end you're glad you've met them because they're so unbelievable, but at the same time it would scare you to know what they do when no one else is around.

Allow me to elaborate.

On Sunday, June 7, 1998, my partner, Officer Larry Maples and I were on patrol one afternoon in the downtown district. It was a slow day, and we were looking for something to do. While patrolling on North Bainbridge Street, we saw several guys who looked to be in their thirties standing in the parking lot of the local housing project just talking in a relaxed group. I like to stop and talk to people when we are not on calls just to be friendly, and not in the manner of someone investigating a crime.

We got out, walked over, and asked them all how things were going. It was a hot afternoon and they were cooling off with a few beers. I noticed that they were nervously trying to hide the cans.

"Relax, guys," I said. "We're not stopping you because you're drinking beer. We're just stopping to shoot the breeze."

"That's cool man. I really 'preciate it. It's a little hot today and we're just chillin'," one of them said.

"Yeah, we're just bored and looking to kill some time." I said.

As we were talking I noticed one of the guys who had his shirt off had some oval-shaped serrated wounds on his chest.

"Are those bite marks on your chest?" I asked.

He looked down at his chest and answered nonchalantly, "Yeah, I guess they are."

He stepped away from the car and I noticed he had three unmistakable sets of deep bite marks on his chest. I looked at him in somewhat disbelief and asked, "How many bites do you have on you?"

"Oh, I don't know. I guess a couple."

"Who did this to you?" I asked, thinking I might have stumbled onto a domestic violence case.

"My girl did this. She's a real freak. I think I've got some on my back too." He turned around and he had two more sets of similar marks on his lower back.

"Man, are you okay? When did you get into this fight with her?"

"Fight!" He exclaimed. "We wasn't fightin'. We're havin' sex," he replied with pride.

"Sex! What kind of sex are you having where you're gettin' bit?"

"Man, my girls a freak and she was gettin' her freak on. And she was doin' things to me. Man, she was wild!" he explained with great enthusiasm. "If she wants to bite me while we're havin' sex, its okay with me."

Not quite believing what I heard, I decided to humor him. "So you were having that wild monkey sex where you're chasin' each other around the room and squealin' like pigs."

A huge smile erupted on his face as he raised his hand up to me for a high-five. "Oh yeah! You're feelin' me, you know exactly what I'm talkin' about! I think you must have a freak for a girlfriend also."

I quickly responded, "Oh, no! Not me. That's not quite my

speed. I can honestly say I've never been bitten making love. My wife is not the "freak" kind."

"You don't know what you're missin', man," he said.

We chatted another minute or two, but we got a call and had to leave.

I asked Larry later what he thought about the guy and his cannibalistic girlfriend. He said that he thought they were *both* freaks.

I have heard a lot things but that was a first. I've heard stories of similar encounters from other officers, but it's different when someone relates the tale and has the marks to prove it.

I've met some interesting people during my twenty-plus years in law enforcement, but I will always remember that guy as one of the most colorful. He spoke of this peculiar brand of lovemaking as if it were nothing out of the ordinary. I guess being eaten alive in the throes of passion is just another day for some folks.

After he finished telling about his exploits, I felt like he should have warned us all, "I am a trained professional. Don't try *this* at home."

"Yeah, Good Thing"

PATROL OFFICERS SERVE AS FIRST responders to any emergency, and their primary job is to answer calls for help from citizens. First responders have a responsibility to assess any situation, often in a hurry, then decide how it should be handled. Most calls for service are routine, although cops tend to cringe a little when the word "routine" is used. It's usually on a routine call that an officer can find himself in a life or death situation.

Mildred Street runs through the middle of District One. The area is poor and the houses that line it are old, mostly wood-frame structures that hold only memories of better days in years long past. Only a few of the homes are well-kept by the mostly elderly population. The younger people who live there are mostly jobless sorts who have moved in with grandma to avoid paying rent.

Officer Shawn Wright had just graduated the police academy two weeks prior, and I was his first training officer. Shawn was in his early twenties and had spent a tour of duty in the Marine Corps before beginning his career with the Montgomery Police Department.

On Wednesday July 22, 1998, we were dispatched at around 4:00 in the afternoon to an address in the 600 block of Mildred Street on a report of a suspicious person. The dispatcher relayed by radio that an elderly woman called and complained that someone was in her house and wouldn't leave.

These types of calls can be anyone from an ex-husband, boyfriend, roommate, or even one of the homeowner's children who refuses to move out. In this case, however, the clerk who spoke with the woman seemed to think the woman might be mentally ill. This always adds an interesting twist to any call. Mentally ill people often call the police because they hallucinate or imagine things that aren't really there. To them, of course, the illusions are real, but we always have to check and make sure the person in distress is facing an actual threat. Either way, you have to be prepared for anything and to expect the unexpected.

We pulled up to the house and climbed the old uneven brick steps onto the rickety porch. Some of the boards looked rotten and were patched with plywood. We had to take care making our way up. Repairs to these old homes are often done poorly and in haste. I knocked on the door and a woman who looked to be in her late seventies answered the door.

"How are you, ma'am?" I asked. "Did you call the police?"

"Yes, I did!" she replied. "You gotta do something about him. He won't leave my house!"

"Who is he?" I asked.

"That boy that comes into my house all the time and won't leave."

"What's his name?"

"I don't know what his name is," she said. "Just make him leave!" I could hear anger and desperation in her voice.

"How's he getting in the house?" I asked.

She pointed toward the air conditioner unit mounted in a nearby window. "He comes in through there," she said.

I looked at my partner. He had this look on his face that said. 'Great, another crazy person.'

I composed myself a little and tried to keep the amused smile off my face. "So, where is he right now?" I asked.

"He's in the back bedroom."

We walked to the back bedroom of the three bedroom house and she opened the door

"There he is!" She pointed toward the full size bed against the far wall.

"Where exactly is he?" I asked.

She put her hands on her hips with disgust. "Right there!" She pointed into the room. "Standing on the bed!"

I leaned over to Shawn. "Follow my lead on this one," I whispered.

I pulled my handcuffs out of my cuff case with my right hand and entered the room. "Alright, you gotta go with us now," I said to the phantom standing on the bed. I reached out as if to grab someone's arm and ratcheted the cuffs one time so she could hear me using them. I pretended to handcuff the person then led him from the room.

I walked down the hallway toward the front door. "Okay, ma'am. I got him now," I said. Then I turned to the phantom I was escorting. "Let's go to the car and we will take you downtown, fella."

I told my partner in a voice loud enough for the woman to overhear. "Open the back door so I can put him in."

As I walked to the back door of the patrol car, Shawn opened the door and stood back. I walked up to the door and tossed the handcuffs on the back seat. "Get in the car!"

I looked back at the woman who had followed us outside. "Well, we got him out of your house and we're taking him to the police station," I said. "He won't be back to bother you anymore."

She walked over to the back window of the car and looked in. She shook her finger at the phantom. "Don't come back to my house *no more!*" she shouted.

She thanked us and seemed much happier as we drove away.

"How did you know to do that?" Shawn asked. "You know, pretend that you put handcuffs on him and take him outside to the car."

"Sometimes you just have to improvise when you handle a call," I said. "If they can see someone, then he's real to them, and you have to make them believe you can see him also. She may never have to call us again because we took time to take care of a problem she had. She may have told other people about the person in her house and they didn't believe her."

Shawn paused a moment. "How do you keep from laughing when you do stuff like that?"

"Sometimes it's not always easy," I said. "You just have to do what you have to do to get the job done. But we were lucky on this one. It could have been worse."

"Worse?" Shawn said. "How could it have been worse?"

While trying to keep a straight face, I looked straight ahead while driving down the street and said in my most serious voice, "He could have wanted to fight us. Then things could have gotten really ugly."

My partner thought for a second, then looked at me and started to laugh. I started laughing with him.

He could only reply, "Yeah, good thing."

BEFORE SOMETHING TERRIBLE HAPPENS TO HIM

PART OF THE POLICE OFFICER'S job is making arrests, and for the most part that never bothered me. After all, when someone broke the law, it was my duty to make the arrest if I was able to do so. Occasionally, I felt a degree of pity for the person going to jail because he or she may have used some poor judgment and did something stupid, or in the case of juveniles, got pulled into something illegal through peer pressure.

The good thing about juvenile arrests is that in almost every case those records are sealed when the defendant turns eighteen allowing the person to begin his or her adult life with a clean slate. That's a good thing because a minor run-in with the law shouldn't keep a kid from succeeding in life. The truth is that most kids who do stupid things and get a second chance usually have no further problems within the judicial system.

I did, however, encounter people whose arrest gave me a great deal of satisfaction. Certain people committed crimes against their fellow man that were cruel and mean and scarred their victims for life. A burglar who broke into someone's house could forever remove whatever sense of security the victim had felt in his own home. Those who committed crimes against helpless children, the handicapped or the elderly were what I considered the worst of the lot, with the possible exception of murderers and rapists. I often wished I could have been the judge on their cases because anything less than life in prison without parole wasn't punishment enough.

One person I didn't enjoy arresting, however, was a young man

I knew personally. Unfortunately, the night he broke the law, the duty of enforcing justice fell on me.

On Friday night, August 7, 1998, we were on bike patrol riding the Brentwood neighborhood near Fairlane Drive and Vaughn Road. Sergeant Shannon Fontaine, Officer Genifer Kennedy and I were assigned this detail, hoping to catch a serial rapist who had assaulted several elderly women in the area. The neighborhood had been saturated by both marked and unmarked units attempting to locate the suspect. We decided to try patrolling the area on bicycles in plain clothes for better and more complete coverage. The department had not yet implemented a regular bike patrol unit, so the officers working the detail at that time used our own bicycles.

I suggested that we meet at Harvest Temple on Vaughn Road and Fairlane Drive at eight that evening for a short briefing before we set out into the neighborhood. We left the parking lot and rode down Shamrock Lane. About four or five minutes later, I saw one of my former youth group members, twenty-one-year old, Scott Waldrop,* standing next to a car parked in traffic.

Scott and his family attended our church regularly, but he never seemed interested in learning about the Bible or living a Christian life. He was an intelligent young man with great potential but had recently chosen to live the hip-hop "gangsta" life style. The transition was quite sudden. From one Sunday to the next he transformed himself from an average sixteen-year-old teenager into a modern rendition of Vanilla Ice.

He had his hair combed up with gel in the front like the rapper and he even had gotten a clip-on gold tooth. He also started talking in a gangsta street dialect. He had been in my Sunday school class for several years, so he knew I was a police officer. He frequently asked me if I knew this person or that person. I would often tell him no, but that wasn't always true.

Many of the people about whom he asked were young career criminals destined for a life spent in and out of prison. A few of the people he mentioned were extremely dangerous felons. He liked the idea of hanging out with those guys because of the appeal of the "gangsta" lifestyle portrayed on television and in the movies. I

---

* Name changed to protect the not so innocent

didn't understand his fascination with this because his parents were good God-fearing people, and I know they didn't raise him to be that way.

Once, the youth minister of our church and I sat down and talked to him about the path he had chosen and the dangers that he faced, but he paid no attention. He told us that his hope was to get shot by the police one day so he could sue the city for millions of dollars.

I explained that people who are shot by the police are breaking the law and are perceived as a threat to the officer or the general public when they are shot. Most of the suspects shot by the police do not survive. Those who do and sue the police department rarely win any money from a lawsuit. The simple fact was that in almost every case, a police officer who shoots someone is justified in doing so.

Scott was in my Sunday school for six years and I tried my best to teach him and set a Christian example but he was not interested.

The other officers with me stopped when we approached Scott, and I began talking to him. He had graduated high school three years earlier and was working, and attending college.

"Whatcha' doin' ridin' a bike?" he asked me in his "gangsta" dialect. "I thought you was doin' crime scene stuff. Did ya change jobs?"

"No," I replied. "We're riding a special detail looking for criminals."

I didn't want to reveal too much about the detail we were working on the chance that he knew the suspect we were hunting.

I asked him how he was doing and if he was still in school and where he was working. As we chatted, he seemed nervous, as if he was in a hurry for me to leave. Usually he was talkative and wanted to brag about the latest criminal he'd met as if trying to impress me.

We talked for about five minutes, but as we rode past the vehicle, I smelled the distinctive smell of burning marijuana emitting from the opened passenger window.

I immediately turned around. "What's that smell, Scott?"

"What smell?" he answered quickly. "I don't smell nothin'."

I got off my bike and walked to the car window and bent down. I could smell the distinctly strong odor of burning marijuana.

"Have you got dope in the car?" I looked straight at him.

"No. You know I don't do that, Steve," he replied.

I could tell he was hiding something. I walked around to the driver's side of the vehicle and looked down at the floorboard, I noticed a bulge under the floor mat.

I looked at him again. "You don't mind if I look in your car, do you, Scott?"

"No!" he said. "Go ahead. I don't got nothin' to hide."

I pulled up the floor mat and found two bags of marijuana inside two clear plastic bags tied in a knot.

"What's up with this, Scott?" I asked. I held up the two bags for him and the other officers to see.

"I'm sorry, Steve," he pleaded. "Could you please cut me a break on this?"

"Why should I cut you a break for this?" I was firm with him. "You know this is against the law. You were in my Sunday school class for six years and I have preached to you about being a criminal and hanging out with criminals."

"Man, I am so sorry." An element of panic crept into his voice. "Could you please cut me a break on this? I won't do it again. This is my first time."

"Scott, you know me and you know what I stand for," I said. "You not only broke the law, but you have embarrassed me in front of my fellow officers. Why should I cut you a break?"

"I know. I know. I'm sorry," he said.

"Well, Scott, you know me and I told you one day your sins would catch up with you," I said. "And guess what?"

"What?"

"Today is your day," I told him solemnly. "Put your hands behind your back. You're under arrest for possession of marijuana."

"Please don't. I'm sorry, Steve," he pleaded. "I won't do it again. *Pleeese* don't take me to jail."

"I can't do it, Scott. You know I'm a straight shooter and I told you that if I ever caught you breaking the law I would arrest you."

"I know. I know. You did," he said. His head dropped as I cuffed his hands behind his back.

I looked at Sergeant Fontaine. "I think we have a flaw in our plan, sir."

"And what's that, sir?" he replied.

"How are we going to transport him back to the office?" I asked. "We don't have a car."

We all then realized that we were on bikes and hadn't counted on making an arrest. Sergeant Fontaine rode back to the church a few blocks away, and drove the truck to where we were while Genifer and I waited with our prisoner. We transported Scott to the narcotics office, and I began the arrest paperwork.

I spoke with the narcotics investigator and told him that Scott was a punk whom I'd known for several years and that he would work as an informant and buy drugs from dealers to work off the arrest. If he didn't want to cooperate, then I'd sign the warrant and send him to jail. I never told Scott that I did this for him to keep him from going to jail.

The following Sunday I saw him in the hallway, walking toward the sanctuary and I spoke to him. He ignored me and walked right on by. This didn't surprise me, and I wasn't offended. His parents also refused to speak to me. I never told anyone at church about the arrest. I figured that should stay between Scott, the legal system, and me.

About three Sundays after the arrest I saw him walking down the hall toward the sanctuary. I expected another snub like the many I'd received since the arrest, but he surprised me again.

He walked to me and stuck out his hand to shake mine. "I am so sorry for the way I have acted toward you the last couple of weeks," he said. "I was wrong, and you were just doing your job. I want to apologize to you."

You could have knocked me over with a feather. I was shocked and pleasantly surprised. I never expected him to do that.

"I really appreciate that, Scott," I said. "I hated that I had to do it, but I have a job to do."

"I understand and I just wanted to say I am sorry." He then left and went into the sanctuary.

Eventually even his parents spoke to me again.

I never asked what happened with his case, and I never mentioned it to him again. Afterward, when I saw him in church, we would exchange pleasantries and go about our usual business. I saw him around town from time to time and heard he was still living his "gangsta" lifestyle, but I can only hope that it was only a phase in his life. I always hoped that he would grow out of it before something terrible happens to him.

I Believe this Tactic Saved
my Life that Night

ON THURSDAY, SEPTEMBER **10, 1998,** I was working on the Brentwood Rape Detail from 11:00 p.m. until 3:00 a.m. This was overtime for me because I normally worked second shift patrol and got off at eleven. We were trying to catch a serial rapist who had burglarized and committed sexual assaults on three women in the Brentwood subdivision, located in the east-central part of town.

Several units were assigned to work overtime patrols in the area and stop anyone suspicious walking or riding through the area. We had only a general description of the suspect. All the victims were elderly and were not able to provide us with a specific description. The only thing we knew for sure was that the perpetrator was a white male wearing glasses.

After riding the area of Fieldcrest Drive for about two hours, I decided to park and watch the intersection of Fieldcrest Drive and Winchester Road in the heart of the neighborhood. I looked for a place where I could sit somewhat concealed in a marked vehicle.

We had no idea how the suspect entered or left the neighborhood, so I picked one of the busiest intersections to sit and watch. I sat back far enough so as not to be seen by anyone traveling on Fieldcrest Drive, but where I could see vehicles coming well before they reached the stop sign.

Around 2:00 a.m., after about thirty minutes of watching a few cars roll nonchalantly through the stop sign at regular intervals, I observed a pickup truck creeping slowly down Fieldcrest toward the intersection. The truck moved much slower than normal before it stopped completely about thirty feet from the intersection. The driver sat there for about ten to fifteen seconds. Suddenly he floored the gas pedal spinning the rear tires into boiling clouds of white smoke before gaining speed and zooming like a missile through the intersection. I have been asked many times what I consider suspicious. That was what I considered suspicious.

I pulled quickly onto Fieldcrest Drive and headed after him. I could see the tail lights of the truck up ahead. Apparently, none of the stop signs on Fieldcrest were functioning because he didn't stop at any of them. He would slow down briefly, then rocket, ahead and blow through each one. I called in on the radio and notified dispatch that I was after a suspicious vehicle and requested assistance from any nearby unit.

The truck turned left on McGehee Road and then right onto Governor's Drive. Lieutenant Anthony Price, also working the detail, was close by and responded to assist me. With back-up on the way, I lit up the overhead strobes, blasted the siren, and signaled the driver to stop in the 3300 block of Governor's Drive. The driver pulled into the apartment complex and stopped in the middle of the parking lot.

I carefully got out of my car but paused for a moment before approaching the vehicle. I wanted to watch him for any movement that might present a threat. Knowing that this might be our rapist, I didn't want to take any chances. Lieutenant Price arrived and took a position covering the passenger side of the truck.

The driver lowered his head to the left and watched me in the outside driver's mirror. This has always triggered an alarm with me because on previous traffic stops, this tactic always indicated that the driver had something to hide. I was careful to keep my flashlight aimed at the mirror and keep him blinded.

I walked to the driver's window and asked to see his driver's license. Lieutenant Price approached the passenger window. The driver seemed much more nervous than was typical for a routine traffic stop. Slow and deliberate in his movements, the driver attentively watched every move I made. Standing at the window, I picked up a strong odor of alcohol from him, but something else just didn't seem right.

He quietly handed me his driver's license, and I carefully backed away from his truck toward my vehicle, never taking my eyes off of him. He continued to watch me in the outside mirror. As I got back to my car, I told the Lieutenant that the driver was acting kind of "hinky." When someone acts strange or weird like this, I describe it as acting "hinky." I'm not even sure if that's a word or not, but it works for me.

I ran his name on the computer in my car, but he didn't have any warrants. I also ran him on the radio and had the clerks at headquarters check for any warrants with the Sheriff's Office. I noticed during the warrant check that the driver bent over toward the glove box like he was reaching for something under the seat, but Lieutenant Price was in a position to watch what he was doing, so this didn't particularly alarm me.

I stood there and watched him do all these things like you would watch a toddler doing something he knew was wrong but wasn't smart enough to know you were watching. Once he retrieved whatever he wanted, he sat up quickly and looked around as if no one had seen him.

As I walked to the driver's door again, careful to aim the brilliant beam of my flashlight in his mirror, I saw he had his hands folded in his lap. Between his legs, sitting on the seat, was a black revolver. I thought to myself, *it was not there when I first walked up and spoke to him, and Lieutenant Price had watched him the whole time. So where did he get the pistol?*

He sat motionless and rigid, head up and eyes fixed straight ahead as if he had been called to attention. I told him to put his hands on top of the steering wheel. When he did I reached in, grabbed the pistol and stepped back quickly from the door. I didn't know how he would react once I grabbed the pistol, so I wanted to have some reaction distance between us in case he bailed out of the truck toward me.

I tossed the pistol into the bed of the truck to get it out of my hands, and also to let Lieutenant Price know that I had taken a gun off of him. The man sat there and never moved. I looked at the Lieutenant. He had a bewildered expression on his face as if to ask, *where did he get the gun?* I asked the driver if he had a pistol permit and he admitted he didn't.

I placed him under arrest without incident for carrying a pistol without a permit and sat him in the back seat of my car. I called for a wrecker and was about to search his truck when Price came up to me. "Where did the gun come from?" he asked.

"I don't know," I replied still somewhat confused. "It wasn't there the first time I talked to him."

"Well, I didn't think you would have let him keep it on him." he said.

"He must have gotten it when he bent over toward the glove box."

"No, I watched him. He picked up a cell phone off the floor," Price said.

"He must have pulled it out from behind his back with his left hand while he was reaching for the cell phone with his right," I said grasping at an explanation.

As we talked I kept watching the suspect in the back of the patrol vehicle and he was moving around entirely too much. "Can you check him while I search his vehicle?" I asked.

"Alright."

After searching the driver's side I walked around the back of the truck to search the passenger side when Price called to me to come back to the patrol vehicle. I walked back to the back door and he asked, "Did you put the cuffs in front of him?"

"No, I always put them in back."

Somehow the handcuffs on his wrists had found their way from his back to the front.

"I didn't think you would do that. He's acting very strange," Price said.

We placed the handcuffs behind the man's back again, then I searched the passenger side of the truck and found a small clear plastic bag of cocaine. After the wrecker towed the truck away, I transported the driver and the cocaine to the Vice and Narcotics office. I placed the driver into a locked room that had a hidden video camera.

While in the room, my suspect stepped over the handcuffs again. One of the narcotics investigators came in while we were testing the cocaine and asked me if I had intentionally cuffed him in front.

"Why do y'all keep asking me that?" I replied in frustration. "I always put them in the back. Are they in front of him *again*?" My patience with this suspect was growing thin. "He did that in the back of my car on the stop."

One of the investigators went in the room and moved the handcuffs back behind him again. This time we carefully watched him on the monitor in the other room. After about twenty seconds he bent over, slid his wrists down below his buttocks, stepped backward through his connected arms and put the cuffs in front of him again.

"You know on the stop he pulled a gun out from somewhere and tried to hide it between his legs." I said quietly to the other officers.

This time after he stepped through the cuffs he stood just inside the door and raised his arms as if to attack the first officer to come through the door. The man didn't know we could see this, so the three of us grouped together, burst through the door, and slammed him hard against the wall. We took him by surprise and got control of him immediately. When he was able to get up off the floor, we shackled his feet and cuffed him securely to the desk. That would be the last of that little trick that night.

I charged him with cocaine possession as well as the pistol violation and booked him into the county lockup.

Looking back on the traffic stop, I believe from his actions that he was under the influence of cocaine. He probably took a hit when he first stopped on Fieldcrest Drive, then boiled the tires when the drug hit his system. I'm convinced that he had enough of his faculties and was planning to shoot me if he got the chance. The cocaine, however, must have slowed his reaction time and allowed me to get the gun away from him.

On the rape detail, we were under orders to request a saliva sample for DNA testing from everyone we stopped. Following the unique encounter and the subsequent arrest of this subject, requesting a sample simply slipped my mind. Because of this oversight, I was immediately removed from the Brentwood Rape Detail along with my supervisor that night, Lieutenant Andrew Signore. The Captain told us that the operation was a rape detail and not a drug detail.

Sometimes even when you do a good thing you can't please some people.

Go figure.

Four days later I was jogging on Fieldcrest Drive at around 12:30 a.m. after getting off from work. Lieutenant Jamie Reynolds was working the detail that night and had a vehicle stopped on Fieldcrest Drive at McGehee Road. As I approached, I could see that it was the same pick-up truck.

I stood back behind the patrol car about six feet so the driver couldn't see my face in the blinding flash of the strobe lights. The subject was standing at the rear of his truck. I called Lieutenant Reynolds to the back of the patrol vehicle and told him that this was the guy I had stopped on the previous Thursday. I told him that he was the guy with the gun who, I believed, wanted to shoot me.

I also warned him to avoid my mistake. "You better get a saliva sample or you'll get kicked off the detail, too," I cautioned.

I stood behind the patrol vehicle while Reynolds asked him for a saliva sample. He consented but wanted to know who I was. Reynolds told him I was only a concerned citizen.

He turned out not to be the rapist. The actual rapist was later identified through a DNA match and lived in the neighborhood east of Zelda Road approximately one mile from Fieldcrest Drive as the crow flies. When the investigators went to arrest him, they asked for a patrol unit with a veteran officer to assist. Once I arrived on the scene, they were glad to see me because of my Evidence Technician experience. The arrest went well, and the suspect didn't resist.

It's ironic that even though I had been removed from the detail, I was present for the arrest. Even though the guy I stopped wasn't our rapist, every stop has the potential for danger. Observing the driver watching me in the outside mirror tipped me off yet again that the driver on a traffic stop was up to something. An officer survival school taught me to shine my flashlight in the driver's outside mirror to blind the driver as I approached. I believe this tactic saved my life that night.

You Realize You Just Made a Difference

WHEN YOU'RE A COP, CATCHING a burglar gives you a wonderful feeling. The fact that a person would rather break into something and steal rather than get a job and work for a living has always irritated me. I've been on hundreds of burglary calls in my career, and I've seen first-hand how upsetting it can be to have your home burglarized. I recall many people telling me, "I can't stand the fact that some stranger broke into my house and went through and touched all of my things! We worked so hard for the things we have and someone just came in and took them!"

It wasn't uncommon for people to take every piece of clothing they owned and common items disturbed by the thief and to wash them just because they'd been touched by an invader in their home.

On September 20, 1998, Officer Terrance D. Smith and I were riding the downtown district. Most of the businesses there closed between 5:00 and 6:00 p.m., and as night fell, our biggest problem in the area were the burglars looking to make a quick, dishonest dollar.

Terrance had worked in the jail for several years before transferring to patrol. I found this to be helpful because he was familiar with most of the regulars who did time in our jail and knew the real names of so many people who wandered the streets at night. People often asked us if he and I were related since we had the same last name. The joke there was obvious, because I'm white and Terrance is black. However, I usually responded by saying, "Yes, we're brothers."

Some people don't have a clue.

350

I called him "T" or "Coach," and he also called me "Coach."

We called each other that because we often listened on the radio to the Mike DuBose and to the Pat Dye football call-in shows. At the time DuBose was the head football coach of the University of Alabama, and Dye was the coach at Bama's rival in Auburn.

We would make fun of all the goofy callers with their questions that no one really cared about. Everyone who called into these shows would either say, "Roll Tide, Coach" or "War Eagle, Coach," quoting the rallying cry from each school. Each coach would always respond with, "Roll Tide" or "War Eagle to you too," respectively.

Then the caller would ask something about a fourth or fifth string player known only to very few people other than the coaching staff for that school and the parents of that particular player. Sometimes they'd ask one of the coaches if they remembered meeting the caller at some obscure function from several years earlier. I often wondered how either coach was able to tolerate the ridiculous nature of most of the calls.

Terrance and I would then make fun of the callers with the dumbest questions by asking each other about players that played at Alabama or Auburn five or ten years earlier.

I would look over at Terrance and say, "Hey, Coach! Roll Tide, Coach!"

He would always respond, "Roll Tide to you."

"Hey, Coach, whatever happened to that David Palmer kid who played at Alabama?" I would ask, laughing.

He would respond, "He graduated about five years ago."

"I wondered why I hadn't seen him playing lately," I would answer back, trying to keep from laughing.

This helped pass the time on the slow nights, we both found it terribly amusing. When you ride with someone five days a week, eight hours a day for six weeks you find ways to pass the time and will talk about almost anything.

While patrolling on Mildred Street, we were dispatched to The Hamburger King, a small lunch restaurant on Decatur Street, on a burglary in progress. An employee from one of the neighboring businesses observed a young man climb into the building through the walk-up window. We were about a minute and a half away

351

from the business, so I punched the Crown Vic and pushed it for all it would do. While en route, the witness on the phone with the dispatcher relayed that the man had climbed back out of the same window and had taken off running east from the building.

I decided to drive several streets past the business in hopes of spotting the suspect running. I drove east on Grove Street, turned right on Decatur Street and drove the wrong way on a one-way street before turning left onto another section of Grove Street. Since Decatur Street was one-way, I was hoping that the suspect wouldn't expect us to sneak in behind him if we came from this direction. One part of the job I enjoyed was trying to think like a criminal and to figure out where they'd go when they made their escape.

As we slowly drove east on Grove Street, we observed a young man fitting the description the witness had given us. He was walking calmly away from us.

I pointed him out to Terrance. "That looks like the guy right there."

"He looks like a runner," Terrance replied. "I sure hope he doesn't want to run."

We approached him slowly, but he never looked back at us and we were able to get very close to him. Terrance began to mutter under his breath, "Please don't run. Please don't run. Please don't run."

I pulled up directly behind him, and as we opened the doors to get out he glanced back only for a moment before bursting into a full sprint dead ahead and away from us. Terrance and I jumped back in and I punched the accelerator sending the cruiser lunging after him.

"I knew it. I knew it," Terrance said. "He's a runner. I really don't feel like runnin' today."

I grabbed the radio mike. "2-0-1, we're in pursuit of a suspect running east on Grove toward Ripley," I said, trying to contain the excitement in my voice.

"10-4," she replied. She quickly directed the other units in the area toward us. I heard the other units on the radio. The racing engines behind each voice echoed the strained roar of the big V-8 in my own car as I pushed the cruiser closer toward the young man fleeing ahead of me.

The man jumped a fence at a house on South Ripley Street. I screeched up to the curb and bailed from the car, Terrence behind me, both sets of our legs pumping hard as we flew toward the fence. I reached it just in time to see the man enter the storage room of the house in back of the house.

Terrance jumped the fence. "He's trying to get into the storage room!" I shouted to him and pointed toward the door he was trying to enter. The door was locked, so the man ran toward the back of the yard where I met him at the fence. He bounced away and tried to run to the side fence and scale it, but we were too close. He was fleeing from Terrance running in the yard with him, and me on the opposite side of the fence matching his every move. He looked like a caged rabbit running from a snake.

Several other officers arrived and we surrounded the yard.

"Each of you take a side and he can't get out!" I shouted.

He finally just gave up, lay face down on the ground and put his hands behind him. Terrance cuffed him, and we took him back to our car without any further incident.

After a minute or two, Terrance caught his breath.

"That's some kind of running for a person who didn't want to run today," I told Terrance.

"I told you he was a runner," he said. "I can always spot 'em."

Burglaries happened much too frequently in my years on the job, and in my experience most of the suspects were able to elude the police. Sometimes, though, we got lucky and an alert citizen reported it in time to allow us to catch the bad guy. To me, catching a burglar, a robber or anyone else who had just committed a major crime was like scoring a touchdown.

Being a cop isn't always easy or rewarding, but the sweet victory of a felony arrest is always satisfying. You train for and always anticipate that moment, and when you finally catch the suspect, you realize you just made a difference.

If He Got the Chance

It's no secret that there are those who dislike the police. There are even those who hate the police to the point where they wish bad things upon them. A few even hate police officers so much that they'd kill one if given the chance. I have dealt with people like this in my career, but on one particular day I encountered someone who told me that to my face. On Thursday, November 12, 1998, I was riding in District One with Officer Alan Thompson. Alan had some previous police experience before coming to our department, and I was one of his training officers. I enjoyed training new officers with previous experience because I didn't usually have to teach them about officer safety or the fundamentals of the job. I could focus mainly on department procedures and paperwork. Alan was a smart officer and I felt comfortable with him as my partner.

District One lies in the heart of downtown, and after 5:00 p.m. most of the businesses and government offices close. After 6:00, with a few exceptions, the commercial and government centers are like a ghost town. The intersection of Mobile Street and Mildred Street, however, lies on the periphery of the commercial center and is a center for drug and criminal activity, so I tended to concentrate my evening patrols in this area.

After a while you learn who the local characters and criminals are and whom you need to be watching. The drug dealers have their corners they prefer to use and eventually you come to associate certain places with certain people. Rose Garden Apartments, formerly Cleveland Court Annex, on Rosa L. Parks Avenue was one such area. When an apartment complex gets a bad reputation, the owners will often change the name of the complex to make it more appealing to tenants. The complex was a small, run-down group of apartment buildings completely enclosed by a brick and wrought iron fence. Drug dealers like to sell drugs in the complex because there is only one narrow entrance to the complex, which gave the lookouts an easy job of spotting the police. The dealers could then run and jump the nearest fence or step inside an apartment and elude us.

The manager had asked for our help in eliminating the drug dealers. I had asked her to give me a list of all the tenants who lived in the complex no matter what their ages. Once I knew who lived in the complex, I began to eliminate the problem.

In every district you have your problem people. These are the small group of people who are always causing problems. On this particular evening, we were driving into the apartment complex and I observed Jonathan Randall,* one of my "problem children," driving his vehicle. I had stopped him several times and knew he had a suspended driver's license.

I stopped him again. "Jonathan, why do you continue to drive without a driver's license?" I asked.

"Why you always messin' with me?" he snapped back defiantly.

"I'm just doin' my job and you keep breaking the law by driving without a license," I said.

"You just always harrassin' me and I'm gettin' tired of it!"

Jonathan was a young man of about five-foot ten inches and weighed around two hundred and fifty pounds and was a known drug dealer on Mildred Street. He had bragged on occasion to other officers that he carried a police scanner in his car, and that he knew when the police were out on calls in the area. At the time he was out of jail awaiting sentencing the following Monday for possession of seven assault rifles and stolen credit cards. He had already served time for attempted murder as a juvenile. The sad thing was that Jonathan was only nineteen years old at the time.

"Let me ask you a question, Jonathan," I asked him. "And I want you to be honest with me. If you had the chance, would you ever try and shoot me?"

"If I need to and get the chance, I'll shoot you to get away," he

---

* Not his real name

quickly replied. I could see in his eyes that he meant what he was saying.

"What type of situation would you shoot me?" I continued.

"If I gots lots of dope or guns in my car and I don't want to go to jail, then I'll shoot you or any cop, if I got to," he replied adamantly.

I didn't arrest him that night, nor do I recall what later happened to him, but Jonathan was in every sense a dangerous person. I truly believed in my heart that he would have shot any police officer without hesitation if he'd had the chance. I notified Sergeant Jerry McQueen, my supervisor, of what he had said. Sergeant McQueen distributed a memorandum to all personnel about the threat Jonathan posed.

Dealing with people like Jonathan was part of my job, and I was always on alert as any officer should be. Its one thing to not like the police, but anyone with the nerve to tell a police officer to his face that he would kill him if given the chance elevates a criminal to another level. But I would rather a person tell me that so I am aware of it and can be prepared, than not to know. If any harm had come to me or another officer in the Mildred Street area, it was also documented that he'd made the statement that he would kill an officer if he got the chance.

"It Wasn't Red — It was Yella!"

WHEN PATROLLING A DISTRICT IT doesn't take long to get bored if it's a slow day. If there are no calls for service, and the criminals are off doing other things, you get tired of just riding around the district over and over. When this happened, I usually found a place to sit and watch people and traffic just to see what I could see.

On Thursday, December 31, 1998, I was riding the downtown district with Officer Kyle Haynes. It had been slow all night, but it was New Year's Eve, and we expected the activity to pick up as the night went on. Until then, though, we parked at Rosa L. Parks Avenue and Mildred Street, one of my favorite spots. This particular intersection gets a lot of foot and vehicle traffic. It was a great spot because I could back up next to the liquor store on the corner and watch the stop sign at the intersection relatively unobserved.

We watched drivers headed north on Rosa Parks Avenue as they approached the stop sign. As they slowed, Kyle would type in the tag number on our mobile computer and have the registration back before they could pull through the intersection. If the vehicles were stolen or the tags were swapped, we could stop them before they got out of sight.

We had been sitting there for about twenty minutes and witnessed several vehicles run the stop sign and a few with switched tags, so we made a couple of stops and wrote a few tickets. As I backed into our spot to watch the stop sign again, we saw a 1985 Chevrolet Chevette approach the intersection, barely tap the brakes, and then run the stop sign to make a left turn. I pulled in behind the vehicle and turned on my blue lights. The driver ignored my lights and continued west on Mildred Street. I tapped the siren a couple of

357

times, and the driver finally stopped in the parking lot of the Deluxe Social Savings Club, a local night spot.

I cautiously approached the driver, who appeared elderly. "Sir, can I see your driver's license please?" I asked.

He handed me his driver's license.

"Sir, do you know why I stopped you?" I asked.

"No, officer, I don't," he replied.

"You ran the stop sign back there at Mildred and Rosa Parks."

"What stop sign?" He seemed confused.

"The stop sign there at Mildred and Rosa Parks," I explained pointing back at the intersection. I looked again at his driver's license and realized that he wasn't just old—he was *ninety-two* years old.

"There's no stop sign there," he said.

"Yes, sir, there is one there," I explained. *Maybe he didn't see the stop sign* I thought. *After all, he is ninety-two years old.*

"Oh wait. I seen it," he said. "It wasn't red – it was "*yella!*"

"Yella!" I replied. "Oh, okay. I'll be right back."

I wrote him a ticket for running the stop sign. He calmly folded the ticket and put it in his wallet, then he and his wife went inside the club.

"That's the oldest person I have ever written a ticket to in my whole career," I told Kyle.

At the end of the shift, I told the guys about him running the stop sign and they could not believe I wrote him a ticket.

I tried to explain. "It would not have been fair to all the other people I wrote tickets to for running the stop sign and not write him one for the same violation." I said. "I don't care how old he is."

I have had a few officers tell me how they have told the story about him running the stop sign and how he told me, "It wasn't red – it was "yella!"

One Hot July Afternoon

MONDAY, JULY **26, 1999,** STARTED out like any other day. My off days were Saturdays and Sundays, so I was rested for the beginning of another work week. It was a hot summer day with a high heat index, but that was typical for July in Montgomery, Alabama. My partner, Officer Charles Dougan and I were assigned to District Nine as Unit 209. This district is in the south part of the city. The district is mostly older homes with older families and not much criminal activity. The busiest part of the district is Baptist Medical Center. We answered all the calls where injured people are brought to the Emergency Room for treatment that involved criminal offenses. Shootings, stabbings, and people assaulted were the usual calls. The other part of our time was spent backing up units in the surrounding busy districts where there is substantially more criminal activity.

On this particular day Unit 216 was dispatched on a family disturbance call in the 3800 block of Macedonia Drive. Macedonia is a poor community in the southern most part of the city limits. The community is made up of several generations of families that grew up in the area. As one sibling became old enough to move out of the house, they purchase a mobile home and set it up on the adjoining property to where they grew up. A lot of the streets are named after the families that live there. This area is not yet on city water or sewage even though they have been in the city limits for years. The neighbors are close and it is also what is considered a high crime area.

Officer Jenny Gola was the senior officer in Unit 216 and had been on the force for approximately ten years. She is about five foot four inches tall and weighs about one hundred and five pounds. If you ask how she would describe herself, she would say "scrappy." She and her partner, Officer Wayne Gaskin, were dispatched to Macedonia Drive on a family disturbance and we notified the Dispatcher that we were en route to back them up. We arrived a few minutes after they did and they were wrapping up the call as we arrived. We met with Jenny and Wayne at the church about a mile up the road. She told us that the subject causing the disturbance ran out the back door when they arrived. We decided to wait approximately fifteen minutes, then go back to the residence and see if the subject might have returned to the house. While we waited in the back of the church parking lot, we talked about the latest gossip at the police department and Jenny smoked a cigarette. After fifteen minutes, we drove back to the address to see if the subject had returned. Jenny spoke to the home owner and she said that he had not returned and was probably going over to his cousin's house.

As we were walking to our vehicles, we heard multiple gun shots coming from the direction of the entrance. Macedonia has only one way into the area and the gunshots grew louder and were coming in our direction.

We took cover behind some large pine trees in the yard and I was the first to observe the faded yellow 90's model Cadillac moving in our direction. The road curved to the left and then back to the right in front of the house where we were parked. I saw a subject with a "Tech Nine" semi-automatic pistol sitting in the front passenger seat shooting out the window. As the car turned in the curve in front of where we were standing, I hollered at the other officers, "Tech Nine! Tech Nine! He's shootin' a Tech Nine out the window!"

As the vehicle moved slowly passed us, the subject with the gun rolled up the window and we could not see through the dark tint. The vehicle slowly passed us but moved to the other side of the road. As the vehicle moved by, I fired one shot at the rear passenger tire in order to stop it. As soon as I fired, the other officers opened fire on the vehicle. The vehicle lurched to a stop and sat still for about two seconds.

I have heard people tell stories about things that have happened to them and they talk about how everything seemed to move in slow motion. Well, this actually happened to me. It's actually a neurological condition called Tachypsychia that is usually induced by physical exertion, drug use or a traumatic event. As the events unfolded, everything seemed to move in slow motion after I fired at the vehicle. I remember seeing the back window shatter out and the bullet holes from the other officers shooting. I remember thinking, 'Don't shoot! The vehicle is leaving!' But with everything happening so fast, some action once set into motion cannot be stopped. The vehicle then sped off into the neighborhood.

Jenny immediately tore the mic of her hand held radio off her uniform shirt to call in that we had been involved in a shooting. She screamed into the radio something about shots fired, including several profanities. Later, when I listened to a tape of the radio traffic, it was completely inaudible.

I held up my right hand at Jenny and said in a firm, but calm controlled voice, "Jenny, I got it. I got it, Jenny." She just dropped the mic and it dangled in front of her. I keyed the mic of my radio, and in an excited but calm voice, called in to the Dispatcher, "2-0-9, 10-33! 2-0-9, 10-33!" The code 10-33 means emergency radio traffic. This is a universal code used in law enforcement that is part of the Ten Codes.

The Dispatcher answered, "Go ahead."

I answered back. "209! We had a yellow or beige Cadillac pass by us, had a Tech Nine pointed out the window, firing at officers! Officers have returned fire! Get us some units down here!"

Dispatcher: "Attention all units! We have a 10-33 in the Macedonia area. Have a yellow or beige colored vehicle firing at officers! Officers have returned fire! Last seen going into Macedonia."

Dispatcher: "216"

Unit 216: "216, we're with 209!"

Jenny and her partner ran to their vehicle to pursue the suspects. I ran to their vehicle and told them to block the road; that we would set up a road block.

I knew the roads in the neighborhood were narrow and the houses sat close to the road. I did not want a running gun battle between the suspects and the police that might accidentally injure or kill an innocent bystander. I was familiar with the area and the last time I had been in the back of the neighborhood there was no exit. However, I discovered since I had been in the back area, a dirt road had been cut through to where they were doing construction for new businesses. The suspects rammed the metal gate and fled from the area.

We set up a roadblock and started checking every vehicle leaving to see if the suspects may be hiding, trying to leave the area. A traffic motorcycle unit was first on the scene and secured the entrance of the neighborhood at Woodley Road. He advised the dispatcher that he had casings in the road and he had them secured for investigators. I knew that a lot of backup was en route to the scene and that many were headed to the area of Troy Highway looking for the suspect's vehicle. I remember hearing Corporal Ben Harrison, who was riding in Unit 201 getting 10-17 (arrived on scene) in the area of Troy Highway. I guess it stood out because he seemed to arrive so fast, considering he came from the Montgomery County Detention Facility which is in the middle of downtown. The State Troopers were advised of the incident and had a helicopter flying around looking for the suspect's vehicle.

It was about 3:30 in the afternoon and was the hottest part of the day. From all that had just taken place, and standing in the road, the heat was taking its toll on us. Sergeant Frank Bennett, our immediate supervisor arrived and then Major Larry Armstead and Major Charles Duffee, the Patrol Commander and Assistant Patrol Commander came to check on us. After they talked with us a few minutes to make sure we were okay, Major Armstead noticed how hot we were and had a unit bring us some water and Gatorade. Investigator Guy Naquin arrived to investigate the shooting scene. He allowed us to call home to let our family know we were all right but not to talk about the case.

The wanted vehicle was located approximately twenty minutes later at the entrance to Brewbaker Elementary School on Bell Road. K-9 units attempted to run a track from the vehicle but were unable to locate the suspects. The driver was arrested inside one of the businesses on Bell Road. A resident spotted the suspect by his description and called the police. We went back to Police Headquarters to sign warrants on the suspect and do the paperwork that took the rest of the night to complete.

The shift ended at 10:30 and Jenny, Wayne and Charles sat outside the back door and tried to relax from the afternoon's events. I was downstairs briefing the supervisors on what had happened and how the other officers had handled themselves. As I was leaving the patrol room, Officer Omar Suro, coming in off his shift, walked up and hugged me. You really can't imagine what you mean to others until something like this happens. The thing about police work is that when you are involved in a dangerous, life threatening situation, the other officers you work with hear everything that is happening on the radio.

As I walked out the back door of Police Headquarters, I saw Jenny and several officers standing outside. They were repeating what had happened for about the sixth or seventh time, as other officers came in from off their shift. Everyone was telling me what a great job I did with the radio traffic and how calm I was. I felt pretty good about all that had happened and how I had handled the incident. As the senior officer with more than eighteen years experience, I was expected to be a leader. I saw Jenny, and as I went over to her, she said, "We were already issued our replacement ammo and here is yours. Here's your one bullet."

That was just what was needed to break the adrenaline tension of the day. Everybody began to call me "one bullet Barney" and making jokes asking, *how long did it take to get my bullet out of my pocket.* I took all the ribbing in stride. Officers can be rough, brash and even insensitive at times, until "one of their own" is in danger. Then they become very concerned and are willing to risk their lives for you. Once the danger is over they go back to being their old selves; glad you are okay, but still having a little fun with you.

On August 24, 1999, we went to Municipal Court on the shooting case. Since I was the senior ranking officer on the scene that day I testified on the events that occurred that afternoon. As I testified and described in detail how the suspects drove passed us shooting and how we fired back, Judge Lewis Gillis, the presiding judge, listened intently, but at the same time had a look of *why is this case in my courtroom?*

The driver of the vehicle was convicted of four counts of Reckless Endangerment and one count of Discharging a Firearm in the City

Limits. He was given ninety days for each charge. The actual shooter was never taken into custody, even though I believe that one of the suspects questioned was the shooter. He was a known "thug" who I had arrested and fought with twice in the past for gun charges and I would later arrest for a third time and have to fight him again on another gun charge. He's not the sharpest tool in the shed and has an extensive arrest record. He denied ever being there but I believe it was him. When he was about seventeen or eighteen years old, he was shot in the head at point blank range. Maybe this explained his obscured sense of right and wrong.

District Sixteen was later split into two different districts, due to its large size. It became District Eighteen and District Seventeen. I was moved to District Eighteen and Jenny was moved to District Seventeen. I had the Macedonia community in my area and Jenny had the district next to me. Jenny and I developed a close bond as fellow officers do after a shooting and we knew that we could count on each other when times got tough.

We rehashed the story many times while working together and repeated the story to the new officers that heard about it. They all wanted to go and see where the shooting took place.

I look back at how all those units responded to us when we were involved in the shooting. I had responded on many occasions to other officers who needed help without even thinking about it, but it seemed different when they were coming to help me. To think about how other officers came to our aid reminds me of the scripture verse John 15:13, "Greater love has no one than this, than to lay down one's life for his friends." And it all happened on one hot July afternoon.

Rookies! Sometimes They Have to Learn the Hard Way

BEING A TRAINING OFFICER WAS a great responsibility. It could also be very challenging. Having to teach someone straight out of the academy how to be a police officer required constant attention. Sometimes it was easy, but sometimes it was a royal pain. There were times, however, when it was funny to see a hardheaded rookie officer learn a valuable lesson.

Wednesday August 18, 1999, my partner, Officer Daniel Motley, learned a lesson he'd never forget. Daniel was a young officer and hadn't been out of the police academy for very long. We were finishing up a detail at headquarters around 4:00 that afternoon when Unit 211 was dispatched to Mill Street on a possible Code 13 (dead body). I heard the dispatcher tell the responding unit that the resident at that address hadn't been seen for several days and that there was a strong, unpleasant odor coming from inside the house. When the unit arrived, the officers entered the house and confirmed that the occupant was inside and had been dead for quite some time.

"Did you hear that, Steve?" Daniel asked. He seemed excited as we walked out of headquarters.

"What's that?"

"2-11 has a code 13 on Mill Street that has been there a couple of days," he said eagerly. "Let's go by and take a look."

"If it's been there a couple of days in this weather it's really going to stink," I said. "I've seen one too many of those in my career."

"I haven't. I need to see one. You know, as part of my training," he said as if trying to justify his own morbid curiosity.

"Believe me, you don't want to go over there. It's gonna be pretty nasty."

"It can't be that bad," Daniel said. "C'mon, let's just ride by on the way back to the district."

"It's not what it looks like," I tried to explain. "It's the smell that's so horrible."

"C'mon, it's on the way. The supervisors won't care. Just say it's part of my training."

"Okay, we'll ride by, but don't say I didn't warn you." I could see that there was only one way to convince him.

We pulled to the front of the house. Sergeant Shawn Smith, the second shift robbery-homicide supervisor, was standing out front.

As I pulled up I rolled down my window. "Hey, Shawn," I said. "My partner wants to see a dead body."

"Well, send him on in. It won't be hard to find," Shawn replied with a sinister chuckle.

Daniel walked around the front of the car and looked back at me. "Aren't you comin' in?" he asked, somehow surprised that I wasn't following him.

"Oh, no," I said with a slight smile. "You just go on inside there, mister. You wanted to see a dead body."

He bounded up the steps and went on inside through the open front door.

I looked at Shawn. "The rookie wants to see a dead body," I said. "I tried to tell him, but he won't listen."

"Sometimes they have to just learn the hard way," Shawn replied.

After about three minutes, Daniel came out. The color was gone from his face except from the green tinge of the nausea distorting his features. His cheeks puffed slightly as if he were struggling to keep down his last meal. He silently walked back to the patrol car and sat down quietly in the passenger seat.

I looked at Shawn. "Thanks, Shawn," I said. "I'll see ya later."

We pulled away and Daniel managed to choke back the bile and find his speech again.

"Why didn't you tell me that it was going to be like that?" he asked. His tone was much more humble than before.

"I did tell you," I replied.

"You didn't tell me it was going to be like that!" He seemed upset like he'd been slapped unexpectedly.

"Did I not tell you it was going to be really nasty?" I asked. "Did I not tell you it's going to stink really bad?"

"Yes, but you didn't say it was going to be that bad." he continued.

"What part of really nasty and really bad did you not understand?" I asked.

"Yeah, but...."

"Daniel," I said interrupting him. "I worked as an Evidence Tech for eight years, and I've been to a few decomps. When I tell you it's going to be really nasty and really stinky, it's gonna be *really* nasty and *really* stinky. I know what I am talking about. Did you not notice that Sergeant Smith was standing *outside* the house?"

"Yeah, I noticed," he said, more quietly now.

"Why do you think he was standing *outside*?" I asked.

"Yeah, I see now," he said in agreement.

"It could've been worse, though." I said.

"How could that have possibly been worse?"

"Because, if we had gotten the call, you would have to helped DFS load the body in the body bag and carry it out," I said. I couldn't resist a smile.

"What?" he snapped. "I don't think so!"

"Oh, yes," I said. "I *think* so, because you're the rookie, and the rookie does the dirty work. I did it when I was a rookie and now it's your turn."

Daniel never forgot the lesson he learned that day but he still had his hardheaded moments. Whenever he didn't believe something I told him I would remind him about Mill Street.

"Oh yeah," he would laugh. "I remember."

I always enjoyed it when a rookie learned and retained something I taught him. I loved it when I told one something and he wouldn't believe me then later learned a lesson like the one Daniel learned that day.

Rookies! Sometimes they have to learn the hard way.

"Ewww, Nasty!"

THE VAST MAJORITY OF CALLS to the police involve relatively ordinary things like thefts or accidents, or maybe even a robbery, but on Tuesday, September 14, 1999, I encountered something on my job that I'd never seen before or have seen since. Officer Daniel Motley and I were partnered together riding District Nine that day. He was eager to learn and see as much as possible. Daniel's father had been a police officer in Tuskegee, Alabama, but had been killed in an on-duty traffic accident six years earlier.

Things had been fairly busy for us that Tuesday when we were dispatched to Lynwood Drive about 5:30 that evening. The dispatcher advised us that the caller had found maggots in his chicken and wanted to see the police.

Daniel looked at me and asked, "Did she say maggots?"

"Yeah, sounded like it." I replied.

"That's just nasty!"

"They probably bought a raw chicken at the grocery store and it had sat out too long somewhere before being sold. I don't know why they need to see us. Just take the chicken back to the store and get another one."

We pulled up to the house and saw several people in the back yard. It appeared to be a family get-together. This seemed strange since it was Tuesday afternoon.

As we walked to the fence I asked, "How's everybody doin' today?"

A gentleman met us at the fence and answered, "We're doin' okay. How are you doing?"

"Fine," I answered. "Who called?"

The gentleman who met us at the fence said, "I did. I got something I want to show you."

He led us through the gate into the back yard and showed us a chicken box from Church's Chicken. He opened it and pointed inside and said, "Look at that."

I didn't notice anything out of the ordinary, so I asked, "What am I looking at?"

He moved a piece of chicken and said, "Right there, what are those?"

In the corner of the box were some small brown round things that I couldn't identify. I had worked as an Evidence Technician for eight years and I had seen maggots but they were always alive and these did not even resemble what I'd seen in the past.

Daniel picked up a piece of chicken from the box and broke it open. A dozen or so live squiggling maggots crawled out all over his hands.

"Ahhh!" he screamed, and threw the piece of chicken back into the box. He violently shook his hands flinging the sticky yellow maggots in every direction.

"You see!" shouted the gentleman, as he pointed to the box of chicken.

"When did you buy this chicken?" I asked.

"I buried my wife this morning and this afternoon around two-thirty, I had some friends stop by and buy some chicken to bring back to the house for everyone. Everything was going well until we found the maggots."

"Where did you buy the chicken?" I asked.

"Church's on Fairview."

Thinking he might have bought the chicken earlier that week, I asked to see a receipt. Some people try to pull scams all the time so I wanted to be sure to verify what he claimed. He showed me the receipt and it was in fact bought that day.

"How much chicken did you buy?" I quickly asked.

"Eight, ten piece boxes."

"So that's a total of eighty pieces of chicken." I said. "How many boxes of chicken had the maggots in them?"

"Only one that we know of and that is this one," he replied.

"How many people ate chicken today?" I asked.

"Oh, I don't know. At least twenty or twenty-five including some small children."

Since the restaurant was in an adjacent district, I had the unit in that district call my cell phone. I spoke with Corporal Jeff Davis in District Eleven. I told Jeff that he needed to go by the Church's Chicken of Fairview Avenue and close the restaurant.

"You want me to close Church's Chicken?" he asked with disbelief in his voice.

"Yeah, we're on a call on Lynwood where these people bought some bad chicken and it had maggots in it." I explained. "I'll be over there in few minutes to meet you."

I asked the gentleman for two, one-gallon zip-lock bags. I followed him into the house with the box of chicken. He gave me the zip-lock bags and I put one piece of chicken in the bag, zipped it up and told him to put it into the freezer. I put another piece of chicken in the other and told him I was going to take it to the restaurant to show the manager.

"What do we need to do now, officer?" the gentleman asked.

"Everyone who ate some of the chicken needs to go to the E/R and be checked out, especially the young children. Tell the doctors you ate some fried chicken that had maggots in it and it was reported to the police and you need to be checked out. Keep this chicken in the freezer in case anyone gets sick. You will have a sample in case the doctors need it."

"Will Church's pay for the doctor bills?" he asked.

"I would go to the hospital first and see if anyone of you are sick. Then contact Church's about the bill." I answered. "If they don't want to cooperate then you may have to sue them. Just keep the chicken you have in the freezer as evidence. I am going to Church's and talk to them right now."

We left, and I told Daniel to call our supervisor and have him meet us at the restaurant. This particular Church's Chicken restaurant was the busiest in the city. On Sundays, especially, they sold tons of chicken. I knew that closing them down was going cause problems, and I wanted to brief my supervisor before the complaints started. I handled this call as much by phone and did not release information over the radio. I did not want to start a panic in case someone from the media happened to be monitoring our traffic.

I also called my friend Susan Luckie, a good friend of Cindy Goocher, a health inspector for restaurants in Montgomery. I wanted to contact Cindy and ask her what I needed to do about the restaurant. My first reaction was to close the business to prevent any more bad chicken from being sold. Susan gave me Cindy's phone number and I called her and told her about the situation. She told me that since it was after 5:00, she would have to talk to her supervisor. She said she would call me back.

I showed Corporal Davis the bag of chicken and you could see the maggots crawling inside. I went inside and spoke with the two employees. I told her that she had sold some chicken with maggots in it. I showed her the bag with the piece of chicken and the maggots.

"How do you know it was sold here?" Her tone was sarcastic.

"Because the person who bought it said he did and he still has the receipt showing it was bought from this store," I replied.

My supervisor showed up and I advised him on what we had. I also told him that I had talked to a health inspector and she was checking on what to do and she would call me back. We inspected all the chicken in the cooler and the employee explained how the chicken was brought to the store. I asked how long it was cooked and at what temperature. She told us it was cooked for 15 minutes at 450 degrees. I don't know how the maggots could have survived those temperatures.

She told us she remembered taking the order and cooking the chicken. I asked her if she might have taken the chicken out of the grease early to speed up the process since it was so much chicken. She denied doing that, as I expected. The chicken looked completely cooked to me, so I couldn't explain how the maggots could have survived. My personal opinion was that she took the chicken out early even though I couldn't prove it.

Cindy called me back after talking to her supervisor. I told her we inspected the restaurant but didn't find any more maggots. She told us to allow the restaurant to remain open, and someone from her office would inspect it first thing in the morning. The employee asked me who was going to reimburse the store for the money they'd lost in the hour they were closed.

I told her that she was lucky that we hadn't closed them down for the rest of the night. I advised her again that the health inspector would be in first thing in the morning and that she might want to call and advise her supervisor of what had happened.

More than a year later on Wednesday February 14, 2001, Daniel and I met with Howard Mandell, the city attorney, at the mayor's office regarding a lawsuit the family had filed against Church's Chicken. Also present was an attorney representing the company. The attorney for Church's Chicken took a short, recorded statement from Daniel and me. He asked about the chicken and if I knew what maggots looked like. I explained that I had worked as an evidence technician for eight years and had seen plenty of them. I also explained that we examined the receipt and saw that the chicken had been purchased that day. Daniel told him how he had broken the piece of chicken apart and how the maggots had crawled out all over his hands. The attorney turned off the recorder and asked if he could talk to us "off the record."

I looked at Mr. Mandell. He nodded his approval. "Okay," I replied.

"You've been around a long time, and seen a lot of things like this, Corporal. What's your opinion of this? What do you think we should do?" he asked.

I thought for a second then looked him square in the eye. "My opinion?" I replied. "In my opinion, you need to settle."

He made a quick note, stood, shook our hands and thanked us for our time. I have to say this is one of the strangest calls I had ever been on.

I've told this story many times to my friends, and other officers, and the usual response is, "Ewww, Nasty!"

It's All Part of Being a Family

WHEN I GRADUATED FROM THE police academy in June of 1983, I was assigned to third shift patrol, which began at 10:00 p.m. each night and lasted until 7:00 the next morning. Although weekends, especially during the summer, were usually busy all night long, weeknights were usually pretty slow. After midnight we spent most of our time checking closed businesses to make sure they were secure and hadn't mistakenly been left unlocked inviting someone to commit a crime of opportunity. But you can only look at locks, doors and windows for so long before you are searching for something to keep your attention. That's usually when you decide to continue the age-old tradition of picking on the dispatchers.

Senior officers teach the junior officers this great art, and then those officers over the years pass it down the line. One of the gags we would pull on the dispatcher's worked like this: we would write down the tag number of the dispatcher's personal vehicle before we left the parking lot of headquarters, then wait until things got slow on the street. We'd then go to one of the local drug houses or some sleazy bar and notify the dispatcher that we were investigating a suspicious vehicle at that location. Then we'd give her the tag number of her own vehicle at that seedy establishment. Of course she never recognized her own tag number until the NCIC check came back. It was usually then that her flustered voice would come on the radio urgently requesting that we call the desk as soon as possible.

"Why is my car parked *there*?" she'd nervously ask. The anger and fear were usually a delicious blend that added a certain urgency to her voice.

This gag never worked on the more experienced dispatchers,

but it was a great way to break in the new ones. We would usually make up some story and keep her in suspense for a few minutes before finally letting her off the hook. This may not sound like the greatest joke to some people, but at 3:00 a.m. it was a great way to pass the time.

I've worked with a lot of dispatchers over the years, too many to try and name them all, but Cindi Hicks worked as a dispatcher my entire career and was one of the best. She was extremely good at what she did—with one minor exception. Try as she might, poor thing, she could never properly pronounce the word Mitsubishi, the Japanese-made sports car. She always stammered through it and it usually came out "Mit-sa-bit-chee."

The first night I noticed this, I decided to have a little fun with her. Another patrol unit had run a tag over the radio and when she gave the vehicle information back, she mangled the word Mitsubishi.

"Did you hear how she said that?" I asked my partner.

I decided to run all the Mitsubishi's I could find on the streets just to hear her try to say it again. This amused my partner and me all night long. We'd cackle with delight each time Cindi made another attempt to pronounce it. We could tell by the end of the shift that she'd caught on and was just a little irritated.

The next morning, my partner had turned in all our paperwork and we were walking out the door when I heard a voice behind me. "Well, were you able to run *all* the tags in the city last night?"

I turned around and saw Cindi looking straight at me. She had a look of irritation on her face but it was just a look, because I knew she wasn't really mad at me.

"I don't know what you are talkin' about," I replied. I couldn't suppress a grin.

"You know exactly what I am talking about!"

"I think it's *cute* the way you say Mit-sa-bit-chee," I replied, still picking at her.

"I'll make you think cute," she replied with a smile, shaking her fist at me.

I decided to look for Hyundai's the next night.

On another occasion, my partner, Corporal Kinney Bishop,

and Corporal Jack Clark and I were attempting to locate a suspect shooting a shotgun in the area between Union Street and St. Margaret's Hospital. The suspect was always one block ahead of us, blasting the phone booths on each corner with his 12-gauge shotgun. Every time we heard a shot, we would run to the next corner and the suspect would be gone. All that was left was the shattered glass of the phone booth and a fired 12-gauge shotgun shell lying in the street.

After about the fourth or fifth shot, Cindi's voice came over the radio. "Attention, all units on Union Street, y'all be careful."

Being a young rookie officer, I began to understand how the dispatchers cared about their officers on the street.

Things really got interesting November 9, 1983, when her husband Vic came to third shift patrol as a lieutenant. This led to some interesting exchanges with Vic in charge of the officers on the street while Cindi was dispatching. Sometimes they would have a disagreement over the air and the next thing you would hear was her voice, stern and demanding over the radio, "One-Twenty-Five, PX the desk *right away!*"

PX is a police code for a phone call. Usually his response was, "I'm callin' now." Knowing both of them, I found it amusing but I could also tell by the tone of their voices that I did not want to be on either end of *that* phone call.

One of the most amusing moments came on December 31, 1999. I was working on second shift patrol and the whole country was preparing for Y2K on the eve of the new millennium. I remember reports of some people actually believing that it was the end of the world. In reality, we were bracing for any disruption caused by computers worldwide when their internal calendars flipped past 12-31-99 at midnight to 01-01-00. It seems crazy now, but at the time it seemed that the whole country lived with a real terror of what might happen. Some experts were saying that all the world's computers would shut down and we would lose electricity, water and gas.

We were also prepared in case some radical groups decided to sabotage electrical substations, natural gas mains and water supplies. The police department had come up with a contingency plan if we lost electricity. Before the dispatchers worked off of computers, complaint clerks would take the calls, write down the information on a 3x8 card, commonly called an IBM card. They would then place it in a slot over a moving belt that would carry the card to the dispatcher sitting behind a glass. The dispatcher would relay the information to the units in the field by radio then place it in a numbered slot to keep track of the call. Once the unit was out of service, the light designated for that district was turned off. This made it easier for the dispatcher to keep track of the units available for calls.

On this particular night, everyone in the police department was scheduled to work in the event of some major catastrophe. We came in at 5:00 p.m. instead of the normal time of 2:30 and were given maps of all utilities in the city for extra patrol. Cindi came in to brief all the officers at roll call on how dispatch would operate in the event of power loss. She also showed us the old-style IBM cards that the complaint clerks would be writing on when the computers went down.

I was the senior member on second shift patrol and was the only officer who remembered when dispatch actually operated this way. I brought a Montgomery Police Department yearbook that was printed in 1984, the one and only yearbook the police department has ever published. In the corner of the patrol assembly room are two long benches that are against the wall in an L shape. That was where we sat waiting for roll call. There were about ten to fifteen officers sitting and standing in the corner and the average ages of the officers were probably twenty-one to twenty-four years old.

"Miss Cindi, what did you do before you were a dispatcher?" one of the officers asked her very politely.

"I was once in *Playboy* magazine," she replied without hesistation.

"What!" several of them said with great interest?

"No, you weren't," one officer answered back.

"No. Seriously. I had my picture in *Playboy* magazine," she said without cracking a smile.

"When?" another officer asked, disbelief in his voice.

"The October 1985 issue."

"You're makin' that up. You weren't really in *Playboy*, were you?"

"She really was. I saw the photo," I chimed in.

They all looked at me and one officer said, "You're a Christian, Steve. Why were you lookin' at *Playboy*?"

"She brought it to work and showed several of us the picture."

"Seriously?" another asked.

"Seriously." I replied.

"How did the picture look?" another officer asked.

"It was a good lookin' photo," I said. I let a wry smile creep onto my face.

You could see the gears in their young minds turning. Some looked back at Cindi—and I mean, *really* looked at Cindi! I know some were thinking, '*Where can I get a copy of that issue?*'

She let them think about it a few moments. Then she told them the story. Cindi and Vic had gone on vacation in Tennessee and had stopped by the Jack Daniels distillery for a tour when a photographer saw them and asked if they wanted to be photographed for an ad. The photograph was of an old bearded hillbilly sitting in a rocking chair on the front porch of an old wooden mountain cabin. Vic was seated in a rocking chair next to him. Cindi was sitting on the steps of the cabin. It was an advertisement for Jack Daniels liquor. We all laughed and I was most amused by the looks on the other officers' faces when I told them I had seen the photo of her in the magazine. I wish I'd had a camera at the moment.

When roll call finally began, Cindi took charge and briefed everyone from the major on down on what to expect, which was— we really did not know *what* to expect. Not only were we celebrating a new year, but the beginning of a new millennium. Each district car was given a map marked with the locations of all the utilities in the city, including all the power company substations, gas mains, water mains and the phone company's junctions. If anyone was going to sabotage the city, those were the areas we figured they'd target.

My partner, Officer Glen Parcus, and I were assigned District Seventeen, which mostly had neighbors with businesses on the main roads. We had to cover the area from Ray Thorington Road, down Vaughn Road to the Eastern Bypass, from the Bypass to Troy

Highway to Taylor Road. It was a lot of territory to cover but the outer areas were mostly pasture and wooded areas.

We answered calls for several hours, until third shift came on duty, then they handled all the calls and we patrolled from utility to utility, making sure everything was okay.

The streets were extremely quiet for a New Year's Eve. I had worked many New Year's Eves and they were usually very busy with fireworks and idiots shooting guns. That year was different. It seemed quieter than in the past, but I knew that the closer it got to midnight the more "shots fired" calls would be dispatched. At about 11:45, I decided to park in front of my church, Thorington Road Baptist Church on Ray Thorington Road and wait until after midnight. At the time we were in the process of moving and the new church was still under construction. I expected a lot of shooting and with that being the new millennium, I expected more than usual.

My wife had packed a cooler filled with sandwiches, chips, cookies and soft drinks for the long night. I was not sure if any restaurants would be open and in the event of a power loss, so we were prepared. We were scheduled to work until at least 4:00 in the morning, maybe longer, depending on what happened.

As far as that night went, nothing out of the ordinary occurred. As a matter of fact, it was extremely quiet because a lot of people were at work waiting on their computers to crash so they could take whatever action needed to fix the problem. That never occurred. About thirty minutes after midnight, people began to leave their parties and drive home. Traffic picked up a little, but it never got as heavy as we expected. I did take the time to write a traffic ticket about ten minutes into the new year.

Y2K turned out to be much ado about nothing, but we were ready. Had the worst happened, I'm sure our dispatchers would have been right on top of everything. Our dispatchers did have a tough job nonetheless. I'll be the first to tell you that. They were our lifeline when things got hairy. Whether it was getting us help in an emergency, or calling for the medics, or simply getting us information on tags and warrants checks, they had a thankless job. I never was a dispatcher, but I watched them at work and I really never understood how they were able to keep track of all the units when things got so terribly busy. It was a skill you had to learn and took a great deal of time and patience to master.

I do know that not just anybody can be a dispatcher. The dispatcher on each shift looked out for her officers almost like a mother hen and took it personally when something happened to any of them. You could read tiny changes in her voice when something wasn't right. I could always tell by the inflection in Cindi's voice when she called out a unit number if she was about to dispatch a hot call.

Even though dispatchers worried about their officers, they would get irritated when units in the field made frivolous or silly requests. Time to a dispatcher was extremely important, and for a unit to waste her time on things she considered ridiculous or unnecessary sometimes led to a stern reprimand over the phone. Of course, none of this went out over the radio other than to perhaps affect the way a dispatcher would reply when she said, "Ten-four." Sometimes it was pleasant, but sometimes a simple *"ten-four"* could convey more fury than any four-letter word.

I have often suggested that dispatchers ride with the patrol officers more often to better understand the perspective of the officer in the field and why an officer might ask for certain information. In return, I believe that every patrol officer should be required to spend some time sitting next to a dispatcher and see exactly how frustrating that job can be.

Officers and dispatchers with our department had a high-stress job and we often vented to each other off the air. Even though we fussed at each other sometimes, it was all forgotten by the end of shift. It's all part of being a family.

SOME PEOPLE ARE JUST SHARP AS MARBLES

MONDAY, JANUARY **24, 2000,** MY partner, Officer Luther DeLoach and I were riding District Seventeen on second shift patrol. I was Luther's second training officer out of the police academy. Around 6:20 that evening we were notified by Juvenile detectives that a runaway named Tricia Russell*was hiding in an apartment on Gaslight Curve with friend. We arrived at the apartment and were let in by the residents. We found Tricia watching television. She and her friends were watching M.P.D. M.P.D. is a local show based on the national television show COPS. We took her into custody and escorted her to our patrol vehicle. On the way to police headquarters she told us that M.P.D. had her boyfriend featured on the most wanted segment just before we walked in. She told us his name and after we dropped her off with a juvenile detective, we verified that he was still wanted.

We drove back to the apartment and knocked on the door. We were let in and found her boyfriend still sitting in the same chair that he was in when we arrested his girlfriend. He had five felony indictments and two felony warrants and was wanted by the AUM (Auburn University of Montgomery) Police department.

I couldn't believe that he watched himself featured on the show as a most wanted, and was still there when we returned. I was more surprised that we were let back into the apartment. Some people are just sharp as marbles.

★   Name changed

I Did Not Have to Take a Life

I T WAS TUESDAY, MARCH 28, 2000, and Officer Mary Butler and I had been riding together for a couple of weeks. She was doing well in her training, and since we'd only been assigned District Seventeen for a short time, we were both still getting a feel for the area and learning where the trouble spots were. At around 5:30 that afternoon, we received a call to the area of East Brookwood Drive to investigate a suspicious black male in his twenties reportedly armed with a gun. According to the person who called, he was wearing a green windbreaker and blue jeans and was walking through the neighborhood with a badge, a radio and a gun.

Montgomery is the capital city of Alabama, and there are many law enforcement agencies with jurisdiction in the city whose agents wear badges and carry radios. There are also private security officers and bail-bonding agents who frequent high-crime areas and are often mistaken for the police.

"Who do you think it is?" Mary asked.

"With all the different agencies in the city, who knows?" I replied, "It could be anybody."

We turned left off of Elsmeade Drive onto Brookwood Street and drove slowly toward East Brookwood Drive. I saw two young black men standing at the corner and made eye contact with one of them. He calmly nodded in the direction across the street. We drove slowly through the slight curve and came upon a young man fitting the description walking toward us on the passenger side of our cruiser. I stopped about fifteen feet short of him and let him walk to us. Our training tells us never to let anyone walk directly up to the car while you're sitting in it. It puts an officer at a severe disadvantage if the subject were to pull a weapon.

Mary and I got out of the car and I kept an eye on the two young men across the street. They continued to watch us as if they knew something was going to happen.

I stepped to the front quarter panel of the vehicle and Mary stayed behind the open door.

"Hold it right there," I ordered the man as he approached. I wanted to keep the car separating us in case I needed some cover.

He stopped immediately.

"What's your name?" I asked.

He spoke hesitantly. "Jimmy,"*he replied.

There was still plenty of daylight, and I looked carefully for any bulges that would reveal a concealed weapon. The young man's windbreaker was buttoned up half way, and I really couldn't tell if he was armed or not.

"Keep your hands where I can see them, Jimmy," I said.

Before I could say anything else, Jimmy reached into his jacket with his right hand. Mary and I reacted immediately and drew our Beretta .40 caliber automatics and leveled them at the man's midsection.

"Hold it!" I yelled.

As his hand emerged slowly from the jacket, I could see an automatic pistol in his hand. I could see that he held the grip by his fingertips, but he wasn't gripping the weapon.

"STOP!" I screamed. I could feel myself in a fully defensive mode. I was prepared to fire if he made any aggressive movements with the pistol. I could feel my finger tense on the trigger as more of his weapon revealed itself.

Jimmy had a terrified but confused look on his face. For a moment he froze, but after a couple of seconds he began to draw the weapon still further from his jacket. I saw he was still holding the grip with the tips of his fingers and not in a normal shooting grip. Because he slowly pulled the gun from his jacket it this manner, I made the decision that he was removing it to disarm himself and not threatening us with it. As the gun cleared his jacket, I saw it had an orange tip on the end of the barrel.

A toy! I thought to myself. I was suddenly relieved that I had not

---

*   Name changed to protect the innocent minded

taken the shot. Other than the orange tip on the barrel, the toy gun looked *exactly* like a Smith and Wesson automatic.

I rushed over and snatched the pistol from his hand tossing it onto the hood of our car. I holstered my own weapon then grabbed him by the jacket with both hands. Fear filled his face as I tore open the snaps exposing a toy badge, a Radio Shack scanner and plastic handcuffs.

I was still shaking. "What are you doing with this stuff?" I asked.

As he began to speak, I could immediately tell that the mind inside the man's body was that of a child. "I was patrollin' the neighborhood checkin' things out," he said simply. "Them bad boys is always messin' with me when I tell them to stop selling weed."

He was referring to the gang members in the area who sold drugs, burglarized homes and occasionally shot at each other.

By this time my stress level had subsided. Mary took down his name and ran a check for warrants on him.

"I know you are trying to protect the neighborhood," I told him, "But you cannot carry a gun and a badge and pretend you are the police. You are going to get yourself hurt or even killed. Do you realize how close we came to shooting you?"

"I'm sorry," he said. He bowed his head in shame.

"We appreciate you wanting to help out, but you need to leave the police work up to us." I said. I tried to speak calmly and not upset him any more than he was. "If you see those bad boys selling weed, you need to call us and we will handle them."

"Okay. Can I go now?" he asked.

"Yeah, you can go now. But you need to go straight home and put all this stuff up," I said.

"Okay," he said. The young man turned and walked slowly away.

I turned and looked at the two guys still standing on the corner across the street. They knew the whole time that Jimmy was mentally handicapped and carrying a toy gun. I sensed that they were just waiting to see what we were going to do. Based just on the nature of the call and on Jimmy's actions, we would have been fully justified in shooting the young man. I think in a sick twisted way, the two guys watching wanted to see us shoot poor Jimmy.

I'm just glad I noticed he held the toy with only the two fingers. Something on an instinctive level told me that he wasn't a threat. Mary and I talked about the incident and I explained that this was a perfect example of why we are trained to always 'Watch Their Hands.'

As you enter the police academy that's painted in large letters on the wall. If it had been dark outside, I wouldn't have been able to see his hands as clearly. It could have easily been a tragic situation. Mary told me later that if I had fired, then she would have fired.

I'm thankful that tragedy was averted in this particular instance. Unfortunately, misidentifying a weapon or a deadly threat happens to police officers across the country all too often. I thank the Lord that he gave me the vision to see the incident for what it was that day and I did not have to take a life.

HE DID NOT SERVE ANY TIME

SOMETIMES, WHEN YOU DO EVERYTHING right, things still don't go your way. As a police officer you have laws to enforce. It's not always easy to go "by the book," but you do it because it's your job. The most discouraging thing for a police officer is risking his life to make an arrest and do the right thing only to discover that the judicial system later hands out little or no punishment to those who commit the crimes.

Friday, April 7, 2000 was one of those days. Around 3:30 that afternoon, Officer Lonnie Harris called me on my cell phone and advised me of several subjects hanging out at the 3080 building of Stonebridge Apartments on Strathmore Drive. Lonnie had security of the apartment complex and informed us that the management had received several complaints of gang and drug activity there. Officer Chris Gruhn was riding as my partner because my regular partner, Officer Mary Butler, had taken off that day. The apartment complex was having problems, subjects loitering around the complex, selling drugs and firing guns. Lonnie had asked me to give the apartment complex extra patrol to try and eliminate the problem over the past several weeks.

We were on another code 12 (disturbance call) and it took us a little while to make it to the area. When we drove up, we saw a crowd of about ten subjects standing on the sidewalk next to parked vehicles.

I saw three subjects sitting inside a white Dodge Neon. As I walked to the driver's door of the Neon a young man wearing a gray t-shirt and baggie blue jeans immediately got out of the car. He was watching me in the outside rear view mirror as I approached. He was holding something in the front of his jeans with his left hand. The t-shirt could not cover up the fact that the front of the pants had a bulge along the pants line and the pants drooped. The subject had a gun in the front of his pants. I had seen this many times before while approaching subjects. Sometimes the subjects would run and sometimes they would try to act cool and try to drop the gun before you patted them down for weapons.

I called to him as I was walking toward him, carefully watching his hands. He started to back away and then he quickly said, "I ain't got time for you, Dog!" and turned and ran. He grabbed the front of his pants to keep the gun from falling. I did not chase him because I did not want to leave my partner alone with the other two subjects in the vehicle. I then looked inside the driver's side of the vehicle and saw T.J. Vernon*. T.J. is a known drug dealer in the area sitting in the front passenger seat. I had many complaints on him in the past dealing drugs and shooting at people, but it was hard to catch him. He was one of those suspects you are warned about that are to be considered 'armed and dangerous'.

The driver's door window was rolled down and as I looked in I saw T.J. quickly thrust his right hand under a light weight jacket sitting in between the front seats. I reacted by drawing my Beretta 40 caliber automatic pistol and ordering the subject to slowly show his hands. Chris pulled the subject from the vehicle and he began to resist. After a brief struggle he was placed in handcuffs. He had ten small zip-lock bags of marijuana in the side pocket of his camouflage BDU pants. We placed him in the back seat of our patrol vehicle. I went back to the Neon and lifted up the jacket and found a Bryco 9mm pistol fully loaded. Also found was fifty rounds of 9mm ammunition and a box of fifty .25 cal rounds in the backseat. T.J. was reaching for a gun to shoot me and I beat him to the draw. I retrieved the pistol and ammo and placed it in the trunk of my patrol car. The third subject in the Neon had no drugs or weapons on him.

Chris and I approached the other subjects standing around and ordered them several times that if they did not live there they needed to leave. The subjects slowly began to walk off then stood next to

---

*   Name changed to protect the guilty

one of the apartment buildings approximately thirty feet away as if they had the expectation of more action to take place. One heavy-set female decided she did not want to obey Chris' commands and stood by the vehicles defiantly. Chris approached the woman who out weighed him by more than 100 pounds. While he questioned her I observed another subject walking behind me from the parking lot. I asked him his name and he looked at me but did not respond. I asked his name again and he did not answer but he had a nervous look in his eyes. I paused a second and then ask him to open his mouth. He actually opened his mouth and I could see several small clear baggies of crack cocaine. One of the things crack dealers will do is hold bags of crack cocaine in their mouth. If you stop them and pat them down you would not find drugs on their person because it is in their mouth. Usually when you ask them to open their mouths they would just turn and run. I was amazed that he opened his mouth to let me see. As I grabbed the subject he began to pull away. I went to grab him with my other hand when I heard my partner start fighting with the female. I looked over to my left to see him throw her to the ground. The subjects standing next to the apartments started to move toward him and I let my guy go and went to help my partner. The subject ran behind the apartments. I immediately called for back up, advising him that we had several subjects with drugs and possibly armed.

We placed two sets of handcuffs on the female because of her size and Chris placed her in the back seat of our patrol vehicle with our first prisoner.

Additional units started arriving and the other subjects ran from the area.

I charged T.J. with Unlawful Possession of Marijuana and Violation of License to Carry a Pistol, otherwise known as no gun permit. The female was charged with Harassment. We went to court several weeks later and I testified to the events that occurred. The female was found guilty of harassment but the subject I arrested was found not guilty of the gun charge. The judge ruled that once the subject was arrested for the drug charge and placed in the patrol vehicle, the 'threat was no longer there' and I could not charge him with the gun. I disagreed with the verdict but I was not the judge.

Now, here's the part of the whole deal that just chaps my hide. The first subject that had the gun in his pants was known on the streets as Dragon. He later murdered a guy. The second subject is a known drug dealer and was in possession of ten bags of marijuana. The third subject had several small bags of crack cocaine in his mouth and was slightly mental and that's why he showed me the drugs. I stopped him later in the same complex and found that he is the brother of T.J. The female was one of the assistant managers of the Four Seasons Apartments on the Southern Boulevard and was tipping off her boyfriend who sold drugs in the apartment complex when the police drove through. What it boils down to is the fact that I beat the guy to the draw and he did not get a chance to shoot me.

Would he have shot me? I don't know but he was reaching for the gun for some reason. But I guess I will never know. We later went to circuit court on the drug charge and he pled guilty and was given probation and no jail time.

Yes, that's right. He did not serve any time.

Because You Just Never Know

WEDNESDAY, **A**PRIL **26, 2000, O**FFICER Mary Butler and I were riding together in District Sixteen, a pretty busy town located in the southeast part of the city, mostly residential neighborhoods with many businesses along the main roads. I was new to the area having just been moved over from District Seventeen.

Mary had just graduated from the police academy and had been assigned to me about seven weeks earlier as her first training officer. We were moved to sixteen only a week after being partnered together so Mary and I were learning the district together.

I had asked a supervisor about the district reassignment and was told that the move was not for any disciplinary reason. Rather, he told me that District Sixteen needed some "cleaning up," and I had been chosen to be the janitor. Afterward, I viewed the reassignment as a gesture that reflected the confidence my supervisors had in me. I took that as a compliment.

Whenever I worked in a new district, I liked to ride it for two or three months and just answer calls and try to determine where the problems were, as well as learn the streets. I was careful to identify the areas where young men up to no good tended to congregate and the areas where I received the most calls. I then focused my attention on those areas when not busy with other duties and worked on solving the recurrent problems responsible for repeat calls. The hangouts that drew idle young men and women were usually the same places where drugs were bought and sold. By aggressively patrolling these areas and targeting those most likely to possess the narcotics, I began to eliminate the problem in this district.

One of the ways I worked to cut down on my response time to calls was keeping detailed maps of the apartment complexes in a notebook. When responding to a call in one of these complexes, my partner could look up the exact location of the apartment and save time hunting the address. Every apartment complex has a different layout and numbering system. Some make sense and some don't. By knowing where the apartment was before we arrived saved us from having to stop at each building, searching for the numbers on the side of buildings.

On this particular Wednesday, that preparation paid off.

Mary and I had been busy answering calls non-stop from the time we came on duty at 2:30 p.m. until 10:00 p.m. At 10:19 p.m., we were nearing the end of our shift when we received a burglary in progress call to Stone Crossing Apartments on Woodley Road. We were close, and as we approached the complex, Mary looked up the apartment number and told me it was the first building on the right as we entered the complex. Very seldom do you get a call on a crime in progress when you're right down the street. The dispatcher advised us that the victim was at home and that the suspect had kicked open the front door.

I switched off the headlights and entered the complex slowly. I saw a young man running through the breezeway of the building and pointed him out to Mary. We watched him cross the parking lot and crouch by a chain link fence, just to our right.

It was obvious that he hadn't seen us creeping through the darkness. He appeared to be about six-one and about one hundred seventy pounds, so I told Mary I would drive around the corner quickly and for her to bail out and grab him.

I turned the corner. Mary quickly bailed out and attempted to grab the man, but he managed to scramble over the fence. Mary followed after him, and the chase was on. I radioed in that my partner was in foot pursuit and gave a description of the man. Mary radioed that the suspect had crossed Woodley Road and entered the back yard of the house at the corner of Woodley and Eagerton Road. This house had a privacy fence, and I was concerned that he might try to hide and ambush my partner.

Mary lost sight of the suspect, and I spotted her walking around from behind the residence. I picked her up and we drove through the area looking for the man. After catching her breath, I told her to give the dispatcher an update on the suspect's clothing. She was angry with herself for not catching him.

"Did you give it your best?" I asked. "Did you give it all you had?"

"Yeah, Steve," she said heaving to catch her breath. "I did."

"That's all the department can ask of you," I said wanting to encourage her.

A third shift unit responded to the address to verify if a burglary had taken place and if the owner wished to press charges. Very often, crime victims refuse to press charges for a variety of reasons. When the unit arrived at the scene, they advised the victim in the apartment had been stabbed several times and appeared to be dead.

What may have started as a burglary had suddenly escalated to murder. The dispatcher immediately advised the units in the area that the suspect was wanted for a homicide. I called the dispatcher and began coordinating the setting up of a perimeter to try and contain the suspect.

Mary was even angrier now because she let a murderer get away. I tried to calm her down and once again told her that if she did her best that's all anyone could ask of her. I told her that it might have been the Lord's will that she didn't catch the suspect immediately after committing the crime. She was chasing him for a burglary, but he was running from a murder.

Third shift patrol units relieved the second shift units on the perimeter and in the wee hours of the morning, the suspect walked out from behind a house and gave himself up.

Sergeant Byrne commended us at roll call the next day for the great job we did in securing the area where the suspect was captured. He said that even though third shift took the suspect into custody, we all worked together to make it happen.

After roll call, Mary and I drove back to the Stone Crossing Apartments. Being a former crime scene investigator, I wanted to look at the crime scene in the daylight. As we pulled into the entrance we saw two men standing at the entrance. We approached the men and one of them quickly pulled his closed fist from the front pocket of his blue jeans, walked over to a tree and stood behind it.

I ordered the man to walk over to me. He ran his hand over a bush, dropping something small. Mary detained him by our car and I retrieved two small plastic baggies containing marijuana. I arrested the man, cuffed him, and placed him in our patrol vehicle. The other man was the owner of the residence where the murder suspect had jumped the fence fleeing from the crime.

I asked the guy if we could go in his backyard and look at where he climbed the fence. The three of us walked in the backyard and found a pair of blue shorts, with what appeared to be blood on them. Also, there was a pair of sandals, which also appeared to be bloodstained and blood on the fence post. We notified detectives and the scene was turned over to Corporal Stan Wilson of the Robbery-Homicide Bureau. We transported the young man with the drugs to the Montgomery County Youth Facility and charged him with possession of marijuana.

★★★

On Monday, March 26, 2002, five months after I retired from the MPD, I testified in the murder case and the events that occurred that night. I was asked a few questions by the defense. I later spoke to the defense attorney and I told him that I expected him to ask more questions. He said the judge asked him the same thing.

He explained to the judge that I was retired from the Montgomery Police Department with twenty years experience, and eight years of crime scene investigation experience. He told the judge that I went back to the crime scene the next day and found evidence missed by all the other investigators and crime scene investigators. He said he did not even want to open that can of worms and felt it was best for his client not to ask me too many questions.

The defendant in the case was found guilty and sentenced to prison.

I used this particular case as an example of how a simple call can turn from bad to worse. We responded to a burglary in progress and it ended up being a murder. I always taught my trainees that they should be prepared for anything when approaching a situation—because you just never know.

Able to Catch All of His Suspects

OFFICER ROBERT LAVALLEY HAD BEEN out of the police academy only a short time when I was assigned to be his training officer. He is tall and lanky with a distinct twang in his voice. He had ridden one night with me earlier before graduating from the academy during his ride-along week we called "OJT" for "on the job training." He'd been amazed at how we could keep up with everything being said on the radio.

"How do y'all keep up with all that?" he'd asked me.

"You'll learn once you have been on the streets for a little while," I said. "All you have to do is listen for our unit number (216), and the units around us and everything else will take care of itself."

When Robert was assigned to me he was extremely eager to work and to do a good job. Rookie officers like him have to be watched closely because they seem to want to rid the city of all the crime in one day. You have to teach them that you can do only so much in an eight-hour shift and that you have to pace yourself.

On Saturday, May 13, 2000, I got to see what the young rookie was made of. We got a lookout at roll call for a sixteen-year-old male wanted for armed robbery. I was familiar with this juvenile suspect from a couple of prior encounters, so we started looking for him as soon as we hit the street.

Around 3:30 that afternoon we spotted a van parked in the 5900 block of Cherry Hill Road around which several people were standing. We stopped to talk to them to see if we could get a lead on the whereabouts of our suspect. I walked to the driver's window as Robert approached the passenger side.

Suddenly I heard Robert. "Hold it!" he yelled.

At that moment I saw a young man running away with Robert right on his heels. I quickly grabbed my radio and told the dispatcher that my partner was in foot pursuit of a robbery suspect running north on Eric Lane. I would find out later that the suspect had struck my partner in the face before taking off. I fell in behind Robert and gave chase. The suspect fled up the block then disappeared into a house nearby.

The people in the house seemed shocked when he bolted in and hid in their bathroom. They pointed toward the bathroom door as we entered the house. Robert and I lunged through the door and into the bathroom. Robert snatched back the shower curtain. The young man hiding there drew back his fist. I swung my metal asp (baton) downward at the young man only to hear a loud *clank*. The metal shower rod caught the blow meant for him.

The man immediately looked up. When he saw that the shower rod had saved him, he slumped down in the tub. He covered his head and cried, "Don't hit me, I give up! Don't hit me!"

Robert snatched him up and snapped the cuffs on him. We dragged him out of the house as other officers and patrol units arrived on the scene. We laid him down in the front yard and searched him for weapons before walking him back to our vehicle several blocks away. A crowd had gathered in the front yard to see what the commotion was all about.

The family in the house seemed angry with us for chasing the suspect into their house. They weren't concerned with whatever crime he'd committed, or that it was the young man who chose to run into their house. They were mad at us because we chased him into their house. Officer Lonnie Harris, who had arrived to assist us, explained to them everything that had transpired and how dangerous the young man was. Afterward, they seemed satisfied.

On the way to headquarters, the young man who had assaulted my partner began his tough talk about we were harassing him, and that he was totally innocent. Just the same old tired gibberish I'd heard a million times before from my back seat. Then he began to complain that he wasn't feeling well. A minute later he vomited in the car. We took him to the juvenile office and turned him over to a detective. We found out there was a pick-up order on him for threatening to kill a police officer. We took care of all the paperwork and got back on the street. I paid one of the jail trustees working at headquarters ten dollars to clean out the back seat of our car.

Robert was absolutely wired for the rest of the evening about the chase and the arrest. I went over the events that led to the arrest and critiqued him about how he'd handled himself. He'd done a good job, but he was young and still learning and had made a few minor mistakes.

Robert got to ride with me for about half of our six-week training period. My second daughter, Kelly, was born May 16, 2000, and I was off for a week afterward to spend some time with my family and get to know her. Then I went on a church construction mission trip and missed another week. During our short time together, Robert chased several young men on foot wanted for felony offenses and was able to catch all of his suspects.

Appearances Can Be Deceiving

WEDNESDAY, **J**ULY **5, 2000,** STARTED out like any other day. It was the middle of the week and most people had been off for the Independence Day holiday the day before. Patrol officers don't get holidays off, unless they're administrative personnel. As the old saying goes, crime doesn't take a holiday.

Officer Richard Lall, a recent academy graduate, and I were riding together in District Sixteen, which included the Palisades Apartments, a large sprawling apartment complex and a haven for drug dealers and gang members. The apartment manager asked us to help with the loitering problem by patrolling the complex as much as possible and running any non-residents off the property. Those who refused were then 'trespassed' and ordered to leave.

Anytime property owners wanted our help in dealing with problem people and were willing to sign trespass warrants, I would do my best to help them. In many cases, by the time managers asked for our assistance, the problem was pretty much out of control.

The east end of the complex was controlled by members of the street gang known as the Bloods. The west end belonged to the Crips. Neither group seemed to bother the other, but both sold drugs in the complex along with other independent dealers without any gang affiliation. I'd been working on the problem over several months and made several felony arrests with different partners.

Around 8:30, Richard and I turned into the main entrance, saw a young man leaning on a set of crutches at the curb in front of one of the buildings. He was wearing camouflage pants and was standing at a location where we'd made several prior drug arrests. We stopped to talk to him to see if he was a new resident or was just hanging out. He identified himself as Jason Killough.* He didn't live there and gave us the usual answer when asked what he was doing out there. "I'm visitin' one of my homeboys," he said.

He told us that he had cerebral palsy that affected the use of his legs and sat down on the curb. He didn't have ID, so Richard got all his information and checked him for warrants.

"Do you have any weapons on you," I asked.

"No."

I had noticed earlier that he had a bulge in the cargo pockets of the BDU pants he wore. I patted him down as he sat on the curb and felt what appeared to be several puffy items in his right pocket. I removed the items that turned out to be eight billiard ball size bags of marijuana.

As I took the bags of weed out of his pocket, he asked, "Whatcha gonna do now?"

"I'm gonna put you in jail, that's what I'm gonna do now." I answered. I was very surprised that he asked me that question.

"Have you ever been arrested for drugs before?" I inquired.

"No."

"How long have you been selling drugs?"

"For a while now."

"How long is *a while now?*"

"Coupla years now," he said.

"Have you ever been stopped and questioned by the police?" I asked.

"No," he replied. There was a tone of defiance in his voice. "Nobody messes with me because I'm handicapped. Nobody until you came along."

"Where do you usually sell weed?" I asked.

"Here."

"I ride out here everyday and I've never seen you," I told him.

"I usually sell before you come on, and the weekends," he answered.

We arrested him and headed toward the narcotics office. He told us he had cerebral palsy all his life and he used it to sell drugs. I asked him if he ever carried a gun and he said he had in the past. He said

---

*   Name changed to protect the not-so-innocent

that other officers had stopped him, but none had ever patted him down for weapons because of his handicap.

We turned him over to narcotics detectives. The marijuana in his pockets weighed in at 21.9 grams. I explained to Richard how dangerous it was that no other officer had ever checked him for weapons. He could have easily injured or killed an officer because they didn't want to be seen picking on a handicapped person. I always try to treat everyone the same no matter who they are but you have to be careful. Appearances can be deceiving.

HE PROTECTED THE LITTLE GIRL

OCTOBER **17, 2000** STARTED OFF like any other Tuesday. At that time I didn't have a regular partner, so I rode with the less-experienced junior officers on the shift. On that particular night, Officer Paul Sampson and I were partnered together in District Sixteen. We started the evening off pretty much like any other; a couple of minor calls, alarms, family disturbances, theft calls and the like—nothing special.

A little after 7:00 p.m. however, things changed. We responded to a domestic violence call on Marlowe Drive. The address was several miles away, and I knew it would take some time to get there. The units in that area were out of service on other calls, and we were the closest help available. Sampson notified dispatch that we were en route from Woodley Road and Virginia Loop Road. Since we were in a more rural area of the district I chose to travel the back way and avoid the major thoroughfares. The route was a little longer but lighter traffic would allow us to make better time.

As we neared Marlowe Drive, the dispatcher radioed that a black male suspect was standing in the front yard with a gun. Now the situation had intensified, so I picked up the pace just a bit.

Often on disturbance calls, the caller will lie and say that someone has a gun hoping that the police will respond more quickly. Whether or not it turns out to be true, it always elevates a responding officer's level of anticipation when he expects to confront an armed suspect.

An update from the dispatcher informed us that the complaint clerk could hear arguing in the background, and she could hear the suspect threatening to shoot everyone at the house. I gunned the Crown Vic and pushed it as fast as I safely could, but it seemed to take forever to get there. I turned onto Narrow Lane Road racing against time as the tone of dispatcher's constant updates told us that the situation had gone from bad to worse.

The cruiser's headlights pierced the darkness ahead then arced broadly as we turned with screeching tires onto Buckingham Drive into the neighborhood. The dispatcher's voice tensed perceptibly as she reported that the clerk could hear the staccato popping of gunfire. I made the right onto Marlowe Drive just a block away, tires now howling against the pavement, as the dispatcher blandly stated that the caller was no longer on the phone.

I rounded the corner pulling to a screeching stop in front of the brick house now surrounded by neighbors, frozen in the street in various states of shock and disbelief. The pale, acrid smoke from gunfire lingered like a haunting mist in the night air. As Sampson and I got out of the car, weapons drawn and scanning frantically for the gunman, one of the women in the growing crowd began to scream, "'Rat Boy' did it! 'Rat Boy' did it!"

"Which way did he go?" I shouted.

She pointed back down the street toward Narrow Lane Road in the direction from which we had arrived, so I assumed that he must have hidden in the darkness of one of the yards as we passed by. We'd missed him by only seconds.

I walked cautiously up the driveway and saw a black female lying facedown on the ground between the house and a car parked in the driveway. I approached her, carefully stepping around the twenty or so brass casings littering the driveway, and saw that many of the rounds had torn jagged holes in her blood-soaked clothing as each one embedded itself deeply in her flesh. I quickly ordered Sampson to cordon off the scene with crime scene tape

Her feet were pointed toward me as I cautiously knelt down looking for any sign of life. It looked to me as if she'd tried to crawl under the car to escape her killer. I holstered my weapon to check the left side of her neck for a pulse. As I pressed my fingers against her lifeless skin, still warm to the touch, I looked up and saw a little girl about two years old standing in the darkness at the side of the house, motionless amid the broken glass of a storm door shattered by a stray bullet. I went to her immediately, and she held up her arms to me. I picked her up, and she locked her tiny arms tightly around my neck.

I thought about my own two daughters as I held her. For a moment I forgot about everything else as my heart went out to this innocent, precious child, now a stunned witness to this gruesome tragedy.

I held onto her tightly. "You're safe now, Sweetie. Everything is okay," I said softly. "I'm not gonna to let anything happen to you."

She held firmly onto me with her head resting gently on my shoulder, never making a sound. I heard the approaching sirens and knew I needed to get back to my job and advise my supervisors of the situation. A lady who lived next door came outside. I walked over to her and asked if she could take the little girl from me. She called the child by name, and the girl reached out to her. I told the neighbor that I didn't think the girl was hurt but I wanted the medics to check her when they arrived.

Additional patrol units soon arrived to help Sampson and me keep the growing crowd out of the crime scene. Since cell phones have become so prevalent, managing crowds at major crime scenes has become increasingly difficult. Once someone at the scene calls three friends, those friends call more friends, and the size of the crowd seems to grow exponentially.

Once the paramedics arrived and pronounced the victim dead, I asked them to check out the little girl with the neighbor. The child wasn't hurt and seemed more at ease now.

Once the detectives arrived, I told them that I was familiar with "Rat Boy" and that he lived in the Stonebridge Apartments. I'd had several previous encounters with him while riding that district. I quickly got on the mobile computer in my car and searched for more information on "Rat Boy." I was able to come up with a full name and current address before broadcasting a more complete lookout on him.

The detectives interviewed the witnesses and determined that the victim in the driveway was not "Rat Boy's" original target. He was actually after the victim's sister, whom he'd been dating on and off. He'd recently been released from jail and had gone over to the victim's house. They also determined that the victim had been holding the child when she was shot and had turned her back toward "Rat Boy" to shield the child with her body as her enraged assailant pumped round after round into her.

★★★

About a year later, as police officers and family members sat in the witness room waiting to testify at the murder trial, I asked one of the relatives how the little girl was doing. She said the girl was doing fine.

"Are you the officer who picked her up that night?" she asked.

I told her I was, and she thanked me for that.

The jury found "Rat Boy" guilty, and the judge removed that threat from society.

So many times when adults can't get along, children become innocent victims of their wrath. In this particular case, a family member lost her life but the child was protected from physical harm through her sacrifice. Only in the fullness of time will any emotional scars become evident. I can only hope that she was too young to remember what happened that terrible night.

As I write this last part of the story, a flood of emotions engulf me, and I just praise God that He protected the little girl.

Mary's Path

ON THE EVENING OF **O**CTOBER 25, 2000, around 6:30 p.m., something happened that altered my Christian walk forever and changed my thinking about certain things. My faith grew in a way that I never thought, and I faced things I thought I'd never encounter.

This particular day started out like any other. I was working second shift patrol on the city's east side training a new officer. I heard the radio traffic about a traffic accident with a fatality on Vaughn Road about two blocks from my house. The description of the vehicles told me it wasn't a member of my family, which was reassuring. I was riding too far away to respond on the call, but I carefully monitored the radio. The nature of the radio traffic from officers on the scene led me to believe that someone important was involved.

Some time later I learned that a lady named Carolyn Kelly had died in the accident. I also learned that the other driver who caused the accident was my former partner, Officer Mary Butler.

I was Mary's first training officer right out of the academy. She graduated from the police academy on Friday, March 3, 2000, and was scheduled to begin her first six weeks of training with me the following Monday. She called me at home the night before to ask if there was anything she needed to bring to work. She also wanted to know what was expected of her when we began our first tour together. I told her to report to work about 1:30 and I'd go over everything she needed to know.

She told me that she didn't want to be "ate up" and wanted to be prepared. "Ate up" is a term that means clueless or unprepared for the job as in "ate up with stupidity."

I could tell by the way she talked that she had a military

background. Of all the officers I trained, Mary was the only one to ever call me at home beforehand to get a handle on what was expected of her. From that first telephone call, I knew there was something different about her, and I felt the Lord had a greater purpose in allowing our paths to cross.

Mary was positive, upbeat, and eager to learn, taking instructions well. She was feisty, with short blond hair, and didn't take crap from anyone. As motivated as she was, I also knew she was dealing with other issues in her life. She was in the Army National Guard, but had always longed to be a police officer. Her ex-husband, whom she'd recently divorced, didn't like the idea of her being a police officer. He was a police officer in Talladega, Alabama, and had vehemently opposed her decision.

She spoke to him often on her cell phone, and I could tell from what I heard that he wasn't at all supportive of her career choice. I never pried, but I allowed her to share her feelings with me if she chose to do so. Being a training officer was more than teaching the proper procedures of filling out paperwork. It also involved helping young adults adjust to the life of a police officer. The average person could make a mistake or commit a crime and in all likelihood it wasn't newsworthy, but let a police officer make the same mistake and suddenly it was the lead story on the six o'clock news.

As a Christian and as a training officer, I made an effort to deal with the spiritual and emotional side of the new officer on the job. This wasn't a department directive, but I felt that my faith in God obligated me to provide this. As a Christian, I believe that God expects me to witness to all of those He brings into my life, more profoundly so those whom I trained to do police work. The six weeks I spent with each one was my chance to be a positive Christian witness.

Notice I said *positive* Christian witness.

I'd met some officers who claimed to be Christians, but for various reasons had strayed from their walk with God. Their witness to the power of God's grace wasn't what I would exactly call positive.

Mary also shared with me the fact that she grew up in church and had been active in her church's youth group until a couple of alcohol related accidents took the lives of some of her friends.

I felt she was a little bitter and even angry with God for what had happened. She told me on occasion that she felt her life was out of control and didn't know what to do. We had several heart-to-heart talks during slow nights and on our dinner breaks. Occasionally her ex would call while she and I were working together. The animosity I sensed between the two became even more obvious regarding her career.

I knew the Lord had placed her with me for a reason, but I had no idea why. I was, however, able to coax Mary and her roommate to attend church with me on two occasions.

Mary completed her six-week training period and moved on to her next training officer. During our time together we handled several interesting calls, and I knew she'd always be there to back me up if I needed her. I had total confidence in her abilities and trusted her completely with my life. That is something I cannot honestly say for all the officers I trained.

Mary was off-duty on the night of the accident and had been drinking. She was late for a birthday party, driving too fast down the center turn lane of Vaughn Road near the elementary school, the cake for the party on the front seat next to her. The center turn lane is often called the "suicide lane," and that night, Mary found out why. She ran a red light and struck Mrs. Kelly's car broadside in the driver's door. Mrs. Kelly died almost instantly.

Following the accident, Mary was relieved of duty and placed on administrative leave, which is standard procedure for any officer under investigation for a crime.

During the criminal proceeding, the department charged her additionally with administrative misconduct. Most of her fellow officers no longer spoke to her, or associated with her in any way. The accident had received a great deal of press coverage and the other officers shied away to avoid any guilt by association. Those who had once been Mary's friends and associates became former friends and strangers.

It was during this period I was walking across the parking lot behind headquarters one afternoon and saw Mary walking out the back door. From a distance I could see she was upset. The Lord reminded me not to give up on her.

I'd never experienced anything like it, but something just kept tugging at my heart. As I approached her I thought about just saying "Hey," then calling her afterward. But I didn't. I stopped her and saw that she was crying.

I asked her what was wrong and she said that the department had brought her up on charges to be fired. I put my arm around her and told her I was sorry about what was happening. I asked her if there was anything I could do.

"No," she replied softly.

I looked toward a picnic table where several officers sat smoking. Their eyes followed us.

"Mary, is it okay if I pray with you?" I asked her.

A weak smile crossed her face. "Yes," she replied. "I would appreciate that."

We walked to the other corner of the building away from the other officers. I put my left arm around her and prayed for her to have the strength to deal with what she was going through and for the Lord to give her overall strength and faith.

After we prayed she thanked me then walked to her car. I walked past the other officers who acted like they weren't looking at me, but I could tell they were. I don't know what they were thinking, but I felt a huge weight lifted from my shoulders.

I knew I'd done the right thing.

Several months passed as she awaited trial. Mary eventually moved in with another police officer and became pregnant.

She, like many others, began to look toward the Lord for guidance. She sincerely wanted to help others avoid the same mistakes she'd made. One night while I was on patrol, she called and asked if she could speak to my youth group. She knew I was a youth Sunday school teacher and was very active with several different programs. I told her I'd love for her to share her story with my group.

I set up a Sunday morning for her to speak. She was waiting in her pickup truck when I arrived at church. She was six months pregnant and had a hard time walking, but I was so excited about her speaking I almost ran ahead of her to the door. She told me to slow down before I realized what I was doing.

Before my group, I introduced her as a good friend who had been my partner on second shift patrol at one time.

She spoke about growing up in church and getting away from God. She told them how easy it was for her to get alcohol in the military because the foreign countries where she was stationed allowed drinking at a younger age than here in the states. Then she told them of her dream of being a police officer and how she finally achieved her dream by joining the Montgomery Police Department. Then she got emotional and told them how her dream came crashing down one fateful night.

"I was all over the news and in the newspaper," she said. "One stupid mistake and my whole career is over. After the accident, I was brought up on charges. After I was indicted, the police department brought me up on charges. I met with the Major and the Chief and they told me I was going to be fired."

The young men and women in the room were intently focused on every word.

Her tone became more solemn at that point. Her voice broke with emotion. "After leaving the meeting, I had already decided to commit suicide and was on my way home when Steve stopped me in the parking lot and asked me how I was doing. I told him the department brought me up on charges and they were going to fire me. He then asked if he could pray with me."

A somber silence fell over the room. I couldn't believe what I'd just heard.

"After he prayed with me," she said, "I decided that I could handle whatever happened and decided not to do it." She then pointed at me sitting on a table to her right and said, "You need to listen to this guy because he is a man of God! If I had listened to him I would not be in the trouble I am in today!"

When her case came to court, she pled guilty to manslaughter. The judge sentenced her to a total of fifteen years, five years of which she would have to serve in prison. She reported to Montgomery County Sheriff D.T. Marshall six weeks after her child was born to begin serving her sentence.

I still get chills whenever I tell this story. I can't believe how close I came to passing her by that day. The lesson I took away from the experience was that when the Lord leads you to do something, you need to do it. You never know how it will affect others.

I began writing letters to her in prison and I sent her a John MacArthur study bible. She wrote back that she was surprised to hear from me but was very happy about it. She said no one else from the police department wrote to her. I received a letter from her once or twice a month and I always replied. I told her all about work, what my family was doing, how church was going, and I sent photos of my daughters as they grew up.

Mary accepted Christ while in prison, and I sensed a change in the tone of her letters. It wasn't just the words, but I could really tell by what she wrote that she was truly saved and knew Jesus. She wasn't the same person with whom I worked as a partner.

I sent several books and study guides for her to read, and she often asked me questions that either she or one of the other female inmates had about the Bible or scripture.

Prior to this, I never placed much stock in the prison religious experience or the true credibility of the person who gets saved in prison. I figured a person messes up their whole life and when it has gotten as low as it can go a person has nowhere else to turn.

God always seems like the last resort to the hopeless. But after knowing Mary and all she went through and reading her letters, my perception of the incarcerated Christian has changed somewhat. I don't believe that everyone who gets saved in prison is truly saved, but I believe it's more feasible than I once did.

I knew the first time I talked to Mary that the Lord brought her into my life for a reason. Because of her, I've grown and matured in my spiritual walk. My grasp of God's word has grown by helping her to understand what He reveals to us through scripture.

From time to time some of those who knew Mary ask if I've heard from her. Occasionally someone wants to know where she is now. Some people actually seem interested; others just want to know if I'm still writing to her. I was the only person from the police department who wrote to her in prison.

Mary was released from prison on September 18, 2006. Her son, Cade, remains in the custody of his father.

I pray only that the Lord will continue to guide Mary's path.

ARE YOU KIDDIN' ME?

TUESDAY FEBRUARY 7, 2001 WAS expected to be a very cold night according to the weather report. The day's high was a cool 65 degrees and was expected to drop in the low 30's and possibly in the 20's. A little after 9:00 p.m., Officer R. A. Wiley and I received a call to Audubon Lane on a code 12 (family disturbance). Officer Jenny Gola and her partner, Officer Charles Dougan, were riding the neighboring district and got en route to back us up. Jenny and I never rode together as partners, but we were always quick to back each other up. As friends and senior officers on the shift, we usually kept track of one another during the shift.

We arrived at the house about the same time and approached the house. By this time the temperature had dropped to the lower 40's and with the wind blowing felt like the 30's. As we crowded around the front door, I knocked and a gentleman in his late forties answered and invited us in. He said he needed to talk to us. All four of us quickly entered the house to escape the bitter cold outside.

I asked the man what we could do for him. He began to tell us about how he thought that the house down the street was a drug house. He explained that his girlfriend left their house nearly every afternoon and went down to this particular house and stayed there for several hours. According to him, all manner of strange people came in and out of the house at all hours of the day and night. His girlfriend would then return home late each night high on drugs.

"I give her money all the time and she keeps blowing it at that drug house," he said. "When I question her about what she's doing with the money, she tells me that she spends it on 'stuff.' When I ask her about always going to the drug house, she gets mad and says the house is not a drug house. I make good money doing upholstery work, but I cannot afford to support her drug habit."

He stood behind a recliner-type chair turned upside down with cotton stuffing sticking out. He pointed around the living room and told us that he did all the upholstery work on the furniture and was working on that chair for someone.

As he sat down he put his head in his hands, took a deep breath and let out a huge sigh and said, "I should have never got involved with this woman. I had a good woman, but I was stupid and she left me."

"Why did she leave you?" I asked him.

He replied, "I started dating this other woman, and she was not going to have it. She is a Godly woman and took care of me and treated me real good. But I had to be stupid and go chasing after this other woman."

"If she was such a good woman, why in the world did you take up with this other woman?"

"She was kinda heavy and was not quite as pretty as this other woman, so I decided to start dating her instead," he said. "I was just stupid! Now I'm paying for it. I wish I'd never gotten involved with the crazy woman."

"Sometimes we don't realize what a great thing we have until we no longer have it," I said.

"Yeah, I had a woman who would cook for me and take care of me, but because she was a little fat, I decided to start seeing this thin, pretty woman," he replied. "I'm just stupid."

At this point the room grew silent.

Jenny, hands on her hips, sashayed up to him, "Hey!" she said, with a big smile on her face. "Fat girls need lovin' too!" Her head bobbed back and forth as she spoke. "All you have to do is put her on some Slim Fast and slim her down and you got yourself a skinny woman."

"Yeah, I guess you're right. I could have done that. I didn't think about that," the man replied without looking up.

Jenny's comment caught me completely off guard. For a moment I didn't know what to say. Charles and I turned toward the living room window both fighting an eruption of laughter welling up inside us. Charles bit his lip trying not to laugh.

The man looked up and noticed us looking out the window. "What are y'all looking at?" he asked.

"We're just looking out the window in case your girlfriend comes home," I answered fighting back tears of laughter.

After composing myself, I put my hand over my mouth so he could not see me laughing. I told the man that we'd turn the information over to narcotics detectives and let them follow up on the complaint. I also gave him the telephone number to the narcotics office and told him that if he got any more information about the drug house to call them. I added that he might want to kick his crackhead girlfriend to the curb and see if the other woman would take him back.

"Tell her that you learned your lesson," I said.

He thanked us and we left. While walking out of the house we waited until we got some distance away before we all lost control and doubled over with laughter in the cold, night air.

I walked over close to Jenny. "Fat girls need lovin, too?" I repeated. "Put her on Slim Fast and slim her down? Are you kiddin' me?"

March 2001 – Kelly (almost one year old)

"Ain't nothin' you can do about it!"

OFFICER BROOKE HERMANN BECAME MY new partner on Monday, April 17, 2001. She was a recent graduate of the police academy, and I was her second training officer. The first thing I usually did with a new trainee was to conduct a guided tour of the district. I did this to point out problem areas and to introduce my new partner to the "problem children" I dealt with on a regular basis. It was the few problem children, mostly young unemployed men, who gave me the most grief during my daily rounds of the neighborhoods. I'd arrested some of them and certainly confronted nearly all of them at some point. This assortment of misfits were the ones who were always arguing, fighting, stealing, or otherwise causing trouble wherever and whenever they could find it. They were the bad apples in the grand barrel of District Eighteen.

I kept track of them as best as I could by stopping and talking to them whenever I saw them out wandering the neighborhood. My rapport with them kept me abreast of events in the neighborhoods in my district, and often during our conversations I could find out if they had any information on other crimes they were willing to volunteer. Some of these guys would freely give me information, if for no other reason than to throw suspicion away from themselves. Others wouldn't give me the time of day.

I also made it a point to keep in close contact with as many as I could so my partners could learn interviewing and interrogation techniques. What might seem like just a casual conversation can be an important investigative tool for a police officer. General conversations on sports, television, movies, current events or recent arrests can generate a great deal of information about unsolved crimes. Those on the fringe of society who populate the subculture of the street are a bountiful source of information, and it takes a certain skill and finesse with people to tap into that rich network.

On this particular afternoon, Brooke and I were patrolling Cherry Hill Road in the Regency Park subdivision when I spotted one of my misfits, Zack Kelly.* He was standing with a group of about four other young men, all in their late teens, in the front yard of a house where I'd been many times.

We stopped and spoke to everyone, and I introduced my new partner. They never seemed to remember the names of my partners and usually referred to them by some physical characteristic. To them, my partners had monikers like, "Blonde Lady" or "Short Dude," or "Country-Talking Officer." My misfits knew me simply as "Corporal Smith" or "Seventy-Seven," which was the number on the side of my cruiser.

Before we got out of the car, I identified Zack to my partner by the description of his clothing so she could pay special attention to him. As Brooke began to talk to Zack, he was very defensive toward her and ignored her questions. The more she talked to him, the ruder he became.

"Why are you disrespecting my partner like that?" I asked him.

"I ain't got to talk to her if I don't want to," he replied.

"All she's doing is just trying to learn who some of the people are around here," I said. "And you're just showing her no respect."

For some reason, he decided he wasn't going to talk to her. Zack was usually very talkative and often bragged about what he had done and things he knew but wouldn't tell us. I can only assume that he was trying to impress someone else there by showing how tough he was. Ignoring Brooke was his way of doing it.

"Look, you may need her assistance one day," I warned. "So you'd better be nice to her."

"I ain't gotta talk to her or you or nobody else if I don't want," he insisted. "And there *ain't nothin'* you can do about it!"

---

*   Name changed to protect the foolish

"Zack, it's like I've told you before," I said. "We can be your best friend or your worst enemy. It's your choice."

He just looked away.

Finally I made an announcement to the group of people gathered in the yard. "Well, apparently we have lost respect in the neighborhood and we're going to have to get it back," I said.

He looked away from us again and gazed off in the distance. "You do what *you* gotta do," he said. "And I'll do what *I* gotta do." His tone was defiant.

"Your choice, Zack," I reminded him. "Just be careful what you ask for." I turned and waved to the rest of the group. "Y'all be good and we'll talk to ya later."

Brooke and I climbed into the car and eased away from the group.

"Don't worry about him," I told her. "He was just trying to be the tough guy around his friends."

"What do you do about someone like that?" Brooke asked.

"We're gonna have to gain our respect back in the hood," I explained. "And we are going to do it at *his* expense."

On my patrols I often overlooked minor traffic violations because I was more worried about protecting lives and property. I'd make the traffic stops and send the drivers off with just a warning as a way to build trust and respect with the people who lived and worked in the community. Later on, when I was looking for a suspect in a crime or information about a particular crime, I could call in a favor from someone who'd received a break in this way. I would much rather make an arrest for robbery or a burglary than to write a ticket for a minor traffic violation. That's a trade-off a cop will take any day.

Because Zack was disrespectful to my partner, things would have to change for a while. Brooke and I began to make traffic stops and writing tickets in the area where Zack lived. Several of the violators wondered why we were suddenly giving tickets when we'd always been so understanding before.

My explanation was that Zack had disrespected us, and we were doing what we needed to do to get back the respect of our authority in the neighborhood.

This may seem like I was picking on one person, but as an officer who patrolled a certain district each day, losing the respect of the people in the community made it much harder to do the job. Occasionally, someone would challenge us to test the limits of our tolerance in front of their peers. Our response largely determined how effective we could be in deterring crime and apprehending the wrongdoers in our district.

Dealing with the neighborhood loud mouth or criminal who always seemed to get away with his crime was like dealing with a bully. Once you stood up to him, or in the case of the criminal, put him in jail, you gained respect from the community. Zack became the neighborhood loud mouth with his attitude, and we were obligated to put him in his place.

On the following Monday afternoon, at around 3:30, we were back on Cherry Hill Road and saw Zack standing on the corner, alone. As we slowly approached, he began waving both his arms, trying to flag us down. He'd never flagged me down in the past for anything, so this caught me a little off guard. We pulled up to him, keeping him in front of our vehicle. Brooke and I got out of the car and he walked toward us.

"Corporal Smith, I'm sorry for disrespectin' you the other day," he pleaded. "These people want to hurt me if I don't make it right. *Pleeease*, you gotta tell 'em."

"You didn't disrespect *me* the other day," I told him. "You disrespected my partner, Officer Herrmann. You owe *her* the apology, not me."

He looked over the hood of the car toward her. "Please officer Herrmann, I'm...."

"Hold it," I interrupted with an upturned hand. "If you are going to talk to her, you walk over to her and talk to her."

He slowly walked around the front of the car and bowed his head slightly, avoiding eye contact. "I'm sorry Officer Herrmann for disrespecting you the other day," he said. His voice was soft, and his tone was respectful. "Please tell everyone that I made it right so they won't hurt me."

"Okay," she replied. "I'll let it go this time."

Then he looked to me. "Can you stop writin' tickets and tellin' everybody that it's cuz of me that they are gettin' tickets?" he asked.

"Okay, you made things right and we'll let up on the tickets," I said. "But remember, I told you that we could be your best friend or your worst enemy. Remember when I said that?"

"I remember," he said quietly. "Just tell everybody that we're okay so they won't hurt me."

"Okay," I said. "We're good and I'll give it a rest."

Zack walked off cautiously. I could see him scanning the area for potential threats. He seemed a little more at ease, but only a little.

Brooke and I got back in the car.

"I cannot believe that," Brooke said. She seemed amazed. "He actually apologized to me."

"I'm a little surprised myself," I told her. "I wasn't really sure what would happen. I knew we'd get some kind of result, but I never imagined him flagging us down and apologizing. I guess we gained our respect back in the neighborhood."

We let up on the ticket writing and went back to just warning people instead. Brooke and I continued concentrating on pursuing offenders for more serious crimes.

Zack continued to be a "problem child," but after that experience he always showed my partners and me the respect we deserved. I also never again heard him say, "Ain't nothin' you can do about it."

People See What They Want to See

ONE OF THE PERKS OF being a senior officer on a patrol shift is the take-home vehicle. It is so much more convenient having the same car to use on duty each night with all your equipment already in place without having to lug your gear and all your paperwork from car to car at the beginning and end of each shift. It was also nice having a free ride to and from work each day courtesy of the city. The trade-off for the department was that assigned cars are better maintained and cared for, and you took pride in something that was yours. Keeping it clean and running well was a small price to pay.

I was assigned vehicle number 77 on the evening shift, but it was in the shop to be serviced, so I was using Corporal Glen Farmer's car from the day shift. Glen lived out of town and couldn't take his assigned vehicle home. The car was brand new and had less than a hundred miles on it. This car was also equipped with one of the newest gadgets, a mobile computer linked to our NCIC database for running warrants and registration checks. Whenever I used a car assigned to someone else, I always tried to take good care of it just as I expected other officers who used my car to do.

It was Monday, April 30, 2001, and other than using Glen's new car, it was starting out like any other day.

After a routine roll call, I drove out to my assigned district with my partner, Officer Brooke Herrmann, both of us enjoying the new car smell. Brooke and I looked over the new Ford Crown Victoria, which didn't seem that much different than the previous year's model.

We arrived and began to patrol the neighborhoods, checking all of our normal trouble spots. At a little after 4:00 in the afternoon we were dispatched to Quality Rentals on the South Boulevard on a dispute between the manager and an ex-employee. The business was a rent-to-own furniture store. The dispatcher relayed that the offender causing the dispute was a male named Randy*who was wearing khaki pants and a black and khaki shirt. Officers Jenny Gola and her partner, Aimee Savell, in the adjoining district to mine, got en route to back us up on the call.

I'd had several female partners over the previous months. Jenny, in the neighboring district, rotated riding with either Aimee or Officer Elizabeth Planer. Several of the supervisors referred to us in that part of town as "Steve and the Girls."

Brooke and I arrived and as we entered the business saw a young man answering the description standing at the front desk. He immediately began to walk quickly toward us. He was angry and shouted as he approached.

"He better give me my mother-f★★kin' check or I'm gonna hit him!" he yelled. "I ain't goin' for this sh★t!" he said.

"Sir, you need to calm down and talk to us about your problem," I said. I was calm but firm.

"That mother f★★ker has my god★★mn check and if he don't give it to me I'm gonna hit him!"

"Don't threaten the manager," I warned.

"I don't give a f★★k!" he replied. "If he don't give me my check, I'm gonna hit him and knock him out!"

"Go across the room and calm down!" I ordered. I pointed, indicating an empty area in the room where I could watch him.

Several customers were in the store watching the events unfold, along with some of the other employees. I spoke to the manager while Randy fumed, stomped and paced around the room. The manager told me that Randy had property that belonged to the store and that when he got it back then he would give him his check.

Randy overheard our conversation. "I told you!" he shouted. "My cousin has that stuff!"

Jenny and Aimee walked in at about that time. Randy saw them,

★   Name changed to protect the angry

then ran at a concrete pole near where he was and struck it hard with his fist. It seemed to me that Randy was putting on a little show for the customers, the other employees, and apparently us too.

Jenny attempted to talk to him and calm him down, but he continued his tirade, spitting out a string of profanities and threats.

Finally I'd had enough. "Place him under arrest for disorderly conduct," I told Jenny and Aimee. "Put your hands behind your back!" I said to the angry, young man.

Jenny grabbed his right arm, Aimee and Brooke grabbed his left arm, but he began to resist and attempt to break free of their grasp. The officers struggled to force his arms behind him, but he fought their efforts and kept his arms out to his sides with quick jerking motions.

I didn't realize it at the time but he had some type of oil or lotion on his arms and they couldn't get a firm grip on him. I also thought he may have been on some type of narcotic because he was unusually hyper and agitated.

Somehow they managed to get him outside. I followed to help in the effort to place him in custody. He continued to resist by pushing and pulling away from the officers to the point that when I approached him, he jumped backward, forcing himself and the three female officers to lunge back into the large plate glass window at the front of the store. The glass didn't shatter, but he and the officers struck the glass so hard that I could see it flex and recoil from the impact.

Before any more damage was done, I grabbed Randy by his shirt and pulled the four of them away from the glass. The girls had his arms stretched out to his side, but couldn't get him on the ground. I pulled my expandable metal baton from my belt and snapped it open with a flick of my wrist. It extended to its full length of twenty inches and locked into place. I swung the baton at his shins, but he saw my swing and stepped back away from the strike. As he did this, Brooke stepped forward without noticing my swing. My baton struck her with full force on the shin of her right leg.

"OH, STEVE!" she shouted. I could tell the pain racing up her leg was agonizing.

Angry now at my own miscue, I pulled him forward and held

him in place this time. I swung the baton again and this time I found my mark. He let out a groan and began to shuffle his feet backward. I struck his shins several more times, each blow of the baton landing with a solid thwack on his shin bones, but he continued to back away from the blows without surrendering. I tried to strike a pressure point on his hip with my knee. The common peronial is a bundle of nerves on the upper hip that can stun and weaken a person's legs when struck. Aimee attempted to strike this area on his other side without much success.

Finally, Jenny and Brooke each grabbed a leg and yanked him down from behind. He fell chest-first on the concrete. This didn't seem to phase him much, and he continued to fight. Jenny had managed to get one cuff fastened to his right wrist, but he pulled his left arm underneath his body and wouldn't relinquish his left hand. I jumped on his back and tried to pull his left hand free, but the oily substance on his body prevented me from getting a firm grasp.

We continually shouted orders for him to comply with us, but he wouldn't give up. I struck him several more times with the blunt round end of the metal baton, but it didn't seem to have any effect. I couldn't get to my mace, so I grabbed Aimee's from her belt and sprayed him in the face. He shook his head violently back and forth several times, but he just wouldn't give up the fight. I whacked him on the wrist a couple of more times before the mace and the pain of the blows began to weaken him enough to get his other hand behind him and secure in the handcuffs.

The whole fight lasted four to five minutes and we were all exhausted. We paused for a few moments to recover a little, and that was when I noticed several people standing in front of the store who had seen the entire event unfold.

Randy began to kick as we were placing him in the back seat, and since we weren't in *my* car, we couldn't find any leg restraints. Jenny called for another unit equipped with a larger set of cuffs for his ankles that we could attach to the bolt in the floorboard.

We picked him up and forced him into the back seat, all the while he kicked and thrashed about. After we got him into the car, he braced himself against the door and pushed his feet against opposite door so we couldn't close it. Jenny pushed as hard as she could with her one-hundred-five pounds, but the strength of his legs was more than a match for her.

"Hold the door closed, Jenny!" I said. "I got an idea!"

I took about a three-step drop then ran at the car kicking the door closed with my foot. The door clicked shut, and Rowdy Randy was finally contained. When the door slammed shut, his knees bent backwards slightly and locked them into place where he couldn't move. He continued to cuss and then started spitting on the windows. I quickly closed the clear Plexiglas partition dividing the front seat from the back.

As we waited for Unit 219 to arrive with the leg restraints, Randy continued to produce a snotty, runny, greenish-colored phlegm and spit huge globs of it onto the windows, doors and ceiling. He was banging his head on the window and Plexiglas partition. All I could think about was this guy spitting this foul, sticky phlegm everywhere in Glen's new car.

When Lonnie got out of the car I told him what had happened and the problems we'd had with this guy.

Lonnie is a huge man. I mean *huge*. He stands about six-five and has been a body-builder much of his adult life and weighs over three hundred pounds. There has almost no fat on his body. He is pure muscle.

Lonnie calmly walked over to our vehicle and looked at the mess inside.

"Nasty!" he said in disgust.

He walked back to his car and donned a pair of rubber gloves. Donald retrieved the leg restraint from their car. Lonnie opened the door and lifted Randy out with little effort. He laid the young man on the ground and placed flex cuffs and legs restraints on him. Any resistance by Randy was met with a powerful grip from a powerful man who could have easily snapped the young man's back like dry kindling. Lonnie made no attempt to quiet Randy's loud and belligerent mouth, however. Randy began to scream and cuss in an attempt to attract more attention, but physically, he was under complete control.

We transported him to police headquarters. Jenny and Aimee followed us in their car. We advised dispatch that we had a suspect maced. Since we had used so much force restraining the young man, we knew we'd all have to write statements about the incident. Pulling into the parking lot, I saw Captain Reid, Lieutenant West, Sergeant Crockett and Sergeant Byrne standing there waiting on us.

Byrne met us at the car. "Are all the officers okay?" he asked.

"Yes, sir. We're all okay," I replied.

"Take him up to the jail and I'll see you downstairs," Byrne said.

I looked over at all the other supervisors. Lieutenant West was motioning his index finger for me to come over to where they were.

As I walked up, Lieutenant West spoke. "We've already gotten several calls of complaints on y'all and what happened," he said. "So tell us what happened."

I recounted the incident in as much detail as I could remember, including the use of the mace and the number of times I struck the young man with a baton as we attempted to cuff him.

"The people who saw all of this, where were they standing?" he asked.

"I remember seeing them standing in front of the store," I said. "I guess they were the customers inside the store who came outside to see all the action." I felt a sudden surge of anger that these people would have the nerve to complain after what we went through. "Are you telling me that they saw everything that happened and still called in to complain on us? What are they complaining about?"

"They said that y'all used too much force and mistreated him for no reason," West said.

"Are you kiddin' me?" I couldn't believe my ears.

"Were these his family members out there?" Reid asked.

"No, sir. Not that I know of," I replied. "They never did say anything to us. They just stood and watched the whole event unfold and never said a word."

"Well, don't worry about it," Reid said. "If anyone comes down to make a formal complaint, we'll deal with it. I'll need each one of you to write a detailed statement on what happened."

After Brooke and I signed warrants on Randy for Disorderly

Conduct, Harassment and Resisting Arrest, we met Jenny and Aimee in the patrol office and wrote out our statements. Sergeant Crockett came into the office and told us that Randy had refused to take a breath test for alcohol. He said he sat stubbornly in the corner of the drunk tank picking at his toes and was completely uncooperative. When the jail staff tried to take photos of his injuries, he became combative again.

Looking back on the whole incident I believe that Randy was on some type of narcotic. This would explain his erratic behavior and his unexplained strength. He was eighteen years old, five-ten and about a hundred and sixty pounds, but something gave him the fight of a much larger man—at least until Lonnie arrived, who actually *was* a much larger man.

I apologized to Brooke several times for whacking her in the shin with my baton as we spent the next hour cleaning dried snot out of the back seat of Glen's *new* car with Windex and water. She had a nice bruise to show for it the next day. I hope she forgave me.

The witnesses who called never came down to file a formal complaint. I just couldn't believe they'd witnessed everything that happened then complained about how we treated him.

But, then again, it really doesn't surprise me. People see what they want to see.

WE DID OUR JOB

FAMILY ARGUMENTS ARE COMMON. SOMETIMES these arguments escalate to the point where someone calls the police. By the time the officers arrive, tension and tempers are often at a peak, and two uniformed strangers called into the situation, suddenly finds themselves in the midst of a pot ready to boil over. These are often the most dangerous of situations for a police officer. Emotions run high, especially so when two cops, the symbol of authority, suddenly step into the room.

Wednesday, May 23, 2001, around 4:30 p.m. Brooke Herrmann and I were patrolling District Eighteen when we responded on a domestic violence call on Kelly Circle at the Strathmore Apartments. Brooke was a young officer, and eager to prove herself on the street.

As we turned and sped toward the address, the dispatcher updated us that a thirteen-year-old girl was threatening her mother with a knife. It took us about five minutes to get there and knock on the door. A heavy-set woman, probably close to 300 pounds, answered the door looking very distraught. I asked her if everything was okay as she invited us in. She told us that she was at her wit's end with her daughter. As she told us about her misbehaving child, her obesity and the stress of the situation were causing her shortness of breath.

"Where's your daughter now?" I asked.

"She's in the bedroom," the woman replied with a breath between gasps.

"Where's the knife?"

"She has it with her." Another gasp.

"Can we speak to her?"

The woman turned and moved slowly toward the back of the apartment. A few moments later the woman returned followed by a

425

young girl who, though not as large as her mother, was clearly big and heavy, and probably strong, for her age. I put her at about five-seven and close to two hundred pounds.

The girl, holding a purse, plopped her large frame into a chair across from me and crossed her large fleshy arms across the purse with some effort. Her lower lip protruded in a pronounced pout, and an I-hate-the-world look was written clearly across her face. She didn't speak at all but clutched the purse tightly to her chest.

"Where's the knife?" I asked her.

She returned a hateful glare. "Ain't got no knife!" she snapped defiantly.

"Don't lie to that man!" her mother scolded.

I looked back at the young girl. "I need to check your purse for the knife," I said.

"NO!"

Our back-up, Officers Todd Brooks and Jeff Walker, arrived about that time. They stood silently across from us in the living room.

I reached to grab the purse, but she jerked it away from me.

At this point I thought that she had the knife in the purse and I needed to disarm her. I grabbed the purse firmly and snatched on it at which time she kicked me hard in the shin. I leaned down to take her into custody and I got a hard kick to my chest propelling me about four feet across the room firmly into the wall. She immediately jumped up and lunged toward me as if to attack.

Brooke, an average-size woman, instantly leaped on her back like a wild spider monkey wrapping her arm around the girl's neck forcing her to the floor. It was an amazing open-field tackle by a free safety on an offensive lineman.

The angry girl then thrashed about trying to loosen Brooke's grip on her. She outweighed Brooke by more than fifty pounds, but she didn't count on my partner's tenacity. I could tell Brooke was mad and her grip on the girl's neck was relentless.

Jeff and Todd rushed forward, each grabbing a big meaty arm attempting to handcuff the girl.

"Let her go, Brooke!" I shouted. "Let her go!" But Brooke, fuming with anger, held on tightly to the girl's neck.

I grabbed the back of Brooke's body armor vest at her shoulder blades and picked her up off the suspect. Jeff and Todd were then able to handcuff the girl.

"Don't *ever* kick my partner!" Brooke screamed at the girl, still struggling against me to get at the dazed girl again.

We transported the girl to the Juvenile Facility where her mother signed a petition, a criminal warrant against a juvenile. The charge was Harassment and Domestic Violence. I signed a petition of my own against the girl for the physical assault.

A training officer never knows how a rookie will react in a stressful situation until it actually happens. Trainees go through sixteen weeks of rigorous training in the police academy, and the instructors prepare them as best they can. But nothing gives an officer experience like experience. In my opinion, Brooke reacted exactly the way she should have. She never flinched or hesitated for a single second to take on a suspect much larger than herself in defense of her partner.

After we completed the paperwork, we were leaving the youth facility when Brooke asked me, "Am I in trouble for jumping on her and choking her?"

"Not at all," I said. I wanted to reassure her. "You saw your partner assaulted, and you reacted. I have no problem with that at all. I think you did a great job, and I would expect nothing less."

The arrested girl's lack of respect for authority seems to have become more common in her generation. Whether showing disrespect to her mother, the police, or other people, I've noticed this attitude more frequently among young people. I see it as a major problem with our society.

Even though some may think jumping on a thirteen-year-old girl might have been extreme or excessive, one must consider the totality of the events as they unfolded. She had already threatened her mother with a knife and was possibly still armed. The girl was big, angry, and certainly capable of causing someone serious injury. She then attacked a police officer and attempted to continue the attack by charging in anger.

Simply put, Brooke and I were called into the situation... and we did our job.

WE COULD NEVER BE ROOMMATES

FRIDAY, MAY 25, 2001, WAS just another day as my partner and I headed for District Eighteen. For the previous five weeks I'd been training Officer Brooke Herrmann and we had about another week to ride together before she was assigned to a new training officer. The trainees were rotated about every six weeks. Brooke had attended Troy State University on a soccer and track/ cross country scholarship before joining the police department.

Part of my training philosophy was to teach each new officer as much as I could in thirty days. Six weeks sounds like a long time but if you eliminate the two off-days each week, it comes out to only thirty days. I required all my trainees to carry all the paperwork they'd need as if they were riding by themselves, so when the day came to ride solo they'd be prepared.

Brooke was doing well in her training, and I was allowing her to handle many calls on her own. I wasn't her first training officer, so she already had some experience handling calls. Burglary and theft calls were easy, just a matter of asking the right questions and writing a report.

Handling disturbance calls, however, took a little more skill and finesse, especially giving advice to people unable to deal with complicated legal situations. A lot of the calls just involved disagreements between people. Sometimes we responded to the silliest situations and were called upon to solve them. I suppose the people who call don't see it as silly, but we come in to see a situation objectively. Often that makes us the bad guy.

A little before 8:00 that evening, we were called to Three Fountains Apartments on a disturbance between roommates who were also students at Alabama State University. While en route to

428

the call, I asked Brooke if she felt confident enough to handle the call.

She said she did, but we worked out a code she would use if she felt the situation getting away from her. I always told my trainees that if they turned to me and ask, "What do you think, Corporal Smith?" That was the signal that the trainee was at a loss for resolving the conflict and needed a little help. Brooke is a bright, educated officer, and I didn't believe she would have any problems with this call.

When answering any type of call I would always ask who called the police, if it was one of the parties involved. I figured that if they called for our assistance then they got to tell their side first. Brooke knocked on the apartment door and one of the females answered. Both of the ladies were in their early 20's. Brooke entered the apartment first and I followed.

Brooke took charge and asked who called the police and began to listen to her problem. The two had met about a week or so ago at the university and were both looking for a place to live and a roommate. They were both standing at the bulletin board and started a conversation. From talking to both ladies, and how they talked and conducted themselves, Katie* appeared to be from an upper middle class family and somewhat naïve, while Kelly** appeared to be from a less affluent background, and street wise. It did not take long to figure out that these two did not need to room together.

"Look, I understand how it is to need to have a roommate to help in rent and share expenses." Brooke explained. "But in looking for a roommate you have to do better than meeting at a bulletin board. I just got out of college and I know how it is."

"We got along real well for a couple of days but then I found out things about her that were troubling," Katie replied.

Brooke was handling the call very well, and since she was a young female their same age, just out of college, I just stood back and let her handle the situation. She could relate to the ladies better than I could. One of the things I taught young officers was if you are on a roll handling the call then I will just go with the flow unless

---

* Name changed to protect the innocent

** Name changed to protect the innocent

you tell them something that is wrong, or illegal. Brooke was on a roll, so I let her go.

"You need to spend more than just a few minutes talking before you decide to be roommates. Just because you get along with a person doesn't mean you can live with 'em. I have been partners with Corporal Smith for about a month now, and we get along fine, but we could never be roommates."

I am not sure if my mouth dropped open or not. Brooke was handling the call but I never expected her to say that. But, since she had their attention and handling the call very well, I just let her continue.

She was right though, we got along very well. But I don't know about us getting along being roommates. Whether it was true or not, it was still funny to hear her say it. I knew I was going to have to ask her about that when we got back to the car.

Katie agreed to move to wherever she was living before she moved in with Kelly. As we were walking back to the car I looked at Brooke and said in a sarcastic tone, "So, we could never be roommates, huh?"

"Oh, I was afraid you were goin' to ask me about that. I just got carried away and it just came out," she said laughing, trying to explain her way out. "I'm sure you and I could be great roommates!"

"Oh, don't try and spare my feelings now," I said, as if I was hurt. "This is goin' to reflect negatively on your training report!" I always said that to any of my partners that were on training. If I was riding with an officer who was not on training, they would say, "But I'm not on training anymore." I would then reply, "Then I will have you put back on training, and then have it reflect negatively!" I really would not do this just because I did not agree with what they may have said, but it was just one of those things I said when I was joking with my partners.

To this day, whenever I see Brooke, I remind her about what she said that night and we still get a good laugh. Those around us will have a puzzled look on their face and one of us will have to tell the story of why we could never be roommates.

I Have to Believe it was True

When I graduated the police academy in June of 1983, our cars were equipped with a radio that had only four channels. There was a small control panel with switches for the blue strobe light on top of the car, the siren and the small spotlights aimed to either side of the car called "alley" lights. We had no computer. We had to quickly scribble down addresses of calls on a piece of paper, which we then wedged in the cracks of the dashboard for safekeeping. We would call dispatch to check the ownership of a vehicle by tag or VIN (vehicle identification number) or check a person for warrants.

After twenty years, the technology had changed dramatically. The interior of a police cruiser resembled the cockpit of the Space Shuttle by the time I retired. Brilliant LED strobe systems had replaced the old motor-driven rotating mirrors. Our digital radios could tune to dozens of channels and link us to other agencies when the need arose. We had computers called MDT's, short for Mobile Data Terminal. An officer on patrol now could run vehicle tags while in traffic or check a person's criminal history before arriving at the scene of a call. This technology has made the police officer much more efficient.

On Friday, July 6, 2001, this technology paid off for me in a big way. Not only did it help put a felon in jail, but also it led to something I never could have foreseen.

I was assigned to District Eighteen on second shift patrol with Officer Elizabeth Planer. Without any rookie officers available to train at the time, I was an extra man on the shift and rode with a different partner each night. Elizabeth was my Friday night partner.

Around 3:30 that afternoon we were patrolling the neighborhoods just to provide a police presence. Most law-abiding citizens liked to see police cars cruising their neighborhoods. It's only the people who were up to no good who wanted us to stay out. One of the things the MDT's were great for was running the license plates on suspicious vehicles. Stolen vehicles were often abandoned on residential streets. We could ride through, spot a suspicious car, and in a matter of seconds pull up the registered owner's name and address. NCIC also told us if the vehicle had been reported stolen or if the car was wanted in connection to any crime.

On this particular afternoon, as we rode down Susan Drive, Elizabeth typed in a tag number of a vehicle parked in front of a house with a young man and a young woman seated inside. For some reason this didn't look right. When the tag information came back it showed that the tag was registered on another vehicle. I pulled in behind the vehicle, and Elizabeth advised dispatch that we would be out with the car to investigate. She relayed the tag number, a brief description of the vehicle, and a description of the occupants inside.

I walked to the driver's window as Elizabeth approached on the passenger side. I questioned the driver while Elizabeth spoke with the young woman in the passenger seat. Neither individual lived in the area or could provide a good reason for being there. When questioned separately, both gave conflicting stories about where they'd been and what they were doing. It was obvious that they were up to something.

While talking to the young man, I noticed he had a tattoo on his right bicep with the initials "PVG." When I asked him what it meant, he told me that it stood for Prairie Vista Gangster. Prairie Vista Drive is a street in west Montgomery with a long history of drug use, violence, and gang activity.

A warrant check revealed that the young man had a felony warrant from the Sheriff's office and was also on probation for a drug conviction. I immediately arrested him and placed him in the back seat of our car. The young woman had one misdemeanor and two capias warrants on her. A capias warrant is an order for arrest issued by a municipal court judge when someone doesn't appear in court as ordered or pay a fine.

Elizabeth handcuffed the woman and placed her in the back seat of the car with her companion. We determined that the car they were in belonged to him and he had taken a current tag from an older car instead of buying a tag for the car. We left it parked where it was.

While en route to police headquarters, we stopped by the Sheriff's office and served the felony warrant on the young man, then booked him into the county jail.

Afterward, the woman asked us if there was anything she could do to keep from going to jail. I told her that if she had any information on suspects we were looking for that we could possibly work out a deal.

I tell the same thing to anyone I arrest. In law enforcement, we're always looking for the bigger fish. Who's more dangerous, the drug dealer or the drug supplier? Get rid of the supplier and the dealers don't have a product to sell.

She told us that she could help us with stolen cars that were being stripped in the area of Prairie Vista Drive. I took her to see Detective Byrd, the auto theft detective, and he spoke with her for a few minutes. He asked her a few questions to see if she had genuine information or to see if she were just lying to avoid going to jail.

She started giving him information on several stolen cars and gave him specific descriptions. He verified the information and had her look at two different photo line-ups of suspects he'd developed in those cases. She picked out the suspects who had stolen the cars in both line-ups verifying that she was telling the truth. She then began to tell Detective Byrd about drugs being sold in the Regency Park area.

Regency Park is the largest neighborhood in District Eighteen and the center for most of the crime. I patrolled the neighborhood frequently, and I was well known in the area. Most people didn't know my name, rather they recognized me by the number 77 on the side of my patrol cruiser. Senior corporals in the department also have a star beneath the corporal stripes worn on the sleeves, so I was also known for the star I wore on my sleeves.

"What do they think about the officer that rides the Regency Park area?" I asked her.

433

"That officer that rides out there, with the star on his sleeve, he drive car seventy-seven. They gonna kill him," she told me with certainty.

I could tell that she did not realize that she was talking about me, but the way she was telling me the information told me that she knew what she was talking about.

"They have scanners and at 2:30 they listen to see if they hear him. If they hear him, they pack up a van with the drugs and leave and don't come back until after eleven when he gets off," she continued.

"How are they going to kill him?" I asked.

"They took out a contract on him, and when they move the drugs, they have a car that follows the van. The car has guys with machine guns. If he ever pulls the van over, the guys in the car are going to shoot and kill him."

"What house do they keep the drugs in?"

"They keep the drugs in a house on Sawston Court. It's the third house on the right. They also have a bullet-proof vest they stole from a police officer's car."

"Would you be willing to talk to some narcotics investigators about the drugs?" I asked.

"As long as I don't have to go to jail, I'll talk to them. I don't know them so I don't care what happens to them," she told me.

I called the narcotics office and asked to speak to one of the investigators. I told them what I had and the information that she gave us. They told me to ask her a question and then hold up the phone to her so they could hear her response. I don't remember the question, and I don't remember her answer, but within ten minutes, two narcotics investigators came over and picked her up. It must have been what they wanted to hear because they hardly ever come over in person to pick up anyone, especially two of them.

She then told me, with concern in her voice, "If you know the officer, tell him to watch his back."

I told her that I would tell him. She never realized who I was. I advised Lieutenant Ed Rogers, my supervisor, of what she'd said. Lieutenant Rogers had been a narcotics officer for several years and also a narcotics supervisor. He spoke to the investigators about her information.

Narcotics officers, by the nature of their work, tend to be very secretive and are very tight-lipped about what they do. They have to know you and trust you to let you know what they are doing. Even though we're all police officers, they deal with extremely sensitive information. One slip of the tongue could cost an investigator a year's worth of work. Some officers were offended by their secretive nature, but it didn't bother me. They had a job to do, and I had mine.

I never approached, spoke with or acknowledged a narcotics officer in public fearing that I might blow his cover, especially if I was in uniform. If they approached me, then I knew they were not on a case or worried about anyone seeing us together.

The next day, Lieutenant Rogers called me into the hallway before roll call and told me that the narcotics investigators had interviewed the suspect. He said that he had even talked to her but he couldn't confirm that a contract had been taken out on me. He also couldn't say for sure that there wasn't one.

With all the information that she had given, it was possible that a contract had been taken out on me and for me to be careful. I asked him if they were going to pull me from the district because of the death threats and he said no. He said that he told Captain Terry Reid about it and he said that he wanted me to stay there because, "I had them on the run and was making them uncomfortable."

I was more alert for a possible set up and I tried not to get on the radio until I was in Regency Park. I prayed for the Lord to watch over my partner and me as we patrolled the area. Psalms 91:11 says, "For He shall give His angels charge over you, to keep you in all your ways." I believe God has guardian angels who watch over Christians who are doing His will. As long as I was doing what I was called to do by God, He would watch over me.

I began to look for the van with the drugs, or any van that seemed suspicious, then looked to see if a car was following it. I would ride by the house in question periodically to keep up with the vehicles parked there. If the drug dealers took out a contract on me to have me killed, then I was going to turn up the heat on them.

I wasn't scared that someone might try to kill me, but I did take the threat seriously. I was not going to be intimidated by drug dealers who think they can run the neighborhood.

Whenever I had a different partner to ride with me, I warned them about the possible contract and to be aware of that fact. Most who'd been on the shift for any length of time were surprised to hear about it, but at the same time, not surprised because of how hard I rode the district. No one ever tried to kill me that I am aware of, and I never did find the van with the drugs. It could have been just talk in the neighborhood, but because of the other information she gave the auto theft investigator and the narcotics investigators, I have to believe it was true.

THE UNKNOWN PHOTO

ONE OF THE ASPECTS OF police work I always enjoyed was hunting for fugitives. Most people envision a fugitive as someone on the run from the police, but simply enough, if a felony warrant is issued for someone and he avoids or hides from the police—he's a fugitive. When riding patrol I was assigned to one patrol district, which limited my hunting area. Sometimes a little trickery was required to "flush the rabbit from the burrow".

One of my favorite techniques was using an anonymous mug shot. I had a photo of a young man who was wanted at one time, but I'd forgotten his name. Another agency had sent the photo to our department years earlier on the outside chance that the suspect may have been in our jurisdiction, but nothing ever came of it. There was no name on the photo, so I decided to use it as bait for other game. I referred to it as *the unknown photo*.

This was how it worked.

We would have a felony warrant for a suspect and a possible address of where the man might live, or hang out. My partner and I would go to the address and ask the residents there if they'd ever seen the man in the photo and give them a bogus name. We'd tell the people theirs was one of the addresses where he might be. Of course they would tell us the man didn't live there and didn't know him.

Occasionally, someone would lie and say, "I *know* him. He hangs out in Ridgecrest," or something like that to send us off on a wild goose chase.

I would then apologize for bothering them, and ask the names of the residents living at that address as an afterthought so we could make a note that our suspect didn't live there. It would be at this

437

point that they would let their guard down and give the names of everyone who lived there. If our actual suspect was among them, we'd enter the house and arrest him.

After we got our guy in custody, we'd usually get complaints from the other people there.

"You ain't supposed to lie when you looking for somebody," they'd usually say. "That's entrapment, and that's against the *law*."

My favorite retort from them was, "All you had to do is ask for who you wanted and he would have gone with you," one of them would say. "You don't have to lie and treat us this way!"

Of course *that* technique very seldom worked. I know, I've tried it.

Friday, July 27, 2001, Officer Elizabeth Planer and I were patrolling District Eighteen. Duncan Lindsey, a civilian cameraman from WCOV-TV rode in the back seat with us taping for *M.P.D.* He was working for the station while on summer break from college.

M.P.D. was our local rendition of *COPS*, the syndicated police reality show. A cameraman from the station rode with different patrol units to show the public what local police work is like from the officer's point of view. Duncan had ridden with me on several occasions and we could usually find interesting stories to air. The show needed three, ten-minute segments to make a thirty-minute episode.

We had been patrolling for several hours with not much going on. Around 6 p.m., a detective from the Juvenile Division called us on the phone and wanted us to try to locate a seventeen-year-old suspect wanted for rape. He told us he was looking for Ethan Zachary,* who hung out in the Regency Park neighborhood, usually near Wimbledon Road and Sawston Road in the heart of our district.

I had a book that I carried in my patrol vehicle of all the people I'd interviewed or arrested since I'd been patrolling in District Eighteen. This book contained over two hundred names, addresses, birthdates, vehicle information, etc. I called it the *Book of Knowledge*.

My partner immediately looked up Zachary's name in the *Book of Knowledge* and found that he lived on South Hampton Drive.

---

* Name changed to protect the sexually depraved

Duncan told me it would be good footage for the show if we could catch him. While on the way, Duncan started taping, and I gave a brief summary for the camera explaining what we were about to do. Afterward, I pulled out *the unknown photo* from above the sun visor. I let go a long, sinister laugh. "Ha ha...ha haaa. We've got a little deception goin' on," I said. "This is not him, *but....*"

"No, but it always comes in handy," Elizabeth said. She pointed at the picture and smiled. "That's our boy from that one day."

"Duncan has seen me do this before," I told her. "I did it on Sawston Road, as a matter of fact." I chuckled softly. "Yeah, that was Morand somethin' or 'nuther."

"Yeah, we know this street." Elizabeth said.

We turned the corner onto South Hampton.

I spotted the vehicle I knew the suspect drove in the driveway. "There's the car," I said.

We parked in front of the house and approached the front door.

"How do you keep a straight face when you're making up those stories?" Duncan asked. He found it fascinating that people fell for this trick and had a hard time keeping a straight face.

I smiled. "It takes practice to be able to make up stories and make it believable. People lie to us everyday, and so I just use it to my advantage to catch fugitives," I said. "If wanted people would turn themselves in, then I wouldn't have to lie to them. But since they don't, I do what I have to do to capture them."

I stood just to the right of the front door, Elizabeth to the left. Duncan stood behind me with the camera aimed over my right shoulder.

I opened the storm door and knocked. Two young children about four and five answered the door.

"Hey, how are you doin'? What's up?" I said, greeting them with a broad, friendly smile.

A man in his forties came to the door, and I showed him the photo.

"We got some information that a guy named Bowman lives here," I said. "This guy here. Do you know him?"

The man studied the photo for a moment. "Nah, I don't know him," he replied.

"Anybody else here who might know him?" I asked.

"My son, Ethan," he said. "He might know him."

"Is he here?" I recognized the name of the young man immediately.

"Yeah. Ethan! C'mere." the older man shouted.

The children went running through the house also shouting, "Ethan, the cops want cha!"

That always made me nervous because if the suspect had any idea why we were there, then he might arm himself with a weapon or try to escape out the back door or a window.

Ethan walked to the door wearing a white t-shirt. His head was through the head hole but his arms weren't through the armholes. He leaned his right shoulder against the doorframe and put his left arm up across the doorway.

"Hey, Ethan. What's up?" I asked. "Do you know this dude?" I showed him the picture.

He glanced at the photo. "Naw," he said quietly.

"You don't know him?" I asked.

I recognized the young man from an earlier encounter, but I always asked any suspect his name to see if he told me the truth. Lying to the police about your name is against the law and would give me another charge against him. Most people just see and remember the uniform when confronted by a police officer, so Ethan didn't recognize me.

"What's your name?" I asked.

"Ethan James," he replied.

He looks at the photo again. "What's that guy wanted for?"

"He's wanted for a gun, or something," I said.

"Naw, I don't know him," He answered apathetically.

I put the photo back in my shirt pocket then looked squarely at him. "I've seen you before. Your last name isn't James." I said. "What's your *real* name?"

He looked at me but didn't say anything. I could read his eyes and facial expression and tell that he was trying to think of another lie.

"He's Ethan Junior," his father said from across the room.

"Uh-uh," the kids chimed in. "His real name is Ethan Zachary."

I looked at the children. "Yeah, I know," I said.

I grabbed the young man's left wrist and twisted his arm behind his back before he had a chance to run back into the house. I placed handcuffs on him and told him he was under arrest.

"What am I arrested for?" he asked.

"Rape, first degree," I told him.

"Who'd I rape?" he asked, somewhat surprised.

"I don't know. We just got the phone call," I told him.

His father came back to the door. I told his father that Ethan was under arrest for rape and that he would be down at the juvenile office.

"Why do you want to lie about your name?" I asked Ethan as we walked to the car.

"I don't know," he said. "Are you trying to say that person in the picture is me?"

"No," I replied laughing softly. "I know that person in the picture is not you."

I placed the young man in the back seat then headed downtown.

Duncan was excited about how well the tactic had worked. "I can't believe that works so well," he said. "This will be great for the show."

This particular episode aired the following week. In the past, I had asked the producers of the show to edit out the details of my technique so our local fugitives wouldn't be wise to it. Since I was retiring the following month, I let them air it in its entirety.

That was the last time I got to use *the unknown photo*.

It's a Calling from God

WHEN THE POLICE ARE CALLED, they respond. It's just that simple. If you have a problem you call the police and they will come to your home, place of business, or wherever you are. But sometimes, calls come to them. You would think standing in the parking lot of police headquarters that not much would happen, but that isn't always true. Sometimes a person running from someone else will drive to the police department for immediate help.

On Friday, July 27, 2001, that very thing happened.

Officers Jenny Gola, Elizabeth Planer and I were standing in the back parking lot of police headquarters a little after eleven one night. We had just finished our shift and were shooting the breeze when a car raced into the parking lot and screeched to a halt near the back door. A woman jumped from the driver's seat screaming as she ran toward the door. Another car immediately pulled up behind hers. A man jumped from that car, outran her to the door and tackled her on the steps just outside the building. She let out a blood-curdling scream as they fell to the concrete.

"He's trying to kill me!" she shouted.

"Hey!" I yelled as I ran toward the couple. "Let her alone!"

Jenny and Elizabeth followed me, and the man stood as we reached the two. I tackled him down the stairs onto the ground three steps below. Elizabeth helped me handcuff the man, who struggled fiercely against us. Jenny got the hysterical woman off the ground and helped her inside to the relative safety of headquarters.

Elizabeth and I both ordered the man to calm down, but he continued to resist. After a few moments, he calmed somewhat. We escorted him inside the building and sat him down on the blue bench in the secure hallway. The blue bench sat between the back

442

desk and the warrant clerk's office. The hallway was secured on both ends by two heavy steel doors with magnetic locks that could only be released by the officer monitoring the camera at the back desk. All suspects arrested sat on this bench until officers completed the arrest paperwork. Injured prisoners waited here for treatment by paramedics before being taken upstairs to the jail. Either way, the hallway was completely secure from escape.

Jenny escorted the woman to the warrant clerk's office ahead of us to sign a warrant against the man for domestic violence. The woman changed her mind and decided not to sign the warrant, but Alabama law mandated that if the victim of domestic violence refused to sign a warrant and the police had enough evidence to show that an offense occurred, then the police were required to obtain and execute the warrant against the offender. Since all four of us witnessed the event, one of us had to sign the warrant.

She came to police headquarters for help scared for her life. We pulled the guy off of her, basically saving her from further injury—even possible serious injury—and she didn't even pursue charges against the guy.

It was obvious to all of us that he intended to hurt her because he chased her to the back door of the police department and committed the assault without regard to any action a police officer might take against him.

Sometimes I wonder why I even bothered doing what I did. So many people always asked for help, but they never seemed to want to help themselves. Fortunately, not everyone was like this. Most of the people I encountered were honest and law-abiding, and I was always eager to help them.

I recall suffering through extremely hot, steamy summers; bitter cold winters; wearing all that equipment, working long, odd hours for low pay, and dealing with people who didn't want you around unless *they* needed something.

Man, I loved that job!

I believe police work is a calling, and those who choose to follow it are called for that special purpose. Not everyone can be a police officer, just like not everyone can be a firefighter. I have the utmost respect for firefighters, who go charging into burning buildings to put out a fire or to rescue someone. To do either job you have to be called. In both cases, whether you're a religious person or not, I don't believe it's just a job; it's a calling from God.

And Now It Was Over

FRIDAY, AUGUST **31, 2001,** WAS bittersweet for me. This was my very last day working as a Montgomery Police Officer. I had turned in my retirement papers and my official date of retirement was September 20, 2001. I'd been hired with the Montgomery County Sheriff's Office and would start work there on October 1ˢᵗ. I planned to burn some leave time and take the entire month of September off to allow myself some transition time.

Thursday night, Sergeant Randy Markham, one of the second shift patrol supervisors, asked me with whom I wanted to ride on my last tour before he made the duty roster. He said I could ride with anyone I wanted.

How do you choose one person out of everyone on the shift?

I considered each officer on the shift a good friend. I'd probably trained a third of them at some point. I didn't want to hurt anyone's feelings, but I had to choose someone. There were several officers I considered right away, but they were all senior officers. Since we were short-handed, there weren't enough senior officers working to pair up two of them. I guess if I had pushed the issue I could have talked Randy into it, but this would have placed a burden on the rest of the shift to cover the other districts.

I chose Officer Brooke Herrmann. She was the last officer I trained. Sergeant Rod Byrne asked me if I wanted to get off early that night, but I told him that since it was my last night, I wanted to work the whole shift.

I had taken the advice of a former officer, Lieutenant Les Brown, and was having my picture made with as many people with whom I'd worked as possible. I had asked him years before if he had any regrets about working with the department. He said the only regret he had was he didn't take enough pictures of his fellow officers during his career. I thought about all the officers with whom I'd worked, so during my time as the department's photographer, I made it a point to do this for other officers who retired or left the department for other agencies. I always got pictures of them with different buddies from the shift with their patrol car. This had been my gift to them.

I was asked to address the other officers on the shift at my final roll call. I told them how much I had enjoyed my time with the department and that second shift, the most active of all the patrol shifts, was the best shift on which to work.

"As the senior corporal and training officer on the shift," I began, "I feel like the winning quarterback on a Super Bowl team. We currently lead in arrests on all three shifts, and I am going out on top."

Our supervisors had been keeping up with the total number of arrests from the entire division, and second shift had led for several months.

Lieutenant J.C. West, a good friend once told me, "You can just go out there and ride around or you can go out there and put criminals where they belong, in jail. It's about making a difference. You should strive to be the best. It's all about winning championships!" He had a habit of using sports references when referring to motivation and teamwork on the shift.

I hung around for about twenty minutes after roll call and shook everyone's hand and hugged a few necks with my close friends on the shift. I had photos made with some of the dispatchers and other officers assigned to the desk with whom I'd also worked.

I then went to the Montgomery Water Works office on Bibb Street. Lieutenant Paul Walker, a traffic shift commander, worked off-duty security there every Friday. I had asked my three remaining academy classmates to meet me there for one final photo of us all together.

Mike Morand was assigned the back desk after being disabled in an on-duty motorcycle accident many years earlier. Lieutenant John Mann worked as the Robbery-Homicide supervisor in the Detective Division. The four of us spent some time reminiscing during our little reunion and swapped a few academy stories before Brooke took one last photo of us together.

"There is a lot of experience standing in this room," I told her. "Almost 80 years of police service standing before you."

One of my classmates asked her how long she'd been with the police department. She told him she'd only been there a couple of months.

"A mere child," he commented jokingly.

At that time, the Montgomery Police Academy Class 83-A had the largest percentage of graduates still employed with the Montgomery Police Department. Since we'd only graduated five officers from our department, and four of us were still actively serving, we held the record with an eighty-percent retention rate.

Brooke and I said our goodbyes to my classmates and left for District Eighteen. It was partly cloudy and had rained on and off all day and looked to continue into the night. As far as calls go, it was a slow night.

Fridays were normally busy, but the rainy weather kept most people inside and out of trouble. Those who did venture out were having trouble with the slippery streets. I think we responded to more traffic accidents that night than we ever had before.

Brooke took several photos of me in different areas of my district; especially the high crime areas where we'd spent most of our time. She said she needed several particular photos for something she was doing for my retirement.

As the night went on, I kept thinking about how this was my last night as a Montgomery police officer.

Several officers met with me during the night to congratulate me and wish me good luck in my new job. All week long, different officers had bought me dinner, and someone bought my dinner that night as well. I appreciated it very much.

After the shift was over, I turned in all my shift equipment, my shotgun, radio, office keys, etc. I stayed around and talked to many of my co-workers for a while. I didn't want to leave because, with a heavy heart, I knew it would be for the last time.

My first day with the Montgomery Police Department was

September 8, 1981. I started my career as a police cadet and after exactly twenty years and twelve days, I was retiring.

I was thirty-nine years old.

My mother said she was too young to have a son retiring from a job. I had attended many retirements and photographed many of them, but a few days from then, I'd be attending my own.

I'd worked at the same place for twenty years and now it was over.

August 31, 2001 – My last night as a Montgomery Police Officer with my partner Officer Brooke Herrmann.

August 2001 – Some of the officers on second shift patrol

I Am Retired

MY FINAL DAY WORKING AS an officer with the Montgomery Police Department was Friday, August 31, 2001. Since Saturday and Sunday were my regular off days, it would be the following Monday before it really sank in that I had officially worn that uniform for the last time.

I'd been hired as a deputy by the Montgomery County Sheriff's Office scheduled to begin work with my new employer on October 1st. Many officers who had retired before me starting new jobs elsewhere had told me that they wished they'd taken more time off before starting the new job to allow themselves some transition time. I took their advice and arranged to be off the entire month of September.

I burned some leave time after the end of August until my official retirement date of September 20th, so I was technically unemployed from the 21st until the 30th. I hadn't been unemployed since I was seventeen years old. My mom reminded me that I wasn't unemployed, just retired.

Okay, Mom, whatever you say.

My brother, Shane, who lived in Ohio, was to fly in the day before my retirement tea on Friday, the 20th. Afterward, he and I were going on a road trip. We'd been planning this trip for about two months, and I was really looking forward to it. I knew I'd never be thirty-nine years old and retired again. Shane had taken a whole week off from work, and we were going to drive and visit our other two brothers. Scott lives in Redfield, Arkansas, and Gregg lives in Bartlett, Tennessee.

Gregg Strawhecker, whom I consider a brother, had come to live with us when I was in high school. He was in the Air Force stationed

450

at Maxwell Air Force Base. My parents treated him like another son, and he was just like one of the family. He and his wife and kids still come home to my parent's house in Birmingham for Thanksgiving every year. We celebrate Thanksgiving and Christmas both on Thanksgiving Day because we can't all be together on Christmas.

Gregg isn't close to his family in Pennsylvania, so he adopted us like we adopted him. Some people, including a few uncles, aunts and cousins, don't understand us bringing Gregg into the family, but that's okay. We never needed their approval.

Each day after my last day of work I took my daughter, Stacy, who was then six years old and in the first grade at Evangel Christian Academy, to school. Afterward, I had the rest of the day off. My wife, Nancy, took Kelly, our one-year-old daughter, to Heritage Baptist Church's Day Care.

Tuesday, September 11, 2001, started off like any other day. I took Stacy to school and was listening to the radio when the newscaster announced that a plane had flown into the World Trade Center in New York City.

"What an idiot!" I said out loud. "I bet some guy was flying his private plane and was pointing out one of the Trade Center Towers and flew into the other."

"What are you talkin' about, Daddy?" Stacy asked.

"Oh, someone had an accident in a plane," I explained, as we pulled up to the school.

"Oh, Okay, Daddy. Bye, Daddy," Stacy said as she climbed out of my truck.

As I was listening to the news of the plane crash, I remember thinking that the pilot just wasn't paying attention and crashed into the building by accident. I never considered the idea that maybe the pilot might have suffered a heart attack or had some kind of medical problem and certainly not that the act was intentional.

I walked into my house and turned on the television in the den then went into the kitchen to fix myself a bowl of cereal. It was then that the news anchor announced that a second plane had hit the other tower.

"What?" I said to myself. "I bet that guy was looking at the first plane crash and he flew into the second tower. What a moron."

451

Boy was I wrong.

I carried my bowl of cereal into the den and sat down in my recliner and began to watch as both towers burned. I was swept up with the images as the newscasters, and the rest of the nation began to consider the unthinkable. This was no accident, I thought to myself and the situation unfolded.

We were under attack.

The phone rang. It was my brother Shane in Ohio.

"Are you watching the TV?" he said. His voice was solemn.

"Yeah, I'm lookin' at it right now!" I said. "What the heck is going on?"

"I can't come down for your retirement." he said quickly. "I've been called into work."

"Why, what's up?" I asked.

"The Pentagon has been attacked, and I gotta go."

The next thing I heard was a dial tone. I thought about it for a couple of seconds and then I remembered. Shane worked for Lockheed Aircraft. The stuff he did was top secret, so he couldn't even talk about what he did at his job.

I knew at this point that whatever he was doing had something to do with national security. I sat down and started watching the news, but I didn't see anything about the Pentagon being attacked. I started flipping channels to see what he was talking about but there wasn't any news regarding the Pentagon... yet.

About twenty minutes after he told me, the first reports of the attack on the Pentagon came in.

At first the reports were unconfirmed, then confirmation of the attack made it real to me. We were under attack, but by whom?

I began to think about Maxwell Air Force Base here in Montgomery being the Air War College. I had always heard growing up that Montgomery was one of the top ten targets to be bombed if we are ever attacked by another country. I began to think about whom to call to tell about the attacks. I immediately thought about the church staff. They don't have a television at the office so I called and spoke with Brother Gary, our minister. I told him about what was going on and at first he thought I was kidding.

"Why would I kid about something like this, Gary?" I asked.

"Well, you're always joking with me," he said. "Are you sure this is not a joke?"

"I promise, Gary, this is not a joke," I told him. "Just find a TV and see what's going on. We're at war with somebody."

"Okay, I'll check it out," he said.

I sat down and watched the news for the rest of the day. I called Nancy at work. She'd already heard about it and had gone into an office where there was a television. I called my parents, and they were already watching it too.

The towers fell, and I mourned the loss of my countrymen who perished that day. I shared the emotion of the traumatic assault with everyone else as a part of America's innocence vanished in a plume of dust and ash.

I sensed that the country was facing a transition of sorts following the attack. I spent the rest of the week preparing for the impending transition I faced on a personal level.

My retirement tea was held that Friday on the 14th at headquarters. I had attended retirement teas for many other officers, but suddenly this was my own. It didn't seem real. Retirement is for old people, and I wasn't old.

The tea was scheduled for 11:00 that morning. My parents had driven from Birmingham, and my in-laws drove from Greenville to attend the ceremony in the patrol assembly room.

Usually someone from the newspaper would attend the retirements and sometimes a television crew would attend. But today they were attending a prayer vigil at the state capital for the police officers and firefighters killed when the towers collapsed.

As friends and co-workers filtered in, Chief John Wilson, Corporal Ben Harrison and I stood in front of the podium and talked for about five minutes, laughing and reminiscing before the ceremony began. Chief Wilson mentioned that he'd had the most fun as a corporal with the police department than at any other rank.

The Chief looked at me with a big smile. "You ready to get this thing started?" he asked.

I returned the smile. "Yes, sir. Let's do it." I said.

We walked up on the platform, and I introduced the chief to my parents, my in-laws, wife and my two daughters. They all sat down in the folding chairs lined up on the platform behind the podium.

Chief Wilson addressed the crowd. "Today, we're losing a real gem, and I really mean that from the bottom of my heart. I've known Steve ever since he came here, and he's a really remarkable individual. He's a very unusual individual."

A collective laugh rose from the dozens of people gathered in the room.

"Did I say something wrong?" the Chief said, with a wry smile. "It's very easy to get down in this job and let morale get the best of you and to not see the good side of life. You certainly in the job don't get to see very much of it. And I've seen a lot of people like you young folks out here go through a transition where you come in here full of vigor and venom and ready to go, and after you see the destruction and how cruel one human being can be to the other, over a period of time, it takes its toll on you.

"You're only human. It can't help but do that. It takes a very special individual to be able to have the moral character, the fiber, and backbone and the attitude that Steve has to go through all the things he's done and be a team leader. He's never been one of those that wanted to be the police chief, and I don't blame him a bit," he said, with a laugh.

"He's that kind of individual. That wasn't his goal when he came here. If he wanted to be—if this man wanted to be part of the staff, he would be there this day. I have no doubt in my mind about that. He's got everything it takes and then some. I've had people—and I'll say this candidly—that have worked on my staff at a far higher rank than he that do not have the values and morals that he's got as a leader. He chose to stay with you, and I admire him for that because we have to have people that will do that. He chose to stay here and be your mentor, to try to show you how it's done.

"And I told a group of business people that I was talking to not to long ago, and—they talk about, you know, we want to pay you some compliment because you never hear any compliments; all you get is complaints. That's not necessarily so. One out of ten letters I get is a complaint. The other nine are usually good, and that complaint, I can almost, by the time I get to the person they are talking about, tell you who it is. There's only about one or a half a percent of this department that I see on a disciplinary basis or get critical letters from. The rest of you all, thanks to people like Steve, are the backbone of this community, and you really do a super job and people recognize you for it.

"Mabel (Lt. Col. Pierce) and I got to have a wonderful experience yesterday. Leadership Montgomery, this is a group of leaders, a cross-section of business people from all across the city. They've ridden with a lot of you in the last week or so. You've gotten to meet some of them. These are people who really know very little about people like Steve and you all. They don't get to see the side of Montgomery that you get to see everyday. They're really a lot of those people are the kind of people who traditionally complain at the drop of a hat about the service they get. You would not believe the rave reviews and the things that they were saying. It was almost like every comment started with, 'Wow! I didn't know we had this kind of police department.'

"They didn't ride with me. I never met a one of them other than the few I knew personally before yesterday. They rode with *you*. That was you they were talking about, not me. They were people like Steve. And I told them in the group yesterday—I stood right out there where you're standing, I saw all those idiotic memos that the chief sent down that made no sense at all. And I knew depending on what that sergeant and that corporal like Steve standing next to me thought of that memo is how much weight I was going to put on it. Not how much weight the chief put on it; how much people like him put on it. So I relied heavily on folks like Steve to keep us motivated at times when it's very easy for us to get down.

"We've gone through some tough years the last couple of years. I wish he wasn't leaving right now because it's fixing to get real hairy. But some of you in the ranks out here are going to have to pick up where he left off. It's going to be hard. This country and our community are fixing to go through some very tough times. And D.T. (Sheriff Marshall) is a winner in this case and I'm a loser, because when it comes to those kind of times and you're out there being asked to work extra hours shorthanded with very little compensation to show for it, I have to rely on people like him to keep you motivated and show you a purpose for what you're doing."

The chief turned and looked at me and continued. "Steve, I haven't given a speech that good for a lot of the high-ranking folks."

"Thank you," I said humbly.

"I can't say thank you enough from the bottom of my heart for everything you've done for this department," he said.

The chief then turned to the crowd and continued, "I mean this with all my heart. If I had joined the police department the same time this guy did and he had any ambition of being chief, I wouldn't have made it."

I have attended a lot of retirements over my career. I photographed many of them and I have seen many awards given but nothing could have prepared me for what was coming next.

The Chief looked at me and began to take the badge off his uniform shirt. "I want to give you something and let you take and just keep as a memento, as a token of my appreciation." His voice was filled with emotion. "Frame it, give to your kids, do what you want to with it." He then handed me his chief of police badge. It had a black mourning band across it in memory of the police officers killed in the terrorist attack.

I was stunned!

All I could say was, "Wow. I don't know what to say. Thank you."

The chief then presented me with my duty weapon, a medal of merit, a retirement watch, the retirement badge encased in acrylic, and a commemorative retirement plaque.

Lieutenant Colonel Gene Cody then presented me with a plaque embossed with the Policeman's Prayer.

"Steve, we're going to miss you, buddy," Cody said. "Steve has helped us out considerably with working with the interdenominational board to name our latest police chaplain who I hope will be with us for a long time. Steve was profiled in the newspaper last week. I don't know how many of y'all saw that, but I wanted to bring that for your collection along with the announcement of your tea. But I've had a police officer's prayer at my house since I came on with the police department that's been on my wall. I kind of changed some things out, and I thought I would like to give this to you to take to the county with you as a token of my appreciation for what you've done for this department. He's a great inspiration to all of us and we're going to miss him."

After that I was given the traditional large card. This card is huge, probably 24 by 36 inches, and is full of good luck messages and well wishes written by my co-workers. I have no idea where they get these giant cards but everyone at the MPD gets one when they retire.

Lieutenant David Warren from second shift patrol then presented me with a plaque from the shift.

"This is from all of us on second shift patrol," David began. The he read the inscription. "It says: 'In grateful recognition for outstanding service and dedication. Your exemplary performance and patrol tactics are an inspiration to others. Grounded in faith, you set a higher standard and left an indelible mark that will remain a part of all who know and respect you. September of nineteen eighty-one—September of two-thousand one—Montgomery Police Department, Second shift patrol. The Rock. There's an inscription. He who rebels against God's institution shall bring judgment on themselves; Romans 13:2.'"

Chief Wilson then spoke again, "Before I turn it over to Steve, are there any of his friends that would like to come up and say anything?" he asked the crowd. "It's a great testament to you, Steve, to have all these people here today."

Captain Terry Reid, the second shift patrol commander then came up on the platform, "I want to say something."

Terry and I are good friends and often referred to himself as 'Captain America.' I always answered his boast by referring to myself as 'Corporal America.'

When he came up I responded with, "Uh, ooooh."

There was no telling what he was going to say.

"I've been out in School Security for about ten years now," Terry began. "I recently transferred to patrol and when I started on patrol, I was real nervous, I hadn't been here since about nineteen eighty-seven. The first person I got up with—we were riding the R.O.T. team together—was Steve Smith.

"I said, 'Steve, what do we need to do to make patrol run better?' And everything that I've done on second shift, a lot of that came from Steve Smith. There is nobody else I asked that question because I knew Steve would have the knowledge that I need to come in and be a good captain. It's been a pleasure working with you." Terry looked over the room and said, smiling, "I'm trying to get him to tear up, and he hasn't teared up yet. I can go further.

"When I was in patrol, I was third shift and Steve was on second and we 'twenty-threed' (met unit to unit) on Lower Wetumpka Road just to pass on important information, Chief," he said looking in the chief's direction. "I've known him ever since then. We might have cut one or two watermelons together, but ever since then..." he paused as laughter rose from the room. "We've had a lot of fun together. Worked on the R.O.T. truck for many years, saved my life several times on the R.O.T. truck."

He then looked toward the crowd and said, "I hear Howie Dave Kenney back there. That reminds me of a quick story I'm going to tell.

"The one time that I saw somebody get the better of Steve was a guy by the name of Tootie. Steve would not go on that side of town in that particular area around Mobile and Mildred for a long time until Tootie was finally killed—God rest his soul—and now Steve can return back to Mobile and Mildred. I'm not going to go and tell exactly what Tootie did but the guy actually did push off on Steve. But the story grew very large and by the time I was through with it. He ended up in the E.R. before I got through telling the whole story.

"Second shift is really going to miss Steve Smith. I'm going to need about three sergeants to take his place, and I just want to take this time to shake your hand and tell you that it's really been a pleasure working with you."

I responded, with a very gracious, "Thank you."

The chief then asked the crowd if anyone would like to come up from the rank and file and say a few words. Corporal Ben Harrison came up and shook my hand and said, "We're going to miss Steve.

He's been an outstanding inspiration to everybody on second shift patrol from people that have come out of the academy to the people that have been here as long as he has. Outstanding corporal, somebody who I'm going to try to be like and try just to carry on what you started on second shift patrol.

"You're going to the county and we're going to miss you. If there's anything that we can do for you—I'm sure I'm speaking for everybody else on second shift patrol—If there's anything we can do for you on second shift or anywhere in the police department, just feel free to call. I'm always home, always there. Just give us a call."

"Thanks, Ben. I really appreciate it," I said.

At that time the Chief turned it over to me and I introduced my parents to those assembled.

"These are my parents, Zane and Janett Smith, my wife, Nancy, my daughter, Stacy. And for those of you that rode with me on training, she is better known as Sweet Pea, as you know when I called her every night. These are my in-laws, Mr. and Mrs. Mullins and this is my daughter Kelly, who is fifteen months."

I grabbed the edges of the podium and addressed everyone.

"Ummm, I tell ya, I can't believe it's been twenty years," I began. "Time has just flown by and I know a lot of y'all are sayin', yeah, well, maybe, but believe me when you cross that ten and it goes that-a-way it's unreal. Some of y'all I remember when you were here and left—retired, some of y'all are still here. I took the job because I was seeking what the Lord wanted me to do. And this job went from a career to a ministry. And all I can say is that I hope and pray that everything that I have done, every decision I have made, everybody that I have trained, I've set that Christian example, of how to be, because that's really my goal, is to be that example of Jesus Christ. And, I just appreciate all y'all being here and I'm changing uniforms. I'm going from blue to brown, I'll have a different colored car and I've got more territory to cover but I'm still there, y'all call me anytime, I'll be there for ya'. And so I appreciate it and I guess that's it, I'm goin' to miss all y'all."

Chief Wilson came back to the podium. "I don't want to put you on the spot and I'm going to leave it to you or the police chaplain or whomever you designate, but I think a short prayer for all the folks in New York and the officers and everything that's going on right now would probably be appropriate. Do you want to take on that duty or would you rather..."

I interrupted because I knew where Chief Wilson was going by saying, "Well, I tell ya, one of the things I shared with the Interdominational Chaplaincy Committee was that, it's kinda funny that, I worked with Cops for Christ trying to get a chaplain all the years and we worked on it and worked on it, and now as the plan comes about, that door has opened but yet it's closing for me, because I'm moving on to the county and all I can say is that I think the Lord may have plans for me when I go to the county, my ministry, so I'm going to ask our new chaplain, to come up and do a prayer, and my pastor, if he would, to come up with him and lead a prayer for the officers and fire fighters and everyone in New York and this department."

Eric Jackson, the new police chaplain came to the podium, followed by Pastor Gary Aldridge. Eric prayed first, and then my pastor, Gary, prayed and wrapped up the event. Everyone came up afterward and shook my hand, hugged my neck and wished me well.

Officer Jeff Walker and Officer Chris Gruhn came up later and presented me with the "original" weapon I was issued when I first started with the department. It was an old unclaimed black powder pistol replica that they had talked Mr. Ducker into giving them from the Evidence Room. Jeff and Chris are quite the characters, and I will truly miss their sense of humor. Officer Brooke Herrmann, the partner I rode with on my last day, gave me several photos that she took that night.

Debbie Hooks, the Director of Church and Community Ministries, attended the retirement with Eric Jackson. She said that when Chief Wilson gave me his badge, Eric commented that this was the highest honor that could be given to a retiring police officer. I didn't think about it at the time, but as far as I know no police chief in the history of our department has ever honored a retiree with his own badge. Chief Wilson didn't even do that for his secretary when she retired, and she had worked for the city for over 30 years. It was truly a great honor to be presented with that badge and one I will always cherish. I am retired.

September 2001 – Police Chief John Wilson presents me with the Medal of Merit at my retirement (Photo by Montgomery Police Dept)

September 2001 – Zane and Janett Smith (dad and mom) at my retirement

September 2001 – (l to r) Stacy, Nancy and Kelly (acting up) Erlene and Graham Mullins, my in-laws.

August 2001 – The Class of 83-A (l to r), Lt. John Mann (retired), Investigation Division, me (Cpl Steve Smith) (retired) Second Shift Patrol, Lt. Paul Walker, Traffic Division – Solo Motors, Cpl Mike Morand (retired) Administrative Division.

*Painting entitled "Who is Steve Smith? Romans 13:4" painted by
my good friend William (Billy) Gordon after my retirement*

About the Author

Stephen Z. Smith retired from the Montgomery Police Department in Montgomery, Alabama in 2001 after 20 years of service. He started his career at nineteen years old as a police cadet working for a year and half before attending the Montgomery Police Academy. He turned twenty-one years old while in the academy and after graduation was assigned to third shift patrol. Throughout his career he has worked in traffic, crime scene investigation and on a high profile zero tolerance drug unit before retiring from 2nd shift patrol as a senior training officer. He retired at 39 years old and is currently employed with the Montgomery County Sheriff's Office in Alabama as a Crime Scene Technician. He also teaches Crime Scene Investigation to other law enforcement agencies.

While with the police department, he organized the local Cops for Christ group in 1992 which lead to the creation of the River Region Chaplain Service. This ministry provides chaplains to assist law enforcement officers and fire fighters with pastoral care and emotional support due to job related stress. He is certified through the International Conference of Police Chaplains (I.C.P.C) as a police chaplain and chaplain liaison

Contact Information:
Stephen Z. Smith
P O Box 230745
Montgomery, Alabama 36123-0745

MPDmemoirs@knology.net